THE OLDER MIDDLE WEST
1840–1880

The American Historical Association

THE
OLDER MIDDLE WEST
1840-1880

Its Social, Economic and Political Life and
Sectional Tendencies Before, During
and After the Civil War

BY

HENRY CLYDE HUBBART

PROFESSOR OF HISTORY, OHIO WESLEYAN UNIVERSITY

D. APPLETON–CENTURY COMPANY
INCORPORATED
New York   London

1423

F 484.3
.H 885

PREFACE

To write the chapter in human experience which covers the life of the Middle West in its older period, 1840–1880; to capture from old newspapers and fragmentary memoirs the local color so necessary to sectional history; to hew a path between the romance of western history on the one hand, and the tragedy and sordidness of "Spoon River" on the other; to reduce to readable dimensions the endless story of political controversy in a half-dozen politics-ridden commonwealths in an ultra-political age; to give due emphasis to economic factors; to seek to understand History as she seems fumblingly and tragically to lead a baffled people into civil war; to reappraise the careers of Stephen A. Douglas, Clement L. Vallandigham, and in fact a whole generation of rather discredited western leaders; to trace the beginnings of middle western culture as it revealed itself in Cincinnati and elsewhere—these are some of the tasks the author has set before him.

The early frontier West—or rather the successive frontier "Wests" as they have developed—have received considerable attention from the historian; the far West, too, has not been neglected. But the Middle West as a settled section has not been given extensive treatment. This is especially true of its older portion and of the period from 1840 to 1880. While as a whole it had marked sectional characteristics, the Middle West of that day was composed of two or even three subsections. First the older portion, the lower West, the region of the river valleys, the description of the social, economic, and political life of which occupies the major portion of this book; secondly, the upper, newer, more aggressive and more quickly industrialized Great Lakes region; and third, the newest part, the emerging corn and wheat prairie belt. Since the term Middle West to us of to-day comprehends rather the two newer regions and since the record of the older West of southern Ohio, Indiana and Illinois tends by the passage of time to be dimmed, there is all the more reason why its story should be told.

The region we describe in this book was for two or three decades one of the focal points around which American history revolved, and one of the testing grounds of American democracy; its hardy yeomanry were compelled to face and strive to solve the national issues of expansion, slavery, war, peace and reconstruction. Among its people there were many who felt the age-long sense of frustration so characteristic of the West. What we have called "Copperheadism" appears to be the manner in which thwarted westerners showed their sectional discontent; it was not primarily pro-southern in sympathy. Jacksonian democracy so vigorous and powerful in earlier decades, was not, as our histories imply, crushed out between an aggressive industrial North and a slave-holding South, but persisted in the Middle West and made great contributions to our national life.

When the attempt is made to paint the complete picture of sectionalism in the United States, of our contentious and multiple society, the vast resultant composite canvas should contain a large measure of middle western and even lower western detail. And this old-fashioned sectionalism of the historian is after all—to use up-to-date terms— akin to the occupational interests, the regionalism and pluralism of the political scientist, to the market systems and the metropolitical areas of the economist, and to the group life of the social psychologist. Sectional behavior is a complex of geographic factors, economic needs, partisan, religious, traditional and other psychological bonds.

The task of the author would have been easier if he had not been compelled to delineate not only the larger lines of cleavage but intrastate division as well. The better types of state histories, say those of Illinois, have already shown this; the difference between Chicago and "Egypt" is well-known. But to blend the stories of the cleavage in the various states, and at the same time delineate the larger sectional lines and to mark a careful trail between these on the one hand and our national history on the other, all this has been a very difficult task.

To all who have aided him, to writers of state histories and of special monographs on middle western subjects, to those in charge of the collections of the state historical societies and in particular of such great newspaper collections as those at Madison, Chicago, and Columbus, the author cannot give adequate thanks. And to Professors A. C. McLaughlin, William E. Dodd, Marcus W. Jernegan and Ferdinand Schevill of the University of Chicago, he owes what is always due to those who inspire and patiently wait for whatever harvest of truth or error the work of their former students brings forth.

HENRY CLYDE HUBBART

Ohio Wesleyan University

CONTENTS

PAGE

PREFACE v

CHAPTER

I THE AGE OF POLITICS—THE PROGRESSIVE WESTERN
DEMOCRACY, 1840–1850 3
Introduction 3
The Progressive Western Democracy, 1845–1848 . 9
Would the Progressive Democratic West Support
Polk and the Southern Democracy? 14
Economic Origins of the Republican Party in the Lake
Region 21

II SOCIETY IN THE LOWER WEST, 1840–1860—SOCIAL AT-
TITUDES 30
Life in the Interior Counties 33
Illiteracy—Public Schools 37
Local Disorder and Feud 39
Religion in the Back Settlements 42
Southern Influences—Black Codes 44

III MIDDLE WESTERN CULTURE, 1840–1860 52
Literature, Music, and the Theater 53
The Cincinnati School of Writers 56
Theological Debate 64
Middle Western Liberalism 66
The Beginnings of the Middle Western College . 69

IV TRADE WITH THE SOUTH BY RIVER AND RAILROAD,
1840–1860 73
Steamboat Disasters—Trade Conventions . . . 84

V THE UPPER WEST BREAKS FROM THE DEMOCRATIC
SOUTH, 1850–1854 88
Upper Western Development, 1850–1854 . . . 90
The Lower West Champions Expansion—Kansas-
Nebraska Bill 98

vii

CHAPTER   PAGE

VI THE LOWER WEST, THE NATIONAL POLITICAL BATTLE-
    GROUND, 1854–1857 103
    The Doubtful Central Counties 105
    Gains and Losses, 1855–1857 109

VII STEPHEN A. DOUGLAS—WESTERN INSURGENT,
    1857–1860 116
    Popular Sovereignty Becomes Popular 116
    Lincoln and Douglas Not Far Apart in the Great De-
    bate 124

VIII WINNING THE DOUBTFUL WEST, 1860 130
     Parties and "Partyism," 1860 130
     The Lower South Breaks from the Douglas West . 132
     The Lakes and the East Reluctantly Accept Lincoln . 138

IX DEMANDS FOR COMPROMISE AND BORDER STATE RECON-
    STRUCTION, 1860–1861 146
    Trade with the South, 1860–1861 154
    Border-State "Reconstruction" 161

X   WOULD THE FREE WEST FIGHT TO PRESERVE THE
    UNION? 166
    The Growth of Coercion Feeling in the Upper West . 171
    The Lower West and the Call to Arms, April–May,
    1861 173

XI THE FREE WEST REPUDIATES ABRAHAM LINCOLN, 1862 178
    Origins of the Peace Democracy 181
    Opposition to Emancipation and the Draft . . . 183
    Patriotic Ardor 186
    The Free West Repudiates Abraham Lincoln, 1862 . 188

XII DEMOCRACY IN CONVULSION—WAR STRAIN, 1863 . . 194
    Attacks on the Press, 1862–1864 203
    Legislative Opposition to War, 1863 206
    Vallandigham, 1863 208

XIII WAR PROSPERITY—THE SOLEMNITIES OF 1864 . . . 218
     War Prosperity and Extravagance 219
     Conspiracy, Ill-Timed and Poorly Executed,
     1863–1864 223

CHAPTER   PAGE
    The Western Peace Bolt, 1864 230
    The Reëlection of Lincoln, 1864 234

XIV EXTRAVAGANCE AND PROTEST, 1865–1880 240
    Republicanism Triumphant 240
    The Revival of the Democratic Party in the West,
      1867–1872 244
    Western Protests Against "Grantism" 249
    New Parties and New Issues, 1873–1880 . . . 253

XV THE GILDED AGE IN THE WEST—SOCIAL LIFE . . . 261
    "Spoon River" in the Seventies and Eighties . . . 266
    Progress in Higher Living 271
    The Sources and Validity of Middle Western Culture 275

  BIBLIOGRAPHY 278

  INDEX 293

THE OLDER MIDDLE WEST

1840–1880

CHAPTER I

The Age of Politics—The Progressive Western Democracy

(1840-1850)

Introduction

We can well imagine then, that here in the Great Valley, humanity is to be displayed on a scale of magnificence which has yet been unknown. . . . It is a vast thought and to many it may seem a hazardous assertion but we venture the prediction that from what is now called the West—the Great Valley . . . is yet to go forth a spirit which shall rouse the nations, reform the civilization of the world . . . and all this is to be accomplished through the agency of the much derided Democratic Principle, as a means in the hand of Him who accomplishes all things in His own good time.

B. B. Taylor in *The Democratic Monthly Magazine,* June, 1844, p. 196.

The part of the United States now called the Middle West cannot be said to have become a distinct section until about 1840; it was not then, of course, called by its present name. The record of earlier developments in the region stretching north of the Ohio and along the upper Mississippi and the lakes—the record of the Jesuits and of the French occupation, of Vincennes and of George Rogers Clark— all this lies in the past and is a part of the history of the colonial conflict between the French and the Anglo-Americans for control of this outlying territory. Even the achievements of the early frontiersmen— their battles of Tippecanoe and the River Raisin, as well as the beginnings of political life north of the Ohio—all these are rather a part of that earlier winning of the West, by which men from Virginia and the Carolinas established Kentucky and Tennessee and they, or their sons in turn, crossing the Ohio, joined with men from Pennsylvania to set up outposts in the form of the infant commonwealths of Ohio, Indiana, and Illinois and to protect them from the Indians and the English.[1]

[1] C. W. Alvord, *The Illinois Country, 1673-1818* (Chicago, 1922) ; C. E. Carter, *Great Britain and the Illinois Country, 1763-1774* (Washington, The American Historical Association, 1910) ; B. A. Hinsdale, *The Old Northwest* (New York,

By 1825, although Ohio had been occupied in all but its north-western part, Indiana's population did not reach north of the line of the National Road, or the fortieth parallel, and was still timidly fringing the Ohio or the lower Wabash rivers, while Illinois was peopled only sparsely north of Alton. Towns which had served as territorial capitals or those which became the first state capitals were near the southern border—Chillicothe, Ohio, Vincennes and Corydon, Indiana, Kaskaskia and Vandalia, Illinois. No more representative political leaders could be found than men who had been born in slave states such as Nathaniel Massie of Ohio, William Henry Harrison of Ohio and Indiana, Ninian Edwards of Illinois and A. C. Dodge of the Iowa country—not to mention Abraham Lincoln, the great leader of a later day. The Illinois Legislature of 1833, with only one native son among its members, contained fifty-eight natives of slave states, principally Kentucky and Virginia, nineteen from Pennsylvania and New York, four from New England and two from Ireland.[2] There is every evidence that the West at that day was an appendage of the upland South, with Pennsylvania population influences a very important factor.[3]

About 1840, however, men who had been born in the region were more and more taking charge of its affairs; a new era was beginning, a new section emerging. A much more diversified population was pouring in from the South, the East, and Europe; southern influences were becoming relatively less important, although until the new lake region became more densely settled, they were to remain the most predominant single population element. The zone of settlement was reaching farther and farther into the region of unoccupied lands to the north recently "acquired by treaty" from the Indians; the state capitals had been moved farther to the north—from Chillicothe to Columbus, from Corydon to Indianapolis and from Vandalia to

1888) ; A. C. Boggess, *Settlement of Illinois* (Chicago Historical Society *Collections* Vol. 5, Univ. of Chicago Press) ; W. V. Pooley, *The Settlement of Illinois, 1830–1850* (Madison, 1908).

[2] *Western Monthly Magazine,* May, 1833, p. 199.

[3] The best authorities that can be given for these statements are: R. E. Chaddock, *Ohio Before 1850,* pp. 18, 20, 37, 40–45, 60, 63; W. E. Henry, "Some Elements of Indiana's Population," *Ind. Hist. Soc. Pub.* IV, No. 6, pp. 384, 387, 389; A. C. Boggess, *The Settlement of Illinois (1778–1830),* pp. 91–93, 120–123, 126–127, 145, 156–159; W. V. Pooley, *The Settlement of Illinois, 1830–1850,* pp. 23, 34–37, 41–42, 91–94, 96, 113, 133; F. I. Herriott, "Whence Came the Pioneers of Iowa," *Annals of Iowa,* 3rd Series, VII, pp. 459, 461–465; *Ibid.,* VIII, pp. 196–198; T. C. Pease, *The Frontier State, 1818–1848, Centennial History of Illinois,* Vol. II, Ch. I.

Springfield.[4] From about 1845 to 1855 a migration movement from the East by way of the Erie Canal and the lakes, embracing in its zone of settlement the Western Reserve of Ohio, parts of southern Michigan, the Chicago region, southern Wisconsin, and parts of Iowa, laid firmly the foundation for the "upper Northwest" or "upper West" as it was variously called. For the purposes of this book much of our attention will be directed to the lower West—the West of the river valleys, the north bank of the Ohio, the valleys of the Muskingum, the Scioto, the Miami, the Wabash, the Illinois, and the upper Mississippi, as far north as, say, Dubuque, Iowa.

The population of the whole free West in 1840 was nearly three millions, all but a few hundred thousand of these living in Ohio, in southern and western Indiana, and southern and central Illinois.[5] Ohio's million and a half was composed largely of immigrants and sons of immigrants from Pennsylvania, Virginia and Kentucky; Indiana and Illinois were much more nearly southern. Immigration into these states had been determined by the geography of that section; the settlers had gone down the Ohio and up its tributaries, the Muskingum, the Scioto, the Miamis, and the Wabash; or up the Mississippi and its great tributary, the Illinois. Or they had followed transverse trails or "traces," roads such as the National Road which stretched from Cumberland, Maryland, through to Columbus and finally to Indianapolis, Vandalia, and St. Louis. They had settled the lower West by 1840—before the era of the railroads which played so large a part in the settlement of the upper or lake region in the late forties and the fifties.

By 1850, the population of the whole region north of the Ohio had increased to nearly 5,000,000. The growth in Ohio, Indiana, and Illinois during the ten years (1840–1850) was by far the greater in absolute numbers, but Wisconsin and Iowa had made greater pro-

---

[4] An analogous change was observable in Iowa, i. e. from Iowa City to Des Moines.

[5] *Sixth Census of the United States, 1840; Census of 1850.* The population for the whole Northwest in 1840 and 1850, by states was as follows:

	1840		1850
Ohio	1,519,467		1,980,329
Indiana	685,866		988,416
Illinois	476,183		851,470
Michigan	212,267		397,654
Iowa Territory	43,112	(state)	192,214
Wisconsin "	30,945	(state)	305,391
Total	2,967,840		4,715,474

portional gains. A significant fact regarding population origins is that of Indiana's population in 1850 the combined total of those who had come from New England, New York and Pennsylvania did not equal the number of those who had migrated from the slave-holding South. In that year in the States of Ohio, Indiana, Illinois, and Iowa there were half a million natives of the South, and the children of natives of southern states constituted, no doubt, an even greater element in the population. There were also New Englanders, or the descendants of New Englanders, at Marietta, Ohio, in Cincinnati, and in Albion and Edwardsville, Illinois; Germans were to be found in large numbers in Cincinnati, in Belleville, Illinois, and in Mississippi and Illinois river towns; French strains lingered at Gallipolis and Vincennes. In contrast, in northern Ohio and the lake region around Chicago, the predominant elements were from New York, New England, and Europe.[6]

When we begin our story—in the forties—the whole free West was, in a general way, united. The lower and the more sparsely settled upper region possessed a common spirit of western optimism and progress. Men were here consciously engaged in the great task of commonwealth building. Such fulsome words as those quoted at the beginning of the chapter were commonly indulged in. A page of history was here to be written by nothing less than the hand of God; a destiny of universal importance was to be achieved here in this "Great Northwest," this "West," this "Free West," this "Great Valley." Here was popular romanticism on a grand scale. Whether or not the wordy predictions of the forties have been fulfilled, there have indeed been important developments in the Middle West that make its history worth the telling. It early became the center of the political life of the nation. From 1840 to 1860, it was the most democratic section in the country and the testing ground of American politics. On the great questions of slavery extension, secession, and civil war, this section proved to be the deciding factor; and since that war, most of the great political battles of the nation have been fought with reference to it. Here was the zone of doubtful states for whose control the leading political parties contended. From this region since the forties have come "available" candidates for the offices of President and Vice-President of the United States. After the war Ohio became known as the mother of presidents and, farther west, vigorous, if ill-fated,

[6] *United States Census of 1850,* Table XV, showing nativities of the population of the United States.

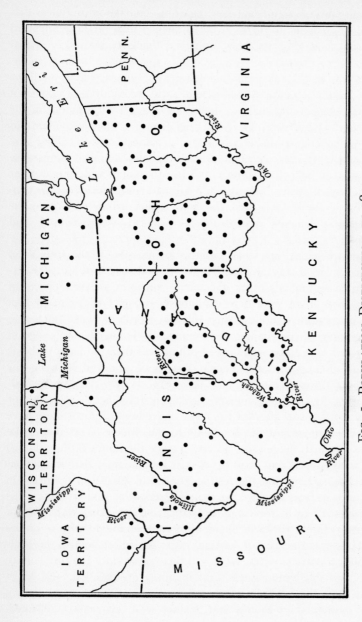

Fig. 1. Population Distribution in 1840

Each dot indicates a county having more than 5,000 people, the lower West showing the greater population density.

third party or insurgent political movements developed. If it be asserted that the study of politics has become somewhat stale and profitless and that turbulent currents of life overflowing narrow political channels make that kind of history less important than other types of development, then it may be said that other aspects of life in the Middle West during this middle period also demand attention.

This is especially true of economic developments. First in the lower West with its southern trading interests, then in the upper or lake regions centering in Chicago, and finally in the prairie corn and wheat belts stretching across the Mississippi and the Missouri—problems of land settlement, economic activity, discontent, and demand for markets, constitute perhaps the most significant phases of the westward moving conquest of the continent. The Middle West supplied first the South and later the East with grain and meat; it has been called a granary of the world. Immigration into it from the South, the East, and Europe, taken as a whole, constituted one of the great population movements of history. However, the difficulty of access to markets due to its inland location, resulted in its subordination and financial dependence upon the East and Europe. The Middle West became the victim of sporadic cheap money crazes, the center of farmer discontent and insurgent protest.

The task of describing social and cultural conditions is equally important. Less realistic writers have emphasized the West as the land of opportunity, have pointed out its wholesome contributions to American individualism and democracy. They have stressed the high adventure of the frontier and the ideal aspects of farm and village life. We should not allow them to carry the romance of the frontier too far. More realistic writers have dwelt upon the harsher features of the conquest of the continent, the exploitation of resources, the waste of human material, the narrow Puritanism, and the cultural degradation that have accompanied the westward movement. To join too readily in this "revolt from the village" would be unhistorical. It may be frankly admitted that the novelist and the poet have been more successful than the historian in depicting social life in the West. The tales of Mark Twain, *The Spoon River Anthology* of Edgar Lee Masters, the *Main Street* of Sinclair Lewis are notable contributions. History owes a great debt to those novelists who in recent decades have been creating for us an invaluable series of "sagas" of the Middle West.

The Progressive Western Democracy, 1845–1848

It was during the years from 1840 to 1860, from the Harrison campaign to the election of Lincoln, that the Middle West became what we have already suggested it was—the storm center of American politics. Local politics in town, county, and state offered a turbulent training ground for the many restless lawyers, newspaper editors, and country school-teachers whose meager preparation for public life proved no obstacle in view of the increase in the number of elective offices and the low qualifications to be met. Geographical location, the sectional divergence between the East and the South, and the general trend of national economic and political development made the whole free West—particularly the States of Ohio, Indiana and Illinois—the political battle-ground for the whole nation. The sturdy, struggling, western farmer of these states with his hand on the plow and a formal education that went little beyond the third grade became the juryman before whom were tried the vast concerns of a great people—expansion, freedom or slavery, war or peace. His descendants in the Middle West have had to face questions of equal importance.

American democracy put off the knee-breeches of gentility, the livery of a trained public service, and the robes of the august Roman republicanism of Washington, Hamilton, Madison and J. Q. Adams. Under the influence of Jefferson, Jackson, Clay, and Harrison, it appeared in equalitarian long trousers or in the coarse, democratic dress of the frontier. American practical politics was taking on the aspect of a hand-to-hand tussle, a battle of wits, or a game to be won. These changes, at work on a national scale, were given added impetus in the West. It was a turbulent, youthful, rampant democracy. The people, now that universal white manhood suffrage had been granted, were to pass on all things political. Nearly every year an election, local, congressional, state, or national, raised the popular pulse to fever heat. Rough and ready campaign methods, exciting and demagogic tricks, were indulged in. Huge mass meetings, originating in Jacksonian days and becoming conspicuous in the hard cider and log cabin campaign of 1840, remained the characteristic form of popular political manifestation through to the days of the Lincoln-Douglas debates in the fifties and on into the Civil War period.

Although the size of these assemblages is no doubt exaggerated in contemporary accounts, we are justified in saying that never before or since have there been such political meetings; they were literally assemblages of the whole masses of the people.

That which was held at Dayton (in 1840) which was one of the largest, presented a most novel and picturesque spectacle. The number was estimated at from 100,000 to 300,000 souls. For two or three days all the roads leading to the place were crowded with carriages, horsemen and pedestrian travellers. . . . The excitement was intense . . . but there was no anger, no uproar, no violence; . . . they bore distinctly and without ostentation the marks of a people who were strangers to poverty and to oppression.[7]

Years afterward, to a Lincoln ratification meeting held at Springfield, Illinois, people came from points two hundred miles away. Lines of wagon trains, one of them seven miles in length, converged on that town from all sides.[8] An observer of the campaign of 1840 held out this warning: "Such excitement as we have lately witnessed must almost necessarily be demoralizing; it unfits men for somber and calm action; it leads to constant resort to grog shops." [9]

Thus the people of the free West in the forties and fifties were a political people. This was true in all senses of the term "politics" whether the word be held to mean political ideals and philosophy; or social attitudes that arise because of sectional, geographic, ethnic, economic or deep-seated environmental factors; or, in a narrower sense, political party programs or activities; or, in a still narrower sense, the designs and manipulations of politicians and petty factions, the meaning usually given to it under American conditions. In Ohio, Indiana, and Illinois, American political life was in its heyday; never before or since in our history has politics occupied such a position. For weal or woe, the Middle West took on political habits and a political tone that colors its life until to-day. Indeed the age was too political, a fact recognized even in that day. "Who can be insensible to the fact that our universal mind has assumed a political character? . . . Political pursuits do not lead to the full development and vigor of mind," were the words of a complaint in 1835.[10] But, since it was a major stream in the life of the people and left so great an impress, politics, in both its deeper and shallower currents, must constantly engage our attention.

[7] James Hall, *The West, Its Soil, Surface and Productions* (Cincinnati, 1848), pp. 168, 169.
[8] W. H. Smith, "Old Time Campaigns," *Journal Illinois State Historical Society*, XIII, 23 (April, 1920).
[9] *Western Messenger*, 1840, p. 285.
[10] *Western Monthly Magazine*, January, 1835, pp. 23, 29.

The free West was, in 1840 and until the middle fifties, controlled both in the lower part and in the lake region by the western wing of the Democratic party. Being the heir of the Jeffersonian and Jacksonian tradition, the party at its best was a good expression of the higher political ideals of the people and of the type of life that most of the people in the West were in fact living. There were among its members social radicals and revolutionists who rejoiced that their great prophet, Jefferson, was a radical.[11]

The true democrat wars earnestly against the existing state of society which is built upon the supposition that men are of less value than property. The real character of the contest of which this country is the scene is a war between man and money. The democracy advocate the right of revolution, of universal suffrage, of freedom of trade, of overthrow of banks, of the establishment of a constitutional currency.[12]

Profiting by the mistakes made in overemphasizing internal improvements, canal-building, ill-managed banking systems, and the importance of merchants in general—mistakes which were usually ascribed to Whigs—this Democracy reasserted Jeffersonian individual liberty, private initiative, agrarianism, and simplicity. This western version of the rights of man was coupled with praise for the farmer, the laborer, and the mechanic; the newly arrived foreigner and the Catholic, too, found defenders in it.[13] The organization was called the "Progressive Western Democracy" party and has much in it that reminds us of the Populists, Bryan Democrats, and insurgent Republicans of more recent years. Its program, it is true, was conspicuous by its lack of concern about the Negro, whether slave or free. "Sumptuary legislation" in the form of regulation of man's habits and of prohibition of liquor was not a part of its creed. But the "common man" was exalted, and there was a deep consciousness among these western Democrats of the forties that they were citizens of no mean country. Their nation had, in fact, special missions to perform for mankind.[14]

In 1847, Clement L. Vallandigham, in a speech on "Constitutional reform," said:

The capacity, once doubted . . . of the people for self government in its vast expanded limits, has been demonstrated; the tyrants of the old world have looked on with blanched cheek at the progress of the Demo-

[11] *The New Constitution,* September 22, 1849, p. 329. This journal was edited by Samuel Medary.
[12] *Western Review,* 1846, p. 208.
[13] *Democratic Monthly Magazine,* 1844, *passim.*
[14] See William Allen Papers, Library of Congress.

cratic principle, which has stricken out a new path. . . . The Spirit of Progress . . . it is vain to resist. . . . I belong to what is sometimes sneeringly called the progressive school of politics, I am proud to belong to it. It teaches faith in man as God made him.[15]

Samuel Medary, a prominent western journalist said, "There is a progressing, reforming, radical spirit spreading over the civilized world, and let Ohio not be the last to partake of the regenerating spirit." [16] This progressive democracy, believing in world revolution, had a conscious feeling of sympathy with revolutionary movements in the France, Austria, Hungary, and Germany of 1848–1850. "It belongs to the United States to stir up free principles over the world." [17] The lake region was to differ from the lower West in demanding a somewhat different type of reform, emphasizing prohibition of the liquor traffic, woman suffrage, and free soil. But everywhere there were demands for popular election to all offices, hostility to monopolies, limitation on a state's power to incur debt, a more extensive public school system and various kinds of judicial and legal reform. More advanced reformers demanded legal equality of married women with men, exemption for the debtor of his homestead, and a ten-hour day for working men.[18] Most of the states north of the Ohio in the forties and fifties were to frame new or make over old constitutions. At constitutional conventions held in Ohio, Indiana, and Illinois, Iowa, and Wisconsin, these reforms were urged and some of them adopted.[19]

Western Democrats in their exuberance and optimism were ardent expansionists; to them, however, expansion meant a vague manifest destiny or the spread of the American government and the "democratic principle" which, if need be, they, like French revolutionists, were ready to extend by the sword. It was agrarian and democratic, not capitalistic imperialism. It might indeed, though it probably would not, imply the expansion of slavery, an institution well-established, American, and "constitutional." Too often the mistake has been made of concluding, because the lake region became antislavery and radi-

[15] *Speeches, Arguments, Addresses, and Letters of C. L. Vallandigham* (New York, 1864), p. 91.
[16] *The New Constitution*, May 5, 1849, p. 48.
[17] *Ibid.*, pp. 221, 381.
[18] *Ibid.*, pp. 24, 48, 55, 119, 191, 256, 322, 327.
[19] *Debates Ohio Constitutional Convention* of 1850–51; *Report of the Debates of the Indiana Convention* of 1850; *Constitutional Debates* of 1847, *Illinois*, A. C. Cole (ed.); *Ill. State Register*, Jan.–Aug., 1847, *passim*; F. L. Paxson, "A Constitution of Democracy, Wisconsin, 1847," *Miss. Valley Hist. Review*, II, 3–24 (June, 1915).

cal, that the spirit of the lower West was pro-southern. To maintain that Samuel Medary, William Allen, Stephen A. Douglas, Clement L. Vallandigham, Thomas A. Hendricks, and George H. Pendleton were pro-southern rather than western leaders is to fail to see the main significance of their careers. It is true that they showed a marked degree of unconcern about Negro rights, and that in the counties along the Ohio and Mississippi rivers there were thousands of men who were pro-southern. But these leaders as a group and their millions of followers were western men and progressives. When, in the fifties and sixties, their allies in the South became pro-slavery secessionists, and the lake district went over to antislavery Republican "radicalism," these western men, though thwarted and embarrassed, nevertheless held to their ideals. They proved, in fact, that the West was the center of two types of progressivism. Before, during, and after the Civil War, they kept alive a spirit of democratic western discontent opposed to the East, the South, and the lakes alike, a spirit which later took the form of the Greenbackism of Pendleton and the free-silverism of Bryan. The preservation of the party of Jefferson and Jackson seemed entrusted to their hands, and these ideals were under their leadership to show remarkable vitality and recuperative power— as they have so often done in our history.

In the forties, the Whigs were the minority party in the free West. Accused by Democrats of upholding property rather than human rights and of attempting to build up in America a stratified social system, they were actually quite democratic, as were, in fact, almost all westerners. Especially in the lower West, there was little to distinguish them from Democrats. But as followers of Clay they would not admit that they were like Jackson and Polk men; they claimed that Democrats were demagogues; they sought to justify the banker and the merchant and to make apology for "moderate wealth."

A fell spirit of demagogism has swept over our land; it has become fashionable to flatter the agricultural and laboring classes, because they are the most numerous and wield the greatest power at the ballot boxes; while a systematic effort has been made to decry the merchant and banker . . . I am happy to believe that the acquisition of wealth does not necessarily, nor as I hope usually, blunt the sensibilities nor destroy the manliness of a generous character. . . . If money be sought with moderation, . . . no employment affords exercise to higher or nobler powers of the mind and heart.[20]

[20] James Hall, *The West, Its Commerce and Navigation* (Cincinnati, 1848), pp. 2, 3, 25.

The Whigs of the lake region were more antislavery than those of river valleys and together with Free Soilers and Free Soil Democrats were in time to form the chief elements in the new Republican party, the economic beginnings of which appeared, as we shall see, in the forties.

Would the Progressive Democratic West Support Polk and the Southern Democracy?

Polk had entered office in 1845 with the support of all the free West except Ohio, which had given its vote in 1844 to the Whig candidate, Henry Clay. The old Jacksonian alliance of the Democratic West with the slave-holding southern Democracy seemed destined to continue. In the lower West especially the Democratic party was strongly entrenched in the Cincinnati region, in "the pocket" (southwestern Indiana) and in "Egypt" (southern Illinois). In these places southern leaders could look for a large degree of support for their measures in all the period up to the Civil War. But even here, there came repeated revolts of Democrats and an assertion of their rights, the progressive western Democrats holding some such relation to the national Democratic party as insurgent or progressive Republicans now hold to those of the East. In the lake region, more serious defections occurred as early as 1845. As we trace in this chapter the political development of the West from 1845 to 1848, our attention will repeatedly be brought to these more constant factors in the situation.

The whole West was, as Polk entered office in 1845, on the eve of great development. Another cycle of prosperity was at hand. Land settlement was again active, and the population was increasing rapidly. Recovery from the panic of 1837, and from over-indulgence in canal-building and reckless banking, was on the way. In Ohio the recovery was almost complete, and Indiana and Illinois were slowly but surely coming out of the nightmare of the late thirties and early forties, out from under the staggering incubus of debt, putting aside their chagrin at the failure of their canal systems or other undertakings and gradually losing the stigma attached to them by British bondholders of being in the third class among the states in their ability and willingness to pay interest on and the principal of their debts. No more were taxes to be so hated and oppressive and the names of their states to be such bywords that foreigners would refuse to settle in them. Never again were their bonds to be worth only seventeen cents on the dollar in eastern markets; their credit was being established; the lessons of economy were being learned; there was less hesitation in paying "pro-British" taxes; even "soulless" Whiggish banks, if well-regulated, were coming into favor among Democrats.[21]

The West was becoming more and more assertive in national politics. Two new states, Iowa and Wisconsin, were within two years to enter the Union and to add to the voting strength of the section in Congress. As we have said, constitutional conventions were to be held in Ohio, Indiana, Illinois, and other states during the next few years to give effect to desired changes in government and finance. A great trade convention was to meet at Chicago in 1847 which would call attention to the economic growth of the region. By conserving the strong hold they had on the lower West and properly using the advantage already gained, the national Democratic leaders might hope to control the expanding energies and appropriate the voting strength of the West for an indefinite period.

No seat in the cabinet was given by President Polk to the free West, but it was clear that in Congress the region was to play an important part in national affairs. John Davis of Indiana was elected Speaker of the House, William Allen of Ohio became chairman of the important Senate Committee on Foreign Affairs, while both Senate and House Committees on Public Lands were headed by western men, Senator Semple and John A. McClernand, both of Illinois. James Shields of that state was Commissioner of the Land Office and a personal friend of Polk. Stephen A. Douglas, representing the Quincy, Illinois, District, became Chairman of the House Committee on Territories. These men together with Lewis Cass of Michigan, Edward A. Hannegan, and Jesse Bright of Indiana and, after the admission of Iowa, Senator A. C. Dodge of that state, were the leaders of the free West at Washington. Most of them lived in the lower part,[22] and four of them, Allen, Semple, McClernand and Dodge, had

[21] For these economic conditions see: R. H. Rerick, *History of Ohio*, 287; Logan Esarey, *History of Indiana*, I, 423-425, 436, 524; Dunn, *Indiana*, p. 491; *Ill. Con. Debates* of 1847 (Cole), Intro. xxi, xxiii, xxiv, xxx, 87-89, 253, 256, 263, 264, 269, 273, 274; article in *London Times*, Dec. 8, 1842 quoted in *Coll. Ill. St. Hist. Lib.* Vol. VII, xxxix (note); G. M. Thompson, "A Study of the Administration of Gov. Thos. Ford," *ibid.*, lvi, lvii, lix *et passim; Ill. State Register*, Mar. 12, Apr. 9, 1847; T. C. Pease, *The Frontier State*, Ch. XVII.

[22] Allen at Chillicothe, Ohio; Bright at Madison, Indiana; Hannegan at Covington and Davis at Carlisle, Indiana, in the Wabash valley; Semple at Ed-

been born in slave states. In 1845 there were only two Whig Senators in Congress from the whole region north and west of the Ohio River and the representation in the House was overwhelmingly Democratic. The admission of Iowa and Wisconsin did not change the proportion.

The harmonious action of southern and western Democrats that had put Polk in office had for one of its slogans the acquisition of Texas and Oregon. The western men willingly voted in the winter of 1844–1845 for Texas. Their vote carried with it little or nothing of a distinct desire to extend slavery in Texas and the Southwest. They voted, as Douglas of Illinois said later, "upon broad national grounds, elevated far above, and totally disconnected from the question of slavery. [They voted for] . . . the extension of territory, of commerce, of navigation, of political power, of national security, and glory . . . without especial reference to any particular section." [23] Would southern men be equally national in spirit and vote for the seizure of all of Oregon? President Polk, indeed, in his message of December, 1845, asserted the claim of the United States to the whole of that territory, and even the *Washington Union,* the administration paper edited by Thomas Ritchie, had come out in its favor.[24] Being practical expansionists, large numbers of western people had already emigrated to Oregon, and the question of the formation of a separate nation in the far Northwest had been freely discussed and approved by men in Congress. A group of western "progressive" Democrats headed by Allen of Ohio, Cass of Michigan, Hannegan of Indiana in the Senate, and Douglas in the House—called radicals and "hot-spurs"—began a strenuous campaign for all of Oregon.[25] They insisted on the immediate cessation of joint occupancy by England and the United States, the building of a road across the Rockies, the preparation of a plan of territorial government, the reaffirmation of the Monroe Doctrine, an increase in the navy, and, if necessary, a

wardsville, McClernand at Shawneetown and later Springfield, Douglas at Quincy, Illinois; Dodge at Burlington, Iowa.

[23] *Cong. Globe,* 31 Cong., 1 Sess., XXII, 1; Albert J. Beveridge, *Abraham Lincoln,* II, 106.

[24] *Cong. Globe,* 28 Cong., 2 Sess., 362, 372; Clark E. Persinger, "The Bargain of 1844 as the Origin of the Wilmot Proviso," *Annual Rep. Am. Historical Ass'n.,* 1911, I, 189; W. E. Dodd, *Robert A. Walker, Imperialist* (booklet); Polk, *Diary* I, 110; J. D. Richardson, *Messages and Papers of the Presidents* IV, 395; C. H. Ambler, *Thomas Ritchie,* 260, 262.

[25] *National Intelligencer,* Nov. 8, 1845; *Niles' Register,* Vol. 69, p. 165; Chicago *Daily Journal,* Feb. 7, Mar. 24, 1846; A. C. McLaughlin, *Lewis Cass,* Ch. VIII.

war with England, some of them expecting that if war came, "away would go the Canadas." [26] "Fifty-four Forty or Fight" became the slogan, coined, it is thought, either by Allen himself or by Sam Medary of Ohio.[27] Resolutions calling for a larger army and navy and for better defenses on the Great Lakes were introduced in Congress by western men; the Chicago City Council held a meeting to consider defense against attack by Lake Michigan.[28] There were reckless statements for the conquest by "democracy" of all of Oregon, all of Mexico, and "the whole continent." Allen was besieged by letters from the West making these demands. Oregon was needed "for the extension of free institutions" and for poor men who wanted homes there. Great Britain was the enemy of progress and the Whigs who stood against all of Oregon were "Tories." [29] Romantic exaltation raised this democratic imperialism to high levels and made it coincident with fate, with manifest destiny, and with the progress of the suns in their courses. Said a western editor giving expression to the expansionist spirit of that day and coupling it with the spread of democratic principles:

The United States must be a conquering republic; and if they should not use the sword so freely as former republics have done, it will be because circumstances will pave the way to their comparatively peaceful absorption of adjacent countries. . . . If we advance for the next half century at the same rate that we have since 1789 our dominion must embrace all that portion of North America which is capable of sustaining human life. . . . Shall Democracy or shall Aristocracy be the governing principle of the World? That is the question which must be decided by the settlement of the rival claims to Oregon. . . . We are the depositories of the Democratic principle. . . . It claims for itself this continent as a rallying ground from which to move the world. . . . It is a fact which . . . stirs patriotism, the love of glory, . . . a desire of territorial aggrandizement and that ardent wish which every man must have felt to make his country the first in the world, the sun in the system of nations. . . . Louisiana, Florida and Texas have been acquired; and now we propose to assume rule over the whole of Oregon and the Californias are soon to fall into our hands; . . . the probabilities of a larger portion of the Mexican republic being annexed to us, within fifteen years, are much greater. . . . By a sad necessity they [the British] are compelled to govern the East, by a necessity

[26] *Niles' Annual Register,* Vol. 62, pp. 241, 242; Jan. 3, 10, 1847; Indianapolis *State Sentinel,* Jan. 13, 1846; Chicago *Daily Journal,* Feb. 2, 1846; *Cong. Globe,* 1 Sess., 29 Cong., 263.
[27] R. C. McGrane, *William Allen, A Study in Western Democracy,* pp. 104–120.
[28] Chicago *Daily Journal,* Jan. 5, Feb. 10, 1846; *Niles' Register,* Jan. 10, 17, 1846.
[29] William Allen papers, Library of Congress.

equally imperious . . . we are compelled to monopolize the West, driven
to absorb all the country lying and being between the farthest line of the
northern inhabitable regions and the isthmus of Darien.[30]

Allen, himself, in the Senate, pointed to Athens, Sparta, Rome, Car-
thage and Venice and said, "the United States must be a conquering Republic; . . . step by step we have advanced until the idea of
controlling the whole continent is what every village voter discusses;
. . . we now propose to assume rule over the whole of Oregon." [31]

But the Democratic party of the South sought to check its reckless
progressive western wing. Under Calhoun's leadership, they opposed
any war for Oregon and favored "masterly inactivity" or compromise
at 49°. President Polk and Senator Benton of Missouri reversed
their earlier positions and, following Calhoun's lead, agreed upon
compromise.[32] Against the wishes and vote of almost all western
Democrats, compromise carried.[33] When events took this turn, a cry
went up of treachery to the West; Stephen A. Douglas said a "game"
had been played; Allen resigned as Chairman of the Senate Committee on Foreign Relations and such leading Democratic papers as
the Indianapolis *Sentinel,* the *Illinois State Register* and the Galena
Jeffersonian resented the action of their own administration.[34] Senator Hannegan of Indiana said, "When the Nueces boundary was

[30] *Western Review,* 1846, pp. 183–188; see also speeches of the following men
on the annexation of Oregon in the United States House of Representatives
(1846) : Robert Dale Owen of Indiana, Jan. 28; W. W. Wick of Indiana, Jan. 30;
Allen G. Thurman of Ohio, Jan. 28; Jacob Brinkerhoff of Ohio, Jan. 14; William
Sawyer of Ohio, Jan. 31, *Cong. Globe,* 1 Sess., 29th Cong., 268; Appendix, pp. 101,
199, 226. See also U. S. Senate speeches of Edward A. Hannegan of Indiana,
Feb. 16; William Allen of Ohio, Feb. 10, 11; *Cong. Globe,* 1 Sess., 29th Cong.
351, 357, 370; Appendix, pp. 62, 834–842 (Allen's speech).

[31] In commenting on the filibustering expedition of William Walker in Central
America, the Chicago *Times* said in 1856: "The rod of Empire which the fathers
of the Spanish race grasped so strongly in Central America is falling from their
relaxing hold. They must give way before the advance of the North American;
. . . they have not the strength to stay the tide of conquest which sooner or
later will overwhelm them." *Daily Chicago Times,* May 2, 1856.

[32] *Niles' Register,* Nov. 8, 1845; Chicago *Daily Journal,* June 27, 1846; Polk's
Diary, I, 339.

[33] *Niles' Register,* May 2, 1846; Aug. 15, 1847. Two Democratic representatives
from Ohio River districts voted with the South; they were J. J. McDowell of
southern Ohio and Robert Dale Owen of southern Indiana. Perhaps it is true
that except for the "bluff of 54° 40'," we would not have received even up to
49°. McGrane, *Allen,* pp. 115–119.

[34] *Niles' Register,* Jan. 10, 1846, p. 289; Polk's *Diary,* I, 471; *Indiana Daily
State Sentinel,* July 8, 1846; Chicago *Daily Journal,* Aug. 25 and 31, 1846.

concerned we took the whole; if it (the Oregon territory) was good for the production of sugar and cotton it could not have encountered the opposition it has done. . . . I dreaded on the part of those who were so strenuously in favor of the annexation of Texas at the Baltimore convention, I dreaded on their part, Punic faith." [35] The slow, compromising methods of diplomacy had betrayed the West. Aged, grave, and experienced "grannies" of the South and East had humiliated the nation by treating with England. J. C. Calhoun was only an aristocrat, a patrician, anyway, "There never was a solitary grain of democracy in him and his clannish state." [36] The whole Oregon episode is significant as showing how Democrats, even in the lower West, broke away from southern leadership. Repeated disregard of their interests in the future and more "insults" of this type and Democrats in the lake region would not hesitate to break away and form a new party.

But feelings of resentment for the time being gave way before the need of party unity under southern control, and most of the vigorous projects of the Polk administration received enthusiastic support. It was to be expected that a region that had favored the annexation of Texas would give enthusiastic support to the Mexican War, and when the war began, expectations were borne out by the vigorous participation of southern Illinois, Indiana, and Ohio in it. In answering the war call, the free West did not shrink from a possible extension of slavery into Texas, but in their conscious desire to extend "American institutions" and "the seed of freedom," it was an ardent expansionist zeal and war spirit rather than pro-slavery feeling that carried them on. At any rate the lower tier of states north of the Ohio gave more ardent support than any part of the country except Texas, Louisiana, and Missouri; Illinois furnished five times as many volunteers as pro-slavery South Carolina.[37] In southern Illinois and Indiana the enthusiasm was especially high, and Whig and Democrat were united for the war; in the radical Whig and Free Soil cen-

---

[35] *Niles' Register,* Jan. 3, 1846, p. 278; Feb. 16, 1846, pp. 411, 413; Clark E. Persinger, "The Bargain of 1844 as the Origin of the Wilmot Proviso," *Annual Rep. Am. Hist. Ass'n,* 1911, I, 194.

[36] Allen Papers, Library of Congress.

[37] *Ex. Doc.* No. 62, 30 Cong., 1 Sess.; W. E. Dodd, "The West and the War with Mexico," *Journal Ill. St. Hist. Society,* V, No. 2, 162, 163, 168, 169; *Ill. St. Register,* May 28, 1847; Gustave Koerner, *Memoirs,* I, 494-505; Indianapolis *State Sentinel,* June 10, 1848.

ters of Chicago and the Western Reserve there was, it is true, strong opposition.[38]

"The West is agricultural," said the *Illinois State Register* in 1846, "it has no manufactures and it never will have any of any importance." [39] A West not yet industrialized might well use such language in support of the Democratic tariff of the Polk administration, the Walker-McKay Tariff of 1846. Democratic congressmen from southern Ohio, Indiana, and Illinois gave unstinted support to this low tariff measure. Indeed, the states of the free West, when the final vote came, gave large majorities in its favor.[40] However, the time was near at hand when not only western Whigs but Democrats, especially those in the lake region, seeing the industrial revolution already spreading for better or worse through eastern and northern Ohio and realizing the need of protection to Ohio wool growers, were to calculate the values of a high tariff. In fact, in the debate on the bill, there were, among Democrats, hints of a bolt. Jacob Brinkerhoff of Mansfield, Ohio, and John Wentworth of Chicago, Democratic representatives in Congress, together with the Cleveland *Plain Dealer* and a considerable local following, threatened to oppose the bill and to refuse to vote for a special war tax on tea and coffee. They complained that the administration wanted them to pay for a war of southern conquest, after having "given away millions of acres of territory in Oregon." [41] But the threat was not carried out; Brinkerhoff, contrary to expectations, voted for the bill.[42] However, this discontent continued to grow; Brinkerhoff was soon to show decided free-soil tendencies and to become the reputed author of the famous Wilmot Proviso; this early, both he and Wentworth were showing signs of a restlessness in the Democratic party that can be only partly explained on the basis of their opposition to slavery. The free-soil Republican party of the lake region was to have deep-seated origins, sectional and economic in nature; this fact is evident even though we admit the deep moral, religious, and humanitarian origins of its abolitionist left wing.

[38] Chicago *Daily Journal*, Sept. and Oct., 1846, *passim; Ill. State Register,* May 28, 1847, June 4, July 4, 1847.

[39] Issue of Sept. 25, 1846.

[40] *Niles' Register,* Vol. 70, p. 309.

[41] *Ibid.,* Vol. 70, p. 273; Polk's *Diary* I, 498. Polk says Brinkerhoff's threat was due to the fact that he was not appointed to the position of paymaster in the army.

[42] Chicago *Daily Journal,* July 13, Aug. 4, 1846; *Niles',* Vol. 70, pp. 301, 309, 356.

ECONOMIC ORIGINS OF THE REPUBLICAN PARTY IN THE LAKE REGION

The lake region has only incidentally engaged our attention; we have, however, already noted that as early as the late forties this district was emerging as a new section in the West. The Western Reserve, Michigan, Chicago, and settlements in Wisconsin and upper Iowa constituted the "new West," a "new Northwest," and like Texas and, a little later, California, they were centers of expanding energy that compelled recognition in national affairs. Here were to be reflected social and political tendencies different from those of the older and still dominant West of southern and central Ohio, Indiana, and Illinois. This upper West was becoming more and more a region of diversified native, eastern, and European population elements. Railroads were to affect its growth more than that of the older settled portion lying just north of the Ohio; it was to prove less fundamentally agricultural and to be much more quickly industrialized. Farther away from the slave-holding South, not bound either by ties of kinship and tradition, or by the Mississippi-Ohio river-trading interests, it was to be more favorable seed ground for anti-southern movements such as the Free Soil party and, later, the Republican party. Though at first Democratic in politics and, under such men as Cass of Michigan and Dodge of Iowa, mildly "pro-southern," how long could such a growing region remain loyal to a party that looked southward or southwestward in its policies? Would the Democrats of the lake region long remain tied to southern apron-strings?

The action of this region on another important issue of the Polk administration, the Harbor and River Bill, is a partial answer to these questions. On this, many Democrats from the lakes stood in opposition to Polk, while those of the lower West stood with him. The divergence was later more clearly marked on the Wilmot Proviso and on other questions. The free West was destined to split politically into two parts with consequences that were very quickly to be of grave national importance.

The Harbor and River Bill of 1847 came as a result of the increase in population in the upper West and of the demand for the recognition of the economic interests of the section. This great region desired better communication with the East and in particular pressed upon Congress the need of improvement of the condition of the lake traffic —the same kind of demand that now expresses itself in attempts to obtain a deep waterway from Chicago to the sea. The growth in population was great in the forties; in the fifties, it became nothing less than tremendous.[43] During these years, as has been previously noted, Iowa and Wisconsin were admitted as states; thousands of people migrating from New York, older parts of Ohio, and Germany and Ireland settled in the region stretching from the Western Reserve to the southern shores of Lake Michigan and out to northern Iowa.[44] The "great exodus" from Ireland and Germany in 1847 and 1848 due to famine and revolution was the largest movement of foreign immigration that the country had yet seen. While many of these foreign immigrants, especially the Irish, remained in the eastern states, others went to the West to swell the population of the towns of the lake region and to work on canal or railroad construction. The Germans, in many cases, brought one or two hundred dollars with them to buy farm land. During the decade 1840 to 1850, especially the latter half, hundreds of thousands of acres of the best corn and wheat lands in northwestern Ohio, northern Indiana, Illinois, and Iowa, and southern Wisconsin and Michigan were bought up by farmers from New York and from the valleys of the Weser and Moselle in Germany. The sales of public lands at the offices located at Upper Sandusky, Defiance, Ft. Wayne, Winimac, Chicago, Dixon, Dubuque, and Milwaukee were much the largest in the United States from 1843 to 1850. The next largest amounts—sold in Missouri and the southern states —were far below these, and the sales in the lower West at Jeffersonville, Vincennes, Shawneetown, Kaskaskia, and other offices were small in comparison. In 1847, the year that the number of immigrants into the United States rose from 154,000, the figure for 1846, to over 234,000, over 600,000 acres were sold in southern Wisconsin, and about 500,000 acres in Illinois. Nearly three fourths of this latter amount was sold in the Chicago and Dixon offices.[45]

---

[43] *Report Corps of Topographical Engineers,* House Ex. Doc. No. 19, 1 Sess. 30 Cong., pp. 22, 23. See also *Census of United States 1850 and 1860.*

[44] The migration direct from New England was smaller than that from the sources named. Into Michigan and Wisconsin there was also a movement of English and Canadians.

[45] For foreign immigration 1840–1860 see *Eighth Census of United States,* 1860, *Population,* XIX. For land sales in northern Illinois see *Sen. Doc.* 30 Cong. 2 Sess. No. 2 (*Report of the Sec. of the Treas.*) For reports of the Land Office for 1843 to 1849 see *Sen. Doc.* 28 Cong., 2 Sess., Vol. I., No. 7; *Sen. Ex. Doc.* 29 Cong., 1 Sess., Vol. II., No. 12; and *Sen. Doc.* 30 Cong., 2 Sess., No. 2; *Sen. Ex. Doc.* 31 Cong., 1 Sess., Vol. II, No. 1, etc. For German and Irish settlement in Illinois see Pooley, *Settlement of Illinois,* pp. 394, 395, 420, 430, 435, 436, 496, 500.

The urban population showed the same increase during this decade. Small towns in 1840, Cleveland, Detroit, Chicago, and Milwaukee became, by 1850, places of from 15,000 to 30,000 inhabitants. Chicago grew from 4,000 to 30,000, displaced Detroit as the largest lake city west of Buffalo and was given its first great honor when it was chosen as the meeting place for the big convention of the lake interests in 1847. Although these towns were as yet far surpassed in size by the Ohio river cities and St. Louis, they were undergoing a marvelous growth.[46]

In 1845–1846, over 1,500,000 people, over half of them living in Ohio, but probably no less than 150,000 located in and around Chicago and Milwaukee, were dependent on the lakes for a market. The interior was opening up. The Wabash and Erie Canal was carrying increased quantities of the produce of northwestern Ohio and northern Indiana to the lake outlet.[47] The Illinois-Michigan Canal was turning a part of the produce of northern Illinois to Chicago.[48] Farmers living one hundred miles distant would haul wheat to that city when the roads were good.[49] Passage by the lakes was for most of this produce the only outlet, since the through railroad routes to the East were not to come into use until after 1850. Though the season during which navigation on the lakes could be carried on was shorter than that on the Ohio and Mississippi rivers, the grain of the upper West was in better condition when reaching New York than that of the lower West reaching New Orleans by river, and it commanded a better price.[50]

To carry the grain and flour of the lake district eastward and bring the settler, his household goods, supplies, and manufactured articles westward, there were engaged in 1845 on the lakes above Niagara Falls 375 vessels with a tonnage of 76,000 tons and a value of over $4,000,000.[51] In that year 1,500,000 barrels of flour passed by this route to the East, and the lakes were soon to surpass the Mississippi in the amount of grain destined for Europe.

But the shipping here, as on the great rivers, was exposed to great

[46] Population of the lake and river cities 1840 and 1850, Compendium *Sixth Census of the United States 1840*, pp. 26, 74, 78, 82, 86, 90, 94, 102; *Census of the United States 1850*, CIII–CXXXVI.

[47] *Indiana Weekly State Journal*, Dec. 3, 1847; E. R. Johnson, *History of the Domestic and Foreign Commerce of the United States*, I, 227.

[48] *Ibid.*, I, 228.

[49] *Niles'*, Oct. 31, 1846; Chicago *Daily Journal*, 1846, *passim*.

[50] *Niles'*, Oct. 31, 1846, p. 134.

[51] *Ibid.*, Oct. 17, p. 46, quoting *Bicknell's Reporter;* Chicago *Daily Journal*, Aug. 31, 1846.

dangers. The mouths of the small rivers that flowed into the lakes became filled with sand; the harbors afforded an unsafe shelter; the St. Clair Flats between Lakes Huron and Erie were dangerous and often impassable for many ships. In 1845, it was estimated that there were sixty lives lost on the lakes and thirty vessels driven ashore of which twenty were total wrecks.[52] Works of improvement which had been begun would be suspended before completion; dredge boats would have to stop operations because of insufficient appropriations. Money was wasted in improvements of small inlets and rivers. A demand went up from the lakes for larger appropriations. The region felt that it had not received its share of the government money. Congress had been relatively much more generous to the lower West in its appropriation to the Cumberland Road. That work of improvement in southern Ohio, Indiana, and Illinois had, up to 1845, received nearly $3,000,000 from the national treasury, while the principal lake improvements at Cleveland, River Raisin, St. Joseph, Michigan City, Milwaukee, and Chicago had totaled about $700,000.[53]

Bills were introduced in the winter of 1845–1846 for various harbor improvements and dredge boats for the lakes. Coupled with these were provisions for certain improvements on the Ohio, at the port of St. Louis, and also some appropriations for the Atlantic coast.[54] Although it contained log-rolling features, the final Harbor and River Bill was felt to be distinctly in favor of the lake interest. There seemed little doubt in that region that the bill as a whole would be passed and receive the President's signature. Many Democrats had already lost the constitutional hostility to internal improvements at national expense that had characterized the period of Jackson. The population of the lake region was urgently demanding the bill, and articles on its merits filled the columns of the Whig and Democratic papers near the lakes.[55] The Whigs of the Reserve approved it, and its most ardent advocates were Jacob Brinkerhoff of northern Ohio, John

[52] *Niles'*, Mar. 21, 1846.
[53] See *Statement of the Appropriation for the Construction and Repair of Roads and for the Improvement of Harbors and Rivers* by J. J. Abert of the Corps of Topographical Engineers. *Sen. Doc.* 29 Cong., 2 Sess., No. 44, pp. 17–20.
[54] *Cong. Globe*, 29 Cong., 1 Sess., 530, 1186; *Niles'*, Jan. 10, 1846, p. 290; Chicago *Daily Journal*, Aug. 12, 1846. There were to be appropriations for harbors at Buffalo, Cleveland, Sandusky City, Michigan City, Chicago, and other places, and dredge boats for Lake Ontario, Lake Erie and Lake Michigan.
[55] See Chicago *Democrat*, Chicago *Journal, St. Joseph Valley Register* (South Bend) January to August, 1846, *passim*.

Wentworth of Chicago, and the Democratic delegation from Michigan in the House.

But the South opposed the bill and predicted that even though it passed, a Presidential veto would defeat it. R. B. Rhett of South Carolina was a leader in the opposition. There were Democratic representatives from southern Indiana and Illinois who would vote with the South and stand by the President if he thought best to use his veto. They disliked it partly because it did not contain sufficient appropriation for their rivers, partly on local grounds, and partly on constitutional grounds. John A. McClernand from southern Illinois opposed it; Douglas was not active in its favor and refused to vote for certain items; the *Illinois State Register* was ready to support the President if he should deem it "unconstitutional." [56] Brinkerhoff seemed to foresee trouble and tried to have the vote on the tariff delayed until the Harbor and River Bill was safe,[57] but there seemed to be good majorities for it and even the Washington *Union* purported to be in its favor.[58]

The bill was passed by the House and Senate with good majorities. Democrats from both the upper and lower West voted with the Whigs in its favor. Three Democratic representatives from southern Indiana and Illinois, however, voted with southern Democrats against it.[59] On August 3, 1846, the President, as southern Democrats had predicted, sent a message to the House vetoing the bill on strict constitutional grounds.[60] The upper West had again been deceived.

The Democrats and Whigs from the lakes were determined to force the issue with the President and his southern advisors and to over-

[56] Polk's *Diary* II, 63; *Illinois State Register,* Apr. 3, 1846; Chicago *Daily Journal,* Aug. 29, 1846; *Cong. Globe,* 29 Cong., 1 Sess., 1183, 1184; Chicago *Daily Journal,* Aug. 25, 1846; *Illinois State Register,* April 3, 1846, July 15, 1847.

[57] *Cong. Globe,* 29 Cong., 1 Sess., 1187.

[58] This paper which had earlier given false hope to the upper West for all of Oregon, again seemed to favor the lake region. It was thought, perhaps rightly, that this was a trick on the part of Thomas Ritchie to get the vote of the Northwest for the tariff bill which was then pending. Chicago *Daily Journal,* August 10, 1846.

[59] Polk's *Diary* II, 54. It passed the House March 20, 1846, Owen of southern Indiana, Ficklin and McClernand of southern Illinois voting against it. *Cong. Globe,* 29 Cong., 1 Sess., 530. The bill received the vote of seven of the eight Democratic and Whig Senators from the Northwest. Jesse Bright of Indiana, for some reason refused to vote, but had been in the Senate just before the vote was taken. *Ibid.,* p. 1136.

[60] *Cong. Globe,* 29 Cong., 1 Sess., 1181.

ride his veto. Brinkerhoff of Ohio said the President was an abstractionist who was ignorant of the interests of the lakes. The attempt to override the veto resulted in a majority of ninety-six to ninety-one against the President but failed in obtaining the required two-thirds.[61] Again the Democrats of the West were divided. Eight representatives of that party from lake districts voted with the Whigs to rebuke their President—among them Brinkerhoff and Wentworth—while from southern Ohio, Indiana, and Illinois, six representatives voted with the South to sustain him.[62]

When the news of the veto reached the lakes, flags were put at half-mast and distress signals displayed by the ships in the harbors. The effect created was intensified by the failure of another bill which the President killed by a pocket veto.[63] The leading Democratic papers in the lake region, the Buffalo *Courier,* Cleveland *Plain Dealer,* and the Chicago *Democrat* disavowed the action of the administration.[64] The *Plain Dealer,* usually an intensely partisan Democratic paper, exclaimed: "We do not belong to the blubbering party," threatened a combination of the East and West to check the South and called upon freemen from the North to rally under the cry of "let the boundaries of slavery be set." [65] River and harbor bills are usually unimportant and are nearly always associated with "pork-barrel" and log-rolling politics, but this lake bill of 1847 and its veto possess unusual historical significance.

The Democratic party was clearly endangering its hold on the lake region. It was hard for Democratic papers to explain the President's action to puzzled constituents, and it was thought that Democratic

[61] *Cong. Globe,* 29 Cong., 1 Sess., 1186, 1187, 1189.

[62] *Ibid.,* 29 Cong., 1 Sess., 1189. The following Democrats voted to pass the bill over the President's veto: St. John from the Sandusky District; Brinkerhoff from the district lying south of the Reserve and dependent on Lake Erie for an outlet (*Ibid.,* 1186, 1187); Pettit and Cathcart from the two districts of northern Indiana lying nearest Lake Michigan; Wentworth of Chicago; Chapman, Hund and McClelland of Michigan. Douglas of the Quincy district also voted to overrule the veto. Those who voted with the South to sustain the President were Cunningham and Parish from southern Ohio; Owen from Posey county, Indiana, and Wick from the region south of Indianapolis; McClernand and Ficklin of southern Illinois.

[63] Polk's *Diary,* III, 116, 166, 169, 244, 249; IV, 64; Chicago *Daily Journal,* Sept. 9, 1846.

[64] *Indiana State Journal,* Sept. 23, 1846; Chicago *Daily Journal,* Dec. 4, 1846; Chicago *Democrat, passim.*

[65] Cleveland *Plain Dealer,* quoted in Chicago *Daily Journal,* Aug. 25, 1846.

losses in the elections of 1846 were due to it.[66] The great trade convention held in Chicago in 1847, an event of great importance and a significant proof of the commercial connection of the lake region with the East, though purporting to be non-partisan, drifted into Whig control.[67] The defection in Democratic ranks continued. It is not surprising that within a week after the veto of the lake improvement bill and two months after the treaty of compromise on Oregon was ratified, the Wilmot Proviso, in which Brinkerhoff was actively interested, was introduced into the House.[68]

It provided for the exclusion of slavery from the territory to be acquired from Mexico. It was to cut through party lines in the free West like a two-edged sword and to show that the interests of the upper and lower West were becoming divergent. The Democrats, Whigs, and Free Soilers of the lake region all showed themselves clearly hostile to the South and slave extension on this question. Leading Democratic newspapers, among them the Chicago *Democrat* and the Cleveland *Plain Dealer*,[69] joined with Whig and Free Soil organs to support the Proviso and check the South. In the Illinois Legislature, Democrats representing northern districts—Norman H. Judd of Chicago among them—voted with the Whigs urging Congressmen at Washington to pass the Proviso.[70] And, in turn, in the national Congress, Democrats from all parts of the upper West, following the lead of Brinkerhoff and Wentworth, voted with Whigs and Free Soilers of the Western Reserve in an effort to block the "pro-southern" tendency of their party. They were accused of party disloyalty and of advocating an "authority higher than the Constitution"; they an-

[66] *Indiana State Sentinel*, Aug. 12, 1846; *Indiana Tri-Weekly State Journal*, Apr. 2, 1847 quoting the Goshen *Democrat*; *St. Joseph Valley Register*, Jan. 7, 1848; Chicago *Daily Journal*, Nov. 6, 10, 1846; the Ohio election was especially unfavorable to the Democrats.

[67] For this convention see *Niles'*, Vol. 72, p. 208; Chicago *Daily Journal*, Nov. 13, 20, 28, 1846; Jan. 25, March 24, June 9, 10, 15, 21, 28, July 5, 6, 7, 17, 1847.

[68] Polk's *Diary* II, 75; *Cong. Globe*, 29 Cong., 1 Sess., 1214, 1218. It cannot be interpreted as the reply of the same Democrats who felt the insult over Oregon so keenly. The article on the "Bargain of 1844" and the Wilmot Proviso by Clark E. Persinger (*An. Report Am. Hist. Ass'n*, 1911, I, 195) does not take into consideration several influences that were at work in the lake region to intensify hostility to the South. It was from Brinkerhoff and Wentworth, Democrats of the lake region and not from Allen, Hannegan and Cass that the Proviso received its main support.

[69] Chicago *Daily Journal*, Jan. 23, 25, 1847.

[70] *Journal, House of Representatives*, Ill., Vol. III, 1846–1847, pp. 384, 385; *Senate Journal*, 1846–1847, pp. 170–171; *Ill. St. Register*, Feb. 5, Mar. 26, 1847.

swered that the spirit of the lake region was such that they must vote against slavery extension or lose office at the next election.[71] Even in the lower West, many Democratic leaders appeared for some time to show free soil tendencies. Later, however, under the leadership of Douglas, their favorite plan for dealing with this problem was to apply the doctrine of popular sovereignty.[72]

Thus, as early as the late forties, the Democrats of the Reserve, of Michigan, Chicago, and southern Wisconsin, showed their discontent with southern leadership and joined with Whigs and Free Soilers to give the lake region a more distinct attitude in national politics. The belief that their section was suffering neglect was more intense among the lake Democrats than among Whigs or Free Soilers who had nothing to expect from the Polk administration. Brinkerhoff and Wentworth and their followers opposed the administration on the Oregon question, on the Harbor veto, and even threatened a bolt on the tariff; in their support of the Proviso, they reached a high point of party disloyalty. When we say that in these changes the economic and political beginnings of the Republican party are clearly marked out, although the thoroughgoing revolution did not occur until 1854, we do not deny that other factors are contributing to this same end. For years the Free Soil party, which in its western form was confined largely to the same region, had been at work in this direction. In addition, the earlier antislavery impulse of the thirties had given a strong moral and religious basis for opposition.[73] Though only a few people even in this upper West really believed in "Negro rights," the existence there of so few Negroes and the distance from the South made it easier to take issue with the lower West on the treatment of the free Negro and, in national affairs, to challenge the South on the extension of slavery. Moreover, the eastern or European origin of the population of the lakes, the rapid expansion of the region, and its commercial connection with the East could not fail to affect its attitude and

[71] Four Democratic Representatives from Ohio, Brinkerhoff, Cummins, Fries, and Starkweather (all from northern districts) ; two from Michigan, McClelland and Hunt; and Wentworth of Chicago, voted steadily in favor of restricting slavery in the territories. Senator Cass of Michigan and Representative Sawyer of northwestern Ohio and Chapman of Michigan voted against the Proviso. *Cong. Globe*, 29 Cong., 1 Sess., 1218; 2 Sess., 425, 442–3, 573; 30 Cong., 1 Sess., 39.

[72] W. O. Lynch, "Anti-Slavery Tendencies of the Democratic Party in the Northwest," 1848–50, *Miss. Valley Hist. Review*, XI, 319–331.

[73] T. C. Smith, *The Liberty and Free Soil Parties in the Northwest;* Gilbert H. Barnes, *The Antislavery Impulse* (D. Appleton-Century Company, 1933).

give it different social ideals. Sooner than the lower West, it was to feel a sense of frustration at the hands of the southern Democracy. A growing demand for woman suffrage and for temperance reform coincided to some extent with this feeling. In short, the Democratic upper West was all but ready in the late forties to break with the slave-holding South—a step which the lower West was not ready to take until the late fifties under Douglas' leadership.

CHAPTER II

SOCIETY IN THE LOWER WEST 1840-1860—SOCIAL ATTITUDES

Although in the early forties the southern element in the population of the West gave it a nearer approach to social homogeneity than it has ever attained since, it was already realized that it was the meeting place of the divergent eastern and southern types. As was said in 1844:

Each of these two fountains of our civilization (Virginia and New England) is pouring forth its columns of immigrants to the Great Valley, forming thus a new and third type which will reform and remold the American civilization. (The Virginian) is less complicated, with less apparent paradoxes, hospitable, generous, liberal and even profuse in his indulgences, less scrupulous than the New Englander. (There is) an absence of that thrift which is characteristic of New England. A tendency to philosophize has made the Virginian so marked an advocate of abstract truths. (The New Englander is) unique and peculiar. He reduces everything to the standard of utility; he is frugal, not mean. He scrutinizes; his curiosity sometimes leads him into impertinence. He has a fine fund of quiet humor. Their religious opinions and their system of education, give to the male portion of the population an appearance of austerity in their manners, but it surrounds the females with a peculiar charm. The two distinct types of character are brought into contact, the one losing its rugged asperities and sharp angles, the other correcting unnecessary habits. If we may judge from present appearances, the traits of mind which characterize the Virginian type will predominate in the Western man. He has the hardihood to encounter obstacles to which he joins the chivalry of the South. The impulses are all generous. There is a certain moral grandeur in his mind suited to great conceptions. The mere forms of etiquette which throw a chill over the warm and gushing affections of the heart, he lays aside. As a speaker he is apt to be florid in his style,—a peculiar fault to young people.[1]

This quotation from a detached and intelligent observer differs of course from the common estimate that these two elements of the population had of each other as in the forties and fifties they were brought into contact—a contact that resulted in some cases in rapid adjustment and harmony, and in others, in conflict. Deep-seated differences were

---

[1] *Democratic Monthly Magazine,* June, 1844, pp. 186, 187, 192, 193. The words of the original are kept but in condensed form, with some minor changes in punctuation.

in some cases intensified by false impressions derived from the past, and the process of blending was hindered somewhat. Yankees, in the eyes of many southern-born westerners, were miserly, scheming and ungenerous, for such had been the trafficking and tricky peddlers who sold tinware and wooden clocks to the people of the Ohio and Mississippi valleys. These neighbors from the East were inhospitable and stiff-necked. Did they not refuse to invite a stranger to stay for a meal and, indeed, have contempt for all natives? [2] The Yankee, on the other hand, often held the opinion that all southerners were "long, lank, lean, lazy and ignorant." There were, in fact, in Indiana and Illinois, southerners possessed of much natural shrewdness and philosophy, zestful, rollicking Kentuckians and Virginians, not interested in accumulating fortunes, but given, like Abraham Lincoln, alike to humor and gravity, delighting in epigrams and in keen observation of life and manners. The Yankee in the West, too, was often liberal and public spirited. An earlier recognition by each group of the merits of the other would have helped to prevent prolonged political bitterness and social cleavage.[3]

By 1840 the first great tasks of road-making, of planting of settlements, of state-making, of laying county lines and establishing county seats, of framing the first constitutions and laws, had been done. This was more true of Ohio, a comparatively well-settled commonwealth by that year, than it was of Indiana and Illinois where much pioneer work was still being done in the central and northern parts. Iowa was still in the territorial stage. Nearly everyone in the West in 1840 could remember one frenzied period of settlement and development, and older settlers had experienced two of these "booms" followed by the reaction-cycles that were so recurrent in western history. From 1814 to 1820 and again in 1836–1837, there had been feverish spells of land-selling, town-lot plotting, and purchasing of land on credit, to be followed by dropping land values, debt, closing of banks, and much distress.[4] The cycle was to be repeated in 1857 and 1873.

Self-made lawyers had framed constitutions and were busy drawing up enactments that became more confused and contradictory with every session of the various legislatures. There were intricate ques-

[2] Carrie Prudence Kofoid, "Puritan Influences in the Formative Years of Illinois History," *Publ. No. 10, Ill. St. Hist. Lib.,* 1905, pp. 261, 303.

[3] Gov. Thomas Ford, *History of Illinois* (Chicago, 1859), pp. 280, 281; T. C. Pease, *The Frontier State,* p. 18.

[4] Ford, *Illinois, passim;* Logan Esarey, *History of Indiana* I, Ch. XVI, XXI; Pease, *op. cit.,* p. 178.

tions of law to be decided. The floating of great bond issues for canals or other public improvements was rushed into recklessly, only to prove a failure, to be suspended or abandoned. How to meet the popular demands for rapid development, for communication with the market by canal and later by railroad and yet not tax too heavily a public subject to waves of panic and poverty, proved a difficult problem for the lawyer-politician. The extravagant bond issues were floated even though state legislatures could not pay interest on their debts, and repudiation was again and again threatened and to some degree practised. Conditions were thus favorable for an aggressive lawyer class. Young men of little training would be rapidly promoted to the office of judge. In Indiana, especially, the requirements for legal practice were low. As to law enforcement, many crimes were entirely overlooked by authorities or were dealt with by "personal law"; even murder, if arising from sudden heat or anger, often went unpunished.[5] It is reasonable to suppose that the confusion in the laws and the many civil disputes regarding claims, mortgages, and land titles helped to make the western lawyer as litigious in his own field as the frontier preacher was polemical in his. Lincoln and Douglas grew up in this country-lawyer atmosphere; it proved, no doubt, stimulating to them and to many another ambitious young man.

The local politician was, like the preacher and lawyer, a leader of the people, and his standards were only a little higher than those of his constituents. He and the lawyer had taken on from the frontier preacher the habit of making loud, wordy speeches. He was able to mount a stump and deliver a rough and ready political harangue. He, or his more able colleagues, had founded commonwealths and established constitutions and laws—this, his greatest work, should be mentioned first. It is his enduring monument. But he was, of course, part and parcel of the exuberant and reckless political life of the day. He took part in the bitter quarrels involved in moving state capitols from one town to another, and in the establishment of other state institutions with all the manipulation, favoritism, and log-rolling that went along with such changes. He had led in local fights over the location of county seats. Now, in the forties and fifties, he was involved in long, continued fights in state legislatures over the election of United States senators; in "bolts" to cause no quorum; in the gerrymandering of legislative districts; and in extravagant misuse of people's taxes or,

[5] O. H. Smith, *Early Indiana Trials and Sketches,* 5, 6, 117; Ford, *Illinois,* 86; Esarey, *op. cit.,* II, 1012; Pease, *op. cit.,* Chs. X, XI, XVII, *et passim.*

perhaps, even in forms of bribery.[6] All such economic, social, and political phenomena may seem to us abnormal and excessive and due to the designs of selfish men. They were rather social growing pains and accompanying diseases; they were groping attempts of an untrained people to build up new commonwealths and make their individual fortunes in a competitive and enthusiastic age.[7]

LIFE IN THE INTERIOR COUNTIES

While the leaders labored with tasks of state or engaged in petty rivalries, their constituents in the interior counties back from the Ohio and Mississippi river towns were held fast by stern and exacting conditions of living and were bound to the hard tasks of building-up settlements, towns, and farms and rearing their families. The matchless description of the rise and decline of the mean log-cabin town of New Salem, Illinois, given by Senator Albert J. Beveridge in his life of Lincoln, and indeed, the general picture he draws of grim conditions in Illinois and around Gentryville, Indiana—of pioneer striving, success and failure, energy and lassitude, poverty, sickness, and death— make an indelible imprint on the mind of the reader. Pioneer tasks, though at times stimulating, involved back-breaking toil for men, hard work, suffering, privations, and lonesomeness for women, and early breakdown for adults of both sexes. A nervous drive and an impelling urge to undertake with one's own hands almost impossible tasks of clearing and building took possession of many fathers and mothers. To others the temptation to shiftlessness was as great as that to thrift and success. Crop failures were common; when the crop was good, the market was often lacking; with corn selling at times for ten or fifteen cents a bushel and in the remoter districts so cheap as to be burned for fuel, seasons analogous to the starving times of colonial Virginia and Massachusetts were not unknown. Gravestones in the old cemeteries of the Middle West show that there was a very high death rate for infants and children, and that men and women in large numbers died before their time, forspent at what is now considered early middle age. There was a wastage of human life in building-up these agrarian communities analogous to that in the rising factory system of the East and on the more ruthlessly managed slave plantations in the

[6] Ford, *Illinois*, 40, 104, 187, 189, 226.
[7] *Ibid., passim.* Gov. Ford is one of the severest critics of early middle western politics, politicians, lawyers, booms and extravagance. His book, however, is an invaluable source; see also A. J. Beveridge, *Abraham Lincoln*, Vol. I, Ch. II, III, IV, *et seq.*

South. The somber drama that has been played on so many frontiers in American history was here enacted by the "hardy yeomanry of the forties" with local variations suited to this setting.

The task of laying the material foundations of middle-western civilization, of making possible the introduction into these new lands of the religious and ethical inheritance of Anglo-Saxon peoples—a stern and unrelenting task—was, it is true, often met with buoyancy and humor. But esthetic and polite considerations, and refinements in learning and religion were crowded out by the pressure of immediate things. It is not surprising that stern Calvinistic fatalism settled down on many persons as did also forms of melancholia such as we associate with Lincoln himself. It was the epic and heroic age of the Middle West, if ever this section had such an age. The work of building-up the river and lake cities and the inland towns and farms was one that gave to some of the great builders qualities of strength, mystery, and heroism to which poet, novelist, and historian alike pay tribute.

> *I went to the dances at Chandlerville,*
> *And played snap-out at Winchester.*
> *One time we changed partners,*
> *Driving home in the moonlight of middle June,*
> *And then I found Davis.*
> *We were married and lived together for seventy years,*
> *Enjoying, working, raising the twelve children,*
> *Eight of whom we lost*
> *Ere I had reached the age of sixty.*
> *I spun, I wove, I kept the house, I nursed the sick,*
> *I made the garden, and for holiday*
> *Rambled over the fields where sang the larks,*
> *And by Spoon River gathering many a shell,*
> *And many a flower and medicinal weed—*
> *Shouting to the wooded hills, singing to the green valleys.*
> *At ninety-six I had lived enough, that is all,*
> *And passed to a sweet repose.*
> *What is this I hear of sorrow and weariness,*
> *Anger, discontent and drooping hopes?*
> *Degenerate sons and daughters,*
> *Life is too strong for you—*
> *It takes life to love Life.*[8]

It is not so much among the vigorous pioneers themselves, but rather among the stragglers who fell by the wayside and became weak and pauperized, and among their children and grandchildren, that the

[8] A characterization of "Lucinda Matlock" from Edgar Lee Masters' *Spoon River Anthology.*

drab conditions described by recent writers were to be found. In the larger river towns, there was a vigorous and aggressive spirit; indeed, they were at their heyday in the forties and fifties. A profuse optimism for western development prevailed in the more prosperous centers. In the towns along the Mississippi, such as Alton and Quincy, and on or near the Illinois River, such as Jacksonville and Springfield, a turbulent competitive life was lived. Later Stephen A. Douglas came to represent these more aggressive and materialistic elements. He saw mankind as divided into groups with their economic demands paramount; he distrusted "isms" and righteous causes and was the champion of western interests.[9]

It was natural that there should be much crudity in manners and disregard of social refinements. The basis of much of Mrs. Trollope's stricture and extravagant caricature is found in the social life of the Ohio valley.[10] Saying "thank you," and "I beg your pardon," were amenities not often practiced on the farms and in the smaller towns.[11] Amusements in the more advanced rural localities were horse-racing, fiddling, dancing, wrestling, shooting matches, "gander pulling," and other sports of a rude sort which were kept from becoming grossly immoral or merely frivolous by the lack of time for over-indulgence and by the influence of the preacher, the school, and the slowly rising standards of taste.[12] The austerity and stern naturalism prevailing in the more remote frontier districts allowed little time for pleasure except that derived from simple diversions, such as hunting and fishing. Cards, dice, and excessive drinking were little known in the earliest years. In the period before, during, and after the Civil War, however, many men and women in the rising towns and cities were to give way to the ravages of drunkenness, gambling, and immorality.[13] The "freer" doctrines of salvation held by the Universalist denomination which spread among many of the lower classes did not check, and perhaps did much to encourage, these tendencies.[14]

The dress of the masses of the people, as higher standards arose, changed from the buckskin, the jeans, the linsey-woolsey of the first

[9] Edgar Lee Masters, *Children of the Market Place.*
[10] Mrs. Trollope, *Domestic Manners of the Americans.*
[11] Herbert Quick, *Vandemark's Folly* (The Bobbs Merrill Company, 1921), p. 133.
[12] Josephine Craven Chandler, "The Spoon River Country," reprinted from the *Jour. Ill. State Hist. Soc.,* Vol. 14, No. 3, p. 265; Esarey, *Indiana,* I, 486.
[13] R. W. Patterson, *Early Society in Southern Illinois; History of Williamson County, Illinois, The Bloody Vendetta.*
[14] James Shaw, *Twelve Years in America* (London, 1867), pp. 162, 163, 234.

period to the calico, ginghams, and delaines of the middle period of a family's social history. "The silk and lace period did not dawn in the smaller towns of the West until the Civil War suddenly scattered bank-notes broadcast through the land and brought in its train tumult, movement, money and the latest fashions." [15] Food likewise changed from corn-bread, hominy and salt-pork to wheat-bread, apple-butter, dried apples, peaches, and more savory meats.[16]

But there was little knowledge of the rules of health and little attention paid to diet. Typhoid and Asiatic cholera were devastating and frequent. So common was "fever and ague" or "walking malaria" in the low-lying regions that it was scarcely noticed. Pneumonia was called "winter fever" and typhoid, "slow fever." The press complained of the "decay of female health in our land." [17] A terrible visitation of cholera swept the Ohio and Mississippi valleys in the years following 1848; it carried off thousands of persons in Cincinnati alone in 1850 and as many as one in seven in smaller towns in the interior of Illinois where it was ineffectually fought by the burning of piles of wood "to purify the atmosphere." [18] While in Cincinnati, medical science, under the guidance of Daniel Drake and others, was reaching higher standards, in the interior there was much use of quack remedies, and "botanic" or herb doctors competed with "calomel doctors" for favor.[19] In the river towns and, to a less degree, in the interior, drunkenness was common. Around Cincinnati vine-growing and wine-making had developed under the auspices of Nicholas Longworth, and in Belleville, Illinois, the making of beer was a leading industry. It was hoped that the Ohio would become the Rhine of America and that the moderate use of wine would check the excesses of whiskey-drinking. Vice was flagrant; one account claimed that in Cincinnati alone in 1860 a thousand prostitutes were walking the streets and added, "the number ascertained is known to be but a small proportion of the number veiled under secrecy with which this vice of all others most conceals its deformities." [20] Articles appeared in papers attacking saloons and

[15] Francis Grierson, *The Valley of the Shadows* (1909), p. 111.
[16] Chas. B. Johnson, *Illinois in the Fifties* (Champaign, Ill., 1918), pp. 18, 19.
[17] *The Genius of the West* (Cincinnati, 1856), pp. 27, 28; C. B. Johnson, *Illinois in the Fifties*, pp. 128, 129.
[18] Chas. Cist, *Sketches and Statistics of Cincinnati* (1851); A. C. Cole, *The Era of the Civil War, Centennial History of Illinois,* Vol. III, 217; Esarey, *Indiana,* I, 489; S. A. Latta, *The Cholera in Cincinnati* (1850); *Annual Report Commissioner of Statistics* (Ohio, 1857), p. 50.
[19] Esarey, *Indiana,* I, 490, 491.
[20] *The Dial,* Cincinnati, edited by M. C. Conway, 1860.

degraded conditions and citing the success of license and the "Maine law." This, however, made little appeal to the Germans and to the Kentuckians living in southern and western Illinois, where "moral and intellectual darkness" or "dangerous liberalism" prevailed against the efforts of reform forces in the Western Reserve and around Chicago. Violence was resorted to by long-suffering wives who, in several towns, "visited grog shops and demolished decanters and stove in barrels." [21]

Such sordidness was not lessened by the fact that there was a poor, listless or roving element in the population, remnants of a less heroic type of pioneer who had brought with him from the upland South or Pennsylvania less energetic traits, and by the fact that some settlers lost their grip in the grim battle of life. Such names as "hoosiers," "Egypt," "suckers," and "pukes," suggest these conditions and these classes of people in Indiana, southern and western Illinois, and in Missouri.[22] Literary treatment has been given them in Eggleston's *The Hoosier School-Master,* the dialect sketches of John Hay, and the Mississippi River novels of Mark Twain. It is, no doubt, a still more backward class that is referred to by the writer of the following:

> In almost every county [in Illinois] there was a race of the original pioneers many of whom were ignorant, illiterate and vicious. These were apt to be such as wore the hunting shirt, the buckskin trousers, the racoonskin cap and leather moccasins. They delighted to wear a butcher knife. . . . They claimed unbounded liberty and were naturally hostile to any action of government tending to their improvement and civilization. . . . They were also called half horse and half alligator men. . . . In all elections, and in all enactments of the legislature, great pains were taken by all candidates and men in office to make their course acceptable to these 'butcher knife boys.'. . . Since the butcher knife has been disused as an article of dress, the fashion has been to call this class of people 'barefooted boys,' 'flat-footed boys' and 'huge pawed boys,'. . . and their influence is yet considerable in all elections.[23]

ILLITERACY—PUBLIC SCHOOLS

There was from 1840 to 1860 much illiteracy in Ohio, Indiana, and Illinois, and the establishment of a public school system was achieved only in the face of great difficulty. In 1840, a report claimed that there were in the West 400,000 children destitute of schools in a population

---

[21] *The Genius of the West* (Cincinnati, 1856), p. 224; A. C. Cole, *The Era of the Civil War,* p. 211, citing Illinois newspapers.
[22] Ford, *Illinois,* p. 68.
[23] *Ibid.,* p. 88.

of 3,000,000; that over 100,000 adults could not read or write; and that in Indiana two thirds of the children attended no school whatever.[24] The Census of 1850 indicated that illiteracy was greatest in southern Illinois and in certain counties in Indiana; in Jackson county, Illinois, for instance, one adult in three could not read or write. Indiana as a whole had about 70,000 illiterates in that year. Negroes constituted only a small portion of these, most of them coming from the class of native-born Americans. Three counties in southern Illinois were without schools of any kind.[25] The State Superintendent of Public Instruction for Indiana said in 1853: "The school houses, where are they and what are they? In some townships there is not a single school house of any kind. In other townships there are a few old leaky dilapidated log cabins wholly unfit for use even in summer and in winter worse than nothing." Teachers received as low as ten and fifteen dollars a month and schools were maintained in some districts only two months in a year. There were almost no public high schools, but private "academies" and parochial schools were numerous in more settled communities.[26] The school-teacher was usually a New Englander, though sometimes an eccentric immigrant pedagogue from England, Scotland, or Ireland held this position.[27] Scenes only slightly less uncouth than those pictured in *The Hoosier School-Master* were enacted in more backward regions of Illinois and Indiana.[28] Governor Ford of Illinois said:

In almost all the south part of the state there were complaints that the legal standard for qualification for teachers was *too high,* the law (of 1844) requiring the knowledge of reading, writing and arithmetic, English grammar, geography and history, and the people being scarce of materials for such learned teachers, were desirous of getting back to the old standard of reading, writing and ciphering to the rule of three, or at farthest through the arithmetic.[29]

[24] James L. Batchelder, *The United States, the West and Ohio as Missionary Fields,* pp. 45, 46.
[25] *United States Census 1850,* p. 725 *et passim; Debates Indiana Constitutional Convention 1850,* Vol. II, 1890; A. C. Cole, *The Era of the Civil War,* 230. The counties in Indiana having the most illiterates were Martin, Brown, Scott, Perry, Pike.
[26] *Annual Report of the Superintendent of Public Instruction of the State of Indiana, 1852, 1853, 1857.*
[27] Meredith Nicholson, *The Hoosiers,* pp. 88, 89.
[28] Edward Eggleston, *The Hoosier School-Master;* Isaac Phillips Roberts, *Autobiography of a Farm Boy* (Albany, 1916), pp. 117–121; Esarey, *Indiana,* I, 328–330.
[29] Ford, *Illinois,* p. 60.

In some of the private schools, however, well-educated Germans often served as tutors, and some very good work was done under self-constituted teachers in "subscription" schools.

The obstacles in the way of an effective state-wide system of public schools were many. The feeling that public schools were a public charity, the disinclination of the more well-to-do classes to send their children to them, the poverty and the opposition in certain southern counties in Indiana and Illinois to taxation for school purposes, the distrust of Yankees, who, it was felt, were sure to control the schools, the fear that the system would drift into sectarian management, difficulties in the courts and problems of administering properly and honestly state school funds—these were among the most important. Ohio and Michigan made progress more rapidly than did Indiana and Illinois. Finally, laws being passed extending the principle of state control, establishing state superintendents, and distributing the tax so that the poorer counties would be benefited, by the late forties and early fifties all these states had established what might well be called a state-wide "free school" system. The prosperity preceding the panic of 1857 seems to have helped this movement along; in the five years preceding the panic, the people of Indiana alone built over a thousand new school-houses.[30]

LOCAL DISORDER AND FEUD

To one who reads in local newspapers and county histories of the more intimate life of the people, the forties and fifties appear to have been a time of much neighborhood disorder and feud. There were numerous local gangs of thieves or of rough, though not criminal, bands, such as the "Clary's Grove boys" who were such ardent supporters of Lincoln in his early career. There was, in places, the most intense hostility to abolitionists; in the thirties James Birney's press at Cincinnati was twice mobbed; at Alton, Illinois, an armed mob besieged Elijah Lovejoy, his press, and his abolition followers in a

[30] For Ohio see: Edward A. Miller, "History of Educational Legislation in Ohio," *Ohio Arch. and Hist. Society Publications*, Vol. XXVII, pp. 1–271; *History of Cincinnati and Hamilton County* (S. B. Nelson and Co., 1894) ; Chaddock, *Ohio Before 1850*, p. 146; *Western Quarterly Review*, April, 1849, p. 301. For Indiana, *Annual Report of the State Superintendent of Public Instruction*, 1852–1859. For Illinois; C. P. Kofoid, "Puritan Influences in the Formative Years of Illinois History," *Pub. No. 10 of the Illinois Hist. Lib.*, 1905, p. 335; Paul E. Belting, "Development of the Free Public High School in Illinois to 1860," *Jour. Ill. State Hist. Soc.* Vol. XI, Oct., 1918, Jan., 1919, pp. 269–369, 467–565.

warehouse. They attempted to burn the building, killed Lovejoy, and threw his press into the river.[31] Horse thieves and tricky counterfeiters preyed on old settlers and on the newer immigrant trains. Activities such as we associate with the James boys and other outlaws in Missouri and districts farther west after the Civil War, were carried on in this region extensively.[32] Western ideas of respectability and law and order found expression in "regulator" movements against lawless people or in threatening with mob violence or killing such undesirable characters as temperance advocates, Mormons, "free-lovers," social radicals of the Fourier type or pietistic communists who settled here and there. With the enactment of the Fugitive Slave Law of 1850 and the legal attempts to rescue escaped slaves under it, another cause of social disorder was added; along the numerous branches of the underground railroad stretching in parallel lines or in irregular network from the Ohio River to the lakes and covering Ohio, Indiana, Illinois, and Iowa dramatic scenes were enacted and, at times, intense excitement prevailed.[33] Foreigners, especially the Irish, were very much disliked by the natives in certain places; Catholic and Protestant antagonism was intense; and Jacksonian Democrats opposed "Federalistic" Whigs in turbulent political contests. There might here be cited as one of the most outstanding examples of domestic disorder and local strife, the Mormon War which occurred in western Illinois in 1845–1846.

The Mormons had settled at Nauvoo, Illinois, and had been welcomed as a persecuted people. They established what was then a large city with a large temple. Joseph Smith, the prophet, became the head of the city government. Their control of the city council and of the courts in Nauvoo and of a local militia with peculiar powers gave them the position of a state within a state. Although their vote was much sought by both Whig and Democratic parties, popular suspicion soon became aroused and thefts and rogueries came to be ascribed to them. Their desire for "plural wives," and their alleged designs to conquer the land as the children of Israel conquered Canaan gave rise to fears of religious war. Finally the Mormon militia and several hundred armed men from nearby towns met and violence resulted. Joseph

[31] One of the most detailed accounts of this is given in Ford, *Illinois*, pp. 234–245; see Pease, pp. 363–368.
[32] Ford, *Illinois*, pp. 437, 438; Herbert Quick, *Vandemark's Folly*, pp. 177, 178.
[33] W. H. Siebert, *The Underground Railroad from Slavery to Freedom*, 1898, Chs. III, IV.

Smith was jailed to be later mobbed and killed; the whole of western Illinois determined to expel the ten or fifteen thousand Mormons from their midst, and an anti-Mormon army marched on Nauvoo. All this created a difficult situation for Governor Ford. However, the Mormons finally decided to leave peaceably and spent a winter preparing wagons and acquiring cattle for their long trek across the plains and mountains to the far West. In February, 1846, the great emigration began; the first group of saints, with Brigham Young at their head, shivering but dauntless, left the country whose liberality and tolerance had welcomed them six years before. Others followed, the poor and weak remaining behind only to be further harassed and persecuted.[34]

In southern Illinois the "Massac War" occurred in 1846. "An ancient colony of horse thieves, counterfeiters and robbers had long infested the counties of Massac and Pope," says a writer. In Massac County they secured the election of a sheriff not over zealous in his duties. Regulators took matters in their own hands, in the name of law and order, used violence and torture against the "rougher elements," collected sympathizers from neighboring counties and from Kentucky, drove the sheriff out of the county, marched against the jail and released some of their sympathizers who had been arrested, called a convention, and—to sum up—finally became a greater problem to the governor and authorities than was the criminal class itself.[35] Among the rougher classes in this region, the "knock down" style of the West came into conflict with the dueling code of the South and brought on many a fight.[36] In Indiana, outbreaks occurred in 1854 and again in 1859.[37] To all this pre-Civil War disorder were added later the intense feelings aroused by that conflict; the practice of carrying concealed weapons given impetus by the war and bushwhacking methods imported from Kentucky did nothing to allay the causes for feud and violence.

[34] Ford, *Illinois*, Chs. VIII, X, XIII; C. M. Thompson, "A Study of the Administration of Gov. Thomas Ford," *Collections of Illinois State Hist. Lib.* Vol. VII, pp. lxxviii–civ; *Niles' Register*, Sept. 27, Oct. 4–18, Nov. 1, 1845; Milo Bennet, "The Building of a State," *Jour. Ill. St. Hist. Soc.*, Vol. 13, No. 3, p. 340; Pease, Ch. XIX.

[35] *Illinois State Register*, Sept. 18, 1846; Jan. 1, 15, 22, 1847; Ford, *Illinois*, pp. 437–444; Pease, pp. 428, 429.

[36] *The Bloody Vendetta, Embracing the History of Williamson Co. Ill.*, p. 226.

[37] See *Indiana Weekly State Journal*, July 29, 1854 for regulators in Parke, Vermilion and Vigo Counties; see also New Albany *Ledger*, July 23, 1859 for outbreaks in Greene, Monroe and Lawrence Counties.

Religion in the Back Settlements

In some settlements and struggling farm communities, there was no religious life whatever; conditions of heathenism or a purely natural, secular life prevailed. What to some contemporary observers appeared to be a refreshing absence of organized religion to others appeared to lend a general degradation and commonness to life and encouragement to vice and immorality. Stark and barren conditions such as those that surrounded the burial of Nancy Hanks, the mother of Lincoln, were not unknown. The following quotation taken from an earlier period describes scenes still enacted in the more isolated districts.

Children are not baptised . . . there is no consecrated burial place, no funeral service. The body is closed in the plainest coffin. Relatives of the deceased convey the corpse into the woods; the grave is prepared and the body quietly placed in it; then trees are felled and laid over the grave to protect it from wild beasts, . . . a few natural tears are shed in silence and the scene is closed.[38]

But most of the remote villages and farms were, by 1840, within reach of the evangelistic and missionary zeal of pioneer preachers and to them was preached a gospel peculiarly fitted to their conditions of life. The extremely violent, pathological Kentucky form of revival had given way to a type more moderate, although we should by no means infer from this that the methods of the circuit rider and the emotionally exciting camp meeting had been discarded. As in an earlier generation, the sudden, mysterious appearance and ministration of such frontier prophets as Lorenzo Dow or the eccentric naturalist-missionary, Johnny Appleseed, so now the more lasting work of J. B. Finley and the strenuous deeds of Peter Cartwright furnished material for many an episode to be handed down in family histories. Accounts of the careers of such men furnish us with a unique body of western American *res gestae* and *acta sanctorum*.[39] Methodist, Presbyterian, Baptist and Campbellite frontier preachers, many of them born in Kentucky or Virginia, had introduced and were still nurturing a rough and fervid

---

[38] Morris Birkbeck, *Letters from Illinois*, pp. 23–25; see also H. T. Stock, "Protestantism in Illinois before 1835"; *Jour. Ill. St. Hist. Soc.*, Apr. 1919, p. 30.

[39] *The Eccentric Preacher or a Sketch of the Life of Lorenzo Dow*, 1841; Peter Cartwright, *Autobiography* (Cincinnati, 1856); J. B. Finley, *Autobiography* (Cincinnati, 1853); O. H. Smith, *Early Indiana Trials and Sketches*.

gospel.[40] A preacher might find it necessary to thrash a hardened sinner before he could convert him; innocent girls and mischievous boys no less than sinful rogues were compelled to agonize at the mourner's bench. The strong man was bound and the kingdom was taken with force. If the preacher often was an uneducated man whose long sermons were little more than loud hallooing of a few ideas, his hearers were usually still less educated than he; his universal call to repentance and his unlettered plea for justice and sound morality helped to rescue human life from sordid heathenism. Under his influence religious and moral sloth gave way to the beginnings of civilization and more tender social relationships. Decency, law, and order settled on many a community. In places where Sunday services were held more or less regularly, the older attitude of Sunday lounging in working clothes or hunting or horse-racing gave way to better dressing and regular attendance at meeting, and with this came a desire for neatness and self-improvement.[41]

The educated missionary preachers from the East, usually college graduates, had little success at first. Their more polished sermons and the "salaries" they were paid were looked upon with bad feeling by the people and by the older native and by the southern preachers who had brought a gospel of free salvation without money and without price. In more settled centers, however, they exercised a refining influence; but at the same time, they helped to make Christianity more dogmatic and formal and less adaptive than the original form in which it was brought to the Middle West.[42] Two sweeping revivals, one in 1836 and another in 1857–1858 must be mentioned in any general survey of the religious life of the time. The former was criticized as being similar to the extravagant Kentucky revivals early in the century, but the latter was praised and participated in even by Episcopalians as a

---

[40] Esarey, *Indiana*, I., Ch. XII; I. F. King, *Introduction of Methodism in Ohio;* J. B. Batchelder, *The United States, the West and Ohio as Missionary Fields,* p. 44 *et passim;* J. C. Smith, *Early Methodism in Ohio,* 1879; Pease, 24–31.

[41] Ford, *Illinois,* pp. 39, 95, 96; Pease, *op. cit.,* pp. 26, 31.

[42] Harry Thomas Stock, "Protestantism in Illinois Before 1835," *Journal Ill. St. Hist. Soc.,* Vol. 12, No. I, Apr. 1919; J. D. Barnhardt, "Rise of the Methodist Episcopal Church in Illinois," *Jour. Ill. St. Hist. Soc.,* Vol. 12, No. 2; James Hall, *The Romance of Western History* (Cincinnati, 1857), p. 137; R. F. Thrapp, "Early Religious Beginnings in Illinois," *Jour. Ill. St. Hist. Soc.,* Vol. 4, No. 3, p. 303; *History of Brown Co., Ohio* (Chicago, 1883), Ch. VI; Meredith Nicholson, *The Hoosiers,* Ch. III; O. H. Smith, *Early Indiana Trials and Sketches,* pp. 97–100.

spiritual awakening of great social importance. It was estimated that it affected as many as 500 towns in the Middle West besides, of course, many country districts.[43]

SOUTHERN INFLUENCES—BLACK CODES

The border state social attitude of the lower tier of northwestern states in the period from 1840 to 1860 is evident in many ways. Since they were, for a long period after their admission, controlled largely by the older Virginia and Kentucky elements in their population, it resulted that in traditions, constitutions, laws, and social institutions the ideals of this older population became rooted and held out long against the resisting tendencies of the newer peoples in the lake counties and in Michigan and Wisconsin.

While the people were, of course, primarily western in ideals and interests, there had been, and still were, pronounced southern influences at work. There was in all the West in 1840 a lively tradition that they were indebted to Kentuckians and Virginians for protection from extermination by the Indians and conquest by the British in the War of 1812. Kentucky was revered for the part her soldiers had played at the River Raisin and for the gift of her gallant Jo Daviess at the Battle of Tippecanoe. Jackson was the greatest popular hero in the region, and January 8, the anniversary of the Battle of New Orleans, was second to no other holiday in public favor. Perhaps the strongest bond was the Democratic party which kept large sections of the lower West in political alliance with the South until the Civil War. Leaders in the South had been friendly to immigration to this region and had favored a lower price for public land when many in New England had opposed it. In fact, opposition to free homesteads did not become strong in the South until after 1845; this was when the upper rather than the lower West was urgently demanding this concession. The same religious denominations that were strong in the South, were strong here—Methodists, Baptists, and Presbyterians together with a newer and more distinctly border state sect, the Campbellites or "Christians." The spirit of southern churches and preachers was for many years to influence political and social viewpoints. The same influence was felt in forms of local government. In Indiana, Illinois, and

---

[43] Bishop McElvaine, *Address to Forty-first Annual Convention of the Diocese of Ohio, Journal of the Convention*, pp. 86 ff.; Francis E. Marston, *After Eighty Years* (Columbus, Ohio, 1886); James Shaw, *Twelve Years in America*, 1867.

Iowa the county or southern type grew up and was during the period 1845–1860 resisting the growth of the township form which found favor in the north of these states.[44] In Ohio a mixed type of local government prevailed. William Dean Howells, born and reared in southern Ohio, says in his *A Boy's Town* that the people in his home town near Cincinnati were overwhelmingly Democratic in politics and "for the most part, bitterly pro-slavery. The South characterized the thinking and the feeling of the town far more than the North. Most of the people were of southern extraction, from Kentucky or Virginia when they were not from Pennsylvania or New Jersey." He knew of only one New England family, Yankees being very much despised. He also notes that corn was sometimes burned for fuel and almost everybody chewed tobacco; there was much fever and ague and much drunkenness and one summer the cholera came and the people died off "like flies." [45]

No better index of the social attitude prevailing can be found than the feeling toward the free Negro. Slavery in the old Northwest—a subject about which much has been written—and attempts by indentures and systems of fines to overcome the Ordinance of 1787, to modify state constitutions and court decisions and to introduce certain forms of servitude or peonage, all this does not concern us here.[46] The number of actual slaves had by 1840 dwindled to about 350, most of these confined to the river counties of southern Illinois.[47] But the free Negro—that was another and a more important question. Whether or not he could vote, serve on juries, give evidence in court, receive poor relief, attend public schools or indeed whether he could even lawfully cross the Ohio or Mississippi and enter the region, these questions were dealt with by constitutional conventions, state legislatures and courts, and the decision was usually against the free Negro. In addition to legal disqualifications, he was then as now in the Middle West the object of unbending social ostracism. The following details will support these statements.

Nowhere in the West could the free Negro vote, unless it was in

[44] Chaddock, *Ohio Before 1850*, pp. 76, 77; Albert Shaw, *Local Government in Illinois, Johns Hopkins Studies*, First Series, Vol. I, No. III; Jesse Macy, *Institutional Beginnings in a Western State, Johns Hopkins Studies*, Second Series VII; E. B. Greene, *The Government of Illinois*, pp. 25–40.

[45] William Dean Howells, *A Boy's Town* (Harper and Brothers, 1890).

[46] J. P. Dunn, *Indiana, A Redemption from Slavery;* N. D. Harris, *History of Negro Servitude in Illinois;* Dunn, *Slavery Petitions and Papers, Ind. Hist. Soc. Pub.*, Vol. II, No. 12.

[47] *U. S. Census, 1840*, pp. 341, 371, 396, 467.

the Western Reserve of Ohio—the clause in the state constitution stating that white men could vote being interpreted in such a way as to allow this. In 1858, however, a new law was passed disfranchising those with a "visible admixture" of African blood.[48] In the Reserve, in the Miami valleys in southwestern Ohio, in eastern and northern Indiana and certain counties in Michigan, Wisconsin and northern Illinois, where Quakers, Free Soilers, and later the more thoroughgoing Republicans lived, there was some sentiment in favor of Negro suffrage.[49] In state legislatures or constitutional conventions, individual members representing these districts would vote for Negro suffrage or present petitions asking for suffrage without distinction as to sex or color.[50] If given a chance to vote, the people of these districts would cast several thousand votes in its favor.[51] But as a whole the feeling of the free West was against giving the vote to the free Negro until after the Civil War. Even the newer states, Michigan, Wisconsin and Iowa, were opposed to it; in Ohio the opposition to suffrage was stronger; in Indiana and Illinois, it was overwhelming.

In the Ohio Constitutional Convention of 1850–1851, delegates from southern counties demanded that petitions in favor of Negro suffrage not be received; the convention voted against such reception, sixty-six to thirteen, all the votes in favor coming from the Lake Erie region.[52] As late as 1865 the people of Ohio voted against Negro suffrage; it was, however, finally adopted by a bare majority in the legislature of 1869.[53] In Indiana the opposition in the southern counties was extremely bitter; there was opposition to receiving petitions on the subject, and the Constitutional Convention of 1850 refused to submit the question to a vote.[54] Southern and central Illinois were likewise bitterly hostile, and the grant of the political right to the Negro was utterly beyond the range of possibility in this state until the events of

[48] G. H. Porter, *Ohio Politics*, pp. 22, 23, 200. The law was on the statute books until 1865 with doubt as to its constitutionality.

[49] T. C. Smith, *The Liberty and Free Soil Parties in the Northwest, Appendix C.*

[50] *Debates, Ohio Convention, 1850–51*, Vol. I, pp. 31, 75, 107–109, 236, 298, Vol. II, pp. 192, 232, 550, 551; *Debates in Indiana Convention 1850*, I, 228, 230, 242–244, 250, 254. For Illinois see Smith, *Liberty and Free Soil Parties*, p. 334; *Debates of the Constitutional Convention of Iowa*, II, 917.

[51] Porter, *Ohio Politics*, p. 248; O. M. Dickerson, *The Illinois Constitutional Convention of 1862, U. of Ill. Studies*, Vol. I, No. 9, pp. 9, 13, 24, 55.

[52] *Debates, Ohio Convention*, 1850–1851, I, 59; II, 550, 551.

[53] Porter, *Ohio Politics*, pp. 248, 254.

[54] *Debates in Indiana Convention 1850*, I, 141, 142, 228, 244, 246, 247, 283.

reconstruction brought it in the form of the fifteenth amendment.[55] Iowa took a stand against it in 1848 and again in 1857.[56]

On the question of the civil rights of the free Negro, Ohio, Michigan and Wisconsin were moderate while Indiana and Illinois, especially their southern parts, were relentlessly hostile. These lower portions were exposed to the immigration of Negroes who wished to settle on free soil north of the Ohio and of fugitives who, attempting to escape from slave states by the underground railroad, often became stranded in the early stages of their journey. All along the southern border and in many of the interior counties of Ohio, Indiana and Illinois, it was felt that the land was being overrun by an undesirable class and that the problem demanded stern action. With the growth of the Free Soil, and later the Republican, party around the lakes, the difference of opinion on this question took on a bitterly partisan and sectional character. Many in the lower West went so far as to approve the institution of slavery in the South, which they maintained held the black man in his "proper place." Sternness on this question did not seem inconsistent with the Jacksonian "democratic principle" so loudly proclaimed. Some, as has been said, had held slaves in the South, and many more accepted the southern social philosophy of the day that society is and should be stratified; that the welfare and progress of the superior class demand the subjection of the inferior, and that the rights of man as outlined in the Declaration of Independence have reference to white men only. While the spread of these ideas was due partly to the influence of certain religious leaders and other teachers of the people, the acceptance of this philosophy is also explained by the partisan alliance of the lower West with the Democratic South and by geographical location. This attitude prevailed in spite of the fact that not until after the Civil War did the free Negro comprise any large percentage of the population.[57]

[55] O. M. Dickerson, *op. cit., passim;* Cole, pp. 338, 417, 418.

[56] *Debates of Constitutional Convention of Iowa 1857,* II, 917.

[57] In Ohio there were in 1840, 17,000 free Negroes; in 1860, 36,000 in a total population of over 2,000,000. They were most thickly settled around Cincinnati, in Greene County, and along the Ohio River. In Indiana, there were about 7,000 in 1840 and 11,000 in 1860, they being largely in the districts near the Ohio and the lower Wabash and in the "abolition" centers of eastern Indiana. In Illinois there were about 7,500 in 1860, scattered through the old Ohio and Mississippi River counties and in Chicago. In Iowa there were about 1,000 free Negroes living in the Mississippi River counties. *U. S. Census* of 1850, IX, 817, 702, 755, 934; *Eighth Census of the United States 1860, Population,* 135, 137, 594, 595.

There was opposition in Ohio, Indiana, and Illinois to the right of free Negroes to serve on juries, to give evidence in court, to receive poor relief, to attend public schools and to migrate into the region. This opposition took the form of constitutional restrictions and in Ohio and Illinois of "Black Codes" of a somewhat notorious character. Ohio had a Black Code until 1849, though in many places the laws were a dead letter. In 1849 men of all parties agreed to repeal this code and Free Soilers in return united with Democrats to elect Salmon P. Chase to the Senate.[58] There were, however, attempts to revive them in the Constitutional Convention of 1850. Their repeal was championed in such words as these:

Ohio was designed for the home of the white man and him only; . . . these United States were designed by the God of Heaven to be governed and inhabited by the Anglo Saxon and by him alone. . . . In this regard the Declaration of Independence was not true. . . . The doctrine of equality contained in it referred to the Anglo Saxon race.[59]

In 1863, after the Emancipation Proclamation and because of fear of increased immigration from the South, even Republicans in southern Ohio favored such restrictions.[60] The laws excluding Negroes from jury service remained on the books in Ohio until 1865.[61]

In Indiana no such tolerance was shown. The free Negro was kept by law from being a witness in any case whatever against a white man, a fact which often led to gross injustice and served as a cover for crime.[62] The debates of the Constitutional Convention of 1850, which serve as a rich mine of information regarding the social ideals of the state at that time, show that delegates from Ohio and lower Wabash counties stood against the free Negro while Quakers and Baptists and progressive Whigs from eastern and northern Indiana stood for him.[63]

[58] Porter, *Ohio Politics,* pp. 19, 20; *Laws of Ohio V,* 53; XXVI, 43; XXI, 94; *Debates Ohio Convention* 1850–1851, II, 600–604.

[59] *Ibid.,* I, 56.

[60] *Columbus Crisis,* Feb. 28, 1861, Feb. 4, 1863; *Ohio House Journal,* 1861, pp. 165, 209, 216, 221, 451. In March 1858 Theodore Parker wrote to Chase: "I wish I thought better of the southern part of your state. What keeps the slaves in the north of Maryland, Virginia and Kentucky? Not the central government nor the slave hunters in the neighborhood, but the public opinion of Pennsylvania, Ohio, Maryland and Illinois." *Chase Correspondence,* Am. Hist. Ass'n. *Report,* 1902, II, 478.

[61] Porter, *Ohio Politics,* pp. 20, 202.

[62] *The Report of the Debates of the Indiana Convention of 1850,* II, 1792; *Indiana Brevier Legislative Reports,* VII, 22; New Albany *Daily Ledger,* Nov. 24, 1858.

[63] *Debates,* I, 836; II, 1406, 1407, 1673; *Journal of the Convention of the People of Indiana,* 1850, pp. 94, 112, 140.

By that convention Negroes and mulattoes were forbidden to come into the state, and all contracts made with those entering the state were to be void.[64] Even so humanitarian and liberal a reformer as Robert Dale Owen felt compelled to vote for these measures.[65] A determined group advocated still harsher measures, such as the confiscation of property used in any way to shelter a Negro or mulatto—this was aimed at hated abolitionists—and the exclusion from the constitution of the principle of the Declaration of Independence that all men are created equal.[66] The people of the state voted overwhelmingly in favor of the exclusion of Negroes and mulattoes when this provision was submitted to them as a separate measure.[67] Although it was difficult to enforce these laws, the insistence on the essential inferiority of the Negro and disrespect for "the abstractions" of the Declaration of Independence was an attitude common to many in Indiana before and during the Civil War.[68] When the propriety of granting the vote to freedman in the southern states was being discussed in 1865, Governor Morton gave the following terse summary of the legal status of the Negro in Indiana:

Let me inquire for a single moment in what condition is Indiana to urge negro suffrage in South Carolina or in any other state. . . . We have perhaps twenty thousand colored people in this state. Most of them can read and write. . . . We not only exclude them from voting; we exclude them from testimony in the courts of justice. We exclude them from our public schools and we make it unlawful and a crime for them to come into the State of Indiana at any time subsequent to 1850. No negro who has come into our state since 1850 can make a valid contract; he cannot acquire title to a piece of land, because the law makes the deed void and every man who gives him employment is liable to prosecution and fine. . . . I sent out the twenty-eighth Indiana colored regiment, recruited with great difficulty. . . . It has been in the field two years. . . . Yet according to the Constitution and laws of Indiana, more than one-half of the men in that regiment have no right to come back again, and if they do come back, they are subject to prosecution and fine.[69]

[64] *Debates,* II, 1788; *Journal,* pp. 753, 754.

[65] *Debates,* II, 1407, 1788, 1791.

[66] *Ibid.,* I, 964; II, 1791; *Journal,* pp. 349; There were forty-four votes from the Ohio and Wabash River regions "against the Declaration of Independence."

[67] *St. Joseph Valley Register,* Aug. 21, 1851; Esarey, *Indiana,* I, 520.

[68] New Albany *Ledger,* Nov. 24, 1858; *Indiana Brevier Legislative Reports,* IV, 60, 62, 161; *Indiana Senate Journal,* 1861, pp. 281, 472; *Indiana Daily State Journal,* Mar. 2, 1861.

[69] *Speech at Richmond Indiana,* Sept. 29, 1865 in pamphlet, *Reconstruction and Negro Suffrage, Indiana and the War,* Adjutant General's Office, Vol. II, No. 15.

Illinois was even more hostile to the grant of civil rights to the Negro than was Indiana. While "Egypt" was the center of hostility, the Illinois valley and even the northern part could muster comparatively few people who would favor him, these few being the Free Soilers, "conscience Whigs," and a new class of antislavery Democrats of Chicago and vicinity. The southern counties insisted that, exposed as they were before 1861 to the inroads of free Negroes and fugitive slaves and after 1861 to "contrabands" and emancipated slaves, they be further protected by law. If protection was not to be forthcoming they threatened to use violence against the Negro.[70] The Black Code of this state resembled that of Indiana, important provisions being the prohibition of immigration, the denial of the right to hold property, to serve in the militia and to attend public schools.[71] The Convention of 1847 was urged by northerners to relax these provisions but the *State Register* rightly estimated public feeling when it said: "No fears need be entertained that the Convention will outrage popular sentiment by authorizing a relaxation of those distinctions between the two races, which are found in human nature and are so essential to the safety and dignity of society." [72] Indeed, rather than relaxation, greater harshness was authorized in later years, the best evidence of this being the notorious "Logan's Black Law" of 1853. This was a bill championed by that aggressive leader of the powerful Democracy of southern Illinois, John A. Logan, its most important provisions being that a free Negro coming into the state could be fined and if unable to pay could be sold for a length of time sufficient to pay this fine and cost.[73] So strange are the changes of history that this strong and bitter advocate of white supremacy later became, as a general in the Civil War and as a political leader in Reconstruction times, one of the idols of abolitionists and stiff-necked Republicans.

This Illinois act a Louisiana newspaper called one of "savage ruthlessness," [74] and the people of northern Illinois became more aroused after this passage. The Supreme Court upheld its constitutionality with regard to Negroes who were not fugitive slaves.[75] Under it there

[70] *Debates in Constitutional Convention in 1847, Illinois State Register,* Jan. 15; Feb. 5, 23, 26; Mar. 5; July 2, 8; Aug. 27, 1847.
[71] N. D. Harris, *Negro Servitude in Illinois,* Ch. XIII.
[72] *Illinois State Register,* July 8, 1847.
[73] *Statutes of Illinois,* 1853, *An Act to Prevent the Immigration of Free Negroes into the State;* Alton *Weekly Courier,* Jan. 19, 28, Feb. 11, 18, Mar. 4, 1853; Cole, pp. 225, 226, 336.
[74] Cole, 225.
[75] N. D. Harris, *Negro Servitude,* 237.

are cases on record of Negroes in Illinois being sold to the highest bidders. While comparatively few arrests and auction sales of Negroes occurred, there were enough to mark the law as a unique social phenomenon. In 1857, Gustav Koerner, an enlightened German of Belleville, Illinois, himself paid the fine of a Negro in order to keep him from being sold.[76] In 1863, Governor Yates pardoned six Negroes "for the crime of being Negroes" and discharged them from correction under the law of 1853.[77] Even the northern part of the state was not aggressive in defending the part of the Negro until well along in the Civil War, in truth many Republicans as well as Democrats feared "Negro equality." In 1862, at the very time Lincoln was planning his Emancipation Proclamation, the state as a whole voted by 100,000 majority to continue the ban on Negro immigration, although by this time a vote of 72,000 against prohibition in the northern counties made it clear to the conservative southern, central and western parts of the state that a change was coming.[78] Not until 1865 was the Black Law of 1853 repealed—by a Republican legislature.[79]

[76] Gustav Koerner, *Memoirs*, II, 31; Cole, pp. 226, 335.
[77] *Reprints of Executive Pardons*, Ill. St. Hist. Soc. *Transactions*, 1910, p. 50.
[78] O. M. Dickerson, *Illinois Constitutional Convention of 1862*, U. of Ill. *Studies*, I, No. 9, 397, 408, 439.
[79] N. D. Harris, *Negro Servitude*, pp. 237, 238.

CHAPTER III

MIDDLE WESTERN CULTURE 1840–1860

We shall secure acknowledgment for a literature partaking the spirit and energy of our people, inspired by our past and full of legend and story of peril and romance, encouraged by our present, full of vigor, independence, and intelligence.

The Genius of the West (Cincinnati, November, 1855), p. 342.

The advance of civilization into the Middle West from the rough beginnings made by the frontiersman's ax to the realization of a mature society is "a chapter in human experience." There is evidence that the earliest intellectual and cultural influences came from Kentucky, Tennessee, and Virginia, especially from Transylvania University, Lexington.[1] For the first two decades of the nineteenth century there was a cultural alliance between the old Northwest and the South, and influences resulting from this alliance persisted for some time. There grew up a polite society in southern Ohio, Indiana, and Illinois that was southern in tone. Town merchants and the older agrarian or lawyer aristocracy in or near towns like Chillicothe, Ohio, Madison, Indiana, and Springfield, Illinois, were familiar with the charms of New Orleans and were brought into contact with the social and cultural stimulations to be found on Ohio and Mississippi steamboats. On these moving palaces, southern planter, eastern merchant, and European traveler spend days together in polite conversation, heated argument, and gay amusement, not to mention drinking and gambling.

But the cultural bonds with the South were much less strong and lasting than the political and economic and were soon to give way to other influences, eastern, European, or native western. New Englanders, while never exerting the influence in the lower West that they were to exert in the lake district, nevertheless proved important

---

[1] Avery Craven, "The Advance of Civilization into the Middle West in the Period of Settlement" in Fox, *Sources of Culture in the Middle West;* R. L. Rusk, *The Literature of the Middle Western Frontier,* 2 Vols. (Columbia University Press, New York, 1925), I, 28; W. H. Venable, *Beginnings of Literary Culture in the Ohio Valley,* p. 171.

elements in Marietta, in Cincinnati, in Jacksonville, Illinois, and other rising towns in the river valleys. They furnished the celebrated Yankee school-teacher, the missionary preacher, and also helped in the founding of colleges. Other factors that helped to develop a higher life were the varied population, German influences, and contact with travelers from the East and Europe. The attractiveness of trips through the West —trips which then usually meant steamboat voyages down the Ohio to Cincinnati and on down the Mississippi to New Orleans or up that river to St. Louis and then by the Illinois River and canal to the small but growing Chicago—brought European and eastern writers, among them Mrs. Trollope, Harriet Martineau, Charles Dickens, W. M. Thackeray, Michel Chevalier, Washington Irving, and Walt Whitman. The visits of the more famous of these could not but be stimulating to the natives who were open to such impressions, this too in spite of the fact that foreign observers of western conditions, though praising the natural beauty of river, hill, and plain, and commenting on the marvelous business enterprise of the river towns, often indulged in severe strictures on western life and manners. In some cases this amounted to gross caricature—those of Mrs. Trollope and Charles Dickens have become proverbial. "Trolloping" the West became a favorite practice and, in fact, still is in certain circles.[2]

Literature, Music and the Theater

As early as 1819 there was a musical club—a Haydn Society—in Cincinnati.[3] Very soon, the place, with a population of only a few thousand, could boast of book-stores and coteries of "literati"; people ceased to ask at the book-shops for "sugar, coffee, the almanac, and spelling books." [4] *The Literary Gazette* appeared in 1824—the work of J. P. Foote and others. Literary and debating clubs arose; Hiram Powers studied sculpture under a German teacher. Impetus was added when the wealthy Nicholas Longworth, lawyer, real estate dealer, and vine-grower, and Daniel Drake, a physician with wide intellectual interests, became patrons of the arts in the growing city. James Hall, perhaps the most prominent figure in the early history of literature in the West, began to attain prominence in the East and in England by his books on western travel, description, and legend. At far Vandalia,

[2] Mrs. Trollope, *Domestic Manners of the Americans* (1832) ; Charles Dickens, *American Notes.*

[3] Greve, *History of Cincinnati,* I, 640.

[4] *The Genius of the West* (Cincinnati, 1855), p. 13.

Illinois, he launched his *Illinois Monthly Magazine* in 1829; then and later his work showed unusual pioneer vigor and sturdy "Americanism." But Illinois was not yet hospitable to literary endeavor, nor was Indiana, so that it was to Cincinnati that Hall felt impelled to come. There he continued his work in a circle that included Timothy Flint, Jacob Burnet, W. D. Gallagher, the poet, and the Beecher family.[5]

The decade of the thirties marked the appearance in Cincinnati of one of its best literary periodicals—*The Cincinnati Mirror*. It flourished from 1831 to 1835 and was widely read; nearly every budding western writer contributed to its columns. This period was

one of the most interesting in the annals of Cincinnati—the proportion of those who looked to literature with hope as a means of support was large. . . . There was a large number of young men then residing in the city; various literary projects were cherished by those ardent youths. . . . The sentinel hills around Cincinnati were then clothed with forests.

In no better way can we feel the intensity and enthusiasm of the native cultural interest and its struggle against financial difficulties, eastern criticism, and western popular indifference than by reading through the columns of the numerous, ephemeral, literary magazines that appeared, of which the *Mirror* was a conspicuous example.[6] There is reason to think that the twenties and thirties, the period of Hall and *The Mirror,* produced the strongest literature that was to come out of the West until after the Civil War.

In the forties and fifties there was evident decline and discouragement. The "ardent youths" of the thirties had by the late forties become disillusioned.

Acquaintance with the practical relieves the heart of its fiction and the prosaic treads close on the heels of the romantic. . . . The sentinel hills . . . are stript of their green glories and the hot sun now [1849] looks

---

[5] Rusk, *op. cit.,* I, Ch. VII; Mary M. Atkeson, "A Study of the Local Literature of the Upper Ohio Valley," *Ohio State University Bulletin,* Vol. XXVI, No. 3, pp. 10–15; *Ohio Arch. and Historical Society Publications,* Vol. XVIII, pp. 468–483; W. T. Coggeshall, *The Protective Policy in Literature* (Columbus, Ohio, 1859), p. 12. Among Hall's books were the following: *The Western Souvenir* (Cincinnati, 1829); *Legends of the West* (Philadelphia, 1833); *Tales of the Border* (Philadelphia, 1835); *Sketches of History, Life and Manners in the West,* 2 Vols. (Philadelphia, 1835); *The Romance of Western History* (Cincinnati, 1857).

[6] See article in the *Genius of the West,* 1855, p. 56; *Western Literary Journal and Monthly Review,* Vol. I, 1845; *Western Quarterly Review,* Jan. 1849, pp. 135 ff.; W. H. Venable, *Beginnings of Literary Culture in the Ohio Valley,* Ch. III.

down on their verdureless and mangled summits. . . . A change as great has passed over the spirits of those young enthusiasts.[7]

But though Cincinnati, now booming and prosperous, was ruthlessly despoiling its splendid natural heritage of river line, forest, and hill and thus making it harder for poets and artists to realize their dreams, still the struggle for a higher life went on. Prolific, amateurish, and sentimental, the short-lived literary monthlies continued to appear every year or two. *The Olio, The Christmas Guest, The Casket,* and *The Parlor Magazine,* were especially weak, as might be judged by their names, and died early and fortunate deaths. A periodical of this type, filled with patterns for dresses and night caps and recipes for the toilet, could, it was said, be found on the center table of every model parlor in every western town.[8] Of a somewhat more substantial quality was the *Ladies' Repository,* a church paper with literary features that seemed peculiarly adapted to the reading habits of the day. It was accorded a successful career for forty years. Still more serious intellectual and artistic effort was represented by *The Columbian, The Genius of the West,* and *The Dial;* in them the standards of the *Mirror* may be said to have been kept alive. Most of the periodicals were printed at Cincinnati; at Columbus and in Indiana and Illinois towns the few weak efforts gave way to the more successful daily and weekly newspapers. Cincinnati's printing and publishing business grew to very large proportions before the Civil War. Besides its periodicals, its presses turned out in a single year as many as a million books.[9]

The three leading newspapers of Cincinnati, the *Gazette,* the *Enquirer,* and the *Commercial* became and continued to be, perhaps, the most influential in the West until after the Civil War. Close seconds were such papers as the *Ohio State Journal* (Columbus), the *Indianapolis Sentinel,* and the *Illinois State Register* (Springfield). All these are invaluable sources of western history and life, and copies of them should be carefully preserved, whenever found. There was, in addition, a flood of country newspapers in the small towns, established by ambitious editors as proofs of local enterprise, or by lawyers or school-teachers seeking to embark on political careers. Some owed their existence to the patronage of a political party and were expected to deal out staunch local partisanship and, in too many cases, bitter

[7] *Western Quarterly Review,* Cincinnati, Jan. 1849.
[8] W. T. Coggeshall, *The Protective Policy in Literature,* p. 17; M. M. Atkeson, *op. cit.,* pp. 10–12.
[9] *The Genius of the West,* March, 1855, p. 74.

party venom of the spiteful neighborhood variety. Such papers were sometimes established only for a single year or "for the campaign."

So great is the rage for getting up papers, that the patronage necessary for their maintenance is thought a secondary consideration. . . . Is there a town or city in embryo with its plot designated, its streets and alleys and public grounds marked out, having within its bounds some half a dozen houses, a tavern, a store, and a blacksmith shop? . . . A press is wanted . . . to give assurance to the world not what it is but what it is to be. . . . Is there a wealthy and ambitious man grasping for office as the only means of obtaining a short lived distinction? The press is the great lever by which to consummate his wishes. Is there a lawyer, brief in years, brief in legal acquirements, with professional prospects briefless, the press is the fulchrum upon which his last hope for political preferment is based.[10]

Daniel Drake, physician, professor, scientist, and lecturer, interested in antiquities, botany, and geology, was one of the founders of the higher life of Cincinnati and the West. While his greatest work was in the promotion of the science of medicine, his wider interests made his home on Vine Street a center of the professional and literary life of Cincinnati. Here he called together a circle of writers including James Hall, Professor Stowe, and Harriet Beecher, in regular meetings called "reunions," and here Harriet Martineau and other foreign visitors were entertained. He delivered in 1833 an address in the chapel of Transylvania University at Lexington on the importance of promoting a literary and social concert in the valley of the Mississippi.

Measures should be taken to mould an uniform system of manners and customs out of the diversified elements which are scattered over the West. . . . Literary meetings should be held in the various states. . . . In short we should foster western genius, encourage western writers, patronize western publishers, and create a western heart.[11]

The Cincinnati School of Writers

In 1841, there appeared a volume of western poetry, "outgushings of irrepressible feeling proceeding from the hearts of those who are daily

[10] *Ill. State Gazette and Jacksonville News,* May 9, 1835, quoted by F. W. Scott in *Coll. Ill. St. Hist. Library,* Vol. VI, p. liv.

[11] *Remarks of Daniel Drake on the Importance of Promoting Literary and Social Concert in the Valley of the Mississippi,* Louisville, 1833. For information on Dr. Drake see C. D. Drake, *Biographical Sketch of Daniel Drake;* S. D. Gross, *Lives of Eminent American Physicians and Surgeons,* 1861, pp. 614–662; Otto Jueltner, *Daniel Drake and his Followers;* E. D. Mansfield, *Memoirs of the Life and Services of Daniel Drake;* Edward Thomson, *Sketches,* pp. 109–132; Dr. Daniel Drake, *Memoir,* Edited by Beverly W. Bond, Jr., *Quart. Pub. Hist. and Philosophical Society of Ohio,* Vol. 18, Nos. 2, 3.

subjected to the perplexities and toils of business." [12] Another appeared in 1860.[13] The Cincinnati literary journals we have mentioned spread widely a knowledge of the aspirations and work of a group of poets and novelists living in that city and in nearby Ohio, Indiana, and Kentucky towns, a group which might be called the Cincinnati school. Coggeshall's anthology published in 1860 listed a hundred western poets. While very few, if any, of these will occupy a permanent place in American literature, the work of W. D. Gallagher, and the early poems of William Dean Howells and Alice and Phoebe Cary, which may be considered the best products of the Cincinnati group, may have some claim to recognition.[14] None of the novels written in the period has survived; it remained for the post-war work of Mark Twain, Edward Eggleston, and the still more recent work of Ed Howe, Hamlin Garland, Herbert Quick, Edgar Lee Masters, Glenway Wescott, Ruth Suckow, and others, to produce distinctive contributions of this type. However, even in comparison with the Indiana writers and with the Chicago, Springfield, and other recent "realist" groups, the Cincinnati school, although antedating these by fifty or seventy-five years, should not be despised. With it came the beginnings of western literature; it set a high standard of enthusiasm, if not a high quality of work, to be emulated. It is to be hoped that there will grow out of all past and present middle western efforts at literary and esthetic achievement, a movement that will realize the dreams of the Cincinnati group, that will find its proper material and will produce a literature "partaking of the spirit and energy of our people, inspired by our past, full of legend and story of peril and romance, encouraged by the present, full of vigor, independence, and intelligence."

It is not surprising that the writers of the forties and fifties produced work less sturdy than that of James Hall and Timothy Flint— they were young; many of them had been born in the West; they wrote for a young people whose tastes had developed little beyond the

---

[12] William Davis Gallagher, *Selections from the Poetical Literature of the West* (Columbus, 1841).

[13] William Turner Coggeshall, *The Poets and Poetry of the West* (Columbus, 1860).

[14] The three last named were early in their careers drawn to the East, as so many western artists have been. The lyrical and imaginative work of "Amelia" (Mrs. Welby of Louisville, Ky.), Coates-Kinney's, "Rain upon the Roof," and Lytle's line, "I am dying, Egypt, dying," in his "Antony and Cleopatra," met with wide-spread popular favor. Others of note were John J. Piatt, Metta V. Fuller, and Otway Curry of Ohio; Louisa Chitwood and Julia Dumont of Indiana; and George D. Prentice of Louisville, Kentucky.

sentimental stage. The countless number of elegant pseudo-romantic poems and novels that appeared helped no doubt to soften the manners of rough westerners, but at the same time they gave to young men and women, now released from the most severe frontier rigors, an unfortunate affectation of refinement, a tendency which a widespread reading of Byron's poetry did perhaps raise to a somewhat higher plane. No great epic of pioneer life comes to us from the period— indeed no such epic has ever been written; and even local color and colloquial humor were inadequately handled. There were novels on far-off subjects, odes to the pioneers and to the West, poems of domestic affection, and of nature strangely elevated and unreal, melancholy treatments of death, the tomb, and other somber themes. It was the plaintive melancholy of the wind blowing through winter pines rather than the heroic melancholy of their own thwarted, pioneer struggles; it was an imported tragedy rather than that of their own lives. Whether or not the treatment of their own frontier environment by these writers was romantic in the sense of a literary interpretation that derived directly from Rousseau and European Romanticism is doubtful.[15] But whatever their faults, better work could hardly be expected from the pens of lawyers, editors, teachers, and preachers vainly trying to make a profession of letters.[16] Most of the energy of the people in country and small town was spent in husbanding the hard-won victories over the wilderness, swamps and forests; those enjoying material success became absorbed in their success; the practice of law, preaching, and politics monopolized the remaining energies. Of the preoccupation with politics a writer said in 1835: "The consequences to literature are obvious . . . genuine literary merit is unnoticed amid the whirl of party." [17]

The writers themselves realized how difficult it was to treat western life in poetic and literary form; the materials for literature existed, but there was needed in the new country the "mellowing influence of time . . . , greater repose, time for individuals for study and labor, time to the people for the mellowing influences which impress popular opinion." [18] Misgivings as to the possibility of a western

15 Rusk, op. cit., I, 1–4; Lewis Mumford, The Golden Day, Ch. II (Boni and Liveright, 1926).

16 W. H. Venable, Beginnings of Literary Culture in the Ohio Valley, Ch. IX; Emerson Venable, Poets of Ohio (Cincinnati, 1912).

17 Western Monthly Magazine, 1835, p. 23.

18 W. T. Coggeshall, The Poets and Poetry of the West; and by the same author, The Protective Policy in Literature.

culture gave way in many cases to more positive discontent with western environment—an early form of "the revolt from the village" which has been a theme so much to the liking of recent midwestern schools. Western writers in the fifties complained that their own West was a region of esthetic poverty and drabness; what the East and Europe had said found echoes in the Ohio and Mississippi valleys. Pork and steamboats, it was said, were given too much attention in Cincinnati; [19] in local satires that city was called "Porkopolis." [20] Then, as now, public indifference quenched artistic fire and left genius restless and bitter. We are not surprised to read that the young John Hay at his home in Warsaw, Illinois, in 1858, having recently returned from an eastern college, was full of dislike for his native land. He considered himself a poet in exile and complained that the "barbarous West" was "a dreary waste of heartless materialism where great and heroic qualities may indeed bully their way up to the glare but the flowers of existence inevitably droop and wither. . . . So in time I shall turn from the rose and rainbow to corner lots and tax titles. . . . (There is) no room in the West for a genius." [21] He later, however, wrote *Pike County Ballads* and found inspiration in the company of Lincoln. Lincoln himself showed much melancholy and restlessness, but we hear no bitter indictment of his "Spoon River" environment from his lips. Nor can the young Mark Twain be classed among the bitter malcontents. Growing up in Hannibal, Missouri, and roving up and down the Mississippi and Ohio rivers, he seemed to observe a pageant of life which exhibited sufficient gusto, variety, humor, and mystery to afford themes for novels and to give color to his best work.[22]

In the work of a few writers, a higher type of self-criticism and social analysis appeared. Puritanical, eastern and European tendencies as well as the "western mind" were in turn objects of praise and of blame. It was counted a tribute to the West that the numerous local periodicals failed to receive support and a point of pride that a Cincinnati book-store sold as many as 5,000 copies of *Harper's*— an eastern journal. "From a thousand fortunate circumstances, the western mind is fortunate; from the unbounded sense of freedom, from the release from conventionalities, from the inspiration which

[19] *Genius of the West,* Nov. 1855, pp. 340-341 *et passim.*

[20] *Porkopolis, a Holiday Satire,* Cincinnati, New Year's Day, 1843.

[21] W. R. Thayer, *Life and Letters of John Hay,* I, 53, 56-58; for a more recent protest in novel form see Floyd Dell, *Moon Calf.*

[22] Van Wyck Brooks, *The Ordeal of Mark Twain.*

awakens in the heart by communion with the magnificence of boundless forests, prairies, streams and lakes." [23] Lyman Beecher's plea for
the young men of the East to go West with New England, Christian
leaven to educate the pioneer and save the land from the encroach-
ments of Catholicism, was derided as a crusade against the "infidels
of the West, inviting pious knights and females of the East to follow
to the conquest of the goodly land which was given up to ignorance
and idolatry." [24] Western authors themselves were not free from
attack. Alice Cary's work was called "over sweet"; people wearied
of "the monody, the wail, the sigh and sob of harp strings sadly
tuned"; and others of the "sobbing school of writers" were held in
contempt.[25] Literary and dramatic criticism in the Cincinnati *Dial*
showed special insight. "Sentimental, moral and anti-slavery or temperance plays fall from grace as soon as they touch the stage" said
its editor in 1860.

In the smaller towns, the imaginative and esthetic life of the people
received inadequate expression through the church and such literary
and musical interests as would be aroused by traveling dramatic
readers, by troops of players and by the "singing school." In these
last mentioned institutions, New England masters sought, usually
in vain, to tone down the habit of loud, strident singing learned at
camp meetings. Historical characters came to the West in the form
of museums of wax figures and, as a substitute for travel, there were
panoramic picture exhibitions entitled "China," "California," or
"Eden." There was also an occasional lecture by an eastern journalist
or author. But in and near Cincinnati, in the Illinois country tributary to St. Louis and in the larger towns like Chillicothe, New Albany,
Peoria, Quincy and Springfield, art, music and the drama in the
forties and fifties assumed higher forms. Among western sculptors
the names of Hiram Powers, and S. V. Clevenger stand high.
The attraction of the East and of Europe for the western man of
talent was then as now often too great to be resisted and his
mature work was more likely done elsewhere than at home. In the
forties Powers' masterpiece of sculpture, "The Greek Slave" attracted attention in Italy and London; it was later carried from town
to town in the United States and placed on exhibition. In the Ohio

[23] *The Genius of the West,* 1855.
[24] James Hall, in the *Western Monthly Magazine,* May, 1835, p. 322, and 1836,
passim.
[25] *The Genius of the West,* Feb., 1856, pp. 57, 58; *ibid.,* Jan., 1855, p. 13;
Sept., 1855, pp. 257, 258.

valley it received marked attention, newspapers giving columns of approval to it or of criticism of its nudity and "improprieties." [26]

Hiram Powers, as a boy, had worked in and around Cincinnati, impressed by the hills and forests that were so beautiful at that time, training himself as clock-maker and mechanic and worker in plaster and wax. Skillful with museum figures and automata, he fabricated a "Dante's Inferno" that worked on the easily excited imaginations of his western audience. Giving up this cheaper, inartistic employment, after doing some of his serious early work under the patronage of Nicholas Longworth, he was called to Washington and the East to make busts of the statesmen of the day, J. Q. Adams, Calhoun, Marshall, Webster, and President Jackson. Then he went to Florence, Italy, where, as he said, opportunities for obtaining marble and for the study of anatomy were greater than in the United States, where living models could be procured and where an artist with a family could live more cheaply. But he remained throughout an American and a westerner and hoped to return to "Cincinnati's hills." He wrote while in Italy:

It is true that music and accomplishment in languages apart, the opportunities for a substantial education for one's children are not as good here as at home. There are, however, less temptations to vice and less exposure to the American habit of hard drinking among young men; but no doubt, the general influences here in the way of developing a manly, energetic, and self reliant character are less favorable than at home. There is a softness, a disposition to take life easy, and a want of moral earnestness in Italy. . . . On the other hand the money getting propensities and social rivalries of America tend to harden human character and to bring out a severe selfishness that is offensive.[27]

While the West produced few if any great musicians and actors before the Civil War, in Cincinnati and other places from time to time the greatest outside artists appeared on the stage and in concert. Germans were everywhere advocates of more and better music. Boys from Illinois and Iowa farms went by boat to St. Louis and there came under the magic influence of Booth and other actors. A dra-

[26] Literary Journal and Monthly Review, Vol. I, 1845, p. 314; Chas. Cist, Cincinnati Miscellany, 1845, p. 60; Vol. II, 1846, pp. 239, 244; also by the same author Cincinnati in 1851, pp. 121–128; Western Quarterly Review, Jan., 1849, p. 95.

[27] For Power's life and work see, H. T. Trickerman, Book of the Artists (1867), pp. 276–294; Lorado Taft, History of American Sculpture (New York, 1903), pp. 57–71; J. D. McCabe, Great Fortunes and How They Are Made, pp. 471–487; Hiram Powers, Letters to Nicholas Longworth, Hist. and Phil. Soc. of Ohio, Quarterly Publication, 1906, Vol. I, pp. 33–59.

matic critic said in 1860: "Shakespeare comes down from the scholar's shelf and through the interpretation of a Booth or a Cushman comes near to the flatboatman." Ole Bull, the violinist, and Jenny Lind were popular in the fifties and "little Adeline Patti" was soon to become an idol in the West. German and Italian opera was at times presented. But already the commercial possibilities of more bizarre amusement were being realized, and popular taste was to be degraded before it had a chance to develop. "Heavy and formal drama" was already giving way to extravaganza and the ballet dancing that was objectionable to many eyes. Almost all the churches protested against these tendencies in the theater. Even the Episcopal church retained on its records until the fifties an injunction against "theatrical amusements, balls and other vain places of amusement" as being "coarse and indelicate" and unfit for communicants to indulge in.[28]

The West had for several decades been a center of communistic societies of various types. Due to the newness of the region and the comparative cheapness of land, opportunities were naturally offered for the adherents of French, German, English, and American sectarian or utopian idealists of that day to undertake adventures in coöperative living. The various forms of religious and economic communism, sectarian, Owenite, Fourieristic and Icarian, grew, flourished, declined and with one or two exceptions, died—the period of their greatest vigor being the twenties, thirties, and forties.[29] The experiment of Robert Owen at New Harmony, Indiana, was, perhaps, the most conspicuous, but at a dozen other places there came to be brotherhoods, utopias, phalanxes, Zoarite or Shaker communities. They served, whether failures or not, as reminders to the masses of the people of the West of the peculiar views of their devotees. The Mormons in Ohio and at Nauvoo, Illinois were not distinctly communistic but rather a religious cult having in the public eye a dan-

[28] For scattered and meager sources on music and the theater before the Civil War see: *Pen and Pencil* (Cincinnati, Jan., 1853); *The Dial* (Cincinnati, 1860), pp. 762–768; C. B. Plattenburg, "In St. Louis during the Crisis," *Jour. Ill. State Hist. Society*, Vol. 13, No. I, p. 18; A. C. Cole, *The Era of the Civil War*, Ch. XXI; *Journal of Proceedings of the Annual Convention of the Ohio Diocese of the Protestant Episcopal Church*, 1852, 1858; see also dramatic notices in Cincinnati newspapers.

[29] Morris Hillquit, *History of Socialism in the United States* (1903); J. H. Noyes, *History of American Socialisms* (1870); Chas. Nordhoff, *Communistic Societies of the United States* (1875); W. A. Hinds, *American Communities*, 2nd edition (1902); *The Herald of Truth* (Cincinnati, 1847); Venable, *Beginnings of Literary Culture*, Ch. VI; various articles on the Shakers by J. P. Maclean in *Ohio Arch. and Hist. Soc. Pub.*, Vols. IX, X, XI, XIII.

gerous polygamous tendency. Followers of William Miller called "Millerites" or second Adventists, were here and there joined together in the forties preparing ascension robes and awaiting the second coming of Christ.[30] Ultra German theorists who had taken part in violent uprisings in their homeland were to be found in and near Belleville, Illinois, in Cincinnati, Chicago, and elsewhere. It was with difficulty that more moderate German liberals influenced them to give up their demands for "uniform compensation for all kinds of labor" and government ownership of public utilities and become more "useful citizens." [31]

More influential, but by no means representing the social philosophy of the region, were abolitionists and Free Soilers who lived in large numbers in the Miami valleys, in the Western Reserve, in Cincinnati and in German, Quaker, or New England settlements in Indiana and Illinois, in fact in widely scattered regions throughout the West where the flaming moral zeal of Theodore Weld and others in the thirties had laid the foundations of the antislavery movement.[32] The editor of a Free Soil magazine, published in Cincinnati, the *Western Quarterly Review,* besides advocating abolition and free soil doctrine, included a wide range of social reform in his platform and thus (1849) expressed his demand for a revision of the harsh and dogmatic *laissez faire* economics of that day:

Europe is rocking like a tempest tossed ship. . . . The social question cannot be blinked down. . . . Political economy must be overhauled. It is a question with some whether truth would not completely annihilate the whole system of Smith, Ricardo, Chalmers, Wayland and Mill and establish a system more hopeful in its promises and more humanitarian in its doctrines. . . . The questions of wages, of accumulation, of distribution and profits are now open for solution.

But such was not the prevailing social thought of the lower or, indeed, of the upper West; we find that rather in the "Progressive Democracy." Believers in that political faith, as we see in another chapter, were, except on the questions of slavery and the Negro, rivals of the Free Soilers as advanced political liberals.

[30] *Western Midnight Cry* (1843), and *The Day-Star* (1846), were organs of the Millerite movement.

[31] R. E. Rombauer, "The Life of Gustavus Koerner," *Trans. Ill. St. Hist. Soc.,* 1904, pp. 290–295; Gustavus Koerner, *Memoirs.*

[32] Gilbert Hobbs Barnes, *The Antislavery Impulse* (D. Appleton-Century Company, 1933), pp. 79–87, 196–197.

Theological Debate

The West before the Civil War was an arena of theological controversy. The recognized creeds and views of life held in common with the East and the South were in the years before the Civil War opposed on every hand by advanced thought along religious, scientific, and philosophical lines. Robert Owen had early introduced a naturalistic view of life, and German agnosticism was common in all the larger towns. Unitarians in Cincinnati were aggressive; "infidelism" also had centers in that city, and in Indiana and Illinois there were many small-town skeptics who antedated Robert G. Ingersoll. Was the earlier Virginia and Kentucky evangelistic and missionary zeal which had brought Christianity into these regions north of the Ohio to be overthrown by such enemies? [33] This was a question that worried the orthodox. Camp meetings were being called "unnatural, forced contrivances for causing great excitement. Do not thousands go to them," it was asked, "as they go to horse races, for amusement, mischief, even debauchery"? In the cities and more settled regions, churches had become fixed institutions, organized into administrative divisions, conferences, presbyteries, and associations. The pagan or loose-living frontiersman was less a problem now than the assaults of these skeptics and Unitarians or the Catholics now coming in large numbers from Europe. Frontier religion was already largely giving way to rationalized theology; the epic of Christianity in the West was giving way to a formula; the camp meeting with its call to universal repentance was being replaced by doctrinal discussion, by a refined but dogmatic orthodoxy, contentious and argumentative.[34] The faith once delivered to hunted and persecuted saints and carried to this midwestern region by intrepid circuit riders was now to be preserved by laborious and formal debates lasting five or six hours a day for six or eight days. The "great debates" of the politicians of that day were equaled if not excelled by these theological contests, perhaps unparalleled in American history and playing a major part in the higher life of the West from 1825 to 1850.

And the champions of various creeds who went forth to battle were men of heroic stature. One of them, Alexander Campbell, the founder of the Disciples or Christian Church, has had few equals in

[33] *The Messenger* (Unitarian) (Cincinnati Sept. 1840), p. 237; Esarey, *Indiana*, I, 541.
[34] Esarey, *Indiana*, II, 573.

representing the better type of Protestant democratic orthodoxy. He proclaimed a "Reformation," a union of churches on a Campbellite or "Christian" basis. On the other side, the still more famous man, in fact, an international protagonist of "naturalism," humanitarianism, and skepticism, Robert Owen, was as eager as any of the orthodox for a verbal battle. The Romanist Bishop Purcell did not hesitate to come into the open in defense of a faith by many considered so accursed and threatening to the free West. Dr. Nathan Rice, the leading old school Presbyterian, argued for a complacent Protestantism divorced from social and political questions, refused to see any revolutionary social message in Christianity, looked upon slavery with little or no alarm and preached "individual salvation" and consolation.

The first debate of importance was held at Cincinnati in 1829 between Owen and Campbell. The question was naturalism versus religion or whether the "laws of human nature" or the evidences and values of Christianity brought more benefit to mankind. From nine o'clock in the morning until noon and again at three in the afternoon, speaking alternately for a whole week, these men argued before a Cincinnati audience presided over by leading citizens as moderators. The report of these debates was published and widely circulated; they fill hundreds of pages.[35]

In 1837 Bishop Purcell and Campbell debated for a week on the history and claims of Catholicism and the danger to society of its doctrines, each of the debaters exhibiting a wide knowledge of European history, culture and religious thought. In a debate in 1843 with Dr. Nathan Rice, Campbell made a remarkable attack on sectarianism in a sectarian age, at the same time he insisted on baptism by immersion, giving half of the time to that contentious subject. The debate continued for eighteen days and the printed volume covers nine hundred pages.[36] In 1845, Blanchard and Rice, progressive and conservative Presbyterians respectively, debated at Cincinnati on slavery; the latter by tortuous, scholastic methods attempting the

---

[35] Owen and Campbell, *Debate on the Evidences of Christianity Containing an Examination of the Social System* (London, 1839); Robert Owen's *Opening Speech* (Cincinnati, 1829); J. J. Haley, *Debates that have made History* (St. Louis, 1920), pp. 57–116. Campbell made twenty-two speeches in the course of the debate, one of which lasted twelve hours and extended through three days.

[36] It was held in Lexington, Kentucky, but the reports were read throughout the West. Henry Clay was chairman. *A Debate between Rev. A. Campbell and Rev. N. L. Rice* (Lexington, Kentucky, 1844); J. J. Haley, *Debates that have made History*, Chs. XVII–XXII.

difficult task of reconciling Christianity and slavery, claiming that the relation of master to slave was not a sinful relation and deprecating the interference of the church in established institutions.[37] The laying of corner stones of Catholic and Protestant churches in Cincinnati in 1867 was the occasion of another contest. Purcell was now an Archbishop and a dominant ecclesiastic in the West.[38] But to point out only a few of these debates is misleading. Theological like political debate spread into the interior; newspapers encouraged the spirit of contention and many people received a large part of their education in this way.

MIDDLE WESTERN LIBERALISM

The spread of advanced ideas among certain classes in the Middle West was not checked by these debates or by the growing social refinement and orthodoxy of the churches. A native paganism or the joyous pantheism of the frontier still lived in the heart of many a stout old pioneer. There continued to be a skeptical tendency in certain places and a lively prejudice against preachers.[39] There was a sense of freedom due partly to traditional frontier absence of restraint, partly to a hatred of "bigotry" and of "autocratic clergy," and partly to dislike of "puritanical" church and state restrictions, all of which was hard to distinguish from a desire to have no interference with western liberty to drink, hunt, race horses, and gamble on Sunday. This was true of central Illinois in particular, but was by no means confined to a few districts. Many public men had an easy tolerance on questions of public and private morals and manners. Lincoln himself, though not self-indulgent, was said to be a man who "ran smoothly in society, complaining of no immorality, no intemperance, no vice, no tobacco-chewing." [40] He was called a deist and he belonged to no church. And over in Missouri the young Mark Twain was growing up neutral on theological and social questions and enjoying rather than condemning "human nature." Indeed, the combined influence of environment, of the tolerant, philosophic Kentuckian, the free westerner, and the radical German was producing in many communities social attitudes far removed from the narrow Puritanism that has been described as typically mid-western.

More pronounced opponents of orthodoxy were M. D. Conway, the

---

[37] *Debate on Slavery* (Cincinnati, W. H. Moore, 1846).
[38] *The Roman Catholic Church and Free Thought* (Cincinnati, 1868).
[39] Caleb Atwater, *History of Ohio*, pp. 304, 305.
[40] W. H. Herndon to Joseph Gillespie, Cole, *Era of the Civil War*, p. 422.

radical editor of the Cincinnati *Dial,* and John Pettit of Indiana who, with the sons of Robert Owen, represented advanced views in that state. Although the social experiment of the father had failed, New Harmony remained a center of considerable culture; and the work of the able sons, Robert Dale, the humanitarian reformer who played a part in Indiana and national politics, and David Dale, one of the first geologists in the West and the author of several important geological surveys, as well as the work of other educators and scientists associated with the colony, were for a long time significant influences in the intellectual history of the West.[41] The advanced views of the liberals shocked the orthodox. An eastern missionary magazine reported this condition in the West in 1841: "Paine's 'Age of Reason' is read with avidity in many families and its doctrines advocated by men of influence. Not a few mothers drink in its poison. Many immigrants from Europe are disciples of Hume and Voltaire. Clubs and associations are found in almost all our towns on the rivers." [42]

In the most advanced circles in the West the theories of geological and biological evolution propounded by Lyell and Darwin were known and accepted before the Civil War. The antiquity of the earth as shown by the record of the rocks was recognized and little difficulty was encountered in reconciling *Genesis* and geology. In 1849 a writer thus set before his readers the new findings of geology:

Until within thirty years the general belief of mankind was that the earth had been in existence only about 6,000 years. . . . Men who have become proficient in the physical sciences now agree, the world over, that our earth and the solar system and the yet unfathomed stellar world have existed hundreds of thousands of years. . . . We may safely estimate its age at millions of years. . . . The first chapter of Genesis does not appear to have been intended as a piece of natural history, and should not be regarded as such. . . . I do not think there is an attempt to . . . give a full clear and detailed description of these stupendous events. The revelation is a moral, not a scientific one.[43]

In 1856 a Marietta College paper said, "Geology is not infidel in its tendency." [44]

The Darwinian theory was somewhat slower in being accepted.

[41] Meredith Nicholson, *The Hoosiers,* Ch. IV.
[42] *The Home Missionary,* quoted by Prudence Kofoid in "Puritan Influences in the Formative Years of Illinois History," *Pub. No. 10 of Ill. Hist. Lib.* p. 326.
[43] *Western Quarterly Review,* April, 1849, p. 225.
[44] *Marietta Collegiate Magazine* (August, 1856).

The *Dial,* a very liberal periodical, in 1860 contained articles treating favorably higher criticism of the Bible, German rationalism and Darwin's *Origin of Species.* This remarkable journal with its unique editor, Moncure D. Conway, forced after a short year of existence to cease publication because in 1860 there was so much slavery and war agitation as to make impossible its philosophical and literary discussion, was indeed what its editor said it would be, a mirror of intellectual and religious history of the West of its day, "of the movements of thought in that period of extraordinary, generous seeking." [45] Among its contributors were Ralph Waldo Emerson and the young William Dean Howells. It introduced Walt Whitman's *Leaves of Grass* to western readers. The editor thus enthusiastically recommended this unusual book:

We have read it at night after following the throngs in New York City by day, we have conversed with its music when the obligato was the whizz and scream of the locomotive which bore us across the continent and have turned to it from the calm rush of the Father of Waters, from the loading here and there on its shores by the glare of pine-knot fires; from the eager crowd of men and women chatting, singing, gaming in the saloon, and we confidently announce that Walt Whitman has set the pulses of America to music. Here are the incomplete utterances of New York City, of the prairies, of the Ohio and Mississippi, the volume of American autographs.[46]

A hearing for most of what the *Dial* sought to convey was accorded only by the New England transcendentalists, liberal southerners, Unitarians, German rationalists, and Jews scattered here and there in the lower West, along with a few college professors and students. Such ideas, of course, spread only slowly to other classes. However, with the evidence before us, it may safely be said that the lower West was far from being out of touch with world thought, and that western orthodoxy and fundamentalism then no less than now were not unchallenged by a certain modernism. What the present-day critic would call the "Bible belt" of that day, found room and some degree of recognition for the radicalism of Conway, the social reform of Robert Dale Owen, the advanced educational ideals of Horace Mann at Antioch College, and the deism and humanitarianism of Abraham Lincoln.

[45] *The Dial,* Cincinnati, 1860; M. D. Conway, *Autobiography,* I, 312.
[46] *The Dial,* Aug., 1860.

The Beginnings of the Middle Western College

In the first decades of the nineteenth century, before there were any institutions of college rank north of the Ohio, higher educational influences were exerted on this region from the South, from Transylvania University at Lexington, Kentucky and from early Tennessee "colleges." That influence, however, soon gave way as there grew up in Ohio, Indiana, Illinois, Iowa, and other states, a large number of primitive "state universities," denominational academies, seminaries and private schools, institutions which played a great part in the training of leaders for a people little removed from the frontier wilderness stage. Some of these, for instance, Ohio University at Athens and Miami at Oxford, Ohio, which had their origin in the appropriation of public lands for educational purposes, survived and became the first "state universities" in the West. Even schools of this type, however, came under a large degree of denominational influence. In the thirties, forties, and fifties a large number of true denominational colleges were founded. The impetus back of some of them was eastern missionary effort; others were native growths. Almost all were in fact children of faith and the object of great devotion and love of men and women who were willing to sacrifice all for their success. A large portion of the semi-private seminaries did not survive in the stern struggle for existence. One who travels by automobile in the Middle West to-day will see here and there in small towns old deserted buildings or heaps of ruins or will be told by native townsmen that at one time a "college" was located in their midst; he can picture in his imagination the story of local intellectual and religious enthusiasm which was followed by disillusionment, struggle, and decline.

If several of the colleges survived, it was not because the path was not hard; they faced poverty and discouragement, lack of support before the Civil War, depletion and set-back during the war, and after the conflict, competition with the newer state universities. Co-education was the rule from the first in a few; others at later periods opened their doors to men and women on an equal basis. Most of them were located in the older and lower West and had their origin before the lake region had reached any high state of development. These colleges, though most of them were sectarian, were distinctly democratic in spirit. One of the objects of some of them was to provide "manual and agricultural training." Among those that came through all the severe tests and promised to become a permanent part of the higher life of the Middle West were: Marietta, Denison, Oberlin, Ohio Wesleyan, Antioch, DePauw, Wabash, Earlham, Illinois College, Knox, Beloit, Grinnell, St. Xavier, and Notre Dame.[47] Among the educational leaders of the forties and fifties, the name of Jonathan B. Turner of Jacksonville, Illinois, editor, originator of the agricultural college idea, and public-spirited citizen, deserves special mention.

The curriculum was modeled on that of the American and English college of the day, and consisted largely of courses in Latin, Greek, mathematics, certain branches of science, and "moral philosophy" with some elocution and composition.[48] There was as yet little or no modern language, literature, history, or social science, and physical science was in some colleges opposed because associated with infidelism or "New Harmony" influences.[49] There was, as we have said, some recognition of the demand for manual training and agricultural education; shop and farm work, or practical training, was required of students in some of the colleges—a feature that was soon dropped in almost all the colleges of this type in the West. This work was required partly as a health measure, partly to help the students pay expenses, and partly for more purely educational values.[50] One of the trustees of Miami University in 1845 asked the colleges to "elevate modern science and language to their true importance, there was too much ancient classics; to elevate the sciences of agriculture, civil engineering, geology, political sciences and modern language to a proper standard; it would greatly tend to equalize the genius and talent of the country and prevent that unnatural rush into the ranks of law, medicine and divinity."[51] As further proof of

[47] *Historical Sketches of the Higher Educational Institutions of the State of Ohio,* 1876; *Denison University Memorial Volume;* E. T. Nelson, *Fifty Years of History of the Ohio Wesleyan University* (Cleveland, 1895); E. J. James, "Life and Labors of Jonathan B. Turner," *Jour. Ill. St. Hist. Soc.* Vol. 8, No. I; E. P. Cubberley, *Public Education in the United States,* pp. 203–210; Esarey, *Indiana,* II, 987–1008; Pease, *The Frontier State,* pp. 436–442; Avery Craven, "The Advance of Civilization into the Middle West" in Fox, *The Sources of Culture in the Middle West,* pp. 57–59.

[48] *Catalogue, Ohio Wesleyan University,* 1844–1860; *The Western Messenger,* 1840, Vol. VIII, which gives the curriculum of Ohio University (Athens, Ohio) at that time.

[49] Esarey, *Indiana,* II, 1006–1007.

[50] *Literary Journal and Monthly Review* (1845), I, 65, 85, 205, 368; *Marietta College Catalogue,* 1855; Howe, *Historical Collections,* pp. 316; N. N. Hill, *History of Licking Co., Ohio,* Ch. XL; Paul Selby, "The Part of Illinoisans in the National Educational Movement, *1851–1862,*" *Transactions of Ill. St. Hist. Society,* 1904, pp. 216, 217.

[51] C. Cist, *Cincinnati Miscellany,* Vol. II, Oct. 1845, p. 145.

progressive tendencies, we may cite the persistent efforts to allow women the advantages of higher education. At Antioch College in the fifties Horace Mann, the educator, and others with him sought to introduce advanced views of "health and life" and a Unitarian philosophy and to admit women and Negroes on terms of equality with white men students; a policy which, of course, brought much opposition from professors and constituents.[52]

Attendance at chapel or prayer service was required daily and, in some of the colleges, as often as ten times a week. Classes would sometimes convene at six o'clock in the morning. Evangelistic services were held in most of these colleges with the idea of winning all unconverted students. The room rent of students was as low as $1.50 "per session," boarding $1.75 to $2.00 a week, and some students are said to have boarded themselves "at from sixty cents to one dollar a week." "Parents and guardians are earnestly advised that young men at college have little need of pocket money," said one college catalogue, "and in all cases, it is safer that their funds be intrusted to one of the professors, whose discretion may regulate their expenditure." [53] Thus the atmosphere was a mixture of classicism, evangelical orthodoxy, and frontier sternness. For all that, it no doubt proved intellectually stimulating to young men and women used to still greater privations and hard work at home.

The attempt to develop a Latin and Greek culture in the West was in the end doomed to failure; nevertheless for many a keen-minded farm boy it broadened the imagination, sharpened the vocabulary, and spurred ambition. Grimly humorous, as we now see it, was the attempt of certain professors to impart a truly Greek atmosphere by themselves dropping their Christian names, urging their students to do so and assuming such rôles as Ajax or Pericles; for many students straight from the prairie farm and struggling to live on a dollar a week such "culture" was hardly appropriate.[54] Literary societies for men and women called by such names as Chrestomathian, Erosophian, and Clionian served a good purpose in providing training in public speaking for many men who later became prominent in public life.[55] These unique centers of self-expression were to last for several decades, only to die out finally

[52] J. W. Allen, *History of Antioch College; Historical Sketches of the Higher Educational Institutions of the State of Ohio,* 1876; S. A. Dean, *Dedication of Antioch College, 1854.*

[53] *Catalogue, Ohio Wesleyan University,* Delaware, Ohio, 1853, 1854.

[54] Meredith Nicholson, *The Hoosiers,* p. 75.

[55] *Literary and Monthly Review,* I, 338.

and to leave no trace except perhaps curiously lonesome looking
Greek names printed on doors in the upper stories or out of the way
rooms in the older college buildings. Several Greek letter "social"
fraternities had their start at Miami University and others founded
in the East spread to these western colleges. If other forms of classicism were doomed to failure, here was found a use of the Greek
alphabet that proved to be eminently "practical" and that fitted in well
with the American tendency to form secret societies. The story of
these fraternities and that of the later formed college sorority together
with the influences they have exerted on the middle western college,
is not a part of this study.

Certain students were discontented with what they considered the
narrow social vision of their college. At times there was open rebellion. Lane Seminary students (Cincinnati), in the thirties, rebelled
against a board of trustees that forbade the discussion of slavery; after
a debate which lasted for eighteen successive evenings, a group of
the students took matters in their own hands and, impelled by an
evangelical antislavery zeal, migrated to Oberlin and made it a center
of abolitionist influence that spread through northern Ohio and over
into Indiana and Michigan.[56] College societies, graduating classes,
and student lyceums sometimes invited radicals, such as Unitarians
or Emersonian transcendentalists, to speak to them, against the wishes
of college presidents.[57] Student periodicals of that day—as we examine the few remaining dusty copies scattered here and there in
middle western libraries—are clearly less clever and pictorially daring than those of to-day; though written in the formal and stilted
style prevalent at that time, they reflect a more serious cultural tone
and a more general acquaintance with good literature.[58]

[56] Gilbert Hobbs Barnes, *The Antislavery Impulse 1830–1844* (D. Appleton-
Century Company, 1933), pp. 74–78, 231–233; D. L. Leonard, *A Century of
Congregationalism in Ohio* (1896), p. 51; *Western Monthly Review*, Jan. 1836,
pp. 2, 4; Chaddock, *Ohio Before 1850*, pp. 99–100.
[57] *Western Messenger* (Unitarian), Cincinnati, Vol. VIII, Aug. 1840, p.
150; *Marietta Collegiate Magazine*, Vol. II, 1856, p. 269.
[58] *Beloit Monthly*, 1855; *Knoxiana*, 1856; *Kenyon Collegian*, 1856; *Marietta
Collegiate Magazine*, 1855, pp. 56, 57.

CHAPTER IV

Trade with the South by River and Railroad 1840–1860

We now address ourselves to the question of the economic interests of the lower West, in particular its trade with the South, and the political attitudes that were associated with this relation. Our concern being with the trade of the period 1840 to 1860, we shall here only remind the reader of the larger epic of the Ohio and Mississippi valleys, a theme that is more and more attracting the attention of the novelist, historian, and poet;[1] a theme that begins as far back as LaSalle and De Soto with the French and Spanish occupations and leads on to restless pioneer migration up and down the great rivers, to intrigue and war between white man, Indian, and Spaniard, to "the shady paths of forest diplomacy," to half-mythical characters like Mike Fink, the last of the boatmen, and to early steamboat days. Being engaged as we are with less romantic parts of the story, with such problems as the amount of territory in the free West dependent on southern states for a market, with the commercial and manufacturing interests of Cincinnati and the river towns, and the nature and extent of the river traffic in the decades from 1840 to 1860, we shall none the less find that the story of those great days of the river trade does not lack zest and an importance of its own. In spite of the fact that it is difficult to draw conclusions on such matters and that available statistics are inadequate and hard to interpret, we shall conclude that in 1840 more western trade went South than went East; and that, in 1860, though the total amount of territory dependent on southern markets was less, due to the rapid growth of eastern trade, the south-going traffic itself was larger in volume and value than it had been in 1840. South-going railroads built between 1850 and 1860 added to the volume.

By this trade is not meant, of course, the trade by southern routes to a foreign market. This was important especially during the few years after 1845 when there was a great demand for the corn and

[1] Mark Twain, *Life on the Mississippi*, 1883; Lyle Saxon, *Father Mississippi* (The Century Company, 1927) ; Vachel Lindsay, *The Great Valley*.

wheat of the West because of the famine in Ireland, the war with
Mexico, and revolutionary movements in Europe. Coffee and other
tropical products were, moreover, brought up the Mississippi and
the Ohio until the Civil War. But, in general, this foreign trade declined after 1845.[2] The competition of the eastern routes by way of
the lakes, the Erie Canal, and the railroads, just now being built,
caused this decline. The produce of the West bound for the world
market was more and more being carried over these routes. Before
1845 New Orleans had been the main outlet for this portion of western trade; in that year about one half of the western surplus passed
through it to the sea.[3] By 1860 the Mississippi had practically ceased
to compete with the lake, canal, and railroad routes eastward, and
comparatively little of the produce of the West reached foreign lands
by the river.[4] It is, therefore, not this trade, but the interstate trade
via the river for domestic consumption in the slave-holding South
with which we are concerned and in which the lower West had so
great an interest.

Above any other one factor, it was the tendency in the South
toward intensive cultivation of cotton and sugar and the resulting
increasing demand for breadstuffs that was responsible for the steadily
increasing southern demand from 1840 to 1860. The production of

[2] Likewise attempts to draw trade away from New Orleans through other
southern cities to the world market had not been largely successful. Southern
statesmen and capitalists had sought to supplement the natural flow of commerce
down the river by means of railroad and river improvements in order to cement
the Northwest and the lower South and make Charleston and Mobile outlets
to the sea. John C. Calhoun had hoped by a railroad between Cincinnati and
Charleston and by the Mississippi and Tennessee rivers and railroad connections to Charleston, to deflect the trade of the Northwest from New York to
Charleston. He had well in mind the political importance of such connection.
Democratic leaders in the lower Northwest like Sidney Breese of Illinois had
met the proposal with favor. (Sidney Breese, *Correspondence,* Reprint in *Jour.
Ill. State Hist. Soc.* Oct. 1909, p. 78; F. J. Turner, "The Ohio Valley in American History," *Ohio Arch. and Hist. Soc. Pub.* XX, 45–47; J. F. Jameson, *Calhoun
Correspondence, Rep. Am. Hist. Ass'n,* 1899, II, 430. Robert Y. Hayne had been
even more actively interested. (Jervey, *R. Y. Hayne and His Times,* pp. 365,
385, 388, 516, 531 *et passim.*) Leaders in Georgia had had similar hopes for
Mobile. (F. J. Turner, *op. cit.,* pp. 45–47.) There was, however, little success
in these attempts to direct the course of foreign trade.

[3] *Report on the Internal Commerce of the United States,* 1887, Gov't Printing Office (1888), p. 210. As early as 1847 the receipts of flour and wheat at
Buffalo exceeded those at New Orleans. *Ibid.,* 211.

[4] *Eighth Census of the United States,* 1860, *Agriculture,* CLVII. In 1860 there
were exported from the United States over 15,000,000 bushels of grain. Of this
New Orleans exported only 224,000 bushels of corn and 80,541 barrels of flour.
Ibid., CXLIV, CLVII.

corn, though large, was not keeping pace with the increase in population.[5] Tennessee and Kentucky, in 1850 and 1860, failed to retain their places as the first corn-producing states in the Union, a place they had held in 1840.[6] Wheat and flour were, moreover, in greater demand in the South than was corn, the South as a whole producing in 1860 only three and a half bushels of wheat per capita, and Mississippi and Louisiana scarcely a peck for each person. Kentucky, Tennessee, Georgia, Alabama, and Mississippi together produced less wheat in 1850 than the single State of Indiana.[7] On the other hand, the surplus grain production north of the Ohio from 1840 to 1860 was so large as to be burdensome.[8] According to the census, Illinois, from 1850 to 1860, was producing sixty-seven bushels of corn per inhabitant; in the latter year this state led the United States, produced one seventh of all the corn raised and at the same time held first place in the production of wheat.[9] The per capita production in the whole West each year from 1850 to 1860 was nearly ten bushels of wheat and about forty-five bushels of corn.[10]

It was of the utmost value to the lower West to dispose of part of this surplus in the nearby slave states or to use it in the production of beef, pork, lard, and whiskey to sell in these states.[11] There were many districts in central and southern Indiana and Illinois that suffered from low prices and inadequate means of communication until the Civil War. At times wheat was as low as forty-five cents and corn fifteen cents a bushel in Peoria, Springfield, and Indianapolis, while, in the much better markets of St. Louis and Cincinnati, prices were often correspondingly low. In 1846 wheat sold for fifty-five cents in Cincinnati and for sixty-six cents in St. Louis.[12] The burden of debt bore heavily on the settlers in the interior counties; Indiana and Illinois had all but repudiated their public debt and the fear of state bankruptcy was still seldom absent; financial bondage to the East

[5] Ibid., CLVIII, li.

[6] Ibid., XLVIII, XLIX.

[7] Ibid., XXIX; XXXI; Emory R. Johnson and Collaborators, History of the Domestic and Foreign Commerce of the United States, I, 250.

[8] Eighth Census of the United States 1860, Agriculture XXIX, XLIX, LI.

[9] Ibid., XLVII, XXIX.

[10] Ibid., XXXI, LI.

[11] James Hall, The West, Its Soil, Surface and Productions (Cincinnati 1848), p. 133.

[12] See Indiana Daily State Sentinel, Oct. 10, 17, 1846; Illinois State Register, June 4, Sept. 17, 1847; Chicago Daily Journal, Nov. 7, 1846. In Indianapolis, Oct. 17, 1846, wheat was quoted at forty-five to fifty cents and corn at ten to twelve cents.

through mortgage, loans, and other forms of dependence was felt by many citizens. By trade with the South, debts could be lifted and the standard of living raised. The return shipments of molasses, sugar, and cotton from the South and coffee from the tropics proved less in volume and value than the products shipped southward and left a balance in favor of the grain-producing states.

When we attempt to arrive at the exact extent of this trade, difficulties are especially great.[13] All evidence seems to point to the fact that in the first decades of the nineteenth century all the West except districts in Ohio and Michigan had looked southward in its commercial relations. In 1845 it was estimated that more than half of the inhabitants of the whole free West, over 2,000,000 people, depended on southern routes for a market. Against this number less than 2,000,-000 around the shores of Lake Erie and Lake Michigan sought an outlet by the Erie Canal.[14] About half of Ohio, more than half of Indiana and Illinois, and all of the settled portion of Iowa in that year looked southward in their commercial relations. This included all the lower and large portions of the upper West. The area extended from Pennsylvania to Iowa, embracing districts far into the interior of Ohio and as far north as Indianapolis, Logansport, Peoria, Galena, and Dubuque, and the territory of Wisconsin. A considerable amount of the territory contributory to Pittsburgh and Cincinnati and practically all that contributory to Madison, New Albany, Louisville, Cairo, and St. Louis was included.

Pittsburgh sent coal and manufactured articles southward through-

[13] The lack of authoritative statistics on the internal trade of the country during this period is unfortunate. A report of the Secretary of the Interior in 1861 said: "The internal trade between the different states of this union is greater than the foreign trade and directly interests a much greater number of people. Yet we possess no agency by which we can ascertain and definitely present to the world the value and extent of this exchange of the products of labor." *App. Cong. Globe,* 36 Cong., 2 Sess., 27. There are available, however, certain helpful sources of information. Among them are the reports of Col. J. J. Abert of the Corps of Topographical Engineers, the statistics of tonnage and steamboat building on the Ohio and Mississippi rivers, the reports of the Chamber of Commerce of Cincinnati and the *River Intelligence* in the newspapers of the river cities. *The Report of the Internal Commerce of the United States,* 1887, and the *History of the Domestic and Foreign Commerce of the United States,* by E. R. Johnson, already referred to, are among the best general studies so far made. E. W. Gould in *Fifty Years on the Mississippi* presents interesting but disorganized facts.

[14] *Report of Col. J. J. Abert of the Corps of Topographical Engineers, House Ex. Doc.* 36 Cong., 1st Sess., No. 19, p. 14. See estimate for 1840 in Hall, *The West, Its Commerce and Navigation* (Cincinnati, 1848), Ch. XII.

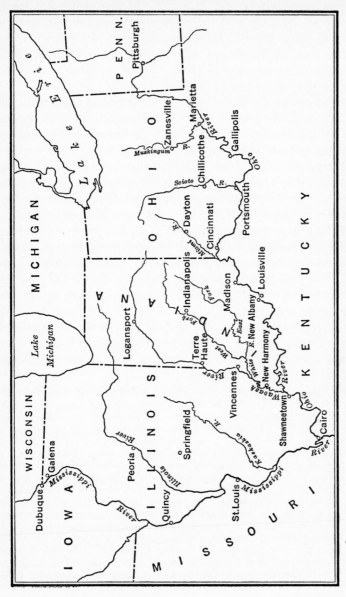

FIG. 2. THE SOUTHERN TRADING INTEREST IN 1845
All the towns indicated on the map with their contributory territory had trade relations with the South.

out the period. Taking no account of the number of flatboats, we find upon examination that the number of steamboat cargoes from that city arriving at New Orleans in 1860 was larger than ever.[15] Cincinnati's trade with the South is a fact of major significance in the history of the West from 1840 to 1860. During these decades that city occupied a comparative importance in the life of America that it has never equaled since. It was the greatest city in the West; its population in 1840 was ten times that of Chicago and, as late as 1860, still outnumbered that of the lake city by more than 50,000. Its leadership in western culture, its literary circles, press, and pulpit have already been discussed; its political importance as the contest between the North and the South became more intense and bitter and finally resulted in war, will challenge our attention repeatedly. Its geographical position, on the Ohio and on the border between the economic and social systems of the North and South, made it a center of manufacture and the emporium of a vast local trade in Ohio and Kentucky as well as an entrepôt for goods in transit to the South.

It was estimated that in 1841, 10,000 workmen were employed in the mechanical and manufacturing industries of this city and the annual value of the product was $17,000,000; that in addition to this $6,000,000 worth of provisions passed through it for the interior.[16] Hides were tanned, soap was made, as were also starch, alcohol, patent medicines, whiskey, clothing, farm machinery and furniture, for all of which there was a ready market down the Ohio and Mississippi. The city was the most important point in an extensive pork-raising region, including Ohio, Kentucky, Indiana, and Illinois. The pork-packing business centering here extended out for a radius of about 150 miles on all sides. In Cincinnati itself every year several hundred thousand hogs were slaughtered and handled by packing processes that suggest those in use in Chicago to-day, with some approach to their speed and efficiency.[17] In this growing city men were already, in the decades before the war, accumulating property and making fortunes that rivaled those in New York City. Nicholas Longworth, lawyer, town-lot speculator, horticulturist, and wine merchant, saw the place grow from a few hundred inhabitants to nearly two hundred thousand. Land that he bought for almost nothing, by the

[15] Johnson, I, 241; *Report on Internal Commerce*, 1887, pp. 214, 222; St. Louis *Daily Reveille*, Sept. 7, 1850.

[16] James Hall, *The West, Its Commerce and Navigation* (1848), p. 193.

[17] *Niles' Register*, Feb. 7, 1846, p. 359; James Hall, *The West, Its Soil, Surface and Productions*, p. 186.

city's growth, brought returns amounting to millions. Due largely to his influence the Catawba grape culture was developed around Cincinnati until at the time of his death in 1863 the banks and hills along the Ohio resembled in small degree the banks of the Rhine. He had wine cellars that became famous, and he was hailed as "the greatest apostle of temperance in America" by Hiram Powers and others who felt that American drunkenness would be reduced if wine could replace whiskey as the native drink. An eccentric, exacting man, he was nevertheless public-spirited, patronizing culture and helping the "worthy poor." [18]

Products sent south from Cincinnati in 1845 included 111,000 barrels and 304,000 pounds of bulk pork, 148,000 barrels of flour, 102,900 barrels of whiskey, and 144,000 kegs of lard. The pork trade of the city with the Mississippi valley was always large; other commodities sent southward were flour, whiskey, corn, horses, and manufactured articles, especially furniture. The trade with other Ohio River cities, St. Louis, Memphis, and New Orleans, employed, in 1850, 233 steamboats and barges with a tonnage of 49,000, the larger part of this being engaged in the lower Mississippi trade. In 1851, the shipments to the South were very much larger than those to the East, and even up to 1855 the city had a larger southern than eastern commercial interest.[19] By 1860, while the eastern trade by the railroads was securing more than half of the exports of Cincinnati and the relative amount of trade with New Orleans had diminished, the river trade of the city still employed 338 steamboats and barges and the interests of many Cincinnati merchants were, as we shall see, bound up with the continuance of good relations with the South.

Southern Indiana produce reached the South through Cincinnati, Madison, New Albany, Louisville, or direct by the flatboat trade of the Wabash River. Indianapolis was connected by rail with Madison in 1847, and produce from central Indiana, previously held up by the cost of transportation, began to yield a profit. The capital city faced southward until the middle fifties. The south-going Indiana produce

[18] Charles Cist, *Sketches and Statistics of Cincinnati*, 1851; J. D. McCabe, *Great Fortunes and How They Are Made*, pp. 152–167; W. R. Houghton, *Kings of Fortune*, pp. 138–153; Nicholas Longworth, *The Culture of the Strawberry* (1855) ; Hiram Powers, *Letters to Nicholas Longworth*, Hist. and Phil. Soc. of Ohio, Quarterly Publication, 1906, Vol. I, pp. 33–59.

[19] *Niles' Register*, Feb. 7, 1846, p. 259; Johnson, *op. cit.*, I, 241, 244, 245; *Report of the Cincinnati Chamber of Commerce*, 1862, 1863; Cincinnati *Daily Gazette*, Sept. 9, 1863.

consisted largely of pork, grain, and hay. Madison, Indiana, packed 100,000 hogs a year, largely for the southern market. And Terre Haute, Vincennes, and Greencastle were likewise centers of the packing industry. In addition to this, the produce of southern Indiana was the basis of much of the trade of Louisville with the South. That city in 1860 sent 172 steamboat cargoes to New Orleans alone.[20]

The interest of southern Illinois, of the Illinois River valley, and of parts of Iowa in the southern river traffic from 1845 to 1860 can best be estimated by an examination of the trade of St. Louis and Cairo, particularly the former. In 1846 as many as 1,000 steamboats, keel, and flatboats arrived at the port of St. Louis; three years later the figure was up to 3,000 crafts of all kinds. A fire on the wharf at St. Louis in 1849 destroyed twenty-three steamboats; in a single day in the year 1850, fifty boats could be seen loading and unloading. Several years later Mark Twain saw the levee packed with freight and "a solid mile of steamboats lying side by side—a towering front of trade." [21] Regular lines of packets brought the produce of Illinois, Iowa, and Wisconsin to the city where much of it was transferred to steamboats of larger draft for the lower Mississippi. Galena, Quincy, Keokuk, and Alton on the Mississippi, and Naples, Peoria, Peru, and other towns on the Illinois, had regular lines of packets with St. Louis during the open season, which in this region usually extended from March to December.[22] Springfield was connected by rail with Meredosia on the Illinois River and thus had intimate commercial relations with St. Louis.

The large output of wheat, corn, and pork of the Illinois valley employed, in 1850, twenty-six steamboats making several trips each to convey it southward. Two years later, 600 cargoes from this valley were discharged at St. Louis to be reshipped to New Orleans. Up the Mississippi, Galena and Dubuque in the late forties were communities little known to Chicago, but in direct connection with St. Louis. Even as late as 1859 heavy products from this region were shipped south-

[20] *Indiana Weekly State Journal,* Oct. 1, 1848; Cincinnati *Gazette* quoted in Chicago *Daily Journal,* Oct. 22, 1847; *Report on Internal Commerce,* pp. 214, 222.

[21] St. Louis *Daily Reveille,* Jan. 14, March 15, June 9, 1850; A. B. Paine, *Mark Twain, a Biography,* I, 120.

[22] St. Louis *Daily Reveille,* Aug. 6, 1849; June 13, July 14, 1850; *Weekly Reveille,* Mar. 10, 17, Apr. 28, 1845; Alton *Daily Morning Courier,* Feb. 10, 1854; W. V. Pooley, *The Settlement of Illinois* (1830–1850) pp. 115, 128, 132, 183, 473.

ward rather than pay railroad rates to Chicago and the East that the traffic could not bear. A third of the surplus of the upper Mississippi was still going south; in fact, much central Illinois produce was flowing toward St. Louis rather than to Chicago as late as 1860.[23]

Like Cincinnati, St. Louis was far ahead of Chicago in manufactures all through the period from 1845 to 1860. These manufactures consisted mainly of hardwood, mill machinery, cotton yarn and batting, pipe, sheeting, shoes, and hemp products, and they found their best market in the South. Though connected with the East by rail in 1855, the southern river trade of St. Louis and all the nearby region in Illinois was not greatly affected; it remained a "river city" until the war. Its population grew from 16,000 in 1840 to 160,000 in 1860. Cincinnati and St. Louis, it was generally believed, would always remain what they were then in fact, the great cities of the West.[24] Even New Albany in Indiana was larger than Indianapolis until after 1850. The vigorous river traffic did much to establish the river cities from Pittsburgh to St. Louis in the supremacy they enjoyed over Chicago and the lake cities as late as 1860.[25]

In the year 1845 there was, according to a report of the Secretary of the Treasury, over $250,000,000 worth of property afloat on the Mississippi and its tributaries. Almost one half of this passed to or from the ports of Cincinnati and St. Louis and other cities interested in the trade of the lower West with the South.[26] In 1849, 700 steamers

[23] Statements in this paragraph based on, St. Louis *Weekly Reveille*, Feb. 4, 1850; Alton *Weekly Courier*, Nov. 19, 1852; Chicago *Daily Journal*, Nov. 27, 1847; *Daily Chicago Times*, Jan. 12, Apr. 1, March 30, 1860; *Report on Internal Commerce*, 1887, p. 215.

[24] St. Louis *Weekly Reveille*, Feb. 12, July 23, Aug. 6, 1849; March 18, 1850; Johnson, I, 244; *Hunt's Merchants' Magazine*, Vol. 42, pp. 325, 331, 332; see *Cong. Globe*, 31 Cong., 1 Sess., 1626, 1627.

[25] According to the U. S. Census returns, the population of the river cities compared to the lake cities from 1840 to 1860 was as follows:

River cities:		1840	1850	1860
	Cincinnati	46,338	115,435	161,044
	Louisville	21,210	43,194	68,033
	St. Louis	16,469	77,860	160,773
Lake cities:				
	Cleveland	6,071	17,034	43,417
	Detroit	9,102	21,019	45,619
	Chicago	4,470	29,963	109,260

[26] Article in the *American Review* quoted in the Chicago *Daily Journal*, July 5, 1846. $120,000,000 were accredited to New Orleans and included the great cotton and sugar trade of that city.

worth $12,000,000 were engaged in the whole river trade, the share of the lower West being again about one half.[27] The growth of the trade is shown by the fact that the number of steamboats increased steadily from 1845 to 1860 and more especially by the fact that there was a great increase in the tonnage, in spite of the very great losses.[28] The yards at Pittsburgh, Cincinnati, New Albany, Louisville and—in the decade 1850 to 1860—St. Louis, were kept busy building new steamboats to meet the increased demand and make good the losses. The steamboats averaged from 200 to 300 tons; certain boats, "queens of the river" as they were called, carried over 1,000 tons. Those used in the lower Mississippi trade were generally larger than those on the Ohio, Illinois and upper Mississippi. They were all heavily loaded in the busy season and often carried in tow two or three barges. In addition to the steamboat trade there was, until the late fifties, a very large use of flatboats, especially in the coal trade down from Pittsburgh and the hay and grain trade down the Wabash River. However, the danger to flatboat navigation and the increase in steamboat tonnage resulted in a diminished use of flatboats before 1860.[29]

The forties and fifties in fact mark the golden age of Ohio-Mississippi trade and steamboating. Apart from consideration of trade relations of the West with the South and resultant political influences, the subject has a social and cultural interest that at the present time is becoming more and more absorbing. The epic of "Father Mississippi" takes on a new form. Abraham Lincoln on a Mississippi River flatboat bound for New Orleans—our minds dwell on the picture;

[27] St. Louis *Weekly Reveille,* Nov. 5, 1846.

[28] The number of steamboats built in 1845, 1850, 1855 and 1860 and the amount of tonnage owned on the same years at Pittsburgh, Cincinnati, Louisville, and St. Louis was as follows:

	Steamboats built					Tonnage owned		
	P.	C.	L.	St. L.	P.	C.	L.	St. L.
1845	46	37	26	—	13,283	14,403	8,751	18,905
1850	14	16	34	5	44,571	17,188	14,820	28,907
1855	51	19	27	7	93,691	28,713	22,680	60,592
1860	53	30	29	13	62,010	33,900	34,551	64,683

See *Sen. Doc.,* 1 Sess., Vol. III, No. 15, pp. 255, 256 and No. 16, pp. 259, 261; *Ex. Doc.* 31 Cong., 2 Sess., Vol. VIII. No. 15, pp. 17, 18, and No. 16, pp. 21, 24; *Sen. Doc.* 34 Cong., 1 Sess., Vol. 16, No. 17, pp. 356, 357, and No. 18, pp. 361, 363; *Sen. Doc.* 36 Cong., 2 Sess., Vol. VIII. No. 21, pp. 658, 659, and No. 22, pp. 663, 666. The intervening years likewise show increases. It is impossible to determine just what portion of this tonnage was used in strictly northwestern trade with the South. No account is taken here of the tonnage owned at New Orleans and engaged in northwestern trade.

[29] *Report on Internal Commerce* (1887), pp. 204, 221, 222.

we are attracted, as is the novelist and poet, by the pageantry of life to be seen on the banks of the rivers from Cincinnati or Dubuque down to New Orleans, and the human cargo on the great floating hotels transcends in interest the heavy loads of grain, pork, whiskey, and hay. For young Mark Twain the vagabond life of boys along the river, the steamboat with its passengers and crew, the magnificently costumed river pilot with his marvelous knowledge of changing river courses, snags, depths, and shallows, his masterly hauteur in the presence of distinguished statesmen or foreign princes whose lives are committed to his care—all this was a world of wonder and inspiration. Writing about these subjects Mark Twain was at his best; living among them, he found himself as he did at no other time or place. The experience he had as a river pilot himself—brought to an end by the Civil War and the blockade of the Mississippi—gave him a real life zest and the "rudiments of a creative education." Before him, as before other writers, river life spread a "marvelous gallery of American types." Would he have written more masterpieces of the type of *Huckleberry Finn* and *Life on the Mississippi* had he not been unfortunately turned from such work to more popular humor and genteel entertaining?[30]

In small compass on a river steamer could be found all classes of men and women—western, southern, eastern, and European society in microcosm. On the boiler deck there were Negro deck hands, slaves, and poor whites; on the saloon deck, first-class passengers, southern planters, northern merchants, European travelers; in another portion there was the part set aside for the women.

The departure of a favorite boat during the ante-bellum days made up a picture for the memory of a life-time. Here came hunters and trappers from the western and northern wilds, men with rifles, pistols, weapons with blades like butcher knives, fashionably dressed planters returning south, men resembling half-breeds, dark, quick-tempered desperadoes, jovial comrades, professional gamblers, negroes, mulattoes, octaroons.

Indeed in the sight of certain persons a Mississippi steamboat was a puffing nightmare of profanity and wickedness, while to a reckless adventurer it meant increased activity, a more expansive feeling of life and liberty. . . . The steamboat was a world in itself, unlike anything ever seen or dreamed of—a floating hotel at whose tables friends and foes, preachers and infidels, card-sharpers and merchants, slave drivers and abolitionists, planters, politicians and cut-throats rubbed shoulders and ate together. . . . The steamboat of those days resembled nothing so much as an architectural

[30] Van Wyck Brooks, *The Ordeal of Mark Twain* (New York, 1920), Ch. II; Lewis Mumford, *The Golden Day.*

tinder-box, ready to disappear in a sudden blaze, sink to the bottom by striking a snag, or go to pieces by an explosion.[31]

STEAMBOAT DISASTERS—TRADE CONVENTIONS

Another index of the extent of the Ohio-Mississippi river traffic is afforded by the annual number of steamboat accidents and losses which, for most of the years between 1840 and 1860, was incredibly large. Many of the wrecks and sinkings were due to rapid and careless steamboat-building; many to overloading and the danger involved in towing heavy barges; others to poor harbors, rapids, snags, and other impediments to navigation; still others to collisions, explosions, and accidental burning. The property sunk or burned was inadequately covered by insurance and the sufferings of crew and passengers and the losses by death were ghastly and terrible. "When a steamboat heavily laden and crowded with passengers strikes upon a snag in the night and is engulphed in a few minutes in the stream, the scene is terrific beyond description." In the explosion and destruction of the *Moselle* in the Ohio near Cincinnati in 1848 over one hundred lives were lost.[32] In 1845 John C. Calhoun said the annual loss equaled eleven per cent of the entire number of boats and that the average life of a steamboat was nine years; in 1847, for the Ohio and Mississippi, the estimate of losses was sixty-five boats; in 1849, eighty-three were totally destroyed.[33] Besides these there were the flatboat losses which were also very great.

It is difficult to estimate what proportion of these total losses occurred in the traffic of the free West with the South. In 1845 Cincinnati owners lost seven; in 1846 in the St. Louis trade thirty-six were wrecked and twenty of these totally destroyed. Newspapers stated that there were, in 1847, ninety steamboats lying in the bottom of the Mississippi between Cairo and St. Louis.[34] Almost every week there were accounts in St. Louis and Cincinnati papers of the wrecking,

---

[31] Francis Grierson, *The Valley of the Shadows*, Ch. XXVI; see also Thomas Boyd, *The Dark Cloud* (Chas. Scribners Sons, 1924).

[32] J. Hall, *The West, Its Commerce and Navigation*, pp. 63, 179–184.

[33] *Report on Internal Commerce* (1887), p. 208; *Niles' Register*, Jan. 31, 1846, p. 352; *American Review*, 1847, quoted in Chicago *Daily Journal*, July 5, 1847 with estimates based on insurance records in St. Louis, Cincinnati and other places; St. Louis *Weekly Reveille*, Feb. 4, 1850; James I. Lloyd, *Steamboat Disasters and Losses.*

[34] St. Louis *Weekly Reveille*, Feb. 4, 1850; Chicago *Daily Journal*, Jan. 15, 1847.

burning, or sinking of a river packet carrying a large cargo and many passengers. Added to this there was, then as now, the danger of flood, of changing river channels, of broken levees and consequent destruction of crops and live stock.

There arose, as a result of all this, frequent demands to Congress for river improvement. They were presented by individual congressmen or in more impressive form by organized trade conventions, which were held in the West or South from time to time in this period. These meetings were significant not only as expressions of the demand for river improvement, but as reminders and monuments of the economic unity and commercial vigor of the Ohio-Mississippi valley market system. One of the greatest was the river convention at Memphis in 1845. The preparations for this meeting were far-reaching throughout the West and South. A western paper said: "The Upper Mississippi, the upper Missouri, the Illinois, the Ohio and the great South all are ready for the day and the good work laid out for it." [35] A very enthusiastic body of over 500 delegates coming from almost all of the slave states and from all the border free states from Pennsylvania to Iowa, met to consider common trade interests, encourage western and southern river navigation and demand aid from the national government for swamp drainage, river improvement, and railroads. Illinois alone sent twenty-one delegates; newspaper editors were present from St. Louis, Cincinnati, Evansville, Springfield, and other cities of the lower West. John C. Calhoun was president, and a long array of vice-presidents included four from the region north of the Ohio, one of whom was A. C. Dodge of Burlington, Iowa. After hearing John C. Calhoun in a speech—later to be widely quoted—on the unifying influence of the Ohio and Mississippi River system and the propriety of national jurisdiction over this "inland sea," the editor of the St. Louis *Reveille* wrote to his paper: "The Union of the South with the great West, the contract which must henceforth command from all respectful attention . . . has been signed and J. C. Calhoun is inscribed in letters of gold upon the record." Resolutions were passed demanding river improvement, national defenses, a national armory in the West, and land grants for railroad-building, and recommending a vast system of reclamation of swamp lands. Investments in railroads to connect the Mississippi valley with the Georgia and South Carolina railroads were recom-

[35] St. Louis *Weekly Reveille,* Nov. 10, 1845. "The whole West and South seem alive to the subject." *Niles' Register,* Nov. 1, 1845, p. 134.

mended to capitalists.[36] This convention seems to have been the most imposing commercial gathering in the history of the nation up to that time and an impression was created by it on western and southern minds that is difficult to realize. As an indication of the identification of the interests of the lower West with those of the South it can be contrasted with the Chicago Convention of the lake interests in 1847, which was prophetic of the approaching alliance of the upper West with the East. Another convention which had for its object the improvement of western rivers, held at Louisville in 1852, was attended by delegates from Mississippi, Alabama, Tennessee, Missouri, Pennsylvania, Ohio, and Illinois.[37]

Whatever the failure or success of these conventions in dealing with the big question of river improvement and flood control—a problem still unsettled—we must repeat that the trade of the West with the South increased until 1860. In spite of the deflection to the East of much of the produce of Ohio, of central Indiana, and of the Galena-Dubuque region, the aggregate amount of the river trade was greater in 1860 than ever before. The fact that the lakes and the railroads East were showing a very much larger annual gain does not affect the truth of this statement. Inadequate statistics—the only kind available—indicate that from 1841 to 1851, produce worth $282,000,000 went South from the free West by river; from 1856 to 1861 an average of 1,150,000 barrels of flour was annually received at New Orleans; and the year 1859–1860 became noted as the "best year on the river." [38]

Moreover, the volume of South-going trade was, as we have already said, much larger than that registered by the river traffic. The building of the Illinois Central Railroad and the establishment of direct connection between Chicago and the South added still further to this trade. The work on this road began in 1851 in both northern and southern Illinois. This important line gradually brought together isolated counties in central and southern Illinois and put them in touch with the southern market. By its river connections with the southern railroad systems, the Nashville and Chattanooga, the

[36] St. Louis *Weekly Reveille,* Nov. 24, 1845; *Niles' Register,* Nov. 29, 1845, p. 196; Dec. 6, pp. 212, 214; *Report on Internal Commerce,* pp. 203, 204; see also W. W. Davis, "Anti-Bellum Southern Commercial Conventions," *Trans. Ala. Hist. Soc.* Vol. V, pp. 123 *et seq.*

[37] Louisville dispatch, Alton *Weekly Courier,* June 11, 1852.

[38] *Report on Internal Commerce,* 1887, pp. 209, 211, 213, 215; Johnson, *op. cit.,* I, pp. 241, 242, 243, 246.

Memphis and Charleston, and the Mobile and Ohio, great inland districts of Kentucky, Tennessee, Mississippi, and Alabama were made accessible to northern products. The sale of lands along the roads brought settlers, and land sold easily at improved values.[39] The Land Graduation Bill of John A. McClernand, whereby unsold lands long on the market were offered for a fifth or even a tenth of the regular price of $1.25 an acre, helped in this development. The immigration into central and southern Illinois greatly increased. There was a marked revival of the movement from Kentucky and Tennessee to this region. An event of special significance was the completion of the road to Chicago and the bringing of northern Illinois into the scope of this trade area. In November, 1857, the first large consignment of sugar reached Chicago and from that time until the war hundreds of hogsheads of sugar and molasses were received each month and even large shipments of cotton. Pork, flour, and grain from Chicago and northern Illinois went to the South in increasing quantities. The freight shipments of the Illinois Central increased steadily from 1858 to 1860, this road being one of the first to recover after the Crisis of 1857.[40] We shall see that in 1860–1861 the business of the Illinois Central with the South was enormous; at Cairo freight accumulated beyond the power of the railroad and steamship companies to handle it. In March, 1860, the completion of the Mississippi Central Railroad made an unbroken connection between New Orleans and Chicago. *The Times,* a Democratic paper in Chicago, owned by Cyrus McCormick and a bitter opponent of the anti-southern feeling that had arisen in that city, urged strongly the strengthening of this trading interest. On January 28, 1860, it said: "It is to be hoped that politicians will not by their loud mouthed intolerance, prevent the establishment of a large commercial business between Chicago and Memphis." We shall see in later chapters how deep-seated was the aversion of large parts of the West to any type of political agitation that would disturb trade relations with the South and how important this issue became in the great fight to prevent slavery extension and in the war to preserve the Union.

[39] H. G. Brownson, *History of the Illinois Central to 1870,* U. of Ill. *Studies in Social Sciences,* IV, nos. 3, 4; Alton *Weekly Courier,* Nov. 19, 1852.

[40] *Daily Chicago Times,* Nov., 1856, Mar. 1859, *passim;* Cincinnati *Daily Gazette,* Aug. 14, 1863.

CHAPTER V

The Upper West Breaks from the Democratic South

1850–1854

The discussion in the first chapter made it clear that there were in the lake region in the late forties materials for a new party. The Compromise of 1850 with its "finality," the approach of another period of great prosperity, and other influences kept that party from actually being formed until 1854. All through the period from 1847 to 1854, the desire in the lake district to "set the boundaries of slavery" was alive and active and showed itself especially in approval of the Wilmot Proviso and in opposition to the fugitive slave provision of the Compromise of 1850. On the other hand, representatives in Congress from southern Ohio, Indiana, and Illinois voted with southerners against the Proviso every time that vexing question came up and forced northern Democrats to take a stand. As often as they voted against it, Democrats, Whigs, and Free Soilers from the Reserve, from Michigan, Wisconsin, and northern Illinois voted for it.[1] The Fugitive Slave Law especially proved to be an acid test. This law which yielded so much to the southern slave-holder received fifteen affirmative votes in the national House from members representing the lower West. It was opposed by fourteen votes from the lake region. Four United States Senators, Douglas and Shields of Illinois and Bright and Whitcomb of Indiana were, for reasons that are not clear, absent when the final roll was called in the Senate; but Senators Dodge and Jones of Iowa went the full length and supported the Fugitive Slave Law heartily. Senator Henry Dodge of Wisconsin, representing that more radical constituency, voted on this question as well as on the Proviso against his son, A. C. Dodge of Iowa, though both were Democrats. In the debate, Jones of Iowa, educated in the South, a friend of Jefferson Davis, and an ex-owner of slaves in Iowa, took an advanced pro-slavery stand. Free soil inclinations among

[1] See votes taken Aug. 10, 1846, Feb. 15, 1847, Mar. 3, 1847, *Cong. Globe* 29 Cong., 1 Sess., 1216, 1218, 2 Sess., 424, 425, 573.

Democrats in northern Illinois and Indiana could not prevail against the sentiment in the southern parts of these states; indeed there was no longer any chance of the break from the slave-holding Democracy and alliance with Free Soilers that had seemed possible in 1848 and 1849. In 1851 the Illinois Legislature reëlected Douglas, an anti-proviso man, to the United States Senate; and in the same year in the Indiana Legislature votes from the Ohio and Wabash valley counties reëlected to the Senate Jesse D. Bright, "avowedly a friend and ally of the South." A further proof of the difference between the lower and upper West is the fact that Illinois and Indiana passed no personal liberty law with the object of nullifying the Fugitive Slave Law, while Michigan in 1855 and Wisconsin in 1858, did so.[2]

But of the lower western senators and representatives who opposed the Wilmot Proviso and favored the Fugitive Slave Law, only a few were distinctly pro-southern and pro-slavery. They were, like those of the lake region, western. Their party in the West was in 1850 already popularizing, in the person of Douglas, the Cass doctrine of popular sovereignty, a new democratic and typically western solution of the question of slavery in the territories, a theory which in the end was to prove only less free soil in tendency than the drastic Wilmot Proviso itself. In the mind of Douglas, popular sovereignty was a combination of the Webster idea that climate and geography would forbid the growth of slavery and the democratic idea of local self-determination. Far from resulting in the spread of slavery, he predicted in 1850 that it would bring freedom to all the West.[3] The inevitable increase of population favoring freedom and a refusal to pass local legislation favorable to slavery would settle the question. To him, the question of action by Congress, whether favorable or unfavorable, was purely an academic one; politicians of the East, the upper West, and the South in agitating the question were only harboring partisan or selfish purposes and encouraging sectionalism.

In the great debates on the compromise measures of 1850, there was great community of feeling between Douglas of Illinois and the grand

---

[2] For the reaction against the Wilmot Proviso in Indiana, Illinois and Iowa, see T. C. Smith, *Liberty and Free Soil Parties in the Northwest*, pp. 192–197, 232; for votes in Congress, see *Cong. Globe*, 31 Cong., 1 Sess., 1778; for the reëlection of Douglas, see E. B. Greene, *Sectional Forces in the History of Illinois, Pub. No. 8 of the Illinois State Hist. Lib.*, p. 82; for the discussion and votes on the Fugitive Slave Law see *Cong. Globe*, 31 Cong., 1 Sess., 1574, 1647, 1660, 1716, 1807.

[3] *Cong. Globe*, 31st Cong., 1st Sess., XXII, Pt. I, *Appendix*, 364–375.

old senators, Webster and Clay. The young western nationalist was receiving his tutelage from these champions of union and masters of compromise. To him, popular sovereignty was the essence of their views on how to deal with the question of slavery in the territories. He felt that even the great Missouri Compromise was of little real value; it merely allayed excitement; slave property like banks and whiskey should be allowed wherever local law sanctioned it, but he was often careful to add that he did not think local law would sanction it. Giving expression time and again to such views in the years from 1850 to 1860, looked upon in anti-slavery circles as a "northern man with southern principles," he was in reality only a little less antislavery than Free Soilers themselves and than his great antagonists, Salmon P. Chase and Abraham Lincoln. He went so far as to say that from the foundation of government the cause of freedom had steadily and firmly advanced, and he believed that the whole West was "destined to be free whether Congress shall prohibit slavery or not." [4] It is not without significance that Abraham Lincoln, who, when in Congress, had been on friendly terms with such southern leaders as Toombs and Stephens, during the great debates of 1850 read the speeches of the great unionists with interest and was like Douglas a staunch supporter of Websterian ideas.[5]

Upper Western Development 1850–1854

The doctrine of popular sovereignty when, through Douglas' efforts, it received enactment in 1854, seemed to the South and the upper West more pro-slavery than it really was. For this reason southerners in Congress, with the exception of a few who saw it in its true light as a western measure, favored it; to the upper West it was the signal for a definite break with the South and its "allies" in the lower West. In the whole region around the lakes in this year, there suddenly came to fruition the tendencies that, we have seen, had begun to assert themselves as early as 1845. Before tracing the break in detail, we must, however, take another look at economic developments in this region, developments which along with those already noted, underlie the antislavery feeling that was developing and lay at the foundation of the "anti-Nebraska" Republican movement that seemed to spring up so suddenly and to attain so large a growth in a few short months.

[4] Albert J. Beveridge, *Abraham Lincoln*, II, 107–110.
[5] *Ibid.*, pp. 131, 155.

In the increase in population and the economic expansion of the lake region from 1850 to 1855, the movement which began in the forties, reached unparalleled proportions. There was growth, it is true, in southern Indiana, Illinois, and Iowa, but the increase in this upper West was far more rapid. A state census taken in Illinois in 1855 showed an increase occurring in the four northern Congressional districts.[6] The very large gains shown by the United States Census of 1860 register a movement confined in great degree to the upper West and occurring before the panic of 1857. That census shows that in ten years the population of Michigan and Illinois had doubled, that of Wisconsin had increased two and a half times, and that of Iowa had trebled.[7] The counties of northwestern Ohio, most of the lower peninsula of Michigan, the "swamp district" in northwestern Indiana and northeastern Illinois, all of southern Wisconsin and the interior of Iowa back of the Missouri border and the river counties, had been filled. The lake cities, Cleveland, Detroit, Chicago, and Milwaukee were growing faster than the large river cities which had led in the previous decade.

The great growth in population was due to the continued migration from New York, Ohio, Pennsylvania, Germany, and Ireland by way of the lakes and the railroads, which, in this period, established through lines to Chicago. Most of the native-born that settled in Michigan and Wisconsin were from New York, while those moving to northern Indiana, Illinois, and Iowa looked for the most part to New York, Pennsylvania, or Ohio as their parent state.[8] During the period from 1850 to 1857 nearly 2,000,000 immigrants arrived from abroad; of this number about 1,400,000 arrived during the years from 1850 to 1854.[9] In 1854, the year of the largest foreign immigration in the history of the country before the Civil War, there entered our borders a

---

[6] *State Census, Illinois,* 1855; *Daily Chicago Times,* May 7, 1859.

[7] *United States Census* of 1850, XXXVI; *Ibid.,* 1860, *Population,* p. 104. In 1850 the population of Wisconsin was 305,391; in 1860, 775,881; in 1850 the population of Iowa was 190,214; in 1860, 674,713. *United States Census of 1850,* XXVI; *Ibid.,* 1860, *Population,* p. 156.

[8] *Eighth Census of the United States,* 1860, *Population,* XXXIV; in comparison with the number from New York, Ohio, Pennsylvania, Germany, and Ireland, the number from New England, England, and Canada was small.

[9] *Ibid., Population,* XIX. Immigrants arrived in this country for the year ending December 31:

1851	379,466	1856	200,436
1852	371,603	1857	251,306
1853	368,645	1858	123,126
1854	427,833	1859	121,282
1855	200,877	1860	153,640

total of over 427,000 immigrants, mainly Germans and Irish. In this same year, there were sold by the Government in northern Illinois over 500,000 acres of land, in Wisconsin over 600,000, and in Iowa over 2,000,000 acres.[10] In 1855, the sales by the Government in Iowa, Wisconsin, and Michigan totaled over 6,000,000 acres.[11] These lands were of the best quality, sold for the highest price charged by the Government, and represent a much larger number of actual settlers than do the sales of the cheap and medium grades which were thrown on the market in 1855 by McClernand's Land Graduation Bill and sold in large amounts in southern Illinois, in Missouri, and the South. In addition, the Illinois Central lands in central Illinois were attracting settlers.[12] During the years from 1850 to 1855, almost 75,000 Germans settled in central and northern Illinois and a like number in southern Wisconsin; the Germans from Prussia, it was estimated, brought on the average $180.00 for each immigrant to buy land.[13] So great was the influx of Germans and Irish that in Chicago and Milwaukee, the foreign-born were threatening to outnumber the native-born. The State of New York was furnishing the largest native American element and the number direct from New England was comparatively small. While in Chicago the Irish were almost equaling the Germans in numbers, in the other cities, and in the rural districts of the lake region, the Germans were far in the lead.[14] The Middle West was looked upon by a foreign observer as "the territorial paradise of the oppressed German and Irish peasant, the land of independent small farmers . . . the most democratic and equal society on earth." [15]

Among the hundreds of thousands of Germans who made up this

[10] *Rep. of Sec. of the Interior, Sen. Ex. Doc.,* 33 Cong., 2 Sess., Vol. I, No. I, pp. 113, 119.

[11] *Sen. Doc.* 34 Cong., 1 Sess., Vol. I, No. 1, Part I.

[12] W. E. Dodd, "The Fight for the Northwest," *American Historical Review,* 1919; Brownson, *History of the Illinois Central to 1870.*

[13] *Eighth Census of the United States,* 1860, Population, XXIII.

[14] *Ibid.,* p. 613. Of Chicago's total population of 109,260 in 1860, Germany and Ireland and other foreign countries furnished 54,636, Illinois 28,093, New York 11,645, while the number direct from New England was less than 6,000. The following figures show the number of Germans and Irish in the lake cities in 1860 (*Ibid.,* XXXI, XXXII) :

	Irish	German
Cleveland	5,479	9,078
Detroit	5,994	7,220
Milwaukee	3,100	15,981
Chicago	19,889	22,230

[15] *Madame Pulszky,* Vol. I, p. 122, quoted in Beveridge, *Lincoln,* II, 107, note.

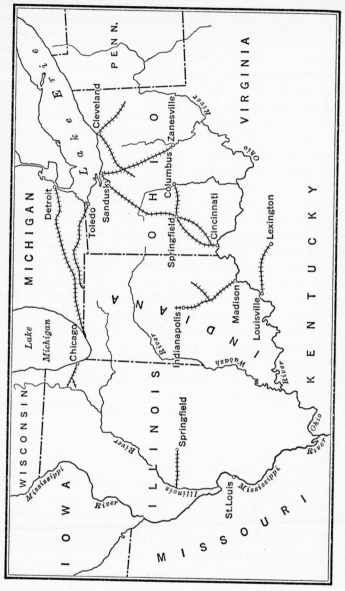

FIG. 3. RAILROADS IN THE WEST IN 1850

large element, there were large numbers of young German idealists imbued with the spirit of 1848 who were to inject, as Carl Schurz says, a new enthusiasm into the older and more conservative German population.[16] The Germans joined the Democratic party and for some years helped to maintain its hold on the lake region. They were won to it by its very name; by its bold aggressive democratic tone which to them embodied the spirit of America; it was the party of Jefferson, of Jackson, and of the free western masses. They were repelled by a prejudice which Whigs seemed to have against the foreign voter and by a rising sentiment in the lake region among Free Soilers and Whigs for a law prohibiting the sale of liquor. The foreigner could vote in Indiana and Wisconsin after one year's residence. To them, this was as it should be, but Whigs rather stood for the Illinois rule, adopted in 1848, that a newcomer should wait longer and become a citizen of the United States before voting. To many Germans, the Whigs were an old party with broken politicians, looking for issues.[17] But the liberal-minded Germans were not long to remain good Democrats, becoming doubtful in their allegiance as they realized that a Democratic party under southern control was not the party of liberty, homesteads, and opportunity that they thought it was. The Irish, however, remained both before and during the Civil War a bulwark of strength for the Democratic party in the cities of the lake region.

The railroad development begun in the earlier decade was pressed with astounding vigor from 1850 to 1857. The Fox River region had been reached by the Chicago and Galena Union Railroad by 1849; by 1852 the connection had been established with Freeport, and in that year this railroad brought 1,658,728 bushels of grain to Chicago for the eastern market.[18] It was evident that the eastern connection would soon turn much of the lead and grain produce of the Galena region and the upper Mississippi to Chicago. Eastern traffic was further encroaching on territory hitherto dependent on southern routes. Indianapolis was beginning to look eastward and northward.[19] While the trade of the lower West with the South was showing only a steady increase, that of the upper with the East was assuming enormous proportions.

[16] Carl Schurz, *Reminiscences,* II, 45, 47.

[17] Gustave Koerner, *Memoirs,* I, 621–623; Carl Schurz, *Reminiscences,* II, 65; *Indiana Weekly State Journal,* Oct. 21, 1854.

[18] *Eighth Census of the United States,* Agriculture, CXLVII; Johnson, *History of the Domestic and Foreign Commerce of the United States,* I, 228; Koerner, *Memoirs,* I, 592.

[19] *Indiana Weekly State Journal,* Mar. 22, 1855.

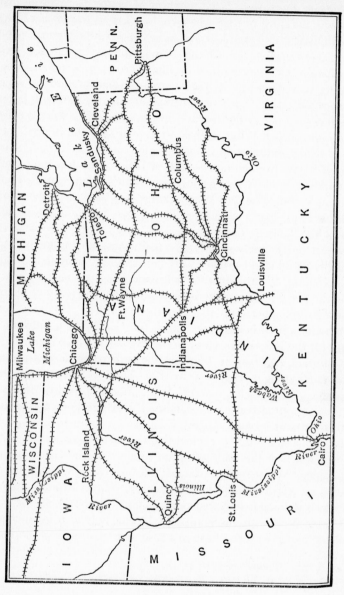

Fig. 4. Principal Railroads in the West in 1860

In 1853, direct rail connections between Chicago and New York were established and the railroads were becoming the competitors of the lakes and Erie Canal in flour, merchandise, and live stock.[20]

The tonnage on the lakes, too, steadily increased.[21] The predictions of the Chicago Convention of 1847 were being more than fulfilled. Chicago, which in 1838 had sent seventy-eight bushels of flour and grain eastward and in 1847—the year of the convention—2,243,201 bushels, in 1854 shipped, by lake and railroad routes, 12,902,320 bushels. The next year this increased to 16,633,645; the city was already becoming the great grain center of the United States.[22] Toledo, at the head of the Wabash and Erie Canal, was next to Chicago in the extent of its grain shipment. It received flour, wheat, corn, and butter from Ohio, and grain, live stock, and lumber from Michigan for the East.[23] There was, singularly enough however, in the upper West, as in the lower, much uncertainty in the demand, and good prices for grain were rather the exception than the rule.[24] The railroad and lake traffic carried westward to the lake cities from Boston, New York, and Philadelphia, dry goods, groceries, hardwood, machinery, boots, shoes, drugs, and coffee and, in years when immigration was heavy, large quantities of furniture. In 1853, the value of this kind of freight shipped westward on the Erie Canal alone was $94,230,720.[25] A new Harbor and River Bill was presented in 1854, similar to earlier bills, having, as did they, the object of improving the navigation of the Great Lakes, and the condition of the harbors of Chicago and other cities, and of the Illinois and Iowa rivers. It was probably inadequate to accomplish these ends, but public opinion in the places affected—especially in Chicago—was greatly in its favor. President Pierce vetoed it—as had Polk that of 1847—and again there was great dissatisfaction in the lake region.[26]

The lake district was, from 1850 to 1860, the section most active in the demand for homesteads. Internal improvements in the form of appropriations for the lakes or land grants to railroads was another demand. The Free Soil party had, with singular insight into the economic desires of the upper West, expressed both these demands in the Buf-

---

[20] Johnson, *op. cit.,* I, 228, 238.
[21] *Ibid.,* pp. 233.
[22] *Eighth Census of the United States,* 1860, *Agriculture,* CXLIX; Johnson, *op. cit.,* I, 235.
[23] *Ibid.,* I, 225, 227, 235.
[24] *Hunt's Merchants' Magazine,* Oct., 1860.
[25] Johnson, *op. cit.,* I, 233, 238.
[26] *Congressional Globe,* 33 Cong., 1 Sess., XXIX, Appendix, 1145–1146.

falo platform of 1848 and had coupled them with free soil. Sooner or later the Germans would join free homesteads and free soil to their demands for "liberty." In addition, as we have already pointed out, there was the growing demand for a protective tariff, especially among the wool-growers of eastern Ohio and the owners of infant manufacturing plants in Chicago and among old Whigs generally.[27] The idea was that the uncertain eastern and European demand for the great surplus grain products of the lake region and the wool of the Western Reserve and eastern Ohio would be supplemented by the encouragement of manufacturing in the East and in the lake cities.

To these influences which were doing so much to bind the lake region with the East may be added a continued growth of those intellectual and social ideas which were common to both these sections. Eastern Congregational and Presbyterian church influence was strong in Cleveland, in Oberlin, Beloit, and Knox colleges and in Chicago. We have noticed that woman suffrage found many adherents in the lake region. In the Ohio Convention of 1850 petitions came from the counties of northern Ohio asking the grant of the ballot to women. Seven delegates from the Western Reserve voted in the convention for this grant against the solid vote of the rest of the state. There was a much greater demand for the prohibition of the traffic in alcoholic liquors. In Ohio, this demand seemed to be strong throughout the state.[28] In the lake region proper, Michigan and northern Indiana and Illinois people were becoming more and more concerned about temperance reform.[29] The agitation was also spreading in Iowa. It was opposed by the Indianapolis *Sentinel* and the *Illinois State Register* and by the lower West generally.[30] To these tendencies in favor of woman suffrage and prohibition should be added the desire of many in this region to repeal the legal restrictions on the free Negro which the people of the lower West favored so strongly.

This general survey of the expansion and of the economic and social demands of the upper West about the year 1854 may help explain the great political revolution which occurred there in 1854 and 1855. As

[27] Koerner, *Memoirs*, I, 588.

[28] For these statements about Ohio, see *Debates Ohio Convention of 1850*, I, 59, 138, 157, 206, 226, 236, 260, 270, 271, 450, 633, 726; II, 232, 555.

[29] *Indiana Weekly State Journal*, Feb. 11, 1846; April 14, 1847; Apr. 15, 1854; *Daily Journal*, June 3, 1854; Alton *Weekly Courier*, Jan. 14, 1853; *Constitution of Michigan, 1850*.

[30] *Indiana State Sentinel*, May 26, 1954; Alton *Weekly Courier*, Apr. 22, 1853.

we look back, it appears to us that to a region experiencing such an economic boom, the expansion and railroad development that would come from opening a new territory like Kansas and Nebraska would make a strong appeal. But it was left to the lower West to champion this expansion and the upper region revolted strongly against it. The Kansas-Nebraska Bill did not seem to fit in with lake district demands for homesteads, for free soil, and for internal improvements at government expense. The feeling long prevalent in the region that the South, which was controlling the nation through the Democratic party, would not grant what the lakes wanted and would continue the neglect of its interests which it had shown at the time of the veto of the Harbor and River Bill of 1847 was now to express itself in action. The bill opening Kansas and Nebraska to slavery, as the people of the lakes claimed, was more than they could bear. This brings us to the author of that enactment, Douglas of Illinois, and to the bill itself.

The Lower West Champions Expansion—Kansas-Nebraska Bill

Stephen A. Douglas was, in 1854 and from that time until the Civil War, the outstanding Democratic leader in the West and in the nation as well. Like Abraham Lincoln, well trained in local legal and political battles, and like him, very ambitious, he differed in being bold and daring; he made a strong appeal to younger men who were imbued with an ardor for western "progress"—expansion, development, and land grants to railroads.[31] As he, outgrowing the local ambitions and politics of central Illinois, moved in the wider circles of Chicago and the national Capitol at Washington, the ideals of the Progressive Democracy of the forties were, under his leadership, to take on a more materialistic tone. In Congress, he had already been the author of several laws for the admission of new states and the formation of territorial governments. With the whole West burning with expansionist fever, with, in the winter of 1854–1855, about twenty thousand settlers waiting along the western border of Missouri and Iowa ready to take possession of land in what is now Kansas and Nebraska, with politicians in Missouri, Iowa, and Illinois aroused and forming competing schemes for the opening of new territories and the laying out of railroad routes to the Pacific, nothing was more

[31] Beveridge, *Lincoln*, II, 165.

natural than that Stephen A. Douglas, the man best fitted for the work, should become the author of a new territorial bill.[32] And further, with popular sovereignty, which in Douglas' opinion had the advantage of combining the values of local self-government with a sure tendency in favor of freedom in the territories, an abstract and unnecessary restriction like the Missouri Compromise could, if southerners so desired, be abrogated—a rather reckless attitude toward that time-honored law, it must be admitted.[33] Senators from the nearby states of Iowa and Missouri—Dodge of Iowa and Benton and Atchison of Missouri—were anxious that the Nebraska region be opened and that a Pacific railroad be built. Territorial delegates to the national government were elected ahead of time in anticipation of the opening. In truth, there was along the border a mania for expansion and the settlement of this territory. The bill was a lower western-southern measure pushed by Douglas in the Senate and Richardson in the House, both lower western men, and was seized upon by most of the slave-holding South as furthering its interests.[34] As the debate in Congress proceeded, it was clear that representatives from Chicago and the lakes failed to grasp whatever economic advantage was offered them, and in the whole section from Wisconsin to the Western Reserve, Free Soilers, Whigs, and Democrats were aroused against it.

Senators Chase of Ohio and Sumner of Massachusetts, by their bitter and in some respects unfair "Appeal to Independent Democrats in Congress and to the People of the United States" helped arouse a spirit throughout the East and the lake district violently hostile to Douglas and the bill. The state of mind in these districts had already become such that to brand any action as a "southern plot to extend slavery" was sure to result in violent opposition.[35] They utterly refused to see the possibilities which Douglas and friends of the bill urged of harmonious and united action between the South and the North and the support of it on national expansionist grounds. Meanwhile, many advocates of the bill North and South frankly stated that they did not expect slavery to develop in Kansas. But to take the stand that Webster had taken and refuse to taunt and reproach the

[32] *Ibid.,* pp. 168, 169, 172–175.

[33] *Ibid.,* pp. 108, 193, 194, 203, 503.

[34] O. P. Ray, *Repeal of the Missouri Compromise;* F. H. Hodder, "Genesis of the Kansas-Nebraska Act," *Wis. Hist. Soc. Proc., 1912; Cong. Globe,* 33 Cong., 1 Sess., *passim.*

[35] Beveridge, *Lincoln,* II, 184–191.

South by expressly prohibiting slavery in the territories was even more unpopular in strong antislavery centers in 1854 than in 1850.[36] In Congress, the representatives and senators from the free West, and, at home, local newspapers and local opinion, split into two sections as Douglas and Richardson engaged in a parliamentary struggle which was carried on for days amid unparalleled commotion. Wilmot Proviso Democrats from the lakes were ready to break forever with their party. It did not long remain in doubt that Douglas and the South would receive loyal support from the lower West. When the final vote came, thirteen representatives from southern Ohio, southern and western Indiana, southern Illinois, and Iowa—along with certain Pennsylvania Democrats and the Tammany group in New York City— voted for this epoch-making bill. To match these thirteen, twenty-six Democratic, Whig, and Free Soil representatives from Ohio, Michigan, Wisconsin, northern Indiana, and Illinois voted against it.[37] To see Giddings, a Free Soiler from the Western Reserve, Colfax, a Whig from northern Indiana, Julian, a Quaker Free Soiler, Wentworth, a Democrat from Chicago, and Dodge and Walker, Democrats from Wisconsin, standing side by side against Bright and English of Indiana, Douglas, Shields, and Richardson of Illinois, and Jones and Dodge of Iowa was to see the growing antagonism of the Western Reserve for Cincinnati, of northern Indiana for the "pocket," of Chicago for "Egypt," and to realize that this cleavage in the free West was to mean much in future issues of national importance.

If a few southern men looked upon popular sovereignty in its true light as a western proposal and one likely to bring freedom rather than slavery to the West,[38] leaders in Congress from the upper West were determined to see nothing in it but a new move of the slavery forces, rash, personal, president-seeking ambition on the part of Douglas, and a violation of the time-honored principle of the Missouri Compromise. Chase of Ohio and others in the appeal claimed that the bill was an "atrocious" pro-slavery "plot" and a "monstrous wrong." The appeal pictured the West from the Gulf of Mexico to Canada as the

[36] Lynch, W. O., "The Character and Leadership of Stephen A. Douglas," *Miss. Valley Hist. Ass'n. Proceedings,* Vol. 10, p. 460; Beveridge, *op. cit.,* II, 197-205.

[37] *Cong. Globe,* 33 Cong., 1 Sess., 1254; in the Senate, Cass and Stuart of Michigan voted for the bill, but Dodge and Walker, Democrats of Wisconsin voted against it; *Ibid.,* pp. 532, 1321.

[38] Among them, Sam Houston of Texas. Beveridge, *op. cit.,* II, 216.

center of a vast slave-holding despotism; a telling moral challenge was made to the clergy of the North and West to stand against this heinous crime.[39] Douglas' failure to gauge opinion in the lake region and the East proved expensive to his reputation and the peace of his country. On the other hand the unwarranted charges of the appeal and its tremendous influence in these same regions were perhaps equally unfortunate.

After tumultuous sessions of the Senate and an exhausting and powerful speech by Douglas, the bill passed that body in the early hours of March 4, 1854. The effect was momentous. The Democratic party in the lake region was not only almost destroyed, but its hold on many districts in the lower West was threatened. Local "Republican," "Fusion," "Peoples," and "Anti-Nebraska" tickets were run almost everywhere between the Ohio and the lakes. Whigs furnished the main body of voters for these tickets with Free Soilers and free-soil Democrats supplying a minority of voters, but more than their share of aggressive leaders.[40] Democratic papers in large numbers refused to support their party.[41] There thus occurred that fusion of interests that was to become the Republican party—a movement which Beveridge describes as a "merging of associated groups into what finally [was] to become a compact and militant army limited to the North, a combination of moral and economic forces, of ancient partisanship and racial prejudice, of industrial philosophy and religious exaltation." [42]

In the national congressional elections of 1854, these opposition fusion tickets carried most of Ohio, three of the four districts of Michigan, two of the three in Wisconsin, all of northern Indiana and Illinois and one of the two districts in Iowa. Districts were carried that had never been anything but Democratic. In state elections, the effects of the reaction were even more clearly seen. The fusion movement carried the lower houses of not only Michigan and Wisconsin but also Ohio, Indiana, Illinois, and Iowa. In Iowa, James W. Grimes was

[39] Beveridge, op. cit., II, 184–187.

[40] George W. Julian, Political Recollections, p. 70; T. C. Smith, Liberty and Free Soil Parties in the Northwest, Ch. XIX; Indiana Weekly State Journal, May 27, June 17, 24, July 1, Aug. 5, Oct. 15, 1854; Chicago Journal and Chicago Democrat, 1854, passim.

[41] Indiana Weekly State Journal, Mar. 25, 1854. Among these were the Sandusky Mirror, Toledo Republican, Ashtabula Democrat, Canton Transcript, Chicago Democratic Press, Galena Jeffersonian, and Alton Telegraph; see these papers Feb., Mar., 1854, passim.

[42] Beveridge, op. cit., II, 218.

elected Governor after a remarkable campaign against the Dodge, Jones, and Douglas Democrats.[43] In the Belleville district of southern Illinois, Lyman Trumbull was elected to Congress. In the Illinois Legislature, an aggressive group of insurgent Free Soil Democrats and anti-Nebraska Whigs seized upon the newly elected Belleville representative and made him United States Senator—Abraham Lincoln as yet not showing radical enough antislavery tendencies to gain their support.[44] In 1855, a prohibitory law was adopted in Michigan, Indiana, and Iowa by the same political forces that were opposed to the Kansas-Nebraska Bill. There were also demands for the "Maine Law" in Illinois and Ohio. In the former state, the Whigs and Free Soilers of the northern counties favored it, Lincoln himself taking no part, however, in the vigorous and noisy campaign. Douglas and the Democrats were generally opposed.[45] These then were the forms that the "wave of moral feeling" took in 1854 and 1855. The upper West had spoken with such decisiveness that the effects are felt in that region up to the present day. It is clear that, important as the slavery issue was, it was only one—though at the time the most conspicuous—of the elements in this great movement in the lake region. There was the element of sectional prestige and rivalry, the sense of strength of a new region and its desire to make itself felt in national affairs. The restlessness of the forties, which was discussed in the first chapter, was bearing fruit. In fact the movement was, as Beveridge says, a complex of sectional, economic, psychological, and cultural forces.

[43] For election returns of 1854, see *Whig Almanac*, 1855.

[44] Beveridge, *op. cit.*, II, 274–287.

[45] For material on this prohibition movement see *Indiana Weekly State Journal*, Apr. 15, 20, June 3, 24, 1854; March 22, 1855; *Indiana State Sentinel*, July 4, 7, 13, 19, 1854; F. J. Herriott, "Iowa and the First Nomination of Lincoln," *Annals of Iowa*, Third Series VIII, p. 215; T. C. Smith, *Liberty and Free Soil Parties in the Northwest*, pp. 271, 273, 280; Gustave Koerner, *Memoirs*, I, 620, 623; Beveridge, *op. cit.*, II, 293–296.

CHAPTER VI

THE LOWER WEST, THE NATIONAL POLITICAL BATTLE-GROUND

(1854–1857)

From 1854 on through the Civil War, the Middle West was diverted from the lines of development that had been set out before it in the decade of the forties. It had become divided; its own sectional interests were not to be realized—to say nothing of the grandiose dreams of ten years before that it was to be a new, progressive center of world civilization. Its bubbling democratic political idealism was to give way to economic concerns which grew ever greater and greater. The building of more commodious homes for the native American population which in many regions of Ohio, Indiana, and Illinois was becoming prosperous and rising to higher standards of living, the rapid growth of the cities especially in the lake region and upper Mississippi valley, the opening and winning of newer lands west of the Mississippi and the Missouri by the incoming Germans and native American settlers and the accompanying interests—town-planning, real-estate development, homestead legislation and railroad-building—these material developments, so marked in the fifties, imparted a spirit of materialism and exploitation more pronounced than the Middle West had ever known. In addition, the development of the region was becoming more distinctly related to national issues, especially the question of slavery extension in nearby Kansas and Nebraska, and on this issue the unity of the West was being broken. The settlement of the new West beyond the Missouri, the building of railroads, the passage of homestead legislation, and other purely western interests were to wait upon the solution of the question of whether slavery could fix itself in Kansas in spite of the powerful forces at work to make it free state. On this question the upper and lower West, which had much in common, developed views sufficiently divergent to align them in different political parties. A difference that was more apparent than real served to divide the two great leaders, Lincoln and Douglas, and the two great political groups they led—western Lincoln Republicanism and western Douglas Democracy.

This western question furnished the issues for the national political battle, and the Middle West was the national battle-ground from 1854 to 1861. The East was called upon to establish some relation to lake district Republicanism, tamed down and moderated as it was soon to be by the spirit of Lincoln; the slave-holding South on the other hand was compelled to decide upon its attitude toward the lower West as represented by Stephen A. Douglas. The views of Lincoln and Douglas on the question of how to deal with slavery in Kansas and Nebraska and on disputed points involved in popular sovereignty and in the Dred Scott decision, became intricate and technical and appeared to be completely divergent. Thus material was afforded for a classic political battle. The East and the radical lake district accepted Lincoln Republicanism reluctantly but definitely; a large part of the border South accepted Douglas, but the lower South was finally to see this contest in its true light as one between two western men, both fundamentally antislavery and national, and was to break away even from Douglas.

The forces in this western contest which came to be of such national importance, met face to face in those central counties of Illinois with which both Lincoln and Douglas were so familiar, and in similarly situated counties in Indiana. The battle line stretched approximately along the fortieth parallel,[1] though in Ohio it was more wavering, the doubtful counties being more scattered. In these meeting points of divided opinion, the western farmer, faced with unwelcome issues forced on him by the divergent South and Northeast, was called upon to make momentous national decisions. In the course of the next six or eight years, the shift of the vote in fifteen or twenty of these counties in Illinois and Indiana was to decide the political fate of the nation. In 1860 and 1861, the issues widened to the question of Union and State rights—again showing how, in our history, western issues, pressing for a solution, have involved the whole nation, have made middle westerners national leaders, have brought forth abstract State rights or Union theories, have made compromise necessary, or, as in 1754, 1812, 1846 and in 1861, have precipitated war.

[1] See map accompanying the monograph "The Fight for the Northwest" by W. E. Dodd, *American Hist. Rev.*, Vol. 16, p. 788.

THE DOUBTFUL CENTRAL COUNTIES

The great movement which, as we have seen, swept down from the lakes in 1854 and 1855, threatened but did not overthrow Democratic control in the lower West; in fact in the next few years that control became stronger. In "the Pocket" in Indiana (the district lying between the Ohio and Wabash rivers), in the "Banner District" in "Egypt," and in Cincinnati (one Congressional district in that city being called the "South Carolina of the North"), the Democratic vote was overwhelming. Even above the National Road, in northwestern Ohio, in the Dubuque region, and among the foreign-born in Detroit, Milwaukee, and Chicago, it was still strong. The strength of the Democracy in the lower West and its continued vitality as a strong minority party in the lake region long after 1854 was, in the first place, due to the continuance for some years of the old alliance with the Democratic South. The second factor at work was the attitude which the Whigs of the lower West, and especially of the central counties of Illinois and Indiana, were to show in the re-alignment of parties after 1854, coupled with the attitude of Germans and Irish throughout the whole West. The third was the fact that the Democrats, being the older party, enjoyed advantages of organization and leadership, and their program of popular sovereignty offered an appealing platform.

The old Whigs along the Ohio, the Wabash, and the Illinois rivers did not, in the stirring years 1854 and 1855, join the party of the lakes in large numbers, and become Republicans. In some counties, parts of southern Ohio, for example, they kept the old party alive by running separate tickets. While their old Whig comrades of the Western Reserve were leading the new party and giving large majorities for it, they ran a separate ticket against Chase in 1855, casting a heavy vote in Cincinnati and elsewhere.[2] There were indeed many of them who (just as earlier their leaders had on the Proviso, the Fugitive Slave Law and on the question of Black Codes, voted with Democrats) them-

[2] They cast 24,310 votes in the state, almost all of which was in the South. How Western Reserve Whigs had become Republicans and Ohio River Whigs were still inclined to hold up the old party banner is shown by the following: Portage County (Western Reserve) cast 2,660 votes for Chase and 10 for Trimble, the Whig candidate; Gallia County (Ohio River) cast 344 for Chase and 1,099 for Trimble. In Hamilton County (Cincinnati) the Whigs cast 6,538 votes; the Republicans, 4,516. *Tribune Almanac*, 1856, p. 44. In southern and western Indiana leading Whig papers like the New Albany *Tribune* and the Vincennes *Whig* were not inclined to desert their party and join the "Peoples' Movement." *Indiana Daily State Sentinel*, July 26, Oct. 27, 1854.

selves favored the Kansas-Nebraska Bill.[3] Others, particularly in southern Illinois, finding themselves not at home in the shift of parties, did not vote at all; still others, including some who had been born in the South, became ardent Democrats.[4] Lincoln himself was slow to leave the old Whig party. Other Whigs, living along the Ohio and Illinois, who did not wish to join the "radical" Republican party and who shared with the Whigs of the East a strong opposition to the incoming foreigner, found themselves joining the anti-Catholic, anti-foreign, American, or Know-Nothing Party.[5] As late as 1860 these Know-Nothing Whigs gave many votes for Bell for President; in 1861, in Cincinnati, they allied with the Democrats, carrying the city against the Republicans.[6]

Many Germans, both in the lower and the upper region, still felt the attraction of the Democratic party, as did also practically all the Irish. The protest against the Kansas-Nebraska Bill in 1854 carried with it only the most radical antislavery Germans, those that were Protestants and free thinkers. Gustave Koerner, himself, the most prominent German in southern Illinois, although opposed to opening the new territories to slavery, considered himself a good Democrat until 1856. Cincinnati in that year sent Groesbeck to Congress as a representative of German Democrats; even in the lake region at that time not many more than the revolutionists of 1848 had joined the new party, and many of the younger Germans still remained Democrats, as Carl Schurz found when, on his arrival, he plunged into the Republican antislavery movement.[7] Many of the new Germans, as well as the Irish, looked on with regret as they saw Whigs and Republicans in the East and in parts of the West allying with the anti-foreign American party, demanding strict naturalization laws and a longer residence requirement for suffrage, and approving prohibition.

[3] Koerner, *Memoirs*, I, 617.

[4] *Ibid.*, II, 22, 23. In Saline County (Illinois) an anti-Nebraska candidate received 11 votes; in Gallatin, 17; in these counties the Nebraska candidate received 1,270 votes and Scott in 1852 had received only 533. *Whig Almanac,* 1855, p. 49.

[5] *Whig Almanac,* 1855–1857. Cook County, Illinois, in 1856 gave Fillmore only 350 votes out of 15,000. Alexander, the extreme southern county of Illinois, gave Fillmore half of its vote.

[6] The statement of Chase that Ohio Americans became Republicans is thus shown to be untrue in some respects. *Letters of Salmon P. Chase, Report Am. Hist. Assoc.,* 1902, II, 278. *Tribune Almanac,* 1861–1862.

[7] Koerner, *Memoirs,* II, 4; Carl Schurz, *Reminiscences,* II, 65–66; see also F. I. Herriott, "Iowa and the First Nomination of Lincoln," *Annals of Iowa,* Third Series, VIII, 215.

They saw that Democrats favored giving them the vote after a residence of a year or two, while the new "Peoples" movement in Indiana and elsewhere kept alive the old Whig opposition to the grant of suffrage to the newcomer until five or even seven years had passed; it was also clear that Free Soilers and Whigs in northern Indiana, Michigan, and Iowa were responsible for the prohibitory legislation that was being adopted in those states.[8] Many immigrants felt that the Republican platform of 1856 was further proof that this party was less favorable to the foreigner than were the Democrats, and that the latter were still the patrons of their class.[9]

The additional advantage which the Democrats of the lower West possessed because theirs was the older party, situated in the older region, and having an older organization and leadership, was to be felt for some years after 1854. In Indiana and Illinois, especially, the apportionment of representation for both the state legislature and the national Congress was in their favor. Attempts of northern Indiana and Illinois to remedy the situation in favor of their newer territory and rapidly increasing population were resisted. Lower western Democrats had already built up a Douglas tradition as the successor of the older Jacksonian allegiance; Douglas had the support of such leading papers as the Cincinnati *Enquirer,* the Indianapolis *Sentinel,* the *Illinois State Register* and the Chicago *Times;* an effective party organization was pushing him for the presidency. If, in view of the more radical developments in the lake region, the party seemed less buoyant, democratic, and "revolutionary" than it had been when it bore the name of the "Progressive Democracy" of the forties, it still kept alive old ideas of individualism, tolerance, laissez-faire, local autonomy, and hostility to the East and to tariffs—ideas to which was now being added popular sovereignty as a western, democratic, fair-and-square method of dealing with slavery in the territories. While the dominant party organization was pro-Douglas, and to be an independent Democrat like Gustav Koerner or Lyman Trumbull was to court political ostracism,[10] there was, as we have seen, the older, more conservative, more "pro-southern" faction led by Senator Bright of Indiana who

[8] W. D. Foulke, *Life of Oliver P. Morton,* I, 44; F. I. Herriott, *The Germans of Iowa and the "Two Year" Amendment of Mass.,* pp. 4, 6, 24, and by the same author, "Iowa and the First Nomination of Lincoln," *Annals of Iowa,* Third Series, VIII, 215; *Indiana State Sentinel,* July 10, 1854; *Indiana Daily State Journal,* June 24, 1854; Koerner, *Memoirs,* I, 588, 623.

[9] Koerner, *op. cit.,* II, 9.

[10] *Ibid.,* I, 618.

owned slaves in Kentucky, ex-Governor John Reynolds of Belleville, Illinois, who was called the "most pro-slavery man" in the state, and Senator G. W. Jones of Dubuque who had held slaves in Iowa and who was considered by his southern friends a "good nigger man" and true to their interests.[11] This small group, much more "regular" and almost constant in their support of the South, was jealous of Douglas and his party and warned southern Democrats not to place too much confidence in this unique leader; they knew him to be too much a western man.

The Republican movement faced certain serious handicaps. Strong in the Reserve, in the Quaker and "Yankee" counties of eastern and northern Indiana, and along Lake Michigan from Chicago to Milwaukee, it had important outposts south of the fortieth parallel in the Marietta region in Ohio, in the Miami valleys, and in the Belleville district in southern Illinois. But for six years after the revolt of 1854 the party strength failed to match the record of that year. The movement was a fusion of parties and lacked unity; it had an old Whig voting strength headed by an undue proportion of aggressive Free Soil and ex-Democratic leaders. The uncompromising spirit of Wade of the Reserve, Julian of Indiana, Chandler of Michigan, and Carl Schurz of Wisconsin was in clear contrast with the humane moderation of Lincoln and antagonistic to the Whiggish conservatism of Cabel B. Smith of Indiana and W. B. Kellogg of Illinois. "Border county" Whigs, as Julian said, made half-developed and compromising Republicans and proved to be a severe strain on radical lake-district abolitionism.

The Republicans felt keenly the injustice of the congressional apportionment of districts. With the census, both in 1850 and 1860, registering tremendous gains around the lakes, the apportionment lagged far behind and the representation in Congress of the full Republican strength of the region was not felt until 1863. A glance at the reapportionment of that year will reveal that the representation of Michigan in the House was increased from four to six; of Wisconsin, from three to six; and, most remarkable of all, of Iowa from two to six.[12] Illinois gained five new representatives, due largely to the great

[11] W. E. Dodd, "The Fight for the Northwest," *Am. Historical Review,* Vol. 16, p. 777. Indiana Democrats were very conservative and often followed Bright's leadership.

[12] *Tribune Almanac,* 1862, 1863.

growth from 1850 to 1855 in the central and northern counties. This increased congressional representation in 1863 was a tardy acceptance of a condition which had existed for almost a decade. It registered, at that late date, the growth in population which occurred almost entirely before the panic of 1857 and largely by 1855. What the presence in Congress during the fifties of more "stalwarts" like Chandler of Michigan, Durkee and Doolittle of Wisconsin, Lovejoy of northern Illinois, and Harlan of Iowa would have accomplished in effectually checking southern "aggression"—or, more probably, in precipitating civil war sooner—it is needless to conjecture.

The course of events from 1854 to 1860 seemed strangely to work in favor of the doctrine of popular sovereignty which the Democrats of the lower West had followed Douglas in upholding in 1854 and which became every year more endeared to them. By this policy the South was not unduly antagonized, and results not unfavorable to the North and West were realized. As real popular sovereignty, notwithstanding the disorders of border war in Kansas and the resultant executive interference of one type or another, seemed in the course of time to be bringing that freedom to the territories which was the corner stone of Republicanism, there occurred a remarkable change in the attitude of many Republicans toward this much maligned doctrine; many came to approve it. The party seemed in danger of losing its reason for existence. Of all the factors which were at work in this great national conflict, factors that rose and fell with varying degrees of modification up to 1860, none was more important than this.

Gains and Losses 1855–1857

If the gains made by the rising forces of the lakes in 1855 are briefly summarized and set over against those of the lower West, the final record will show that a reaction against the high spirit of 1854 had already set in. The election of Salmon P. Chase to the governorship of Ohio and the attempt of the newly elected legislature to protect the slave fleeing across that state by the passage of personal liberty laws, the election of Trumbull of Illinois as a United States Senator and the prohibition successes we have mentioned—these were among the clear gains for lake-district Republicanism. But movements to offset some of these gains were soon on foot. Southern Illinois Democrats, aided by the Germans and Irish of Belleville, Quincy, Peoria, and Chicago, organized a "personal liberty party" and checked a prohibition wave that had its strength in the northern part of the state.[13] Furthermore Indiana's prohibition law was weakened by doubts as to its constitutionality, and the zeal of northern Indiana Republicans for this kind of reform was dampened. With a caution on this question that reminds us of more recent political attitudes, they expressed themselves in Schuyler Colfax's words as follows: "On the whiskey question under the Supreme Court decision until we can reform the judges we cannot get an efficient law; and if we cannot, need we provoke prejudice against us without being able to effect any good? I would not take back my principles, but now it appears that all we can do is to labor for freedom." [14]

In Indiana, also, many local elections went against the Republicans. The Democrats, fearing that the dangerous Republican movement would continue to spread from the eastern and northern counties and finally engulf Indianapolis and the Wabash and Ohio river counties, resolved to use strong methods to keep their power from slipping. To allow a joint session of the legislature with the Republican majority in the House meant Republican control and the election of a Republican United States Senator. The State Senate with its Democratic majority, dominated by aggressive men from southern counties, fell upon the device of refusing to permit a joint session and thus preventing a quorum.[15] To leave one of Indiana's seats in the national Senate vacant was better than to elect a despised Republican. Such methods were more than once resorted to in Indiana in that ultra-political age and were not at all out of keeping with the ideals of public and private morality that were widely prevalent in many western states. The West, then in the midst of the great boom that preceded the panic of 1857, offered great temptations to business men and speculators. The desire to escape from the extreme poverty of an earlier period and the chance of great prosperity in the stimulating early fifties were testing men's characters. Forgery, counterfeiting, and embezzlement were common, and banking conditions were unsettled. Railroad control was extravagant and wasteful, and railroad "smashing" a frequent practice; stock jobbers and fraudulent bankrupts "in and out of the penitentiary" were numerous.[16] The common man, whether farmer or mechanic, was

[13] *Tribune Almanac,* 1856, p. 51; Koerner, *op. cit.,* I, 620–23, 633.
[14] O. J. Hollister, *Life of Schuyler Colfax,* p. 94.
[15] *Indiana Senate Journal,* 1855.
[16] Koerner, *op. cit.,* I, 621.

driving for quick returns with a nervous and exhausting eagerness. Town-lot speculating was rampant; needless to say, lawyers and politicians could not but feel the effects of this reckless western spirit.[17]

In 1856, a Presidential election year, the Democrats of the lower West were to retain their hold on their own region and make a strong appeal to voters in the doubtful border counties of central Indiana and Illinois. Meeting in national convention at Cincinnati, the national Democratic party passed over the popular candidate, Douglas, and nominated the more available Buchanan of Pennsylvania. It is not surprising that the Cincinnati convention adopted a platform that reflected the spirit of southern Ohio, Indiana, Illinois, and Pennsylvania. That document favored popular sovereignty and denounced as anti-Catholic, anti-foreign, and therefore undemocratic, the American and Republican parties. The Germans as a whole were in a state of indecision that made their vote so important to both parties in those years. There is, however, evidence that a majority were still Democrats.[18]

Most of the voters in southern Indiana and Illinois could see in the first national platform of the Republicans, adopted at Philadelphia, nothing but dangerous radicalism, sectional arrogance, and "Black Republicanism"; it went so far as to say that Congress should prohibit slavery as well as polygamy in the territories as twin relics of barbarism. The action of the administration with regard to Kansas was severely criticized, and an attempt was made to revive a dying interest in the democratic principles of the Declaration of Independence, and the equality of all men. Nor would John C. Fremont as a candidate appeal to them. Even Lincoln himself was unenthusiastic about this man who would offer little to attract the Whigs of central Illinois.[19] Millard Fillmore was sure to make a stronger appeal to conservative

---

[17] It has been given good expression in Edgar Lee Masters' *Children of the Market Place.*

[18] The New York *Abend Zeitung* of June 13, 1856 said that hardly one tenth of the Germans would vote for Judge McLean if nominated. (Rhodes, II, 185.) This is no doubt exaggeration. Schneider of the *Illinois Staats Zeitung* on the other hand said that a majority of the hundred German papers in the country were for Fremont. *Ibid.,* 178, note. But account must also be taken of the feeling among the German voters themselves. Schuyler Colfax of northern Indiana said that the three or four thousand foreigners in his district were opposed to him in 1856. Hollister, *Colfax,* 102. Koerner says that all non-Catholic Germans voted the Republican ticket (*Memoirs,* II, 21), while Schurz says the Germans did not in large numbers support the party until 1858 (*Reminiscences* II, 101). Koerner, usually a better guide than Schurz, seems not to be as nearly correct as the latter in this case.

[19] Beveridge, *Lincoln,* II, 395, 396, 400.

Whigs than could the Republicans, and many Whigs preferred Democratic to Republican views on slavery. Even former anti-Nebraska
men were being captured by the idea of popular sovereignty.[20] Southern Democratic leaders had good grounds for the expectation that
Buchanan would carry Indiana and Illinois and possibly Iowa, but only
after a bitter fight; the contest was to be as Alexander H. Stephens
said, "the hottest ever waged in politics." [21] The eyes of the whole nation became focused on Indiana and Illinois, but the keener vision of
knowing politicians was directed particularly to their central doubtful
counties.

Old Whigs, besides distrusting Fremont and showing enthusiasm for
Fillmore, stood against sectionalism, against radicalism, and against
the possibility of war. Abraham Lincoln, whose constant task in those
years was to win the genial ex-Kentuckians who were old followers
of Clay and Webster and who constituted this element in central Illinois, found them stubbornly critical of the Republican party and saw
their old party spirit again growing.[22] They could not be stirred by the
campaign literature and speeches that ascribed responsibility for the
bloody deeds and absence of law and order in Kansas to the Democrats.
The sectional nature of the Republican party was to them a great
danger, and many felt with Douglas that if only the more lawless in
Kansas were kept from doing their rash and bloody work and migration took its natural course, Kansas would become free.[23] Douglas
himself spoke repeatedly on the "Constitution and the Union" as
against Republican sectionalism, and wherever he spoke there were
tremendous crowds and long processions. The campaign in this respect rivaled the Harrison-VanBuren campaign of 1840.[24]

The enthusiasm of the new-born Republican party in this, its first
great campaign, is well known; in both parties, there was extreme
bitterness. There was, indeed, no little violence in word and deed.
The border war between free and slave state men in Kansas was
only one form of the political rough-handedness of the day. Buchanan's
followers were called "Buccaneers"; he himself was "the candidate of
the inveterate old office-holders and office-seekers . . . a melancholy
array . . . clad in the liveries of administrations past and present—

[20] Koerner, *Memoirs*, II, 31.
[21] *Ibid.*, II, 33; Letter of Stephens to Thomas, June 16, 1856—*Correspondence
of Toombs, Stephens and Cobb, Report of Am. Hist. Ass'n. 1911*, Vol. II, p. 368.
[22] Beveridge, *Lincoln*, II, 402, 409, 435.
[23] *Ibid.*, II, 411, 412, 413, 419, 420.
[24] *Ibid.*, II, 426, 430.

a decayed aristocracy." He was a "complacent, frosty, venerable bachelor" who was unable to stir either the intellect or the heart of the American people.[25] Violence in Kansas was matched by violence in the United States Senate when Representative Brooks of South Carolina attacked and beat Senator Sumner of Massachusetts with his cane. Attacks by natives on the foreign-born occurred in Cincinnati and Louisville and elsewhere. Henry Reed, editor of the Cincinnati *Commercial* was attacked in the street by Alexander Walker, the editor of *The Enquirer*.[26] J. B. Finley, the aged missionary evangelist, was assaulted and knocked down at Lewisburg, Ohio; "it must have been," he said, "by some one who hated me for my firm opposition to whiskey and slavery." The social and political philosophy of this aggressive leader was, in his own words, "free grace, free speech, free press, and free territory." [27] It is thought that it was partly as a result of such a high-strung state of the public mind and especially as a result of the attack on Sumner, that Abraham Lincoln abandoned his hitherto uncertain attitude and at last joined the Republican party.[28]

Uncle Tom's Cabin which had been published several years before had already been dramatized, and Democrats made slurs against the crowds it was drawing. "To see Uncle Tom performed, the most pious rushed to the most disreputable holes, nicknamed theaters, and led their families where but for this negro fanaticism, it would have been considered a very vile sin to have entered." [29] Fremont meetings were called "nigger meetings" by the Democrats. George E. Pugh, A. G. Thurman, Clement L. Vallandigham, and Samuel Medary, the Buchanan leaders in Ohio, spoke to English and German audiences in that state "for Union, no North, no South, no East, no West. Let the people of each state and territory govern themselves—no proscription on account of birth or religion." [30] Such was the spirit of the campaign.

It must not however be supposed that all Republicans deserved to be called fanatics. Fusion with Know-Nothings was advocated by many Republicans, and the "Greeley idea of moderation" was widely accepted.[31] Conservative middle western Republicanism of 1856 re-

---

[25] Cincinnati *Daily Commercial,* July 1, 19, 1856.
[26] *Ibid.,* Sept. 16, 18, 1856.
[27] *Christian Advocate,* Oct. 9, 1856, quoting *Western Christian Advocate.*
[28] Beveridge, *Lincoln,* II, Ch. V, *passim.*
[29] *Ohio Statesman,* Oct. 7, 1856.
[30] *Ibid.,* Sept. 21, 23, Oct. 4, 11, 1856.
[31] Cincinnati *Daily Commercial,* Nov. 8, 1856.

ceived no statement more true to its real character than one by
F. P. Blair, a Republican slave-owner. He said that the Republican
party did not expect to abolish slavery in slave states; that any program of liberation of slaves under existing conditions would be impossible and ruinous. "Amalgamation or equality with our race . . .
is impossible. My neighbours . . . know that I own slaves, some in-
herited and some that have begged their way into my house from the
slave pen." [32] That this was an attitude much like that of Douglas
needs only to be stated to be recognized.

The count of ballots after a bitterly contested campaign showed that
the verdict of Indiana and Illinois, and therefore the United States, was
that Buchanan should be President. Indiana's South, center, and
West, by their big majorities, carried the state for him. Southern Illinois Democrats, aided by those in the Illinois valley and by the di-
version in favor of Fillmore, overcame the strong Republican movement around Chicago and made it clear that the state that had never
failed to vote the Democratic ticket in a Presidential election could
still be counted on as an ally of the Democratic South. Republicans
were scarce in southern Illinois; twenty counties could be named in
no one of which did Fremont receive as many as one hundred votes.[33]
Democrats with a majority in both houses of the Indiana Legislature,
heedless of Republican attempts to bolt and cause no quorum unless
given the Senator of whom they had been "robbed" in 1855, pressed
through the election of Jesse Bright and Graham Fitch, the so-called
"bogus" Senators.[34] Gains were made in the lower West in the election of Democratic Congressmen over the year 1854; in Illinois the
unequal apportionment gave that party the advantage in contests both
for Congress and the state legislature.[35] In 1857, in Ohio, the Democrats won both houses of the legislature and repealed the Republican
personal liberty laws. In that year, too, proposals in Republican Iowa
and Wisconsin to grant suffrage to the Negro were voted down. It
seemed that only old Free Soil communities like the Western Reserve in Ohio, and Racine and Kenosha along the lake shore above
Chicago, were ready to take any other than a Democratic stand on

[32] Cincinnati *Daily Commercial,* Sept. 24, 1856.
[33] *Tribune Almanac,* 1857.
[34] *Indiana Senate and House Journal,* 1857.
[35] Cook County, with a population of over 100,000, had no more representation in the state legislature than counties in southern Illinois with populations
one half or one third as large, Koerner, *Memoirs,* II, 37, 38.

this question.[36] The vote in the cities of Milwaukee and Detroit with their large Irish population was safely Democratic; far off in the newest part of the Northwest, in the recently admitted State of Minnesota, the Democrats succeeded in electing the governor and the legislature. With a Democratic delegation in the national House of Representatives and two conservative United States Senators, Shields and Rice, that state was for a short time to be allied with the lower West on public questions, rather than with Michigan and Wisconsin.

But such Democratic success along the Ohio River and other localities farther north did not mean that the whole West was Democratic or that the fusion-Republican movement was on a decline. In 1856, due to the great majorities in the Reserve, Fremont electors were chosen in Ohio; Michigan and Wisconsin and Iowa also went Republican. One important result was that Lewis Cass of Michigan and Henry Dodge of Wisconsin, the last prominent leaders of the Democracy in the lake region, were forced to yield their places in the United States Senate to the radical Republicans, Zachariah Chandler and James R. Doolittle. In Illinois, the Republican north reached south to the Belleville district for a governor and carried the state for their candidate, William H. Bissell, even though Buchanan carried the electoral vote. As governor, Bissell proved, however, almost helpless in the face of a Democratic legislature, which, under the leadership of John A. Logan resisted all attempts at a fairer legislative apportionment. As the years 1857–1858 came on with their stirring events associated with the name of Stephen A. Douglas, the strength of the Democrats in the West was still very great.

[36] *Tribune Almanac,* 1858.

CHAPTER VII

Stephen A. Douglas—Western Insurgent, 1857–1860

Popular Sovereignty Becomes Popular

To the ardent follower of Stephen A. Douglas in his remarkable career as a western insurgent from 1857 to 1860, the movement he led was an expression of the best in American democracy. Even a surface glance at this man and his program as he opposed Buchanan's pro-slavery Kansas policies in 1857, as he opposed Lincoln for United States Senator in 1858, and as he, in 1860, led the "Union loving" people of both sides of the Mason and Dixon line from Missouri to New Jersey against the sectionalism of the Republicans of the North and the Democrats of the South, will reveal that his was primarily a lower western movement. The careful student, however, will go further and will not hesitate to ask again and seek an answer to the persistent questions that the name of Stephen A. Douglas suggests, questions that seventy-five years of controversy have not settled. If these questions were stated in a form favorable to Douglas they would be: Was not the movement led by this greatest of lower western leaders in those years the surviving form of the Progressive Western Democracy of the forties? Was it not the saving remnant representing what was best in the national Democracy against old party corruption and "Buchanan's truckling to extreme pro-slavery men"? Was not its doctrine of popular sovereignty the best preventive of civil war and a great principle of progress, which was making the territories free and rendering the Wilmot Proviso and even the Republican party unnecessary?[1] Were not those Republican leaders who sought to support Douglas against Lincoln in the great senatorial canvas of 1858, showing unusual political wisdom? Were not Douglas' ideas the nearest embodiment of the ideals of Jeffersonian and Jacksonian individualism, democracy, union with local autonomy, and regional and sectional rights?

[1] See William O. Lynch, "The Character and Leadership of Stephen A. Douglas," Miss. Valley Hist. Ass'n *Proceedings,* Vol. X, 459, 460.

Is it true, that this Union cannot permanently endure as our fathers framed it, composed of free states and slaveholding states? . . . This theory of the irrepressible conflict rests on the assumption that uniformity in the domestic institutions of all the states is indispensable. . . . The Union is founded on the theory that uniformity in local laws and domestic institutions is neither possible nor desirable. Our fathers knew that a country so extensive . . . must necessarily have a corresponding variety of interests. . . . The right of every people to govern themselves and form their own institutions on the supposition that no two states would form them precisely alike is the fundamental principle on which the American Union was made.[2]

The less favorable interpretations put on Douglas and his spectacular career must also be noted. To many people in 1860 this uncertain man had been for eight or ten years the arch politician, eager for the presidency. His method was to use the West and western principles to gain a party following and then, by shifting, gain now southern votes, and now, northern. He was ready to break the party of Buchanan if only his ambitions could be served. His party was a band of personal followers and contained a large element of rough and reckless men, office-seekers, Catholic Irish, and whiskey drinkers.

Stephen A. Douglas is the most strenuous, persistent and indefatigable of all the hunters for political notoriety . . . the foremost of political tricksters . . . always a schemer and a demagogue, . . . looking both ways, . . . pro Southern, . . . the candidate of the loafers, those who grow noisy on politics and bad whiskey.[3]

He was charged with precipitating under the pretext of fairness and of democracy a four years' struggle between slavery and freedom in Kansas. The free western farmer and the freedom-loving German, it was claimed, saw through his device of fighting for the South by the "trick" of popular sovereignty and left him for the newly formed Republican party. By 1860 the far South, too, was ready to reject him as too sectional, personal, and western, or perhaps—for it—too national. Without hoping to settle definitely this Douglas controversy, we must proceed to a fresh examination of the facts.

President Buchanan, as is well known, desired that Kansas should be admitted with the pro-slavery Lecompton constitution. An old man, tired of the Kansas question and hoping to avoid continued strife, he seemed to feel that the best policy was to admit Kansas as a state and let the people, if they so desired, free the slaves after its

[2] Address by Douglas in the Senate, Cincinnati *Enquirer*, Jan. 25, 1860.
[3] Cincinnati *Daily Commercial*, Jan. 31, May 7, 1860.

admission.[4] This they were almost sure to do, and even southern men who supported Buchanan in his pro-slavery efforts in Kansas could not fail to see that free state men in Kansas with their large majority would not be a long time in turning the tables. But before this occurred, perhaps, the South would at least come out of the deal with two pro-slavery Senators who would for a few years give it aid in the struggle for sectional power. However, the Lecompton constitution itself had been made by a group that did not represent the people of Kansas, and, when it was decided to submit only the question of acceptance of the constitution with or without the further introduction of slavery, Douglas claimed that the principle of popular sovereignty was being violated and broke with Buchanan.[5] The man who had done so much to make Buchanan President, and to energize the Democratic party, was not going to allow the President to usurp leadership and to do violence to his favorite political doctrine.

This action of Douglas'—as is the case in so much that he did—raises for us, of course, the question of motive. Did he act from principle or for political expediency? Was the irregularity of procedure in Kansas so obvious that the author of the Kansas-Nebraska Bill did not dare add to his unpopularity in the North by complying with it? Had Douglas in his close contact with the people of Illinois—mingling, as he had, with them at the state fair and elsewhere—felt a rising antislavery tide?[6] Would not an issue of fair play in Kansas make him strong with the voters in the coming canvas for the United States Senate? Even Republicans might be won over to him. Whatever motives he may have had, his break was spectacular and had far-reaching consequences. He stood up boldly in the Senate and before crowded galleries defied the administration.[7] In a speech at Chicago later he said his action was based flatly on the principle of popular sovereignty. Each state should be sovereign over its domestic affairs; this was a fundamental principle of our complex federal system. "In politics, in religion, in industry, in all the activities and conduct of life, uniformity is the parent of despotism the world over."[8]

In his spectacular insurgent movement against the national administration, Douglas was opposed by such older Democratic leaders in

[4] Beveridge, *Lincoln*, II, 525, 529-531.

[5] *Ibid.*, pp. 528, 529, 537-539.

[6] A. C. Cole, *The Era of the Civil War*, pp. 157, 158; Beveridge, *Lincoln*, II, 529, 539.

[7] Beveridge, *Lincoln*, II, 539, 540.

[8] *Ibid.*, II, 593, 594.

the West as Bright of Indiana and Jones of Iowa; and he had to reckon with Democrats everywhere who were unwilling to brave executive disfavor and the blows of the national party whip. Local politicians and editors and members of Congress in the West in large numbers fell into line with Buchanan as regular party men. Even the Cincinnati *Enquirer,* the Indianapolis *Sentinel,* and the New Albany *Ledger* were not whole-hearted in their support of Douglas against the Lecompton "fraud." [9] About one fourth of the Democratic papers in Indiana favored the admission of Kansas under the Lecompton constitution or were unwilling to follow Douglas in boldly opposing it.[10] The Chicago *Daily Times,* a Douglas paper, said of the Indianapolis *Sentinel:* "it piteously whines about the integrity of the administration and the duty of Democrats to keep out of the Republican organization." [11] In Indiana, the Vevay *News* and in Illinois, the Joliet *Signal* and the Chicago *Herald* supported Buchanan and the Lecompton constitution against Douglas.[12] In southern Illinois, Democrats hesitated to follow Douglas, and if they did, did so "with a heavy heart." [13] The extreme pro-southern wing, together with Buchanan postmasters and federal office-holders generally in Illinois, formed a third party in opposition to Douglas. Its members came to be called "Danites."

Bright and Fitch in Indiana had always disliked Douglas' leadership in the party, and the anti-Douglas movement which they inaugurated in their state became so strong that it proved hard to offset in 1858 and 1860.[14] Douglas, with a spirit of independence that reminds present-day readers of such western insurgents as Robert M. LaFollette of Wisconsin or George W. Norris of Nebraska, boldly defied Senators Bright and Fitch as well as Buchanan, joined in the double fight against "bogus" constitutions in Kansas and "bogus" Senators from Indiana and voted with Republican Senators to unseat them.[15] Senator G. W. Jones of Iowa, besides being a conservative pro-slavery Democrat and favoring the Lecompton constitution, had a personal quarrel with Douglas on the location of the western terminal of the

---

[9] Chicago *Daily Times,* Dec. 18, 20, 1857; New Albany *Ledger,* Mar. 27, Apr. 27, 1858.

[10] Logansport *Pharos,* Apr. 28, 1858 quoting Laporte *Times.*

[11] Chicago *Daily Times,* Dec. 30, 1857.

[12] *Ibid.,* Dec. 24, 1857.

[13] Koerner, *Memoirs,* II, 54.

[14] Lew Wallace, *An Autobiography,* I, 248, 250; see speech of Senator Fitch against Douglas, Dec. 22, 1857, *Cong. Globe,* 35 Cong., 1 Sess., Part I, 137–142; New Albany *Ledger,* Dec. 28, 1857.

[15] See action of Senate, *Cong. Globe,* 35 Cong., 1 Sess., 567–570, 698, 710.

Illinois Central Railroad. Called a "dough-face" by the northern and eastern forces that had captured Iowa, he showed himself in every test a tried and true "southerner" in a hostile environment. The Iowa Legislature asked him to resign if he voted for the Lecompton constitution.[16]

On the other hand, Douglas' course was being watched with favor by many who had formerly opposed him. He was now occupying "high Republican ground." Indeed, many influences favored him in his dramatic break with the President and with the radical pro-slavery South. Despite fraud and executive interference, popular sovereignty in Kansas was felt to be working in favor of a free state. The strong traditional sentiment for the Missouri Compromise was dying out among Democrats and many Republicans were becoming less insistent on the Wilmot Proviso. The latter, too, were receding somewhat on the liquor question and were becoming more like the Democrats in their attitude toward the foreign-born. All Democrats and almost all Republicans in the West were united in opposition to Negro suffrage which a few abolitionists insisted on bringing to a vote in one state or another every few years and which served only to emphasize the differences in the Republican party and to make clear the ideas which many in that party held in common with Democrats. The peculiar position in which Republicans were more and more finding themselves involved was thus stated by Oliver P. Morton of Indiana, ". . . if Kansas and Nebraska come in as free states . . . the other territories will be free, too, and the present issue between the Republican and Democratic parties will be over. Now we have a new party and we must have a living issue." [17]

No more favorable time could be found for Douglas to reclaim the hold he had lost in 1854. Drawn this time to assert western rather than southern interests, he might win the doubtful counties in Illinois and assure his reëlection to the Senate in 1858. The travesty on popular sovereignty and the palpable fraud in Kansas afforded the opportunity. In northern Illinois the Democrats strongly supported him— as finally did also those in the southern counties. Republicans, too, could not help admiring his pluck and courage.[18] The danger lay in losing the support of radical pro-slavery men of the far South. Such was the involved nature of western politics when Douglas launched his

[16] Parish, *Life of George Wallace Jones*, pp. 51, 55.
[17] W. D. Foulke, *Life of O. P. Morton*, I, 64.
[18] A. C. Cole, *The Era of the Civil War*, pp. 159, 163.

great attack on the administration. When the question of admitting Kansas under the Lecompton constitution came to a vote in the Senate, he, along with Pugh of Ohio and Stuart of Michigan, voted with the Republicans against it. Douglas found himself allied with Lyman J. Trumbull, his most able and persistent political enemy. During the session of 1857–1858, Republicans in and out of Congress supported Douglas and contended for the right of the people of the territories to regulate slavery, to that extent undermining their own platform and their own reason for existence.[19]

The Buchanan administration with the high sense of discipline that marked the dominant Democratic party of that day, made the acceptance of this constitution the test of party loyalty, and Senators Bright and Fitch of Indiana and Jones of Iowa, true to form, voted for it, together with Bigler of Pennsylvania and the Senators from New Jersey and Rhode Island.[20] In the House there were Representatives from the lower West equally bent on supporting the party even if it meant forcing Kansas into the Union with slavery. The House Crittenden-Montgomery substitute, which aimed to submit the constitution to a vote of the people of Kansas, this time at a fair election, was opposed by five representatives from eastern Ohio and southern Indiana.[21] These men were willing to go to the length of refusing to allow the people of Kansas to decide whether they wanted slavery or not.

William H. English of southern Indiana was unwilling to go this far; he and others above all else desired harmony in the Democratic party. It resulted that a compromise movement was inaugurated by southern Indiana Democrats, the most partisan Democratic group in the North, and for a few weeks William H. English became the great figure in American politics. With the Senate in favor of the Lecompton constitution and the House opposed to it without a fair submission to the people, he moved that the House and Senate go into conference. The motion brought a tie vote which the Speaker broke by voting in the affirmative. Democrats from the free West who voted for this were the five already mentioned, and English, Pendleton of Cincinnati and Hall of northwestern Ohio. They seemed to Douglas

[19] Cincinnati *Daily Commercial,* Oct. 26, 1858.

[20] *Cong. Globe,* 35 Cong., 1 Sess., 1264.

[21] F. H. Hodder, "Some Aspects of the English Bill for the Admission of Kansas," *Report Am. Hist. Assoc.,* 1906, I, 201; *Cong. Globe,* 1 Sess., 35 Cong., Vol. 36, Part II, p. 1437. They were Joseph Burns and Joseph Miller of Ohio; William I. Niblack, James Hughes, and James M. Gregg of southern Indiana.

to be "going over to Lecompton." The "English Bill" was the result of this conference. It, in turn, became the test of party loyalty.

The bill has, no doubt, been misunderstood. Republicans of that day and historians more recently have been mistaken in condemning it as a flagrant bribe. Its land grant provision was a common feature of territorial bills, but it did subordinate the main question at issue, which was the Lecompton constitution, and emphasized a grant of land in case the constitution be accepted by the people of Kansas. It was silent as to whether the grant would be made if the constitution were not adopted and implied by its threat of postponing admission unless the constitution were adopted, that there were in Kansas "people enough to hold slaves but not enough to enjoy freedom." It was an attempt not to force the acceptance but to bridge a crisis in Congress and in the Democratic party.[22] Like all aspects of the Kansas question and of the question of slavery in the territories, it was a very confused matter, and in the popular mind, hopelessly so. The confusion was not lessened by speakers and editors in their attempts to present the question before the people. Such words as "dodge," "bribe," and "juggle" were used in reckless and misleading ways by both sides.

To prevent Kansas from coming into the Union as a free state when it is the clearly expressed will of her people to do so, the original Lecompton "test" was abandoned and then a test adopted, the merit of which was its incomprehensibility. One thing was to be submitted to the people and as they voted yea or nay upon it, something else was to be decided. Non-acquiescence in this juggle is the test of loyalty to the dominant party of the Republic.[23]

Douglas opposed the bill because it permitted Kansas to come into the Union under the Lecompton constitution with 30,000 inhabitants but refused to admit her, if the people were determined to have a free state, until she had acquired a population equal to the congressional ratio, which was 93,420.[24]

The Democrats of the lower West who were unwilling to force slavery on Kansas, but who did not object if it grew up there, and who were above all else intent on party harmony, eagerly accepted the English Bill.[25] Democrats of northern and western Indiana, more

[22] F. H. Hodder, op. cit., 201.
[23] Cincinnati Daily Commercial, Sept. 6, 1858.
[24] Ibid., Sept. 30, 1858.
[25] New Albany Daily Ledger, Apr. 6, May 8, 12, 1858; Logansport Democratic Pharos, May 5, 1858.

favorable to Douglas, did not receive it so gladly.[26] The Cincinnati *Enquirer,* whose editor was at the time postmaster of Cincinnati, and the New Albany *Ledger,* the leading Democratic papers in southern Ohio and Indiana, approved the bill. Douglas' leadership in Congress was for the moment usurped by English and the rivalry between Indiana and Illinois Democrats was clearly marked. Douglas succeeded in holding only the Representatives from southern Illinois and Senator Stuart of Michigan in opposition to the English Compromise. Senators Pugh of Ohio, Bright, and Fitch of Indiana, and Jones of Iowa favored the bill and in the House it received the support of Ohio and Indiana Democrats.[27] But the English Bill did not settle the question.

Nor had the vexed question of slavery or freedom in Kansas been settled by the Dred Scott Decision, which had been delivered sometime before the Lecompton-English Bill fight. Although the only actual decision was on the status of Dred Scott to the effect that he was a slave and subject to the courts of the slave state, Missouri, the case was portentous and an ominous sign that the judges of the court thought that slavery was national. It supplied the Republicans with arguments and with an issue, which, however technical and legalistic, would help to check Douglas and the rising popular sovereignty tide. To have the Supreme Court say that Negroes could not be citizens and that the Missouri Compromise was unconstitutional looked like a great pro-slavery victory, and Douglas, in supporting the decision was, it was said, merely executing another pro-southern twist. How could he support popular sovereignty and the decision at the same time? Douglas, himself, however, did not consider either the decision or the Missouri Compromise as important as his own principle of popular sovereignty. In his opinion and that of his followers, the public mind was becoming needlessly confused on legal and constitutional questions as to the power of Congress or the Court or a state or territorial legislature over slavery. The territories, if left alone, would become free. Nothing was to prove of any avail if it were against "the laws of nature," of "labor and population, supply and production." The question would be settled if "nature could have her way" and if it were recognized once and for all that it was friendly or unfriendly

---

[26] The Goshen *Democrat,* Terre Haute *Journal* and Logansport *Pharos* yielded "for the sake of harmony." LaPorte *Times,* May 15, 1858.

[27] *Cong. Globe,* Vol. 36, Part II, p. 1899, 1905 (Apr. 30, 1858); *Ibid.,* pp. 1905-1906 (Apr. 30, 1858).

local legislation that would decide the fate of slavery in any territory.[28] We of to-day are still forced to ask the question whether Douglas' treatment of this whole matter was not more realistic than either the southern or the northern view.

The Kansas-Nebraska Bill, the Lecompton constitution, the English Bill and the Dred Scott Decision and Stephen A. Douglas—these were the issues in the state, congressional, and senatorial elections in the West in 1858. The greatest contest was to occur in Illinois as Douglas, fresh from his break with a southern controlled administration, launched his well-known campaign for reëlection to the United States Senate. However strong he was in Illinois, at no time was his position as a leader of the Democrats of the nation and of the West in so much peril. Unaided by Ohio and Indiana Democrats in his English Bill fight, in the eyes of the administration at Washington a proscribed man—he was bitterly opposed by not only the Bright-Jones old line Democrats of the West but by the radical pro-slavery leaders of the South.[29] It was of very great importance that he win the election of his own state. Then in coming years he could with that marvelous recuperative power that such leaders have often shown in American politics, contend with all comers for the presidency. He was the greatest national leader in the years from 1858 to 1860; in the former year he seemed to be emerging as the leader of the anti-slavery forces of the nation; the latter year he again stood forth a powerful and dominant figure.

LINCOLN AND DOUGLAS NOT FAR APART IN THE GREAT DEBATE

Lincoln had been quite slow in joining the Republican movement. Although he had been a Wilmot Proviso Whig in Congress in the forties,[30] nevertheless, when the Republican party was first formed, he remained aloof. Throughout 1854 and 1855, when the anti-Nebraska agitation was at its height, and the new party was in the process of formation, he was not a leader. His greatest biographer says he was "always slow to make up his mind about anything"; he waited to re-

[28] See Beveridge, *Lincoln*, II, 450, 453, 499–508 *et passim;* F. H. Hodder, "Some Phases of the Dred Scott Case," the *Mississippi Valley Historical Review*, June, 1929, pp. 3–22.
[29] Chicago *Daily Times*, Dec. 30, 31, 1858 *et passim*.
[30] Beveridge, *Lincoln*, I, 421.

flect public opinion—"he neither led nor retarded mass movements, but accurately registered them." [31] If he could not carry his old Whig and Know-Nothing friends around Springfield with him into a new party, that was a reason for staying out himself.[32] But in May, 1856, the fusion movement in Illinois now having become stronger and the public mind being aroused over the Kansas question and the attack on Sumner in the United State Senate, he finally committed himself.[33] His Whiggish conservatism, the fact that he, like Douglas, came from central Illinois, together with the remarkable speeches he had made in 1856, made him the candidate against Douglas in 1858. Moreover the split in the Democratic party made it an especially favorable moment for the opposing forces.[34]

The formal contests at the seven towns of western and southern Illinois which constitute the famous Lincoln-Douglas debate are only a part of the battle between these two typical representatives of the West in 1858. There were, besides these, a far greater number of informal engagements, most of them held in the doubtful central counties.[35] All this speech-making, however, was only a single, albeit an important, factor among several that determined the final outcome. Among the most important was the fact that Illinois was still a Democratic state and that, while Douglas was opposed by the strongly proslavery Democrats in the South, there was an able group of southern leaders who were adopting the Douglas attitude and gave him moral support, among them Crittenden of Kentucky, Wise of Virginia, Bell of Tennessee and Toombs and Stephens of Georgia.[36] There was also working in Douglas' favor and against Lincoln the unjust apportionment of legislative districts—the northern Republican counties being inadequately represented.[37] Then, too, the same general influences that had made Douglas a popular hero in the North in his fight with Bu-

[31] *Ibid.,* II, 143, 353; see also A. C. Cole, "President Lincoln and the Illinois Radical Republicans," *Miss. Valley Hist. Review,* Vol. IV, p. 419.

[32] Beveridge, *Lincoln,* II, 354, 355.

[33] *Ibid.,* pp. 358–361.

[34] *Ibid.,* Chs. VIII, IX.

[35] A. C. Cole, *Era of the Civil War,* pp. 169–170.

[36] Allen Johnson, *Stephen A. Douglas,* p. 382; *Toombs, Stephens, Cobb Correspondence Report Am. Hist. Ass'n.* 1911, II, 424, 427, 431, 433; *Sidney Breese Correspondence, Jour. Ill. State Hist. Soc.,* 1909, pp. 82–84; Cincinnati *Daily Commercial,* Oct. 29, 1858.

[37] The Chicago *Daily Times* contended in its issue of Nov. 27, 1858 that the Democrats did not profit by the bad apportionment system. The argument is supported by rather plausible statistics.

chanan over Lecompton "federalism and fraud" the previous winter, were at work. The career of Douglas had already caught the public eye; his campaign was more highly organized and expensive than that of Lincoln; it had spectacular features including chartered trains, paid musicians and newspaper advertisement. Douglas' demeanor was more immediately impressive; Lincoln was lean and lank and his manner self-effacing.[38] Douglas was almost sure of the Irish Catholic vote which was strong in Illinois, while Lincoln, it was thought, would make a strong appeal to the "Protestant church member vote." [39] To many of doubtful mind the fact that much derided "squatter" sovereignty was finally really bringing freedom to the West appealed more strongly than did the keen logic of Lincoln. Indeed, popular sovereignty seems to have been growing in popularity.

Lincoln could point out, as he did at Freeport, Illinois, the inconsistency of adhering at the same time to the doctrine of popular sovereignty and the Dred Scott decision, and could on the question whether the people of a territory might at any time before the formation of a state constitution prohibit slavery in a territory, force Douglas to conclusions which were offensive to the South. But popular sovereignty was already coming under suspicion in that section. Douglas' well-known answer in which he stated that slavery might be excluded by unfriendly local legislation—an answer which was only a repetition of what he had said "a hundred times" before, a fact which robs both the question and the answer of unique importance—[40] might better have been forced from him before a less antislavery audience in the southern part of Illinois, rather than at Freeport.[41] In order to outdo Douglas and make a clear issue, it would have been necessary for Lincoln to take higher ground, to make a broad human appeal against slavery as an institution and a moral evil to be checked in the old as well as the new states. If in some of his speeches he seemed to do this, it was going beyond the Republican platform, was allying him with hated abolitionism and was far too much for central and southern Illinois. At Charleston, Illinois, where old line Whigs were numerous, Lincoln clearly showed his conservatism on the question of race equality:

[38] Cole, op. cit., pp. 167, 169; Lillian Foster, Glimpses North and South (New York, 1859), Reprint in Jour. Ill. St. Hist. Soc. Vol. V, p. 396; Daily Chicago Times, Oct. 10, 1858; Beveridge, Lincoln, II, 610, 618, 619, 636.

[39] Cincinnati Daily Commercial, Oct. 20, 1858.

[40] Beveridge, Lincoln, II, 503, 504, 656, 663.

[41] Cole, op. cit., p. 171.

I am not, nor ever have been, in favor of bringing about in any way the social and political equality of the white and black races; (applause) . . . I am not nor ever have been, in favor of making voters or jurors of negroes, nor of qualifying them to hold office, nor to intermarry with white people.[42]

This shows how near Lincoln was to Douglas except on the issue of slavery in the western territories and the fact that Douglas held the view that popular sovereignty would bring freedom rather than slavery to that region, makes them not far apart even on that question.[43] They were both western men, and keen southerners were recognizing the dangers in both. But by his repeated hammering on the differences between Douglas and the national administration, Lincoln did unquestionably weaken his opponent.

The course of events in Kansas and the promising split in the Democratic ranks caused by the Lecompton issue were leading more and more of the doubtful Republicans and even some of the stalwarts to the conclusion that the North would win more by espousing Douglas and popular sovereignty than by fighting for an out-and-out congressional prohibition of slavery in the territories.[44] Republicans and Douglas men had just been voting together at Washington against Buchanan measures and the points of difference between them had been reduced to what many considered technical abstractions. There were several "practical" Republican leaders who were directly or indirectly supporting Douglas rather than Lincoln, and a unique rapprochement between these leaders and this daring Illinois insurgent seemed to be at the point of realization. It was very alarming to Lincoln and Illinois party men.[45] The newspapers contained rumors that William H. Seward wanted to use Douglas to kill the unpopular Buchanan Democracy in the North, and to this end was helping the Illinois Senator raise a larger campaign fund. More substantial evidence than political gossip can be found for the statement that Schuyler Colfax of Indiana urged Douglas to become the great national antislavery leader and that the two discussed plans of mutual help. "I only give these things to you," Colfax said in a letter to his mother, "to show the

---

[42] Beveridge, op. cit., II, 673.

[43] William O. Lynch, "The Character and Leadership of Stephen A. Douglas," Miss. Valley Hist. Ass'n. Proceedings, Vol. X, p. 461.

[44] George W. Julian, Political Recollections, p. 167; Lillian Foster, loc. cit.

[45] Trumbull Correspondence quoted in H. White, Trumbull, pp. 79, 80, 86, 87, 91; Beveridge, op. cit., II, 545–547.

strange evolutions of politics and what strange bedfellows its whirligigs bring together. You must not repeat them to anyone." [46] For years after 1858, Horace Greeley and Douglas were hard put to it to disprove certain statements of Representative Kellogg of Illinois. Kellogg insisted that Greeley visited Douglas again and again in 1858, that he wrote letters to Illinois urging Republicans to allow Douglas to return to the Senate without a contest, and that many Republicans took the same stand.[47] Gustav Koerner says that Greeley worked hard to induce Republicans to elect Douglas men to the legislature.[48] Whether this activity hurt Lincoln's candidacy and helped along Douglas' success is a question.[49] It seems that far-reaching schemes of a Republican-Douglas alliance were in the air, which, if carried out, would have revolutionized politics in the North.[50]

In the doubtful central counties, in which Douglas and Lincoln at one time or another addressed audiences in nearly every town, there were many who had supported Fillmore in 1856 and who were likely to be diverted to Douglas.[51] This was the real battle-ground, including Tazewell, Sangamon, Morgan, Mason, Macon, Logan, Madison, Coles, Dewitt and Piatt counties. Here were "many old line Whigs—timid, shrinking but able men from Kentucky, Tennessee, Virginia and from other southern States." [52] To them Douglas was represented by editors and speakers as a Unionist, a moderate on the slavery question, a true

[46] Hollister, *Life of Schuyler Colfax*, pp. 121, 123.

[47] See Kellogg-Greeley controversy in the Cincinnati *Commercial*, Feb. 15, Mar. 26, 1860.

[48] G. Koerner, *Memoirs*, II, 53, 54, 57.

[49] From the following material one would conclude that the movement injured Lincoln: George W. Julian, *Political Recollections*, p. 166; A. C. Cole, *Era of the Civil War*, p. 159 (citing the Trumbull Manuscripts) ; White, *Trumbull*, p. 91. But Beveridge maintains that Illinois Republicans were so angered by the pro-Douglas feeling among the Republicans in the East that they worked all the harder for Lincoln. Beveridge, *Lincoln*, II, 549.

[50] A letter of G. W. Jones to Sidney Breese in the *Breese Correspondence* at Springfield says that a union was formed in 1857 between Seward, Douglas, and Crittenden, to reëlect Douglas Senator "by Democrats if possible, otherwise by a union of Douglas Democrats with Republicans and Americans, through the influence of Seward and Crittenden"; that Seward was to be made candidate for President in 1860; that Crittenden would form his cabinet and that Douglas was to follow to the Presidency in 1864. See also W. E. Dodd, *R. J. Walker, Imperialist*, p. 23.

[51] Horace White, *Life of Lyman Trumbull*, p. 92.

[52] Cole, *op. cit.*, pp. 169, 170. A perusal of the election returns for central Illinois counties from 1854 to 1862 shows that in addition to the above named counties, Peoria, McDonough, and Bond were doubtful or close in the various elections. *Tribune Almanac*, 1854–1862, *passim*.

successor of Henry Clay; Lincoln in turn was presented by his friends as a conservative Whig.[53] The more stalwart Republican leaders in and out of Illinois and most of the Republican voters of the state were strongly for Lincoln. They discountenanced the overtures between Douglas and Greeley. Dr. Ray of the Chicago *Tribune* said, "Watch him (Douglas), use him, but do not trust him, not an inch." [54] Chase said that Douglas merely wanted a suspension of hostilities on the part of Republicans until his election was made sure.[55]

The result of the great debate in Illinois is well known. A sufficient number of districts were carried to control the legislature and to return Douglas to the Senate. Through the combination of complex causes we have referred to, a state which in 1854 had been so indignant at the passage of the Kansas-Nebraska Bill and the repeal of the Missouri Compromise that it elected Trumbull, the great enemy of that repeal, to the United States Senate, sent back the author of the repeal to the same body in 1858. Outside Illinois, Republican and "anti-Lecompton" Democrats were in the main successful—this result, too, being not greatly different from a real Douglas success. In northern Ohio, Republican tickets were victorious and in the southern part of that state, the less radical "opposition" composed of Republicans, Whigs, and Americans defeated the Democrats in several districts. In Indiana the legislature was carried by Republicans and Douglas Democrats, who joined in an attempt to displace Bright and Fitch and elect two new Senators. In both these states, while the personal following of Douglas was not as great as in Illinois, and despite the feeling for a lukewarm "harmony" that marked the situation in Indiana, Douglas won more and more adherents and succeeded in holding his own as the great western leader.[56]

[53] Cole, *op. cit.*, pp. 175, 176.
[54] Hollister, *Colfax*, p. 120.
[55] Chase Letters, *Rep. Am. Hist. Ass'n.*, 1902, Vol. II, p. 276; see also Beveridge, *Lincoln*, II, 557–559.
[56] A strong feeling for Douglas in Indiana in spite of the great influence of Bright is seen in the New Albany *Ledger*, Oct. 26, 1858.

CHAPTER VIII

Winning the Doubtful West, 1860

Parties and "Partyism"—1860

The Democrats were, in 1860, the national party. As would any party that presumed to exert strength in all parts of the "confederacy" —as the Union was then so often called—they suffered from serious divisions which even their traditional recognition of local and sectional interests could not prevent. There was the Buchanan administration group, strong in the Senate and in the South, and among federal appointees everywhere. There were the lower South "cotton Democrats," who demanded positive protection to slavery in the territories; there was the Douglas Democracy of the West, the largest single element and the most truly national. The convention of 1860 was to face, as the conventions of this party have so often done, insuperable difficulties in framing a platform and nominating a candidate. Having been in power for decades with little interruption, the Democrats suffered from all the evils of "partyism," and had to face unsparing criticism not only from Republicans but from factions in the party itself. Except in the Douglas group, there seemed to be little that remained of the ideals of Jefferson, of Jackson, or of the Progressive Democracy of the forties. The western Douglas Democrats often joined Republicans in roundly criticizing the administration. No reform movement of recent years has hurled stronger invective against recent "stand-patters" than was aimed at Buchanan and his favorites. Party discipline, it was claimed, pervaded every township, and there were pledged "wire-pullers" in every village. Tests of loyalty like the Lecompton constitution or the English Bill were rigidly applied. Buchanan was called "old Public Functionary." Caucus manipulation, ballot-box stuffing by importing Irish or other voters, office-creating and scrambling for public plunder—all these practices were, in 1860, ascribed to the dominant Democratic party. "Our politics have become so base that few of the better class of men are willing to seek office." "We have been using a very poor article of manhood in the manufacture of presidents for some time past." Multitudes, it was claimed, did not vote and there was a growing indifference on political questions.[1] Party allegiance sat lightly among many Democrats. They had witnessed two great independent movements—that led by Salmon P. Chase in 1854, and that led by Douglas in 1857–1860. Meanwhile the Republican party, formed along rigid antislavery lines in 1856, was as yet largely unorganized and undisciplined in the states north of the Ohio River.[2] The social groups who found themselves drawn together in the Republican movement represented diverse tendencies on many other questions. Would they hold together? Would orthodox Protestants work with radical Germans, many of whom were frankly "infidels"; would not orthodox abolitionists be shocked by those that were atheistic; would strict Sabbatarians tolerate Sabbath-breaking Germans, and temperance people coöperate with the moderate drinkers who were likewise largely German? How would old Whigs comport with antislavery Democrats, Know-Nothings with newly arrived Germans, western farmers with eastern industrialists?

We have on record a remarkable description of the make-up and social attitude of the Democratic and Republican parties in 1860, written by a keen observer of the two party conventions in Indiana in 1860.

[In the Democratic convention] the old veterans of a hundred caucus fights went at it with the system of business men and wolfish appetite. There was the dead weight of a multitude undisciplined in the Republican convention. The Democrats in convention assembled were in an incessant fermentation. The Republican convention was calm on the surface, except at special spells, as a prayer meeting. There was a good deal of the barroom element in the Democratic and some of it in the corners of the Republican convention, but the effects of Sabbath school education could be seen in more faces in the latter than the former body. The Republicans took pride in their decorum. The Democrats rejoiced in the clangor of action. Whereas the use of the very expressive term, *damn,* while not confined to either convention but sadly prevalent in both, seemed most appropriate to and was used with the most consummate skill by the Democracy, the tender word *bless* was more popular and most ingeniously handled by Republicans. Where a Democrat would propose to "damn" anybody or thing, himself, for instance, thus "damme"—the Republican equivalent seemed to be "bless us." The Democrats as a class are not alarmed at the idea or the article of whiskey or of tobacco, and chewed as if they fattened on the rankest form of the foulest weed. The Republicans were few and

[1] For severe attacks on the "partyism" of the day see, Cincinnati *Daily Commercial,* Jan. 7, 18, 23, Feb. 22, 29, 1860.

[2] *Ibid.,* Jan. 21, 1860.

far between who were prevailed upon to indulge in potations beyond a
single glass of ale, or to try the weed to a greater extent than a shy nibble
at a roll of fine cut, or an awkward pull at a mild cigar. There were exceptions, however. . . . As for pluck the Democrats had over much of it,
the Republicans an inadequate supply. The Democrats named out Stephen
A. Douglas, James Buchanan and General Joe Lane and fought over them
man to man. The Republicans said not a word of Chase, Seward, Abe
Lincoln, Bates or Fremont. They talked of the "Chicago candidate" with
bated breath. As for the coming election, the Democrats are most confident,
and, if possible, the Republicans will work the hardest. There are (in both
parties) . . . many conflicting interests. The American and old line Whig
element is not well mixed in the Republican organization and in Indiana, as
in Ohio, the party is one thing in the northern and another thing in the
southern part of the state and still another thing along the National Road.
Commencing in the Ohio river tier of counties and proceeding northward
we find the anti-slavery sentiment gaining in strength constantly.[3]

THE LOWER SOUTH BREAKS FROM THE DOUGLAS WEST

In preparing for the Presidential contest of 1860, the first task of
the Douglas leaders in the states north of the Ohio was to control
the various state Democratic conventions of the party and make sure
that these conventions approved popular sovereignty and chose
Douglas delegates to the Charleston convention. The canvas for
Douglas before and during these state conventions was perhaps the
most vigorous and active canvas for nomination in the history of
American politics up to that time. Douglas' followers in the towns,
counties, and state conventions of the West—as well as at Charleston
later—fought for him in his own vehement and impetuous spirit and
were animated by the "little Giant's" domineering and executive will.[4]
The spirit of these conventions was western and national in the
Douglas sense. Less recklessly democratic and individualistic than
the western Democratic progressives of the forties, the Douglas movement nevertheless retained much of that buoyant spirit. The western
"ism" of the moment was popular sovereignty—now eight or ten
years old with some substantial victories for freedom to its credit.
The attempts of Buchanan and such vigorous supporters as John
Slidell in the South and Bright and Fitch in the Senate "to kill off"
Douglas, only increased the crusading spirit of the westerners. There
was available, too, the charge that the administration party was a nest
of corruptionists and spoilsmen.

[3] Cincinnati *Daily Commercial*, Feb. 25, 1860.
[4] *Ibid.*, June 27, 1860.

The Illinois convention chose a delegation of influential Douglas men to go to Charleston, among them the able leader, W. H. Richardson.[5] Ohio's delegation, somewhat less ardent in its Douglas enthusiasm, was led by George E. Pugh.[6] The Democrats of the lake States, Wisconsin and Michigan, likewise supported Douglas. In Indiana, there was for some time a serious break in the Douglas enthusiasm and a bitter contest in the state convention held at Indianapolis.[7] But Jesse Bright and his seasoned Indiana politicians seemed less clever and able in dominating the situation; contested seats in the convention were generally won by Douglas men; the attempt to send an uninstructed delegation to the national convention failed after a bitter fight. Newspapers reported that there were blows in the streets of Indianapolis between Douglas and administration men; if true, this reveals Indiana politics as again asserting strong-arm tendencies.[8] The final outcome was a Douglas delegation to Charleston; here as elsewhere most of the local Buchanan leaders came over to the Douglas band-wagon. Delegates from the whole West, including the upper western, lake Democrats, went to Charleston pledged to Douglas, stopping at Washington on the way to be primed by their great leader.[9] At Charleston they proved themselves to be the dominant element in the party. First of all Douglas men, they were also nationalists of the western type, and committed to the nomination of their man, to union and to popular sovereignty; they were nevertheless devoted to western interests and were unwilling that Republicans displace them as the true representatives of their section.

As the convention opened the Cincinnati *Enquirer* issued the following challenge to the East and the South:

Opposition to the Homestead Bill and to the admission of Kansas into the Union is dictated by jealousy of the rapid growth and political power of the Northwest. The old Atlantic and Southern states see the sceptre of empire departing from their hands. . . . They vote against extinguishing Indian titles. . . . They advocate a Congressional despotism over settlers in our infant territories and favor their deprivation of the right to regulate their local and internal policy. . . . It is difficult to get their aid in an appropriation of a cent to the Western rivers and harbors. . . . The West

[5] *The Enquirer,* Jan. 5, 1860.
[6] *Ibid.,* Jan. 7, 1860.
[7] *Ibid.,* Jan. 10, 11, 12, 1860.
[8] *Ibid.,* Jan. 13, 14, 19, 1860.
[9] Cincinnati *Daily Commercial,* Jan. 18, May 5, 1860; New Albany *Ledger,* June 28, 1860; Gustave Koerner, *Memoirs,* II, 81; Chicago *Daily Times,* June 13, 1860.

(in a few years) will command peace between the East and the South in this eternal subject of dispute—slavery. The South will make a sad mistake if it neglects to cultivate a cordial understanding with the Northwest with which it is united by the strongest ties of interest; . . . upon the West she can confidently rely to repel any assaults that may be made by Eastern fanaticism upon her constitutional rights. . . . The times are propitious for the recognition of the West. If it is done at Charleston, the nominee will beyond all doubt be elected.[10]

Led in the convention by Richardson of Illinois and Pugh of Ohio and supported by delegates from the East, the Douglas men were more than a match in numbers and in tactics for the Yancey-Rhett group from the cotton states. As for Buchanan and his Federal patronage group, only Fernando Wood and the New York delegation were of any great importance. As is well known, Charleston was a scene of bitter conflicts and dramatic turns; in fact, it was the most important party convention in our history up to that time. The Democracy, as it has so often done, fought it out openly on the floor, showing then, as it has since, a refreshing lack of "political astuteness." The issues were clear. The "Alabama platform" called for a congressional code protecting slavery in the territories; the Douglas men supported the "Cincinnati platform" of 1856 which refused to recognize congressional control over slavery in the territories and left the question to the people to decide.[11]

One needs only to read over detailed accounts of the bitter fight between men from southern Ohio and Illinois on the one hand and those from Alabama and Mississippi on the other, to realize how superficial is the charge that the Douglas Democracy was "pro-southern," "pro-slavery," and "secessionist." It was for a time even more bitter against "dictatorial and rebellious southerners" than were the Republicans of the lakes and the East. These southerners were enemies near at hand to be met face to face in convention. Extreme southern men were called fanatics and fire-eaters as freely by Douglas Democrats as ever they were by Republicans. "A bolting ticket of fire eaters would help us greatly in the North and do us no injury in the South," said the enthusiastic pro-Douglas correspondent of the Cincinnati *Enquirer*.[12] Radical Republicans and Yanceyites were thought by Douglas men to be alike in their fundamental political

[10] Editorial, *The Enquirer*, Apr. 15, 1860.
[11] *The Enquirer*, Apr. 5, 1860.
[12] *The Enquirer*, Apr. 26, 1860; see also Murat Halstead "On the Circuit of the Conventions," Cincinnati *Daily Commercial*, Apr. 24, 25, 1860.

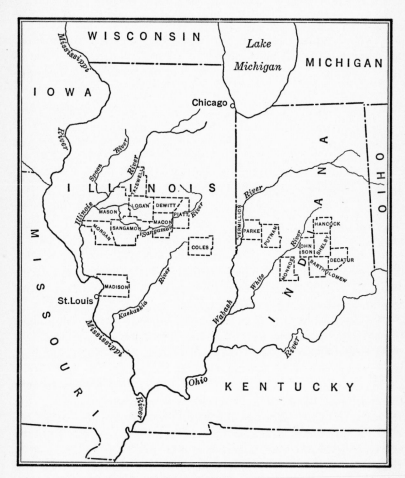

FIG. 5. THE DOUBTFUL CENTRAL COUNTIES OF ILLINOIS AND IN-
DIANA, 1854–1860

thought. "Both are in favor of legislating on the slavery question.
. . . Both are sectional parties. Many of the leaders of both desire a
dissolution of the Union." [13] "Shall a few bullying and blustering secessionists and disunionists be able to thwart the emphatic expression of
the majority of the Democratic citizens of the United States"? [14]

As the convention proceeded amid intense heat and excitement, the
cleavage on platform and candidate became more and more evident;
continued balloting revealed it all the more. The willingness of the
Douglas men to obey all decisions of the Supreme Court on matters
of constitutional law affecting slavery in the territories was not enough
to please the Yancey men.[15] Douglas' doctrine that the people of a
territory could, by unfriendly legislation, check slavery, proved to be
the bogey. Southern men saw clearly what Republicans, too, were
slowly realizing, that popular sovereignty was free-soil in tendency.
In vain did Douglas men ask for southern gratitude for their years of
"fighting southern battles" against "black Republicans" on their own
home grounds. They said they might carry "Egypt" on a platform protecting slavery in the territories but they could not face the doubtful
border counties in central Illinois, Indiana, and Ohio with a platform
offering such a boon to the southern slave-holder.[16] Delegates representing rural districts of Ohio said that a positive slave code for the
territories was more than they could carry.[17] "So help us God," said
Payne of Ohio in a spirit and tone that caused a sensation in the convention, "we will never abandon this principle" (popular sovereignty).[18] Union-loving Douglas men pled for harmony and compromise, while Yancey followers seemed glad that the time had come to
carry out threats of secession and revolution by taking actual steps.
A direct and threatening speech by Yancey was met by another
equally bold by Pugh of Cincinnati.[19] The Douglas men who at first
welcomed a mild secession movement that would rid the Democratic
party of its extreme pro-slavery group and strengthen it in the North,
later realized that the movement was becoming too threatening and
that slavery was showing a tendency to unite all southerners. Demo-

[13] *The Enquirer,* May 3, 1860.
[14] *Ibid.,* May 1, 1860.
[15] Murat Halstead, "On the Circuit of the Conventions," Cincinnati *Daily
Commercial,* May 2, 1860.
[16] *Ibid.,* May 2, 1860.
[17] *The Enquirer,* Apr. 27, 1860.
[18] *Ibid.,* Apr. 29, 1860.
[19] The speeches of Pugh and Payne of Ohio are given in full in *The Enquirer,*
May 5, 1860.

crats from Tennessee, Kentucky, and Virginia, too, had their own "Tennessee plan" that was neither pro-Douglas nor disunionist, and the New York delegation held a peculiarly uncertain and powerful position. Although the Douglas national group was much the largest, the Democratic party found itself dissolving into the three or four divisions, as did the country at large in later months. Douglas men were dismayed but held firm.

The acceptance by a majority of the convention of the Cincinnati popular sovereignty platform with an evasive Supreme Court plank, was the signal for the Alabama group to withdraw. The Democratic party, as Murat Halstead, the young but keenly observant newspaper correspondent said, "was in the agonies of dissolution"; the scene was "a spectacle of prodigious significance"; the party of Jefferson and Jackson was breaking up and there were "mutterings with white lips that the hour of revolution was at hand." [20] If the Democratic party dissolved into fragments, would not the Union also? Douglas delegates with various motives—some of them reckless western enthusiasts, some anxious office-seekers, some devoted followers who had for eight or ten years been planning to make their leader President, some with sincere belief in Union and popular sovereignty— held out to the end. They voted fifty-seven times for Douglas, but could not get the two-thirds vote necessary for a nomination; in spite of the Yancey bolt, there still remained delegates from the South and border slave states who stood out against the western candidate. As slavery had so long found protection in the national Congress in the three-fifths rule of apportionment, so now in a Democratic national convention the anti-Douglas interests were protected by the two-thirds rule. Finally, in despair, an agreement was made to adjourn to meet at Baltimore in June; thus time would be given, it was thought, for depleted delegations to be filled with "Union loving" Democrats from the lower South. Wearied and perplexed by their failure at the Charleston convention, the Douglas Democrats of the West continued to hurl violent epithets at the radical pro-slavery seceders, putting them in the same group with "abolitionist traitors" of the North.

For years the Democracy has been cursed with a restless, unhappy and turbulent set of men, who hung around southern county seats and courthouses, getting up meetings of the people. . . . (They) have been a blight and mildew upon the National Democracy. The Union and Constitution

[20] Cincinnati *Daily Commercial,* May 2, 5, 1860.

loving people of the North have been disgusted with their ignorant, brutal and domineering rule. . . . Let the (Baltimore) convention act fearlessly and boldly and let it put down southern rebellion against the principles and usages of the organization with the same spirit it has exercised against rebellion in the North and all will be well; the flag of Democracy will wave victoriously in all sections of the Union.[21]

The Alabama seceders called themselves Constitutional Democrats and likewise planned a new convention. American history at Charleston had witnessed one of those conflicts of sections and interests that so often seem insoluble. Circumstances were making the Douglas national Democracy into a semi-free-soil sectional party which to the South was as objectionable as "Sewardism" and "Black Republicanism."[22] Later, in the convention at Baltimore, bitterness between westerners and southerners again broke out, but Douglas was finally nominated; the seceders and northern Democratic office-holders nominated John C. Breckinridge of Kentucky. It was clear, even before these nominations were made, that the Chicago Republican convention must nominate a man who like Douglas would be strong in the doubtful counties of Ohio, Indiana, and Illinois. In spite of the Breckinridge defection and the further complications caused by the running of a border state "Constitutional Union" ticket headed by Bell of Tennessee, the vote of the border counties of the lower West was to be a deciding factor. Douglas' candidacy made necessary the nomination of Lincoln of Illinois. In the popular mind and at the polls—if not in the electoral college—the contest was to be between these two adopted sons of central Illinois who so truly reflected the spirit of the doubtful counties of that state, and of Indiana and Ohio, where the decision was to be made. We must, therefore, consider briefly the Republican convention.

THE LAKES AND THE EAST RELUCTANTLY ACCEPT LINCOLN

The Republican party had for some time been receding from the high ground it had held in 1856. A sectional, idealistic party in that year, it had since been attempting to become national and in so doing was becoming more accommodating and conservative. Border state men from Maryland to Missouri were becoming the instruments of this process of nationalization, and the lower West, the prime factor.

[21] Editorial, *The Enquirer,* June 15, 1860.
[22] Cincinnati *Daily Commercial,* May 7, 1860.

The leaders of this movement in the party were the Blairs, of Washington, D. C. and Missouri, Judge McLean of Ohio, H. S. Lane and Caleb B. Smith of Indiana, Lincoln of Illinois and Bates of Missouri.[23] As Douglas persisted in his attack on Buchanan, and, at Charleston, on Yancey and his group, and as California, Kansas, and Oregon were revealed as clearly non-slaveholding, and as New Mexico promised to be the same, Republicanism seemed more and more to be losing its reason for existence. The increase of immigration and the inherent expansive power of freedom were substantiating Webster's great principle of 1850—that it was needless to strive unduly to re-enact the will of God. "While politicians were quarreling about slavery in the territories, in Congress, and the press, on the stump, and in the national conventions, the people of Kansas, Nebraska, New Mexico and Washington were quietly settling it to suit themselves." [24] In southern Ohio and Indiana, it seemed better for ex-Whigs, Americans, and conservative antislavery men to join in a sort of moderate "opposition"; [25] the name "people's movement" was popular in Pennsylvania, and in this latter state also the tariff demand was to many more important than fulmination against slavery. Some Republicans, like the young Murat Halstead of the Cincinnati *Commercial,* were frank "squatter sovereignty" men.[26] There loomed up the temptation merely to strive to overthrow Buchanan partyism and corruption, to look on while the Democrats weakened themselves by division, to elect opposition men and get the offices rather than settle the slavery question. It was urged that to hold old Whigs and Americans the party would have to assume an attitude on slavery in the territories that was no more radical than that of Douglas. About 200,000 voters living in the region stretching from Iowa to New Jersey, who were indifferent on the slavery question and who had favored Fillmore in 1856, must in some way be won. To win Pennsylvania, the party of human rights and ideals would, it appeared, have to foster property through a protective tariff. The Fremont fervor of 1856 was cooling.

The course of events was to prove that no "philosophical radical,"

---

[23] E. C. Smith, *The Borderland in the Civil War,* pp. 55–58; *The Enquirer,* Feb. 5, 1860.

[24] *The Enquirer,* May 4, 1860.

[25] New Albany *Daily Ledger,* Dec. 7, 17, 1859.

[26] Halstead affirmed himself a popular sovereignty man in conversation with a southerner while enroute to the Charleston convention. Cincinnati *Daily Commercial,* Apr. 25, 1860.

like Seward or Chase, no crusader like Wade or Fremont, all of whom breathed the spirit of the East and of the lakes, was to be the candidate in 1860. As early as February, 1860, the *The Enquirer* predicted that the "Blacks" who stood for Seward would go down in convention before the "Mulattoes" who favored Bates or Lincoln.[27] The candidate must of necessity be a man who would represent the spirit of the Republican minority of central and southern Ohio, Indiana, and Illinois. In fact, he was to be a border county Whig who was a comparatively late convert to Republicanism; an able, honest, shrewd country lawyer whose greatness was only later to be revealed. Discontented Republicans were already lamenting the emphasis on success and availability already evident in a party only four or five year old—"this young and vigorous party, so ample in resources, so rich in promise, so strong in the affections of the honest masses of the people at the very outset of its career." To trim the party sails to every wind of availability for the purpose of gathering together odds and ends of defunct organizations would forfeit "the confidence of the honest masses, . . . the enthusiasm of the young men of the nation, the fidelity of the free souled Germans of the West." [28]

What stand would such a party take at Chicago on the question of slavery in the territories and who would be the candidate who could get enough votes in the doubtful counties, carry Pennsylvania with the aid of a tariff plank, and thus gain a majority in the electoral college? To eastern Republicans and those of Michigan and Wisconsin, Seward was the true man—intellectual, bold, an eastern substitute for the gallant Fremont. It is true that Horace Greeley, an ardent admirer of Stephen A. Douglas, had long been on the lookout for a more available candidate.[29] But to most Republicans in the East and around the lakes the author of the challenging words "higher law" and "irrepressible conflict" was the leader. Keen observers, however, saw clearly that there stood in the way of the nomination of this eastern man not only border county objections to the abstractions of "Sewardism," but the commanding figure of Stephen A. Douglas.[30] When the Chicago convention met, it was not long in recognizing that the lower West was going to dictate both the platform and the candidate. The convention did not boldly denounce slavery and po-

---

[27] *The Enquirer*, Feb. 16, 1860.
[28] Cincinnati *Daily Commercial*, Apr. 19, May 14, 17, 1860.
[29] *Ibid.*, Mar. 6, 1860.
[30] *Ibid.*, Jan. 1, 1859.

lygamy as twin relics of barbarism as the party had done in 1856; it did not say it was the duty of Congress to prohibit slavery in the territories; it stated negatively that Congress had no power to legislate slavery into the territories; it vexed Joshua Giddings of the Western Reserve by its hesitation in approving the classic phrases of the Declaration of Independence about inalienable rights to life, liberty and the pursuit of happiness; it favored Pennsylvania by a rather indefinite tariff plank.[31] It did not nominate William H. Seward or Salmon P. Chase. Candidates for local office in the states stretching from Illinois to Pennsylvania, and especially, delegates from Illinois and Indiana, some of whom were accused of having only a "half developed Republicanism," were working incessantly for Lincoln of Illinois.[32] It is said that when the crisis was on, "hundreds of Pennsylvanians, Indianians, and Illinoisans never closed their eyes that night." [33] Henry S. Lane of Indiana, pale and haggard, walked from one caucus room to another in Chicago hotels pleading for votes for Lincoln. Candidates for governor in the battleground states were said to be ready to resign if Seward's name headed the ticket.[34] The party, especially in Illinois and Indiana where the Douglas strength was so great, could never survive a Seward nomination.[35] Only once had Indiana failed to vote Democratic in a presidential election, and Illinois had never failed to do so. As a result of concerted pressure, Bates of Missouri and Cameron of Pennsylvania were dropped and the anti-Seward delegates coming from the middle belt of states stretching from Missouri to Pennsylvania, concentrated on Lincoln, an action which resulted in his nomination on the third ballot. With great keenness of observation a western poet and novelist says that the West of Douglas won in the Lincoln convention.[36]

The campaign of 1860 in the free West was similar in intensity to the Douglas and Lincoln canvas for nomination and to the bitter contest of 1856. Michigan and Wisconsin were conceded to Lincoln from the start. Illinois and Ohio were more doubtful; Indiana was the most doubtful of all, holding the position in the West that Pennsylvania held in the East. The importance of this western state was all the

[31] E. C. Smith, *The Borderland in the Civil War,* pp. 58, 59; *The Enquirer,* May 18, July 10, 1860; Cincinnati *Daily Commercial,* Jan. 24, 1860.
[32] George W. Julian, *Political Recollections,* p. 177.
[33] Halstead, in the Cincinnati *Daily Commercial,* May 21, 1860.
[34] Cincinnati *Daily Commercial,* May 21, 1860.
[35] *The Enquirer,* May 20, 1860.
[36] Edgar Lee Masters, *Children of the Market Place,* p. 433,

greater because of the fact that it, along with Ohio and other states, had an October election which it was thought would be an object lesson to the whole country and the outcome of which would be an indication of the probable outcome of the national Presidential contest in November. Hence efforts that one paper called super-human were made to carry the state. The vote of the central counties, especially those west and south of Indianapolis, was what each party desired and here as well as in the "Republican north" of the state, Democratic speakers of national reputation, including the impetuous Douglas himself—whose health was now visibly breaking—centered their efforts. In the central counties and in the "Democratic south," Republican speakers—for example, Carl Schurz, Thomas Corwin, and Cassius M. Clay—did the campaigning for their party. Speeches in the German language and special appeals to the Irish vote were marked features of the contest. The Germans had been enthusiastic for Seward but were now willing to take Lincoln rather than Douglas. If, by this time, Republicans were more confident of German support, the Democrats were without doubt holding the Irish vote. Indeed the Douglas movement in some places became so closely identified with this group that it was called "Irishism." [37] In Indiana, as well as in Illinois, the heavy Republican vote in the northern counties would in this Presidential contest be counted at its full strength, as it had not in legislative and congressional contests for some years. With some help from the central counties, the north of each state would pull through successfully and Abraham Lincoln would be elected President.

To all except the Germans and abolitionists it was good Republican policy to emphasize the similarities between the party of Lincoln and that of Douglas. In doubtful Indiana and Whiggish-American border counties of Ohio and Illinois, votes were much more likely to be won for Lincoln by emphasizing this likeness than by reminding voters who were lukewarm on the slavery question of such startling doctrines as the higher law and the irrepressible conflict. How could the Webster-Douglas principle of popular sovereignty be put to Republican uses and thus help to turn the tide for Lincoln? As cam-

[37] Cincinnati *Daily Commercial,* May 24, Sept. 4, Nov. 7, 1860; Indianapolis *Daily Sentinel,* Oct. 8, 1860; Indianapolis *Daily Journal,* Oct. 8, 1860; New Albany *Daily Ledger,* Nov. 8, 1860. Counties in Indiana that were especially doubtful or close in the elections from 1854 to 1862 were: Vermillion, Parke, Shelby, Monroe, Putnam, Hancock, Johnson, Bartholomew and Decatur. *Tribune Almanac,* 1854–1862 *passim.*

paign subtleties developed this very end was in some cases accomplished. Republicanism was presented in popular sovereignty garb! Readers were reminded of the Douglas-Republican entente of 1858. Let radical Germans and all Sewardites, if they pleased, vote for Lincoln on the basis of his Cooper Institute speech which made it clear that Congress could legislate to prohibit slavery in the territories; anyone could see that the Republican platform did not say that Congress actually would. Again and again the prominent Cincinnati *Commercial* placed before its thousands of readers in the lower West articles attacking "Federalism" in the territories and insisted that Republican success would not mean Federal interference in the territories against slavery, but would merely bring an end to the use of the Federal Government for proslavery purposes; that under Lincoln popular sovereignty would for the first time have a real chance to function, freed of the doubtful championship of Douglas and the Democratic party; that California, Oregon, and Kansas were free because the question had been left to the people; that the natural forces of free labor and free immigration were worth more than any Wilmot Proviso enactment by Congress. If popular sovereignty failed in any particular case to bring freedom, then perhaps congressional intervention might be resorted to. Besides, was not Douglas' willingness to abide by a decision of the Supreme Court enough to show that he himself was not a real champion of this great principle? This made him after all an interventionist and like radical southerners an interventionist in favor of slavery! Eli Thayer of Massachusetts, who had been a practical "squatter" sovereignty man in Kansas, John Sherman, S. P. Chase, and other Republicans, it was claimed, were not opposed to real or "Republican popular sovereignty." [38]

Attempts were made to prevent such extreme doctrines as Seward's "higher law" from doing their perfect work of alienating lukewarm westerners from Lincoln's party and of keeping Douglas men from voting for Lincoln. This startling phrase was deprived of any revolutionary meaning by such interpretations as the following:

[It is] quite inoffensive, it does not interfere with the obligation of oaths or the binding force of statutes, (it is) but a mere expression for that absolute excellence not embodied in written law, for that superior common law found in the consciousness of enlightened men. In this sense it is not

[38] This remarkable advocacy by Republicans of this doctrine in 1860 has apparently been overlooked by historians. The author found it best exemplified by the Cincinnati *Daily Commercial*. See issues of Apr. 25, July 12, 26. Sept. 14 (quoting *Ohio State Journal*), Oct. 16, 20, 1860.

incendiary. The irrepressible conflict need not be brutal or bloody. The revolution may be peaceful. It may be, probably will be centuries before American slavery shall be extinguished.[39]

The nomination of Douglas had of course put the administration Democrats of the West and especially the Bright-Fitch pro-southern group in a difficult position. The latter, however, in Ohio, Indiana, and Illinois, in 1860, still stood out bravely for Breckinridge for President. There were in addition thousands of "constitutionalists" who voted for Bell of Tennessee. These parties had the support of only a few papers, among them the Vevay (Indiana) *News* which stood for Breckinridge and the Vevay *Reveille* and Cincinnati *Evening Post* which supported Bell and Everett.[40] The latter paper lacked support and expired early in the campaign. Speeches for Breckinridge were made by Senators Bright and Fitch who appeared at various meetings in Indiana and Ohio, roundly charging Douglas with insatiable ambition, calling Lincoln boorish and unpolished and asserting that the Dred Scott decision gave the southerner the right to take his slave property with him into western territories.[41] These men were outspoken in their attack on Douglas, and even Daniel Voorhees of Indiana and John A. Logan of Illinois were considered lukewarm in their support of him.[42]

Republican campaign policies bore fruit. The doubtful West was won, and the course of United States history changed. Many of the central counties of Indiana and Illinois went for Lincoln and this vote, added to the large Lincoln majorities in their northern parts, made it clear that the electoral vote of these states would be carried and the Republican party put in office. Douglas, however, received the vote of the lower West as a whole; Lincoln was a close second, even in these counties; and Breckinridge and Bell received thousands of votes—in Indiana these two southern candidates together drew over 17,000 votes and in Ohio over 23,000. An eight to one vote for the Republicans in several counties of the Reserve of Ohio, along with the losses suffered by Democrats even in Ohio river counties, insured Lincoln's success in that state. In the three states of Ohio, Indiana, and Illinois Lincoln received a total popular vote of 542,804, Douglas of 462,956, Breckinridge of 26,104, and Bell of

[39] Cincinnati *Daily Commercial*, Aug. 17, 1860.
[40] Indianapolis *State Sentinel*, Oct. 23, 29, 1860; Cincinnati *Daily Commercial*, Sept. 15, 1860.
[41] Cincinnati *Daily Commercial*, Aug. 6, Sept. 11, 1860.
[42] Indianapolis *Daily State Sentinel*, Oct. 23, 1860.

22,413. The vote for the two latter candidates came no doubt from surviving anti-Douglas Democrats of a distinctly "pro-southern" type and former Whigs and Americans near the Ohio and Mississippi rivers.[43] The momentous importance of the election of 1860 in the West, an election which broke the alliance between the free West and the Democratic South, was immediately realized; whether the new alignment between West and East was to stand the strain of South Carolina's secession and of Civil War will be the subject of later chapters.

[43] *Tribune Almanac*, 1861; E. C. Smith, *Borderland in the Civil War*, pp. 69, 73-75; in Union County, Illinois, Breckinridge received forty per cent of the vote.

CHAPTER IX

DEMANDS FOR COMPROMISE AND BORDER STATE RECONSTRUCTION, 1860–1861

The secession of South Carolina and other states of the lower South threw the public mind of the North into a state of confusion and change that James Ford Rhodes describes as "chameleon-like." Amid all the shiftings of public sentiment in the critical months of the winter of 1860–1861, the lower West, though alarmed to the last degree, was more constant and consistent in its attitude than any other part of the North. In its most recent expression of political feeling the region, tied as it was to the border South by geography, kinship, and other interests and yet strongly attached to the Union, it had voted for Douglas; it had in addition cast nearly 50,000 votes for the southern candidates, Breckinridge and Bell—thus again showing a tendency much like that of Missouri, Kentucky, and Tennessee. Defeated at the polls and rankling with bitter partisan feeling against the Republicans of the Reserve, the lake region, and the abolition centers in northern Indiana and Illinois, facing political subordination in state and national affairs, it could, without being held responsible for results, urge a mild policy toward the South and could maintain with much reasonableness that it had had nothing to do with causing the crisis. Although, in the critical situation then at hand, it was, in reality, standing for its own western interests and for what it considered the welfare of the Union, it seemed to give easterners and lake-district Republicans only more convincing proof of a "prosouthern" tendency.

Its first attitude, then, was one of compromise and concession. Joined with the border slave states it attempted to bridge the chasm between the extreme North and South.[1] In Congress, men from the lower West were leaders in this movement. In the Senate there were George E. Pugh of Cincinnati, Jesse D. Bright of southern Indiana, Graham N. Fitch of the Wabash region and Douglas of Illinois. In

[1] E. C. Smith, *The Borderland in the Civil War*, pp. 134–140.

the House there were twenty-one Representatives from congressional districts lying south of the National Road or in the Wabash and Illinois valleys. Fourteen of these were Democrats; most of them were natives of the region; three had been born in Kentucky, one in Virginia, and only one of the total number had been born outside of the border state zone.[2] The spokesmen of the region in the House were—it might be said—George H. Pendleton of Cincinnati, C. L. Vallandigham of Dayton, John A. McClernand of the Springfield, Illinois, district, and John A. Logan of the extreme southern part of that state—the "Banner" Democratic district of the United States, where five out of every six persons were devoted admirers of this magnetic leader.

In the Senate, Douglas, with Crittenden of Kentucky, was most active for adjustment and reunion. A prominent member of the "Committee of Thirteen," he favored the Crittenden Compromise, popular sovereignty, a restoration of the Missouri Compromise line, or any plan of adjustment that could be agreed upon. Insisting that he himself was throwing political partisanship and consistency to the winds, he charged the Republicans with unwillingness to restore the compromise, the repeal of which had been the cause for the formation of their party. He presented a plan of his own for the settlement of the slavery question in the territories.[3] Senator Pugh of Cincinnati said that it had been the policy of the government from the first "to allow slave-holding as well as non-slaveholding states an equal opportunity for colonization and development." In an earnest plea that the Missouri Compromise should be embodied in the Constitution, he said, "I call upon you Senators from the northern and from the southern extremes to remember those of us whose homes and families are upon the border. . . . Assist us in averting a calamity that must fall chiefly upon us." [4] Though he, with Douglas, deprecated secession, his bitterest shafts of criticism were aimed at Republicans.

In the House "Committee of Thirty-three" no Democrat from the free West was given a place. The lack of such support on this committee was felt by men in the South. "I would have been glad," said Hawkins of Florida, "to have seen my friends from Ohio, Vallandigham and Cox, and Illinois, Logan and McClernand, noble and true

[2] J. A. Gurley of Cincinnati, a Republican. He was a native of Connecticut.
[3] *Cong. Globe*, 36 Cong., 2 Sess., *Appendix*, 35–41.
[4] *Ibid.*, pp. 29–33, December 10, 1861.

spirits, . . . who have stood by the South and fought her battles." [5]
But on the floor of the House such aid was by no means lacking.
Here men from the West were demanding extreme concession.
George H. Pendleton said: "Fifteen states of this union come to you
with their complaints. Hear them. They tell you they have grievances—redress them. They say they have fears for their safety. Allay
those fears, gentlemen, remove every cause of agitation." [6] John A.
Logan, himself a native of Kentucky, dwelt on the bonds of kinship
that united so many in his district to the South.

The South are our kinsmen and should be dealt with kindly. Their return from their wanderings may be looked for at some future day if our
action shall be tempered with forbearance and moderation. . . . What shall
I say to my gallant constituents when I return to them? . . . Must I tell
those gallant Tennesseeans, Kentuckians and men from different Southern
states that . . . if they should desire to visit the soil of their nativity, they
must be prepared to visit a foreign and perhaps a hostile government? [7]

While these and other men from the border free states, together
with those from the border slave states, were engaged in futile efforts
to play the parts of Clay and Webster in 1850,[8] their constituents at
home in a high pitch of excitement were likewise demanding compromise. At public meetings held throughout the winter in southern
Ohio, Indiana, and Illinois and in parts of Iowa resolutions were
passed and memorials signed which embodied almost every degree
of concession on the slavery question. These were sent to Congress,
to the various state legislatures or were printed in the newspapers.
Though the meetings were called "union meetings" and were often
asserted to be non-partisan, it is clear that they were largely composed
of Democrats. Republicans, however, often attended and approved
the action taken. The press of the region, mostly Democratic, reflected the spirit of these local meetings, as did also the minorities of
the legislatures of Ohio, Indiana, and Illinois. The attitude of the men
that constituted these minorities—so closely in touch with the strong
"conservative" districts in the south of these states—is an especially
good index of the feeling of the section on all questions that arose
during the winter.

[5] *Cong. Globe,* 36 Cong., 2 Sess., p. 36. December 10, 1860.
[6] *Ibid., Appendix,* p. 70.
[7] *Ibid.,* p. 178. Feb. 5, 1861.
[8] Most of the speeches in that invaluable series on "The State of the Union"
in the *Appendix to the Congressional Globe* for the session of 1860–1861, were
made by border state men, and many of them by Senators and Representatives
from the lower West.

In Ohio "union" meetings were held all over the state, but especially in the southern part.[9] At a great mass meeting held on February 22 at the mouth of the Big Sandy, crowds of people from four Ohio, six Virginia, and five Kentucky counties joined in an expression of the common interests of the three states and demanded concession.[10] A memorial from Cincinnati in favor of the Crittenden Compromise presented in Congress by George H. Pendleton had been signed by ten thousand citizens.[11] Editorials in *The Enquirer* left no doubt as to the "pro-southern" bent of that paper on the question of the hour.

The Missouri Compromise was a violation of the constitution . . . was all on one side and had no element of fairness . . . it did not say the South should have what was south of that line for slavery. . . . Where the character of the climate and soil of a territory would invite strife for its possession by the two classes of labor, then there should be a partition of it.[12]

It advocated making intervention by Congress constitutionally impossible. Sam Medary, the prominent Ohio editor and a "constitutionalist," seeing that disintegration threatened American society, seriously undertook the task of reëstablishing it. He founded the Columbus *Crisis* and his plan, as stated in the first number of his paper, was to bring reunion by "fraternal feeling and discussion" and on the basis of State rights.[13] His unique paper, in many respects the most restless and outspoken in the West during the Civil War, increased in circulation at a remarkable rate. So intense was the demand for concession that Democratic factions disappeared in Ohio, and Buchanan and Douglas men, meeting in a state convention, urged the Crittenden or the Border State Compromise and passed a resolution stating that "when the people of the North shall have fulfilled their duties to the Constitution and the South—then and not till then—will it be proper to take into consideration the question of the right and propriety of coercion." [14] The Democratic minority in the legislature took a similar stand.[15]

In the southern part of Indiana there was very evident willingness

[9] *The Enquirer,* Jan. 22, 1861; at Chillicothe, *ibid.,* Jan. 15, 1861; in Pickaway County, *ibid.,* Feb. 2, 1861.
[10] Columbus *Crisis,* Mar. 7, 1861.
[11] *App. Cong. Globe,* 36 Cong., 2 Sess., 70.
[12] *The Enquirer,* Jan. 4, 8, 1861.
[13] Columbus *Crisis,* Jan. 31, 1861.
[14] *The Enquirer, Columbus Correspondence,* Jan. 24, 1861; G. H. Porter, *Ohio Politics During the Civil War Period,* p. 54.
[15] G. H. Porter, *Ohio Politics,* pp. 56, 57.

to yield much to the South and there is no doubt a majority even in the northern part was strongly in favor of a very large degree of concession. It seemed that the reaction following the vote of the state for Lincoln in the previous autumn was complete. At the smaller county seats and the larger towns of the south, Madison, Jefferson-ville, New Albany, Evansville, Terre Haute, and also in the north, union meetings were held, resolutions adopted, and petitions sent to the legislature urging action.[16] This informal referendum is impres-sive in its magnitude and indicates an intense state of agitation. At a mass meeting of citizens of four southern counties of Indiana— Washington, Harrison, Crawford, and Orange—held at Hardinburg on January 11, 1861, a committee consisting equally of Democrats and Republicans, it is reported, submitted resolutions which, while ad-mitting that South Carolina and Mississippi had "acted rashly," pledged the support of the people to the Crittenden Compromise and stated:

It is our opinion that if the border free and slave states come up unitedly in favor of this plan of settlement that sooner or later the extremes must of necessity follow. . . . That it is our ardent desire that the happy relation-ship long existing between Indiana and Kentucky, socially and commer-cially, shall not be destroyed by madness or folly, but that the citizens of Indiana may always be ready to . . . defend all the rights of Kentucky as was [sic] the sons of Kentucky to come to the defense of Indiana when her citizens required defense from the scalping knife of the merciless sav-ages in the War of 1811, when Jo Daviess and his gallant companions in arms poured out their blood on the memorable plains of Tippecanoe, in common with our citizens.[17]

In Vigo County a meeting of 1,000 persons resolved that "no part of the country has a deeper interest in the preservation of the Union than the Wabash Valley, which has ever sought a market at the South as well as the North." [18]

The Democratic state convention meeting at Indianapolis on Feb-ruary 22, under the leadership of Robert Dale Owen, advocated a division of the western territory for slavery and held that an exten-sion of the limits for slaves did not extend slavery, which could only be done by importation. It called for a convention of the border

[16] *Indiana House Journal* (1861), pp. 213, 220, 236, 237, 260, 382, 385; *Brevier Legislative Reports,* Vol. IV, pp. 270, 288, 337, 344; *Indianapolis Correspondence of The Enquirer,* Jan. 22, 1861.

[17] *Indiana House Journal* (1861), p. 221.

[18] *Indiana Brevier Legislative Reports,* Vol. IV, pp. 91, 92.

states at Louisville.[19] In the state senate the minority report of the "Committee on Federal Relations" held that the aggregate of grievances which the South had sustained at the hands of the North furnished good grounds for alarm to slaveholding states and justified them in demanding concession.[20] In the House the minority, headed by Horace Heffron, an extremist from southern Indiana, adopted resolutions of a violent nature, vilifying Republicans and abolitionists and asserting that ministers of the Gospel, even, had

. . . soiled the robes of religion, disgraced decency . . . by their infamous and hellish harangues to aid in the unholy cause of bringing about contention and strife. Their whole theme has been of the wrongs of another race upon whose very form the God of creation has stamped the impress of inferiority to that of the white. We now stand . . . upon the slumbering volcano. . . . Such is the terrible condition of our country today and to this she has been brought by demagogues and fanatics until a portion of the people of the Union seek to preserve their rights by secession.[21]

Such specious argument no doubt influenced many who were not already by partisanship and interest in hearty accord with it.

In southern Illinois there was among many undoubted sympathy with secession. Several leaders in this region were conspicuous by their refusal to take an out-and-out stand for union. Local meetings went as far as to advocate actual separation.[22] The Democratic state convention at Springfield passed resolutions placing the responsibility for disunion on the sectional Republican party, maintained that the Union could be restored by fraternal feeling and that differences in institutions, industry, and modes of thought, rather than being a cause of conflict, should be a basis of lasting unity. Republicans said that this convention went further than the Democratic leaders, Douglas, McClernand, and Morris were willing to go, that it was controlled by demagogues and disappointed office-seekers of the lower orders of Democracy, who were repudiating the sentiment of Jackson, endorsing those of Calhoun and justifying treason.[23] At popular meetings in Iowa, too, compromise was urged.[24] In that state the Democratic party as a whole favored it, but was divided into fac-

[19] *Indianapolis Correspondence, The Enquirer,* Feb. 24, 1861.
[20] *Indiana Senate Journal* (1861), p. 96.
[21] *Indiana Brevier Legislative Reports,* Vol. IV, pp. 142, 143.
[22] A. C. Cole, *The Era of the Civil War,* pp. 260, 261; E. C. Smith, *Borderland in the Civil War,* pp. 138, 139.
[23] Chicago *Tribune,* Jan. 18, 1861; *Illinois State Journal,* Jan. 23, Feb. 13, 1861; Horace White, *Life of Lyman Trumbull,* p. 118; Smith, *Borderland,* p. 137.
[24] Clark, *Politics of Iowa During the Civil War,* pp. 78, 80, 81.

tions, many, as in Illinois, wishing to outdo the Douglas Democrats in yielding to the South.[25] Dennis A. Mahony of the Dubuque *Herald* took advanced ground and in some of his editorials opposed, as did *The Enquirer,* a compromise line on the ground that it restricted slavery.[26]

And what is more significant, Republicans, too, were yielding to the strain. It is well known that before the threats of an aggressive South, the whole spirit of the Republican party became more moderate and gracious. We are here concerned, however, with a tendency that went further; many of the party of Lincoln were occupying the ground of the Douglas platform of 1860.[27] Old Whigs living near the Ohio or in the "border counties" of central Indiana and Illinois again showed their willingness to concede much; and independent Republican papers like the Cincinnati *Commercial* were not willing to follow partisan leadings blindly. Some of the victorious party, satisfied now that they were enjoying the spoils of office, were ready to sacrifice principle as well as policy, and others retracted through sheer fear of the results of a vigorous course.

It was therefore no easy task which the strong-willed members of the party undertook in attempting to hold the moderates and conservatives to their duty. In Ohio, this work of "stiffening the backs of Republicans" fell mostly to men of the Western Reserve. They did not always succeed.[28] In Indiana, the trend toward moderation among Republicans was distinctly observable. The Indianapolis *Journal,* the leading Republican paper in the State of Indiana, sought earnestly to convince the South that the Republicans did not believe in Negro equality.[29] It took its place beside its rival, the *State Sentinel,* in advocating the compromise line of 1820, popular sovereignty, and the right of transit in the North for slave-holders with their slaves.[30]

---

[25] Clark, *Politics of Iowa During the Civil War,* pp. 67, 74–80.

[26] *Ibid.,* pp. 57, 58, 67–68, 75; Dubuque *Herald,* Dec. 12, 1860, Jan. 13, 1861.

[27] Statement of Gov. Dennison of Ohio, *The Enquirer,* Jan. 8, 1861; Smith, *Borderland,* p. 135.

[28] Conservative Republicans joined with Democrats in voting for delegates to the Peace Conference at Washington, *Ohio House Journal,* 1861, p. 112. James A. Garfield tried to delay action on this question, *Senate Journal,* pp. 58, 59. See also Porter, *Ohio Politics,* pp. 65, 66, 68. *The Enquirer* saw even in the intensely partisan *Gazette* a relaxation of its "spinal stiffness." As to the work of Wade and Chase, see *The Enquirer,* Jan. 26, pp. 29, 61.

[29] *The Journal,* Nov. 22, 1860.

[30] *Ibid.,* Dec. 3, 1860.

While Democratic papers complimented it for thus holding out the olive branch and returning to reason, it was accused by members of its own party of receding from the Chicago platform.[31] However, its "latter-day Republicanism" was finding much support. A meeting held in Indianapolis, February 23, called to express, "feelings of conciliation . . . especially on the part of Republicans" and composed, the *Sentinel* said, largely of men of "respectability and worth," favored the border state compromises and opposed a motion to declare confidence in Lincoln. Men in the party who believed in the "rugged issue" crowded into the meeting to disturb it and amid great confusion adopted minority resolutions opposing any declaration of policy at that time and reposing confidence in the incoming administration.[32] Another meeting of a similar kind, held in March, voted to allow slavery south of 36° 30′.[33] Among the Republicans in the legislature there were also "submissionists." [34]

In southern Illinois, in the Illinois River region, and even in Chicago, especially among the commercial classes, Republicans were weakening and coming to favor the Crittenden Compromise.[35] The Chicago *Tribune* was denounced by many in the central and southern parts of the state and by a meeting of conservative members of the party in its own city.[36] Congressman Kellogg from the Whiggish Peoria district broke with his party and attained national fame as a compromiser when he stepped forward with a constitutional amendment allowing slavery where the Chicago platform had declared it should not be.[37] Approved by northern and southern Democrats in Congress and by Democratic papers in the lower West, he was denounced by his own party.[38] The Republicans of Chicago who supported Kellogg in his defection were called by the *Tribune* "the merchants and pork packers of Chicago who desired southern trade," while at the same time the Democrats who seemed more pro-southern

[31] *Ibid.*, Dec. 1, 1860; *State Sentinel*, Nov. 8, Dec. 1, 7, 1860; New Albany *Ledger*, Dec. 4, 12, 1860.

[32] Indianapolis *Daily State Sentinel*, Feb. 25, 1861; Indianapolis Correspondence, *The Enquirer*, Feb. 24, 1861.

[33] Indianapolis *Daily Journal*, Mar. 15, 1861.

[34] *Brevier Legislative Reports*, Vol. V, p. 66.

[35] White, *Trumbull*, p. 117.

[36] *The Enquirer*, Feb. 5, 6, 17; also *Ibid.*, *Springfield Correspondence*, Jan. 19, Feb. 8, 1861.

[37] *Cong. Globe*, 36 Cong., 2 Sess., *Appendix*, 192.

[38] Chicago *Tribune*, Feb. 12, 1861.

than Douglas were the "McCormick-Times-Egypt branch of the Democratic party." [39] Even the *Tribune* was forced to admit that there were many submissionists,[40] and in Iowa there were the same indications of weakening in Republican ranks.[41]

In view of this reaction among Republicans, we may well wonder whether, had the victorious party agreed to submit the Crittenden Compromise to a vote of the people as the Democrats dared them to do, it would not have carried overwhelmingly in the lower West and by good majorities in the whole of Indiana and Illinois, if not in Ohio and Iowa. In that critical hour of our national existence, the lower West was willing to make great concessions to the South.

TRADE WITH THE SOUTH 1860–1861

The West had by the end of 1860 largely recovered from the disasters of the panic of 1857, and, with an abundant wheat and corn crop and chances of a greater demand from Europe, had hopes of a larger degree of prosperity for farmer and merchant. With the slight ripples of a "Presidential panic" which followed the election of Lincoln safely passed over, the future seemed bright, especially for the lake region which, with its eastern market, might easily be less concerned with the economic effects of secession. But the lower West was not in so fortunate a position. Since it looked to continued financial and commercial relations with the South, it could not disregard political movements that threatened those relations. Not all of its indebtedness was credited to eastern and European financiers, many southern Indiana and Illinois railroad and municipal bonds being held by the older communities in Kentucky and Tennessee. It was the trade with the South, however, and the effects that the secession movement might have on it, that caused the more grave concern.

The gradual increase in the demand from the South and in the amount of goods shipped southward which we have noted in a former chapter continued in 1860 and 1861. There was an added demand as a result of a drought and crop failure in Alabama, Georgia and parts of Mississippi. With famine threatening in these states, the demand on the free West for corn alone was estimated at 60,-

[39] Chicago *Tribune,* Feb. 16, 1861.
[40] *Ibid.,*
[41] Clark, *The Politics of Iowa,* p. 62.

000,000 bushels.[42] Even after it had seceded, the lower South purchased the grain of the region north of the Ohio—or accepted its charity. In March, 1861, Springfield, Illinois, gave 1,000 bushels of corn to the starving poor of the State of Mississippi.[43] With the growth of the secession movement the demand, as we shall see, increased still further. Almost all the supply came from southern Ohio, Indiana, Illinois, and Iowa.

The amount of corn and flour received at New Orleans in 1860 and 1861 showed an increase over the years immediately preceding; in the latter year nearly 4,000,000 sacks of corn arrived from the upper river valleys, most of it in the months before the war blockade.[44] But New Orleans' receipts from the North were no longer the best index of western trade with the South; [45] the river trade with Memphis and Nashville and the railroad traffic on the Illinois Central, the Mobile and Ohio and other roads, were becoming more important. Nashville became a great entrepôt to the drought-stricken region of Alabama and to the heart of the Confederacy.

The trade of the river cities with the South in 1860–1861 need not be recounted in detail here. Coal from Pittsburgh; whiskey, pork, and bacon from Cincinnati; manufactured goods, hay, and pork from the Wabash valley; grain, flour, and pork from southern Illinois and the Illinois River region by way of Cairo or St. Louis; and, due to the great demand, even produce from Iowa and the upper Mississippi —all this went to New Orleans, Memphis and Nashville by river in amazingly large amounts. Cincinnati had regular packet lines with New Orleans, Memphis, Nashville, the Red River, Louisville, and St. Louis, some of these lines running several steamboats.[46] On March 13, 1861, eighteen boats were loading at the wharf of this city to leave within a few days on the downstream trade.[47] Boats from Cincinnati ascended the Tennessee River as far as Florence, Alabama.[48] At times during the winter, the boats available at New Albany, Indiana, were not sufficient to carry the south-bound produce.[49] At Cairo each day from ten to twenty steamboats might be seen at

---

[42] *Hunt's Merchants' Magazine,* Vol. 43, p. 412.
[43] Indianapolis *Journal,* Dec. 18, 1860; *Illinois State Journal,* Mar. 27, 1861.
[44] *U. S. Census of 1860, Agriculture,* clvi, clvii.
[45] *Report on the Internal Commerce of the United States,* pp. 216, 218.
[46] Cincinnati *Daily Commercial,* Dec. 14, 29, 1860; *The Enquirer,* Jan. 8, 20, Feb. 2, 13, Mar. 7, 1861, *et passim.*
[47] *The Enquirer,* Mar. 13, 1861.
[48] *Ibid.,* Feb. 22, 1861.
[49] *Ibid.,* Feb. 3, 1861 (quoting New Albany *Ledger*).

the wharf, those south-bound carrying the cargoes of goods we have already mentioned and those north-bound having on board sugar, molasses, coffee, cotton, and empty barrels. Cairo and the South proved a welcome outlet for the Illinois corn crop of 1860 which was so great that corn was burned for fuel in the central counties of the state. For some time during the winter 1,000 tons of produce were shipped daily from Cairo to Memphis.[50] St. Louis, economically a unit with the river cities of the free West, became in a special sense a source of supply for the South; distance and high freights kept it from shipping as much produce to the East as did Cincinnati. Vast supplies from La Salle and Peoria on the Illinois River and from upper Iowa by the Des Moines and Mississippi went through it on their southward journey.[51] The Illinois Central Railroad was in 1860–1861 making the largest earnings in its short history; it increased the number of freight trains to take grain and pork from Chicago to the South and to relieve the vast surplus of central Illinois. One writer counted "one hundred and eighty loaded freight cars on the levee in front of Cairo—being the arrivals on the day previous, and depot and wharf stacks full." [52]

The Cincinnati *Enquirer,* speaking for thousands of people in Ohio, Indiana, and Illinois, repeatedly pointed out that the prosperity of Cincinnati and the lower West were bound up in the furtherance of southern trade, in the continued culture of cotton at the South, and slavery as necessary for that culture; it deprecated any political agitation that would disturb this reciprocal system.[53] Southern merchants who visited the city expressed surprise in finding business men "so conservative." The political strain during the winter did cause some houses, especially manufacturers, to suspend; orders from the South were cancelled; persons were thrown out of employment and soup houses opened to feed idle men and their families.[54] All this distress was to be attributable to Republicanism and to politicians who preferred to see "every merchant in the city fail and every bank suspend than do justice and pacify the South." With a large

50 *Cairo Correspondence, The Enquirer,* Feb. 13, 1861.

51 St. Louis *Republican (Correspondence), The Enquirer,* Mar. 7, 1861; *River Correspondence, Ibid.,* Feb. 24, 26, 27, 28, 1861.

52 *Statement of Mr. Arthur, Supt. of the Illinois Central, The Enquirer,* Jan. 19, 1861; also same paper, Jan. 22, Mar. 3, 9, 1861.

53 *The Enquirer,* Jan. 20, Feb. 6, 26, 1861.

54 *Ibid.,* Jan. 12, Feb. 26, Mar. 7, 1861; *App. Cong. Globe,* 2 Sess., 36 Cong., p. 29. For some time an average of 1,000 families sought relief.

southern trade in spite of conditions, more harmonious relations and the large crops of 1860 would, it claimed, bring enormous profits.[55] A report from Washington that Fort Sumter would be evacuated, made sugar and molasses importers of the city "jubilant." [56]

The New Albany *Ledger* spoke as eloquently for southern Indiana.

The question for the people of southern Indiana to determine is whether they will, to gratify a malignant partisan majority, consent to have their business destroyed and the natural markets for their produce shut up. . . . There is a great and fertile . . . region . . . embracing Kentucky, Missouri and a large portion of Ohio, Indiana and Illinois, whose people are not to any considerable extent effected by the ultraism of either of the extremes, who would in the event of the convulsion of the Republic, be drawn together by the ties of commerce, neighborhood and general coincidence of views and interests.[57]

In all this part of Indiana, as in Cincinnati, the uncertainty of political conditions and the shortage in return products from the South caused discontent and there continued to go up insistent demands to the state legislature and to Congress to take some action toward concession.[58]

The increased demand from the South during February and March was no doubt caused in part by the establishment of the Confederate Government. In the moment of its greatest self-assertion, the economic dependence of the South on the North became quite apparent. South Carolina was buying supplies for its "independent army" in Cincinnati and St. Louis;[59] an order was received from an agent of Jefferson Davis for the "finest dapple-gray horses that could be found in Ohio";[60] a steamboat passed Cincinnati carrying over one hundred tons of metal for Vicksburg to be run into cannon balls for the Confederacy,[61] and numerous agents of the seceding states bought corn in southern Indiana and Illinois.[62] A Commissary General of the Army of the Confederacy visited St. Louis and, with $500,000 to his

[55] *The Enquirer*, Jan. 4, 10, 12, 22; Mar. 8, 1861.
[56] *Ibid.*, Mar. 13, 1861.
[57] New Albany *Daily Ledger*, Nov. 21, 1860; Feb. 5, 1861.
[58] *Indiana Brevier Legislative Reports*, Vol. IV, pp. 63, 116.
[59] *The Enquirer*, Feb. 5, 1861: "Major Hayne of the South Carolina army, brother of Colonel Hayne, was in the city last week and . . . purchased in this city and St. Louis 47,000 barrels of pork, 4,000 casks of bacon and several thousand bushels of corn for the independent army." The New Albany *Ledger*, Feb. 7, 1861, thinks these amounts exaggerated.
[60] *Ibid.*, Feb. 26, 1861.
[61] *Ibid.*, Feb. 24, 1861.
[62] New Albany *Ledger*, Feb. 4, 1861.

credit in New Orleans banks, it was reported, purchased supplies for 20,000 men;[63] a boat was chartered and a full cargo of bacon, lard, flour, and corn was sent from that city.[64] It is not surprising, then, that the southern railroads were, like the Illinois Central, working overtime. The Nashville *Banner* of February 8, said:

> The amount of flour, corn and bacon which has passed through this city *en route* for the Republics of Georgia, Alabama, Mississippi and South Carolina is unprecedented. The receipts by railroad and steamboat have accumulated to such an extent already that it would test the capacity of the Nashville and Chattanooga Railroad for thirty days we are told, to carry them off, without another pound added.[65]

At Florence, Alabama, there was similar congestion; and the Memphis and Charleston stopped receiving freight for days at a time.[66]

Thus the peculiar needs of the South and the willingness of the lower West to supply them, helped to counteract the effects that political events might have in checking trade. While there was a decline in credit relations and in contracts for manufactured goods and some distress as a result, the traffic in grain products and in army supplies seemed greater than ever. Even the firing on the relief ship, *Star of the West,* in Charleston Harbor, did not produce an appreciable decline in the trade of Cincinnati with New Orleans.[67] A more serious obstacle to good relations, however, arose when on January 13 dispatches from Jackson, Mississippi, stated that the authorities of that state had ordered a battery of artillery to be placed on the banks of the river at Vicksburg to hail passing boats and order them to land for inspection. The object in reality was to get possession of the steamers *Marengo* and *Silver Wave* upon which it was thought United States ordnance was being transported to Federal posts in the South. Blank cartridges were fired; in case the boat did not land, the next gun was shotted. Boats whose business engagements did not

---

[63] *St. Louis Correspondence, The Enquirer,* Feb. 28, 1861.

[64] St. Louis *Republican* quoted in *The Enquirer,* Mar. 6, 1861.

[65] Quoted in *The Enquirer,* Feb. 15, 1861; see also Feb. 5, 13, 1861.

[66] *The Enquirer,* Feb. 24, 1861. The secession movement further affected trade by making Memphis and Nashville more important shipping points to the North. Shipments of cotton from Memphis to St. Louis, Cincinnati and to the East by the Ohio River for days and even weeks exceeded those to New Orleans. Nashville, too, began sending cotton by steamboat to Cincinnati in large quantities. *The Enquirer,* Jan. 22, 23, Feb. 14, 24, 28, Mar. 7, 1861. For the week ending Mar. 7 the total shipments from Memphis were 19,455 bales of which 6,166 were for the Ohio River, 1,240 for St. Louis and 2,700 for New Orleans.

[67] *Ibid.,* Jan. 15, 1861.

require them to stop at Vicksburg were compelled to land and pay wharfage rates.[68] Such actions as this vexed even the friends of the South in the West, brought the revolution nearer home and caused bold demands on the South for the freedom of the Mississippi. The old western tradition that the way to the Gulf must be kept clear, again stirred men's hearts and without distinction of party they spoke plainly to the South. Douglas had said early in January: "Illinois, situated in the interior of the continent, can never acknowledge the right of the states bordering on the seas to withdraw from the Union at pleasure and form alliances by which we shall be excluded from all access to the ocean." [69] In the Indiana Legislature both parties joined in a resolution which stated that interference would be considered an offense against the whole Northwest and that it would protect its commerce and its people.[70] The radical Republican *Gazette* of Cincinnati, giving undue importance to the Vicksburg incident, threatened dire retaliation. "William of Orange opened the dikes. . . . The Father of Waters has already volunteered on several occasions to teach this lesson. . . . All the lower country, if aggression is made on Northwestern rights, can be subdued by the work of a single night." [71] Insurance rates on goods for the South were raised and certain packers at Chicago refused to negotiate sales to New Orleans.[72]

But such episodes were only incidentally disturbing to the intimate trade relations. There was little danger that the Confederacy would adopt any commercial policy opposed to the interests of the free West. In fact there was a very evident intention to allay opposition to secession in that region and even to win friends for it by declaring the freedom of the Mississippi, by passing free-trade laws favoring northwestern produce and by encouraging the shipment of foreign goods to the Northwest by New Orleans rather than by New York. This alluring policy was held before the people of the lower West by Democratic papers of that region, the Columbus *Crisis, The Enquirer,* and the Dubuque *Herald,* and was very pleasing to a region where opposition to the Republican Morrill tariff was as bitter as

[68] *Ibid.,* Jan. 22, 23, 1861.
[69] *Cong. Globe,* 36 Cong., 2 Sess., *Appendix,* p. 39. Other Democrats made similar statements, *ibid., passim.*
[70] *Indiana Brevier Legislative Reports,* Vol. IV (January 14, 1861).
[71] *Gazette* of Jan. 15, 1861 quoted in *The Enquirer.* Congressman Gurley of Cincinnati uttered a similar threat. Chicago *Tribune,* Jan. 22, 1861.
[72] New Albany *Ledger,* Jan. 17, 1861.

in any part of the South.[73] In the Alabama state convention on January 25, William L. Yancey offered a resolution in favor of the free navigation of the Mississippi. He maintained that free trade should be the motto of the South . . . that the natural and commercial affinities existing between it and the Northwest should determine that an "enlarged and enlightened and friendly commercial policy" should be adopted.[74] The attractiveness of this program was felt even by Republicans north of the Ohio. The Cincinnati *Commercial* pointed out the injustice in the Morrill Tariff Bill and the bad policy of such action at that time.

Our new and supremely idiotic tariff is a great lever placed in the hands of the secessionists and they are employing it with tremendous effect to pry off the border slave states from the Union; . . . petitions must be circulated throughout the West . . . demanding the repudiation of the miserably shortsighted policy of Pennsylvania.[75]

The Confederacy had already passed an act to go into effect in March which did not materially affect the produce of the farm and left western trade generally free. This was supplemented by an act declaring the freedom of the river trade, thus dispelling all fears of unfavorable action being taken by the South.[76]

Even after the firing on Fort Sumter there was much trade with the South. There was uncertainty as to questions of local, state, and national jurisdiction on this question. Lincoln was slow to take action and such steps as were taken by local officers were resented even by union men.[77] On the other hand it seemed entirely wrong for the free West to be supplying the enemy with grain and provisions. Kentucky's peculiar position as a go-between for trade with the Confederacy added perplexity.[78] The blockade order was finally issued and arrangements were made to carry it out, but even then by smug-

[73] Columbus *Crisis,* Jan. 31, 1861 ; Dubuque *Herald,* Jan. 30, 1861 ; *The Enquirer,* Feb. 3, 1861.

[74] *The Crisis,* Feb. 28, 1861.

[75] *The Commercial* quoted in the Columbus *Crisis,* Apr. 4, 1861.

[76] *The Crisis,* Feb. 28, 1861. Bacon, pork, hams, lard, beef, wheat, flour, corn meal, barley, rye, oats, gunpowder, lead, arms, and agricultural products generally were admitted free. See also *Confederate Laws,* Feb. 28, 1861 ; *The Enquirer,* Feb. 24, Mar. 3, 1861.

[77] *The Enquirer,* Apr. 18, 1861. Two steamboats laden with powder, lead, revolvers, and cavalry accoutrements were stopped at Cairo on Gov. Yates' orders. Koerner, *Memoirs,* II, 129, 130.

[78] *Indiana Brevier Legislature Reports,* Vol. V, pp. 25, 31, 40, 93, 96, 105, 106; Indianapolis *Daily Journal,* April 26, May 2, 1861.

gling and by evasion of regulations a considerable volume of trade continued.[79]

BORDER-STATE "RECONSTRUCTION"

Compromise to preserve the Union "as it was" being the dearest hope of the lower West, should plans looking toward this end fail, the region must face other alternatives. In the distracted state of the public mind, paper schemes offering solutions of the nation's problems —schemes artificial and even fantastic in nature—were proposed in Congress and appeared almost daily in the press. Besides the main compromise schemes, there were several which had for their purpose what may be termed "reconstruction." These appealed to many persons in the southern parts of Ohio, Indiana, and Illinois. This demand was rather a feeling than a program or policy and was indefinite in its nature. It in no sense contemplated coercion and seemed to call for a readjustment of states or larger sections on the basis of geography and economic and political interests. With men everywhere calculating the value of the Union, and the lower South definitely going her way alone, there was, on the part of many, little hesitation in expressing this desire for sectional and even state autonomy. The tendency received concrete expression in certain proposals which, though never assuming the importance and absorbing the public attention that was given to the great plans of compromise, cannot afford to be disregarded. For instance, the Indianapolis *State Sentinel* advocated that Indiana maintain "a separate sovereignty." [80] Kentucky's "neutrality" is an interesting example of such a feeling in a border slave state carried to the point of definite action, an attitude in some respects as thoroughgoing as actual secession.[81]

To others who indulged in the idea of "reconstruction," it meant a dissolution of the old Union and a formation of sectional confederacies with a Federal bond of union. The historian faces difficulty when he tries to estimate these plans and this demand to cast the existing Federal-State system into a different mould. The plans gave expression to a feeling that our country was so large, our interests so multiple and diversified, our sectional needs so marked, that they would not admit of certain forms of centralization nor would they

---

[79] E. Merton Coulter, "Effects of Secession on the Commerce of the Mississippi Valley," *Miss. Valley Hist. Rev.,* Vol. III, pp. 289, 290.

[80] *The Sentinel,* Dec. 3, 1860.

[81] Smith, *The Borderland,* 277.

fit into our formal dual system that recognized only the state and the national government. In the light of the sectional divergence that is so apparent in all our history both before and after the Civil War, divergence confined to no one part but manifesting itself now and again in the East, the South, and the West, the plans of "reconstruction" offered in the crisis of 1860–1861 by Vallandigham and others lose some of their fantastic and impossible character. They may even be listed by the future historian and political scientist among the attempts to evolve a form of sectional pluralism or a regionalism better suited to our needs and more in accordance with existing facts.

To start with the best-known project, that of Clement L. Vallandigham of Ohio, one of the keenest observers of sectional tendencies in our history—his plan sought to divide the United States into four sections which were to operate by a system of concurrent majorities and balance of power. Vallandigham held that fundamental physical features and sectional differences had been disregarded by the makers of the Constitution and advocated the recognition of the North, the West, the Pacific, and the South as distinct units.[82] The West was to include the states north of the Ohio, together with the lake states and Kansas and Iowa. The author claimed that it was a reorganization of the Union for the purpose of preserving it and did not contemplate dissolution in any form.[83] The idea received some support from contributors to the press,[84] and much criticism as being altogether too bizarre and artificial.[85]

Another proposal was "Border State Reconstruction." Vague and elusive in both its provisions and authorship, it contemplated the exclusion of New England from the reconstructed Union and sought to include the border slave states and border free states of the West. Various ingenious names were offered for the proposed grouping of states: "The Northwestern Confederacy," "The Central Republic,"

---

[82] *Cong. Globe,* 36 Cong., 2 Sess., *Appendix,* 235–243.

[83] *The Enquirer,* Feb. 19, 1861.

[84] See letter in *The Enquirer,* Jan. 13, 1861.

[85] It sought to sever the ties that bound the lake states to the East. The Chicago *Tribune* said, Feb. 9, 1861: "Mr. Vallandigham can go up to the head. He has spelled down the whole class." There was, however, in the press and elsewhere a growing consciousness of economic power in the Northwest. There was resentment against merchants in the East who since the Panic of 1857 had favored the South but were with the prospect of secession again seeking western trade. "Let them," said the Chicago *Tribune,* "brood over Southern bills receivable till they become convinced that there is both a West and a South." New York *Independent,* Nov. 15, 1860, Jan. 31, 1861; *Hunt's Merchants' Magazine,* 1861, *passim.*

"The Middle Republic," the "Central United States," and the "Federal Republic of Washington." It received special attention at a time when the far South was seceding without molestation. A strong movement was going on, it was said, in the border states, to form a unit on both sides of the Mason and Dixon Line including the states of the Northwest, Pennsylvania, and New Jersey on one side and Delaware, Maryland, Virginia, North Carolina, Tennessee, Kentucky, and Missouri on the other.[86] Another report said that the New England states were to be invited to stay out and perhaps Michigan and Minnesota unless they revoked their abominable "isms" of freedom. Western New York, northern Ohio, and northern Illinois would have a tight squeeze to get into the reconstructed Union. Some of the leaders said that they were not particular whether the cotton states united with their central republic or not at first. Reliance was placed on the northern Democracy.[87] A meeting at Nashville, Indiana, on January 7, resolved that if the North failed to make concessions to the South, or if the South rejected them and they were dissolved, "we are in favor of forming a Central Republic composed of the middle and conservative states." [88] Resolutions with similar objects were adopted in meetings held in small towns here and there in Indiana; Democratic papers in southern Ohio and Indiana gave much space to the propaganda and conventions of that party in Indiana and Illinois called for a meeting at Louisville, Kentucky, with, it was claimed, some such view in mind.[89]

If it was easy for restless border state Democrats to devise paper schemes for new republics, it was just as easy for Republicans to assert that all such programs were merely cloaks to cover attempts of southerners to unite the border free states with the southern Confederacy. No doubt some aggressive and over-enthusiastic southern leaders, believing in the expansive power of slavery and accustomed for two decades to think along imperial lines, calculated the sphere of influence that their system might exert and indulged in extravagant dreams. As far back as Calhoun's time they had cherished the idea of a permanent alliance of a large part of the Northwest with the cotton South; Douglas incurred the ill-will of southern men

[86] Chicago *Daily Tribune,* Dec. 22, 1860.

[87] *Ibid.,* Dec. 29, 1860; *The Independent,* Jan. 3, 1861; *The Enquirer,* Jan. 15, 1861.

[88] New Albany *Ledger,* Jan. 17, 1861.

[89] *Indiana House Journal,* 1861, 260; *The Enquirer,* Jan. 17, 22, Mar. 6, 1861; Indianapolis *Sentinel,* Mar. 6, 1861.

because more than once he did not work in harness with them. During the first days of the secession movement, Jefferson Davis seems to have had a vague hope of northwestern coöperation. Rumors of a "conspiracy" appeared here and there in the papers. The offer of free trade to the upper Mississippi valley, it was thought, would be an inducement. The Louisiana House of Representatives invited southern Indiana and Illinois to form a pro-slavery state and join the South.[90]

But we search in vain for a substantial basis for these hopes. It is true that older pro-slavery Democratic leaders in the lower West, certain defeated candidates of the rougher sort, and the people themselves, here and there, had given and were now giving some encouragement to the South. G. W. Jones of Dubuque who, since his failure to hold his seat in the United States Senate because of the growth of Republicanism in Iowa, had been provided with a post at Bogota, wrote to Jefferson Davis pledging the support of his family and "hosts of other friends" in the West.[91] Sam Medary's paper at Columbus boldly asserted that the West would set up for themselves or ally with the South.[92] It is well known that Senator Jesse D. Bright of Indiana wrote a letter to Jefferson Davis regarding the use of a new brand of fire-arms. Lew Wallace, a prominent young Democrat of Indiana, is responsible for the statement that the older Democratic leaders in that state held a meeting in Indianapolis, planned to "go with the South" and were ready to offer him, as a Democrat with military experience, leadership in the movement.[93] In at least two public meetings in the lower West the plan was favored. At one held at Cannelton, Perry County, Indiana, January 1, 1861, and at another in Washington County, resolutions were adopted stating that the commercial, manufacturing, and agricultural interests

[90] *The Enquirer,* Feb. 22, 1861. For unconvincing material on the whole question of this proposed union see Illinois *State Journal,* Feb. 6, 1861; Chicago *Tribune,* Feb. 12, 1861; R. D. Owen, *The Future of the Northwest* (pamphlet, 1863), p. 8; *Cong. Globe,* 36 Cong., 2 Sess., *Appendix.*

[91] J. C. Parish, *Life of G. W. Jones,* p. 60.

[92] Columbus *Crisis,* Feb. 7, 1861; Senator Lane of Oregon had said in the Senate, "I look to see if a dissolution takes place, the day when every one of those great Northwestern States shall become a part of that Southern Confederacy." *Cong. Globe,* Dec. 19, 1860, p. 144.

[93] Lew Wallace, *An Autobiography,* pp. 258-260. However, the sweeping report of the Indianapolis correspondent to the Chicago *Tribune,* Jan. 14, 1861, that a concerted movement in Indiana was designed to "drag Indiana into the Southern Empire," that the militia was being enrolled and the "hardest kind of Democrats were being commissioned as Colonels and Captains" was no doubt a great exaggeration.

of the region required that the people could not consent that the Ohio River be the boundary line between the South and the North and that if one were drawn, "that line shall be found north of us." [94] But such words have, after all, a hollow sound. For Indiana and Illinois or any part of them to secede when even Kentucky remained "neutral" and Tennessee and Missouri were for a long time in doubt as to their action, was beyond the realm of possibility. The lower West was to play a unique rôle in the Civil War, but it was to do so in its own name and not as a part of or an ally of the South.

[94] New Albany *Ledger,* Jan. 7, 1861; *Indiana Brevier Legislative Reports,* Vol. IV, p. 5. This sentiment was practically approved by *The Ledger* itself, Jan. 12, 1861; *Daily State Sentinel,* Feb. 26, 1861.

CHAPTER X

Would the Free West Fight to Preserve the Union?

As it became clear that compromise and "reconstruction" were to be of no avail, the dread question of coercion loomed. But there was throughout the lower West the bitterest opposition to the use of force to maintain the Union. The idea of shedding blood to preserve national integrity was abhorrent, and there was intense opposition to any form of military preparation. Believers in preparedness, like the Republican governors Dennison of Ohio, Morton of Indiana, and Yates of Illinois, speaking for the less hesitant Republicans of the northern parts of these states, had urged upon their legislatures the need of improvement in their militias, which at the time compared very unfavorably with the organizations in some of the eastern states. Bills were accordingly introduced in the various legislatures— usually by Republicans from the districts near the lakes—having such objects as the enrollment of the militia, its more adequate organiza- tion and discipline, provision for regular military funds, the collection of state arms and their concentration in the hands of the executive. These bills and such other coercion sentiment as was receiving ex- pression aroused intense feeling in southern Ohio, Indiana, and Illi- nois. Democratic leaders, who, after Sumter, joined the war party, at this time allied with partisan demagogues and extreme "peace men" in crying out against coercion with greater vehemence even than attended their demands for compromise. Douglas said in the Senate, "War is disunion, certain, inevitable, irremediable; I am for peace to save the Union." [1]

This sentiment was repeated by George H. Pendleton and C. L. Vallandigham,[2] and Democratic papers from Cincinnati to Iowa took the same stand. Gratitude once more welled up toward the South and again and again the tradition, harking back to the River Raisin, Tippecanoe and the Battle of New Orleans, that the Northwest was

[1] *Cong. Globe,* 36 Cong., 2 Sess., *Appendix,* 35.
[2] *Ibid.,* 71, 243; *The Enquirer,* Jan. 20, 31, 1861.

the child of the South and owed its preservation to that region, received expression in such appeals as this:

Abolition New England opposed the War of 1812 and gave comfort to the enemy. Her clergy, her orators and her dominant political party sympathized with the Briton and Indian and lamented the fate of the latter as they now do that of the African. . . . It would indeed be an inglorious spectacle to see Ohio and the West . . . following in the footsteps of New England in a crusade against Kentucky and the slave-holding South, letting loose upon them a black population more bloody and ferocious than that from which their gallant sons saved us in a time of supplication and need.[3]

The Columbus *Crisis* maintained that through peaceable pressure only and perhaps only after years the "last Pleiad" must and would return.[4] The Indianapolis *Sentinel* said that if the South could not be reconciled to the Union, there must be "two or more confederacies" and urged a united Democracy in the North to prevent coercion and the horrors of civil war.[5] The New Albany *Ledger* opposed the militia bills and the "war and coercion" policy of the "despotic majority north of the National Road." [6] Iowa papers made similar statements.[7]

The Democratic state conventions in Ohio, Indiana and Illinois, the minorities in the legislatures of those states and the local "union" meetings through the lower West usually added to their resolutions demanding compromise, others vigorously denouncing coercion. Civil means only could rightfully be used to check secession.[8] In the legislatures, the opposition of the men from southern Ohio, Indiana, and Illinois to the militia bills was so strong that little headway was made until after the firing on Ft. Sumter. In Ohio, Democratic members unsuccessfully opposed the bills that such "stalwarts" as James A. Garfield of the Western Reserve and other Republicans favored, the Representatives and Senators from Cincinnati being especially strong in opposition.[9] In Illinois, where the message of Governor Yates on the subject had been very urgent, the militia bill which had been

---

[3] *The Enquirer*, Jan. 20, 24, 1861.
[4] Issue of Mar. 7, 1861.
[5] Issues of Dec. 22, 26, 1860.
[6] Issue of Jan. 30, 1861.
[7] Clark, *Politics of Iowa during the Civil War*, p. 88.
[8] *Indiana Brevier Legislative Reports*, IV, 44, 45; *Indiana Senate Journal*, 1861, p. 95; *Springfield Ill. Correspondence to the Enquirer*, Jan. 20, 1861.
[9] *Ohio Senate Journal*, 1861, pp. 30, 81; *Ohio House Journal*, 1861, pp. 454, 469, 470, 486.

introduced by a Senator Applington from the northern tier of counties was so strongly opposed by Democrats from the southern part
of the state and by some Republicans—who in view of the "agitated
and equivocal state of the country thought no action should be taken"
—that it failed completely.[10]

In Indiana, on the proposals to effect a complete reorganization of
the militia and a concentration in the hands of the Governor, the
warmest support, as in Ohio and Illinois, was from the northern
Republicans and the greatest opposition was from southern Democrats.[11] A man named Wolfe in the State Senate and a Horace
Heffron in the House representing Ohio River constituencies, led
the attacks. In the contest there was involved also the decennial conflict between northern and southern Indiana over the question of
legislative apportionment, the census of 1860 here, as in Illinois,
being clearly in favor of the Republican North. It was claimed that
the successful Republicans were attempting to gerrymander the state,
and they were admittedly "putting the rowels into the Democratic
party pretty strong." The most reckless language was used in the
debates on the militia and apportionment bills. The Democrats, falling back on the effective recourse in Indiana legislative battles—a
minority bolt—caused no quorum, prevented all legislative action,
and threatened to hold out even "if heaven fell." The Republicans
capitulated and even Governor Morton was forced to beg his party
to defer all action on the obnoxious militia and apportionment bills
in order to pass the necessary appropriation measures of the session.[12]
Nothing was done toward military preparation until after the firing
on Ft. Sumter.

Less weight should be attached to extravagant threats against
coercion that came mainly from intense partisans and discontented
placemen deprived of office by the election of 1860. The people "north
of the National Road" were treated with language that differed in
no respect from that accorded northern abolitionists by the "fire-
eaters" of the South. There were loud challenges that the lower
West would come to the aid of the South in case force were used
against her—no doubt gaining currency by the supineness of the

[10] *Illinois Senate Journal,* 1861, pp. 40, 68, 645; A. C. Cole, *The Era of the
Civil War,* p. 259.

[11] *Indiana Senate Journal,* 1861, pp. 72, 304, 305, 518, 667; *House Journal,*
pp. 630, 846; *Brevier Legislative Reports,* IV, 148, 156, 342, 348, 350.

[12] *Indiana Brevier Legislative Reports,* IV, 345, 342, 348; *Indiana Daily
State Sentinel,* March 9, 1861.

Buchanan administration as well as by Republican indecision. To take these reports at their face value would be unhistorical; to disregard them, equally improper. In the most extravagant bravado, the superior prowess of the lower West against the "abolition Myrmidons" of the lake region was asserted. Even a moderate like David Tod of Ohio—afterward a war Democrat—declared that if the Republicans attempted to cross the Ohio for the purpose of coercing the South, they would find the two hundred thousand Democrats of Ohio in front to oppose them.[13] It was stated by Democrats from southern Illinois in the State Legislature and the "treason" state Democratic convention that their part of the state would offer similar resistance and that only by passing over the "dead bodies of the gallant sons of Egypt" would the marching hosts of the Chicago region be able to reach their enemy in the South. If the South invaded the North, moreover, it would be met by a "wall of fire."[14] Nor were the loud talkers of Indiana willing to be outdone by this Ohio and Illinois bravado. Democrats from the south of that state said in their minority resolutions offered in the House of Representatives:

It would become subversive of the very spirit of liberty and of natural right to attempt by the strong arm of the Federal power backed up as it would be by the army and navy to coerce or compel a state to remain an integral part of a government they desire to separate from. . . . We believe . . . we speak the sentiments of more than one hundred thousand of the freemen of Indiana that we will not assist in the scheme, that we will not stand idly by, but remembering the illustrious example of our fathers, fight to keep the fires of equal rights and justice and liberty burning.[15]

Republicans from the North charged that the spirit of treason breathed through these words. In the State Senate, too, the threat was made that the Democrats would "meet the Republicans at Philippi." Heffron representing sentiment along the Ohio River said in a grandiose manner that in case the President should go south with an army to enforce the laws, he would prefer to leave the hearth-stone of his father's house, would do as De Kalb, Lafayette, and Kosciusko did and become a private in the armies of the South rather than a commander-in-chief of a northern army.[16] These words left much to ex-

[13] Porter, *Ohio Politics during the Civil War*, p. 55.
[14] *Weekly Illinois State Journal*, Jan 16, 30, 1861; Cole, *The Era of the Civil War*, p. 273. J. L. D. Morrison and a Mr. Green, a representative of Massac County, were the most outspoken.
[15] Presented Jan. 31, 1861, *Indiana Daily State Sentinel*, Feb. 1, 1861.
[16] *Ibid.*, Feb. 4, 1861.

plain when a few months later Governor Morton offered this man a command in the Indiana troops.

Moreover, during the early months of the winter, it seems evident that there was no general realization of the need of forceful measures even in the lake region. We have seen that in the early stages of the secession movement many Republicans of the West were disposed to acquiesce in it. Their motives were, however, quite different from the social, economic, and partisan interests which influenced the section contributory to the Ohio and the Mississippi. To some Republicans of the lake region, it seems, secession was welcome as the fulfillment of a desire which had been cherished ever since abolitionism first felt moral aversion to a union with slave-holders; to others it offered promise of benefits to be received from the national government which the South had so long prevented; to others the difficulties of any other course than compliance with secession seemed to weigh. For instance, in Ohio, peaceable secession was strongly endorsed by Republicans in the southern part of the state and by some of the abolitionists of the Reserve. The Cincinnati *Commercial* in January admitted that the people were no longer unanimous for the preservation of the Union and favored giving peaceable secession a fair trial.[17] *The Press* of that city pointed out the intermittent economic distress that was sure to accompany an unstable union of sections and maintained that the trade of Cincinnati with the South would increase after a peaceable secession.[18] It said on February 4:

The Union has ceased to exist. . . . The North has ceased to expect that the Union can be preserved. . . . A separation of the sections is peace, the creation of that mutual respect which the people of independent nations secure for each other, the emancipation of trade from all connections with political opinions.[19]

In Indiana the Republican Indianapolis *Journal* stood on the same anti-coercion ground occupied by its Democratic rival *The Sentinel* when it said: "Let the two, three, or four states which are bent on disunion go out. . . . The people of the North will never raise or use an army to force any state to stay in the Union. . . . We can imagine no evil equal to an American civil war." It suggested a commission to settle the question of the debts and common property of

[17] G. H. Porter, *Ohio Politics*, p. 50.
[18] *Ibid.*
[19] Cincinnati *Press*, Feb. 4, 1861 quoted in the Indianapolis *Sentinel* Feb. 5. *The Sentinel* adds: "A Republican paper coolly estimates the blessings of the Union and considers that trade would be benefited by separation"!

North and South. Like the *Sentinel* it gave several columns to Robert Dale Owen's letter in favor of allowing the southern states to depart and deprecating a "baptism of blood" and was complimented by its contributors for its "humanitarian" attitude. The editor's fear of uncompromising Republicanism almost reached the point of distraction.[20] In Illinois and Iowa many Republican papers were in the early winter months outspoken in favor of separation. The Chicago *Tribune* said that if the Union was to be dissolved, a bloodless separation was to be coveted and maintained that by it the North could carry out vast plans of improvement which the South had hindered.[21] The Ft. Dodge (Iowa) *Republican* said it was best to let South Carolina go out and "make her stay," and the Keokuk *Gate City* said, "We shall be stronger in 1870 without the South than with it, however hard the separation may be." [22]

THE GROWTH OF COERCION FEELING IN THE UPPER WEST

As the winter advanced, however, and the secession movement became more ominous, the lake region became conscious of a strong attachment to the Union, and in its cities and towns there developed a willingness to use coercion that was greater than in any part of the West. Having voted so strongly in favor of Lincoln, holding closely to the Chicago platform, and sure to play an important rôle in the next administration, that section felt that it was being deprived of the fruits of its victory at the polls. The danger of isolation should the nation dissolve into fragments and the desire for the aid of a strong national government in further development influenced many to cling to the Union. Politically and economically coming into its own and shown by the census of 1860 to possess greater expansive energy than any part of the country, the whole region stretching from Lake Erie to upper Iowa came to have in the crisis of the winter of 1860–1861 a more decided and less yielding state of mind. The bonds that tied it to the East helped to strengthen this attitude. The distance from the possible stage of civil conflict and the partisan animosity which this "cradle of Republicanism" felt for the South made it possible for stalwarts and irrepressibles to urge a policy of facing the rugged issue and war without weighing too heavily the horrors it

[20] Indianapolis *Daily Journal,* Nov. 10, 15, 19, Dec. 22, 1861; *Daily State Sentinel,* Nov. 28, 1860; Foulke, *Morton,* II, 86.

[21] Issues of Dec. 1, 8, 1860.

[22] O. B. Clark, *The Politics of Iowa,* p. 56.

would entail. Then, too, a disinterested love of the Union and a willingness to fight for it as having a God-given mission, and the hope of democracy, were elements in this lake region fanaticism, as it was called by people living south of the National Road.

Conspicuous among the "rugged issue" men of the upper West were Benjamin Wade and Joshua Giddings of the Western Reserve and Senator Zachariah Chandler of Michigan. The last named man opposed sending commissioners to the Peace Convention and his famous words "without a little bloodletting this Union will not . . . be worth a rush" had considerable influence.[23] Salmon P. Chase opposed all "concessions of principle." [24] Representative Edgerton of northern Ohio said: "Peace is not the first interest of a people. . . . Better encounter war, than suffer the sense of justice and humanity to die out of the hearts of a people." Owen Lovejoy of northern Illinois held that the government had the right to maintain itself.[25] The western members of the Committee of Thirteen, Wade of Ohio, Grimes of Iowa, and Doolittle of Wisconsin were determined that the Republican party oppose compromise.[26] The Chicago *Tribune* which had earlier reëchoed the New York *Tribune* in advocating peaceable separation did not long hold to such a course; and that city and the surrounding country became the strongest outpost in the West for the coercion forces.[27] Republicans of Democratic antecedents were in many cases more energetic in facing the crisis than those who had belonged to the Whig and Free-Soil parties.[28] This is true of Chase, Governor Morton of Indiana, John Wentworth of Chicago, and Lyman Trumbull and Gustav Koerner of the Belleville district in southern Illinois which constituted, together with the German Republicans of Cincinnati, a sphere of influence in the lower West where

[23] J. F. Rhodes, *History of the United States,* III, 307, quoting the Detroit *Free Press,* Feb. 20, 1861.

[24] Chase Correspondence, Am. Hist. Ass'n. *Report,* 1902, Vol. II, p. 295.

[25] *Cong. Globe,* 36 Cong., 2 Sess., *Appendix,* 85, 129.

[26] J. F. Rhodes, *History of the United States,* III, 151–181 *passim.*

[27] Chicago *Tribune,* Dec. 22, 1860, Jan. 3, 1861. Frequent charges were made by the press of the Ohio Valley that the speculators and politicians of Chicago and Milwaukee were opposed to compromise and in favor of forcing the issue for the sake of the development of these cities and from a desire to ruin the rival cities of St. Louis and Cincinnati in the lower Northwest. (New Albany *Ledger,* Jan. 30, 1861). Lake shore lots and northwestern lands would profit by the depopulation of the border region (Cincinnati *Enquirer,* Jan. 31, 1861), and war would bring a higher price for Chicago produce. (*Ibid.,* Feb. 5, 1861) Lincoln at Springfield was being besieged by this class of men, it was claimed.

[28] Gustav Koerner, *Memoirs,* II, 113.

the more radical upper region could hope for support. Governor Morton's Republicanism was much more vigorous than that of many old Whigs of Indiana. John Wentworth of the Chicago *Democrat,* striving to revive the rugged spirit of the Jacksonian Democracy, pretentiously warned the South that everyone who attempted to subvert the Union would be hanged. "We have no feeling in this matter? By the Eternal, the Union must be preserved. . . . The chivalry will eat dirt. . . . They will back out." [29] Gustav Koerner, though always more conservative than Carl Schurz of Wisconsin, was holding out a high standard for the Germans of southern Illinois and St. Louis, and events were to prove that there were many Douglas Democrats who needed but the call to arms and the appeal of their great leader to put them in the coercion ranks. This finally came with the attack on Ft. Sumter; it brought to an end the several months of indecision under Buchanan and Lincoln that had been such a strain on men's nerves. It aroused the upper West almost to a man. Our special problem is, however, the reaction of the lower West in this sudden turn of events.

The Lower West and the Call to Arms (April–May, 1861)

No doubt the most important manifestation was the remarkable response which even this conciliatory region made to the call.[30] Douglas went on his mission through Ohio, Indiana, and Illinois, for the first time in many months speaking in unmistakable terms and calling men to the defense of the government and making his unique confession of having himself leaned too much "toward the South." [31] His influence together with that of John A. McClernand brought many in southern Illinois and in all the districts that had cast a large Douglas vote in 1860, to active support of the administration. In Iowa, N. B. Baker and other Democratic leaders did not hesitate a moment.[32] In Indiana, Lew Wallace, Ex-Governor Joseph A. Wright, and Robert Dale Owen took a similar stand. The great Douglas newspapers, the Cincinnati *Enquirer,* the Indianapolis *Sentinel,* and the *Illinois State Register* seemed willing to follow their leader. To read in *The Enquirer* such words as, "If war comes, our sympathies will be with the stars and stripes" and "We owe allegiance to the Federal

[29] Chicago *Democrat* quoted in the *Indiana State Sentinel,* Nov. 13, 1860.
[30] E. C. Smith, *Borderland in the Civil War,* pp. 168–177.
[31] Allen Johnson, *Stephen A. Douglas,* pp. 478–485; A. C. Cole, *Era of the Civil War,* p. 261; Smith, *Borderland,* pp. 179, 180.
[32] B. F. Gue in *Annals of Iowa,* I, 86, 87.

Government and are in duty bound to sustain, protect, and defend it without any reference whatever to the person who may administer it" and to find that it supported the war bills in the Ohio Legislature, makes us wonder at its later attitude.[33] In the legislatures of Ohio, Indiana and Illinois, which were called in special session, partisan differences seemed for the moment almost blotted out, and vigorous military measures were passed.[34] Possible trouble was perhaps forestalled by the appointment of many Democrats to high military command, among them Grant and McClernand of Illinois, Wallace of Indiana, and Baker and Tuttle of Iowa. Even the Horace Heffron of southern Indiana who, as we have seen, had threatened to join the South, was offered an appointment by Governor Morton, not without objection being raised and suspicions expressed as to his loyalty.[35] In the state election about to occur in Ohio the Republicans appealing to Democratic Unionists dropped their party name and nominated David Tod for Governor. Thus, much of the Douglas following, many of them urged by disinterested patriotism, others won by the traditional western battle-cry for an open Mississippi, and others with an alacrity that left room for doubt, joined the Republicans of the lakes and rallied to the cause of the Union. The wave of martial feeling spread toward the Ohio and, even more than the great radical movement of 1854, was sweeping differences away and producing a spirit of unity never to be equaled in the later years of the war.

But the sweep of such a movement may easily be over-estimated; and this in fact has been. The traditions and interests of the lower West prevented any such easy adjustment. Volunteers, it is true, seemed to come as readily from this region as from Chicago, but this fact is not conclusive of the feeling among the masses. Fears of invasion from the South made many willing to arm, but mainly for home defense rather than coercion. Many conversions were superficial.[36] It is clear that, from this time until the end of the war, the records that we have showing public sentiment here—and many of them have been lost or intentionally destroyed—do not tell the whole truth. Fears of being mobbed by excited Republicans and by the soldiers now being recruited in almost all the towns kept many from

[33] *Indiana Daily State Sentinel*, April 17–30, *passim; Illinois State Journal*, April 17; *The Enquirer*, April 17, May 18, 1861.

[34] *Ohio House Journal*, 1861, pp. 526, 600; *Indiana Brevier Legislative Reports*, V, 19, 35; *The Enquirer*, April 25; *Illinois Weekly State Journal*, April 17, 1861.

[35] *Indiana Brevier Legislative Reports*, V, 342, 346.

[36] W. H. Russell, *My Diary North and South*, p. 330.

opposing what they did not approve. There appeared, especially in the inland towns and rural districts of southern Ohio, southern and western Indiana, southern Illinois, and along the Missouri border in Iowa, a popular sullenness that is at once the interest and despair of the student of this peculiar region.

There was, even at this time, open discontent and opposition. It must here be repeated that Breckinridge and Bell had received nearly 50,000 votes in this region and that Douglas was still distrusted by a number of Democrats now as ever more "pro-southern" than he. He even faced defection in his own following and his early and unfortunate death seemed to release others from their allegiance. There were among these factions many leaders who resisted the call to arms, not afraid even in the thrilling days after Sumter to speak for the sullen thousands who opposed the course of events. They form the nucleus of a small Peace Party as early as the year 1861.

Among those most prominent were Sam Medary of Columbus, Vallandigham of Dayton, Daniel W. Voorhees of Terre Haute, Jesse D. Bright of Madison, Indiana, Ex-Governor John Reynolds of Belleville, Dennis Mahony of Dubuque, Iowa, and LeGrand Byington, also of that state. Close scrutiny of the career of John A. Logan seems to establish the fact that for some time after Sumter he belonged to this group. It is difficult to determine what newspapers really supported this movement. Those most nearly identified were the Columbus *Crisis,* the Dayton *Empire* and the Dubuque *Herald,* though the more influential Democratic papers that spoke for the lower West, like *The Enquirer* and the Indianapolis *Sentinel,* often contained signed articles and even editorials that reflected this extreme tendency, and in later months gave direct support to it.

C. L. Vallandigham on April 17 issued a public statement "for the Republican press" in which he said: "I know that . . . in a little while the sober second thought of the people will dissipate the present sudden and fleeting madness and will demand to know why thirty millions of people are butchering each other in a civil war." [37] D. W. Voorhees made a speech at Greencastle, Indiana, on April 13, in which he said he would not vote one dollar, one man, or one gun to

---

[37] *The Enquirer,* April 20, 1861. He added: "But meanwhile should my own state be invaded . . . then I will aid in defending her to the utmost extremity. As to myself . . . no threats of violence have been made to me personally. And now let me add for the benefit of the cowardly slanderers of Cincinnati and elsewhere who libel me daily . . . that if any man have any business with me, I can be found at my home or on the streets of Dayton."

make "a party war on the South." [38] Senator Bright was charged by both Democrats and Republicans in the Indiana Legislature with southern sympathy and by resolution in the United States Senate was asked to declare his seat vacant.[39] Railroad trains in southern Illinois had to be guarded by soldiers from possible attack by daring sympathizers with secession, and William H. Russell of the London *Times,* who passed through that region in June, was impressed with the signs of disaffection.[40] The home district of John A. Logan might well be so disposed. He himself was for some weeks allied with Voorhees in resisting the appeal of Douglas. His dramatic change of front later in the year brought bitter denunciation from constituents in southern Illinois and was thought by many hardly to bear the grace of an eleventh hour conversion.[41] It seemed to take the combined influence of Douglas and McClernand, the promptness of Governor Yates and General Steele of Chicago in sending troops to Cairo, and finally the weight of Logan's tardy action, to prevent civil conflict in "Egypt." [42] In Iowa, the Iowa City *State Democratic Press* on April 17, maintained that Lincoln's call for troops was unconstitutional and that no honest man's allegiance bade him kill his brothers "in a republic of coördinate sovereignties." [43] The repeated statements in the records that large numbers of individuals from the lower West joined the southern armies cannot be passed without comment. There was, no doubt, some of this.[44] Already the mysterious Knights of the Golden

[38] New Albany *Ledger,* April 13, 1861 (quoting Terre Haute *Journal*) ; *Cong. Globe,* 38 Cong., 1 Sess., Part II, 1544.

[39] *Indiana Brevier Legislative Reports,* V, 151, 253; *Senate Journal,* Special Session, 1861, p. 299.

[40] W. H. Russell, *My Diary North and South,* pp. 342, 350, 351; U. S. Grant, *Personal Memoirs,* p. 244; G. F. Dawson, *Life of Logan,* pp. 16, 17.

[41] Gustav Koerner, *Memoirs,* II, 134; U. S. Grant, *Personal Memoirs,* p. 245. Logan's apology in his *Great Conspiracy,* pp. 265–275, is inconclusive as is also the defense of his biographer G. F. Dawson in his *Life of Logan,* pp. 13, 14, 288, 292. Logan seems to have been closely in touch with certain peace men in Congress for some time after Sumter. Cincinnati *Daily Commercial,* October 7, 1862; see also A. C. Cole, *Era of the Civil War,* p. 262.

[42] Koerner, *op. cit.,* II, 124; Cole, *op. cit.,* p. 262.

[43] It later followed Douglas but kept its columns open for articles by LeGrand Byington, an anti-coercion Democrat, and other anonymous articles of an inflammatory pro-southern tone. Iowa City *State Democratic Press,* April 24, June 19, 1861.

[44] Cole, *op. cit.,* pp. 260, 262; U. S. Grant, *Personal Memoirs,* p. 244. Among the Archives of Iowa at Des Moines there are letters to Governor Kirkwood indicating hostile action in many parts of that state. One from Jackson County, April 24, 1861 said there were "rebels" there; another, May 15, claims that one company in Keokuk County that was asking the Governor for arms was in re-

Circle had begun their secret work in Illinois and Iowa in opposition to war.[45] In short, the year 1861 saw north of the Ohio the beginnings of an extensive anti-war movement that was to grow into alarming proportions in 1862 and 1863.

ality secessionist; another, June 22, 1861, from Moravia, Appanoose County— on the southern border—states that rebel companies were being organized and calls on the Governor for protection; another, June 23, from Montezuma—to the same effect; others state that pro-southern sympathizers threaten the militia, that a company calling themselves "home guards" were really pro-southern, that Missouri agents were busy in Iowa and an appeal is made that certain "apple peddlers" be sent back across the Missouri border; *Archives of Iowa, War Matters, 1858–1888*. See also *Military Archives, Letters to Secretary of State*, July 13, 1861.

[45] *The Enquirer*, Feb. 22, 1861; Keokuk *Gate City*, July 17, 1861, quoting Peoria *Transcript*.

CHAPTER XI

The Free West Repudiates Abraham Lincoln, 1862

The Democrats who had followed Douglas and had come out for war in 1861 proved to be only a minority of the party. Important as the action of prominent Democratic leaders was in thus breaking party bonds, in overcoming all misgivings and difficulties and in joining with conservative and radical Republicans in the "Union Party," [1] the mass of the Democrats in Ohio, Indiana, Illinois, and in parts of Michigan, Wisconsin, and Iowa did not follow them. To support this statement, ample evidence is available. For instance, the regular Democrats carried the municipal elections in Illinois in 1861 and prevailed over Republicans in the election of delegates to the coming constitutional convention to be held in that state.[2] And again, the opposition in Congress which had started early in the special session in the summer of 1861, continued.[3] Already, in July 1861, Democratic county conventions in Ohio were passing resolutions declaring that war to coerce a state was unconstitutional and demanding a peaceful settlement.[4] Anti-Douglas Democrats and Bell and Breckinridge men met in convention in Columbus on August 7, 1861; they adopted an anti-war platform, calling for a national convention to restore the Union; they denounced the corruption and extravagance which, it was claimed, were already creeping into the departments at Washington; they charged Lincoln with illegally suspending the habeas corpus writ and then, paradoxically, nominated for governor H. J. Jewett who was less opposed to war measures than were those who nominated him.[5] They were not destined to prevail against the Union candidate, a War Democrat, David Tod, who strongly advocated the use of force to bring southern leaders to their senses. The Union party in the election won both the governorship and a majority in

---

[1] A. C. Cole, *The Era of the Civil War,* p. 261; G. H. Porter, *Ohio Politics,* Ch. II.

[2] Cole, *op. cit.,* p. 267.

[3] *Cong. Globe,* 37 Cong., 2nd Sess., 880.

[4] Porter, *Ohio Politics,* p. 83.

[5] *Ibid.,* pp. 84–86, 135.

the legislature, thus making it clear that this body was not destined at least for some time to be a dangerous opponent of the administration.

The fires of opposition flared up in the opening session of Congress in December, 1861, on the question of the expulsion of Jesse Bright of Indiana from the United States Senate. The charge against him was that he had written a letter to Jefferson Davis addressing him as "His Excellency . . . President of the Confederation of States" and recommending to him a man who was interested in disposing of a "great improvement in fire-arms." He was accused of disloyalty to the United States and with giving aid and comfort to public enemies.[6] Although Bright had been, along with many of the old guard Democrats of the lower West before the war, very friendly to southern leaders, and frankly hated abolitionism, this letter had been written in March, 1861, before Lincoln's inauguration and at a time when many Republicans themselves were advocating peaceful separation. The Judiciary Committee of the Senate reported that the facts were not sufficient to justify expulsion.[7] But Republican Senators, among them Sumner of Massachusetts and Lane of Indiana, pressed the case, likened Bright to Catiline and Benedict Arnold and the debate became the political sensation for several days. Democratic Senators defended Bright. "Reason and justice and common sense," said one "have nothing to do with it [the resolution]. . . . We have much of the reason of Robespierre, Marat and Danton; none of the wisdom of Washington, Jefferson and Franklin. The Mountain reigns supreme and woe to him who is not of the Mountain." [8] The Republicans won; by a party vote Bright was expelled in the face of the strong support of Democrats from the border states,[9] and the western Democrats began to lay plans to reëlect him in 1863. As further evidence of the opposition spirit, we note that in the House of Representatives, on April 11, 1862, Vallandigham voted against the abolition of slavery in the District of Columbia, as did other Democrats from Ohio, Indiana and Illinois, Vallandigham declaring such abolition to be the beginning of a grand "scheme of emancipation." His right to a seat in the House was also questioned.[10]

A cause contributing to discontent was economic distress in the region north of the Ohio River. The difficulty already indicated, of

[6] *Cong. Globe,* 37 Cong., 2nd Sess., 89.
[7] *Ibid.,* pp. 287, 412, 417, *et passim.*
[8] *Ibid.,* 37 Cong., 2nd Sess., 539.
[9] *Ibid.,* p. 655.
[10] *Ibid.,* pp. 879, 1647, 1648.

making trade adjustments following the outbreak of war, became more serious especially in southern Indiana and Illinois. The spurious prosperity which the war later caused even in this region—and to a much greater degree in the cities of the lakes and the East—did not come in large degree until 1862. Complaints of economic misery were voiced by Democrats in state legislatures and party presses, and their partisan character should not blind us to the reality of the distress. In Indiana a "treason bill" supported by the war party of the northern and central counties and intended to prohibit sales of produce to Kentucky was opposed by men from southern counties on the ground that it would ruin them. They asked that, if southern trade be cut off, stay laws be passed to prevent the collection of debts; that otherwise such action would be too severe a test to the loyalty of the people.[11] The National Government, which, in May 1861, issued an order through the Secretary of the Treasury requiring surveyors of customs at Cincinnati and other places to examine steamboats, flatboats, and railroad trains for military supplies and other provisions bound for persons in seceded states, could enforce its order only with the greatest difficulty and not without occasioning considerable distress.[12] Though a part of the surplus of southern Ohio, central Indiana, and Illinois was turned eastward by the railroads and the lakes soon after the outbreak of hostilities in April 1861,[13] the blockade of the Ohio and Mississippi rivers and the closing of the Baltimore and Ohio and other railroads, proved a detriment to regions in southern Indiana and Illinois which could not pay the additional freight rates to the more distant eastern market and therefore could not make the shift. While the great demand for supplies created by rapidly mobilizing armies offset the decline in some places, it was for many months unequal to the former normal southern outlet that was now so largely cut off.[14]

The result of all this was temporary stagnation and distress. It was asserted that rents declined 33 per cent in Cincinnati by the middle of May.[15] In southern Indiana the demand for a moratorium on debts and for relief laws continued; sheriff's sales were advertised in the papers in large numbers, the plaintiffs being creditors in Kentucky;

---

[11] *Indiana Brevier Legislative Reports*, V, 92, 94; Esarey, *Indiana*, II, 777.

[12] *Indiana Brevier Legislative Reports*, V, 95, May 8, 1861.

[13] *Report of the Commissioner of Statistics*, Ohio, 1861, p. 30.

[14] *Report Cincinnati Chamber of Commerce*, 1861, 1862, Cincinnati *Daily Commercial*, Sept. 17, 1862.

[15] Columbus *Crisis*, May 16, 1861.

general repudiation threatened.[16] Cairo had declined from the busy commercial center of a few months before and by June had become a "desolate, woe-begone place," with distress and pauperism prevalent among the civil population. However, the presence of large quotas of Federal troops in hot uncomfortable barracks lent a new activity which would in time bring a certain kind of prosperity in its wake.[17]

Origins of the Peace Democracy

In the early months of 1862 the opposition to Lincoln and the war crystalized into a formidable party and plans were being laid for the congressional elections in November. In Congress Vallandigham continued to draw around him a group of extreme Democrats from Ohio, Indiana, and Illinois,[18] and back in Ohio, he together with Samuel Medary of the Columbus *Crisis* and Allen G. Thurman, set about the task of making the Democratic party follow their new opposition program. The state convention was held July 4, its shibboleth being "The Union as it has been and the Constitution as it is." [19] Extremely partisan and in some cases petty speeches were made against abolitionists, against the state administration under Tod, and the National Government. Resolutions against "contemplated emancipation," arbitrary arrests and Negro immigration, were adopted.[20]

In Iowa, in the city of Dubuque, the home of G. W. Jones and Dennis A. Mahony, the revived Democratic party carried everything before it in the city election in April. There was extreme anti-administration feeling, though the "pro-southern" sympathy of the movement was probably exaggerated in the following report:

> During the afternoon and evening of election day scores and hundreds of men were swarming the streets cheering for Jeff Davis, the Southern Confederacy, Beauregard and the Merrimac. . . . Dubuque is an example of what Vallandigham, Mahony, Geo. W. Jones and that class of sympathizers with treason would make of the Democracy and people of the entire North.[21]

The Dubuque *Herald,* edited by Mahony, denounced the arrest of Jones, who had been minister to Bogota, whose son had joined the

[16] *Indiana Brevier Legislative Reports,* V, 40, 105, 106.
[17] W. H. Russell, *My Diary North and South,* pp. 330, 335, 344.
[18] E. C. Smith, *The Borderland,* pp. 315–325; Porter, *Ohio Politics,* p. 136.
[19] *Ibid.,* p. 139.
[20] Cincinnati *Daily Gazette,* July 5, 7, 1862; Porter, *op. cit.,* pp. 141–143.
[21] Keokuk *Gate City,* Apr. 14, 1862.

southern army, and whose arrest on his return from his mission was based on the letter he had written to Jefferson Davis. The arrest of the members of the Maryland Legislature was likewise denounced in an editorial in the *Herald* headed the "Progress of Despotism." [22] A state convention in July put out a "Jones-Dodge-Mahony" ticket.[23]

In Illinois, the constitutional convention elected in 1861 assembled on January 7, 1862 and was organized under Democratic control, without a single official who lived north of Springfield. The convention proved to be non-committal on the war, but was an extremely partisan Democratic body; it gerrymandered the state in the interest of the smaller Democratic counties, repeated old attacks on banks and corporations, thereby antagonizing the financial interests of northern Illinois, and submitted to the people two separate articles, one prohibiting Negroes from voting and another attempting to incorporate into the constitution the law of 1853 forbidding Negro immigration. But a constitution framed in political turmoil and civil war and by a party opposed to the administration, would of course meet great opposition. It was rejected by the voters—northern Illinois majorities overcoming all votes in its favor. The old lower western spirit, however, showed clearly in the vote on the separate articles. The article forbidding Negro suffrage carried by a majority of over 175,000 votes, and that forbidding the settlement of Negroes in the state by a majority of over 100,000. Such was the opinion of both northern and southern Illinois regarding Negroes in 1862 just before Abraham Lincoln issued his Emancipation Proclamation.[24]

It was in some respects a new party that was forming, led by comparatively young men, and composed of western sectionalists—ambitious, intense partisans or sincere constitutional Unionists who felt that the Union was being destroyed by war and that the life of Jeffersonian and Jacksonian Democracy was at stake.[25] There were many of the poor farmer class, the "poor whites" of the West, and many Irish Catholics in the cities in the following. The leaders, Vallandigham, Thurman, Pendleton, and Long of Ohio, Hendricks and Voorhees of Indiana, Richardson, W. J. Allen, J. C. Allen, and Melville W. Fuller of Illinois were, most of them, young men; long political careers—except in the case of Vallandigham—lay before them. To call

[22] Keokuk *Gate City*, May 8, 1862.
[23] *Ibid.*, July 23, 1862.
[24] O. M. Dickerson, *The Illinois Constitutional Convention of 1862*, U. of Ill. *Studies*, Vol. I, No. 9; Cole, *op. cit.*, pp. 266–272.
[25] Cincinnati *Daily Commercial*, Oct. 13, 1862.

these men and their rough and turbulent followers "Copperheads"—as in fact they came to be called in the bitter campaign of 1862—[26] is to pass over the issues too lightly. It may seem strange that future United States Senators, a future Chief Justice of the Supreme Court, and a future Vice-President of the United States were identified with this movement, looked back upon by many to-day as so petty, nagging, factious, and disreputable. The ultra-conservative pro-southern group constituted an element in the party, and their leaders, Dodge and Jones and Henry Clay Dean of Iowa and Bright of Indiana, joined with the younger political adventurers whose policies were more to their liking than those of Douglas had been. That the two groups together—the younger ambitious men and the older discarded leaders—succeeded in drawing together so many hundreds of thousands of voters is proof both that the old pre-war Democratic opposition was still strong and that sectionalism, demagoguery, and partisanship together with plausible constitutional issues, still had great vote-getting power. Then too, many old line Whigs, members of the former American Party, and many old Bell and Breckinridge voters joined with them against Lincoln and against Union by means of war.

OPPOSITION TO EMANCIPATION AND THE DRAFT

Repeatedly in 1861 and 1862, Democrats from southern Ohio, Indiana, and Illinois had voted in Congress against resolutions and bills designed to justify or secure emancipation of slaves in rebellious states, or confiscations of rebel property in slaves, or intending to bring about gradual abolition or compensated emancipation or abolition of slavery in the District of Columbia or in the territories.[27] When Lincoln's preliminary proclamation of emancipation was issued after the check administered to Lee's army by McClellan at Antietam in September 1862, the opposition became more pronounced. Many Republicans in the West as well as War Democrats were opposed to emancipation of the type proposed.[28] With these classes not unanimous in favor of it, little less could be expected from extreme Democrats than the most fervid opposition. The Indianapolis *Sentinel* said, October 13, 1862:

[26] Paul S. Smith, "First Use of the Term 'Copperhead,'" *Am. Hist. Rev.,* Vol. 32, p. 799.
[27] *Cong. Globe,* 37 Cong., 2nd Sess., 5, 159, 1563, 2793, 3107, *et passim;* Columbus *Crisis,* Sept. 17, 1862.
[28] Cincinnati *Daily Commercial,* Sept. 22, 1862; Indianapolis *Daily Journal* Aug. 11, 1862; *Indiana Brevier Legislative Reports,* VI, 138.

Do the people of Indiana desire their state to be overrun with lazy, help-less and thriftless negroes? Do they want the state to be Africanized? . . . Large numbers have already been brought into the state in violation of the constitution. . . . If Lincoln's proclamation is carried into effect, our state will be flooded with a population which by an overwhelming vote of the people it was determined to exclude. . . . By order of the Secretary of War thousands of contrabands, men, women, and children, are being carried into Illinois, the same thing is going on in Ohio.

Samuel Medary said the President's proclamation was a Mexican Pronunciamento; "the moment is frightful." [29]

The draft of the year 1862 was objectionable in being the first of its kind. It aroused "Anglo-Saxon" hostility to compulsory military service and, while it was not accompanied with such bounty granting evils as were those of 1863 and 1864, it proved a major cause of pro-test and is directly connected with the arrest of several prominent men in the summer and fall of 1862. Anti-war orators and editors denounced the draft officers and the national authorities; then the editors and orators were themselves arrested. The issue of freedom of speech and of the press thus became involved and opposition Demo-crats became champions of this old English right. A major item in the excitement of the elections of 1862 was that several men who were arrested ran for Congress or for other public office. This is true of Dennis Mahony of Dubuque, Iowa and of Edson B. Olds of Lan-caster, Ohio; the former was nominated for Congress and the latter for the State Legislature of Ohio.

Of the speeches made by opposition leaders in 1863, two or three have been chosen to quote in some detail. These and others were de-livered in great mass meetings and were published in complete form in the party newspapers. At Dayton, Ohio, August 2, 1862, Vallan-digham in the presence of a "vast concourse" of people, said: "Con-scious of rectitude, I mean, face to face with every foe and every danger, to do all and bear all that may become a man." Quoting from Magna Charta, the Petition of Right, the Habeas Corpus Act of 1679, the Bill of Rights of 1689, and the Ohio Bill of Rights, he made a plea for freedom from arbitrary arrest and for due process of law.

I call on all men to demand of the administration that it obey the Constitu-tion. No man should be arrested without due process . . . I was born a freeman; I shall die a freeman. My opinions are unmovable. I defy arbi-

[29] Columbus *Crisis,* Oct. 1, 7, 1862; Porter, *Ohio Politics,* pp. 143–144.

trary power, other patriots in other ages have suffered before me. I may die for the cause, but the immortal fire shall outlast the humble organ which conveys it and the breath of liberty will not die with the prophet but survive him. (loud cheers) I am for suppressing all rebellion, both rebellions. There are two. The Secession Rebellion South and the Abolition Rebellion North and West. I will neither vote for nor against any purely war measure; a Representative and exempt from military service, I believe it my duty to stay at home and fight the abolition rebels of the North and West.[30]

Near Springfield, Ohio, at an outdoor meeting, he spoke for three hours amid wild excitement; there were ten acres of people, bands of wagons, and a "table one thousand feet long loaded with beans and mutton." His subject was "Deliverance from Abolition Despotism." [31]

We are cut off from our southern market. It is a fact in contrast, that the eastern states during the last nine months, have accumulated more wealth than during the same time in any period in their history. . . . For the want of a southern market, the men of Indiana lost nearly one half the rewards of their labor. . . . To encourage and stimulate the people of the South in the production of their peculiar commodities that they may be large buyers from us, has been and will be the true interest of the Northwest —and that political party that would destroy that market is our greatest foe. [An Emancipation policy would] be the destruction of southern labor, and the ruin forever of our rich trade and the value of our products, . . . but if the failure, folly and wickedness of the party in power render a union impossible, then the mighty Northwest must take care of herself and her own interests. She must not allow the arts and finesse of New England to render her labor subservient to an eastern sectional policy.[32]

The arrest of J. W. Kees, editor of the Circleville (Ohio) *Watchman* brought out the following from an editor in Indiana. "The mercenary pimps of Abraham the First . . . tore him (Mr. Kees) from his family. . . . Mr. Lincoln must administer the government according to the Constitution or accept the alternative." [33] When Olds of Ohio was arrested, a Lancaster editor said: "Dr. Olds was dragged from his bed and the bosom of his family . . . by Wm. Scott and other hired tools of the Lincoln, unscrupulous and despotic administration." [34]

[30] Columbus *Crisis*, Sept. 24, 1862.
[31] *Ibid.*, Oct. 1, 1862.
[32] Indianapolis *Journal*, July 29, 1862. Address by Hendricks of Indiana at the Democratic convention at Indianapolis in 1862.
[33] Huntington (Indiana), *Democrat*, quoted in Indianapolis *Journal*, July 12, 1862.
[34] Lancaster (Ohio) *Eagle*, quoted in Columbus *Crisis*, August 20, 1862.

Patriotic Ardor

We shall not attempt the difficult task of judging the sincerity and earnestness of this opposition following. The movement was more than momentary partisan bitterness, malignity, and vociferation; it had a historical, geographic, and economic basis. Its leaders, being so largely out of power, were forced to resort to speeches and verbal invective that often have a peculiarly ranting and insincere sound. To disregard these speeches would be to neglect one of the essential factors in the movement. Making due allowance for the loud talking and hollow threats that discontented minorities always indulge in, it must be admitted that some of these leaders took themselves and their movement with a lofty seriousness. They looked upon themselves as the guardians of the American democratic tradition. Likewise the other side, the Union following and the supporters of Lincoln—in the midst of all of Vallandigham's and Hendricks' attack—went at their task of preserving the Union, of raising taxes, organizing a fighting machine, volunteering, and responding to the draft, on a high level of exaltation. To them these tasks were all important; politics was a middle western luxury or folly to which only carping peace men would devote much time or effort.

Let us balance the fervid speeches of Vallandigham and Hendricks with a document or two that represent the patriotic ardor of the Unionists in Illinois in this same summer of 1862.

To raise 35,320 volunteers but thirteen days were allowed. . . . These new volunteers must come from the farmers and mechanics of the state. Farmers were in the midst of their harvests . . . and it is not exaggeration to say that . . . firmly resolved on rescuing the government from the very brink of ruin and restoring it to the condition our fathers left it, over fifty thousand [in Illinois] left their harvests ungathered—their tools on their benches—the ploughs in the furrows and turned their backs upon home and loved ones, and before eleven days expired the demands of the country were met and quotas were filled!! . . . When I remember the universal liberality of those who were either too young or too old to enlist . . . when I remember the holy ardor which aged mothers and fair daughters infused into husbands, sons and brothers . . . I cannot but feel justified in departing from the dull routine of statistics.[35]

Among the curious documents that the author found as he searched through old newspapers and public records, none proved more inter-

[35] *Adj. General Report,* Ill., 1863, *Illinois Documents,* 1863, I, 490.

esting than a report of the superintendent of the Illinois State Hospital for the Insane for the year 1863. In it the superintendent attempts to treat war strain and excitement in their psychological and pathological aspects and claims that the war was bringing a "vast invigoration of the American mind," in spite of the strain endured by the soldier and the fear and bereavement faced by the soldier's family at home.

The question is daily asked, how far the life or death struggle on which the all of our civil institutions are now staked is influencing the public mind in the production of mental disease. . . . It would be supposed that the issues involved, . . . the absorbing anxieties, the bereavements, the perennial suffering in camp, field and hospital, would assuredly have itself felt in such an institution as this. . . . It may be claimed that war excitement has been healthful in its operation upon the public mind. It is purely an objective, not a subjective emotion. . . . Hence its great contrast with the waves of popular delusion such as Millerism, Spiritualism, etc., which have wrought such ruin in the past and whose melancholy wrecks are still found strewn among our institutions for the insane.

He produces a table to show that for a certain period, of the number under his care, fourteen cases were those of soldiers brought from camps and hospitals, two cases were civilians made insane from sympathy and anxiety, and seven were cases produced "by war excitement generally." Then he proceeds with the following wordy "psychological" justification of war:

Mournful as any table of mortality or suffering must be . . . the true psychologist sees in the above but a small price for the vast invigoration of the American mind which present events are sure to result in, provided the contest is not carried to the point of exhaustion. . . . It is national athleticism on a grand scale—the protracted tournament of a whole people—in which the valetudinarianism of a long peace, and the enervations of an ultra pacific policy are to give place to national vigor and open the dawn of a new national life.[36]

His very doubtful hypothesis does not deprive the document of its very great interest. It, along with all the other sources we are quoting at such length, is proof that the West and the nation as a whole, was torn by war-strain, indecision, party faction and demagogism, anxiety, sacrifice, devotion, suffering, insanity, and death. Democracy was in convulsion.

[36] *Superintendent's Report of the Illinois State Hospital for the Insane, Illinois Documents*, 1863, II, 26–28.

The Free West Repudiates Abraham Lincoln, 1862

In this state of mind the lower West faced the important congressional elections of 1862. There were in the states of the free West half a hundred or more national Representatives to elect and hundreds of state legislators; in Indiana and Illinois the legislatures were in turn to choose United States Senators. The issues discussed in a thousand speeches and hundreds of local newspapers were as we have seen, the blockade, trade with the South, debt, taxation and arbitrary arrests; to these was added, as the battle of Antietam in September made clear that the administration was going to face the slavery question, the burning issue of emancipation. "Armistice and peace"—the battle cries of 1863 and 1864—were not the chief questions in this campaign. The absorption of Republicans and War Democrats with war work, the concern of business men with the production of war supplies, and the absence of thousands of soldiers in the field gave a certain impression of political indifference on the part of administration forces and allowed all the greater freedom for partisan opposition to indulge in excesses that have rarely if ever been equaled in these politics-ridden commonwealths. In view of the great defections the western Democrats had suffered since 1854, the strength displayed in this campaign and in the final vote is difficult to explain. Chase had drawn large numbers of Democrats with him against the Kansas-Nebraska Bill in 1854; others left the party when Douglas opposed the "Lecompton swindle" in 1857; Douglas, Tod, and others had led great numbers of War Democrats with them in 1861. In view of all this, the success of the remaining opposition in causing what was no less than a violent political overturn in these congressional elections of 1862, has far-reaching significance.

When the votes were counted after the election it was clear that Tod, Morton, Yates, the Republican Unionists, and Lincoln himself had good cause to be alarmed. "The fate of the North is trembling in the balance," Governor Morton wrote to Lincoln.[37] Most of Ohio, Indiana, and Illinois and three congressional districts of Wisconsin had gone Democratic or anti-Lincoln. Though Vallandigham was defeated in his own Dayton district, the Democrats won fourteen out of Ohio's nineteen seats in Congress, and it seemed that only the Reserve and the Miami region were left to support Lincoln and the war. In Indiana seven of the eleven seats in Congress were won,

[37] Foulke, *Morton,* I, 208.

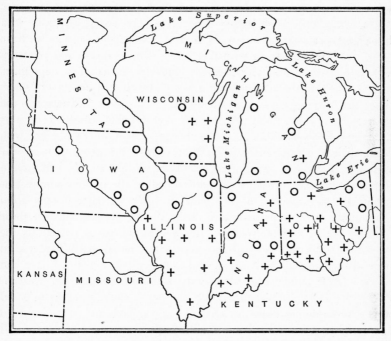

FIG. 6. THE CONGRESSIONAL ELECTIONS OF 1862
+ Districts voting against Lincoln
◯ Districts voting for Lincoln

and an intensely partisan Democratic legislature was elected which was—as it proved—to choose opposition Senators to the United States Senate and to force an obstructionist program on Governor Morton and involve the state government in an *impasse* in 1863. In Illinois a still more sweeping victory was won; the south and center went Democratic; seven Congressmen were elected as well as J. C. Allen, Congressman at large; W. J. Allen, an extreme peace man from southern Illinois, was sent to Congress. The Democratic state ticket went in with a 14,000 majority. A hostile legislature and later a Democratic United States Senator elected by it, William A. Richardson, were further fruits of this political overturn in Illinois. The sweep of anti-administration sentiment even invaded the loyal lake region. Most of Michigan and Iowa did, indeed, remain true to Lincoln, and Dennis Mahony's imprisonment and "martyrdom" had not availed to elect him, yet three of Wisconsin's six districts elected Democratic representatives, and in Milwaukee the redoubtable Congressman Potter met overwhelming defeat. While Garfield of the Western Reserve and Colfax and Lovejoy of northern Indiana and Illinois were left to represent the staunch Republicans of the lake region, they were to face as representatives of Cincinnati, Wabash River and "Egypt" constituencies, Pendleton, Voorhees, and Allen, men who were equally aggressive. The free West showed itself still to be two sections rather than one, but taken as a whole it had repudiated its own greatest man, Abraham Lincoln, and his administration at the polls.[38]

Samuel Medary called the election the greatest revolution since the election of Jackson. The Joliet *Signal* said that the party which had brought on war and had caused the land to be drenched with blood, had been vanquished. At Democratic post-election celebrations in Ohio, Indiana, and Illinois, most extravagant and insolent claims were made. Vallandigham was quickly proclaimed as the proper candidate for Governor of Ohio in 1863 and Edson B. Olds, who while still a prisoner had been elected to the Ohio Legislature, was considered a hero. The Democratic *Enquirer* said that conservative Democrats, old line Whigs, and Americans voting together had won the election. The Indianapolis *Sentinel* attributed the victory to emancipation, abolitionism, arbitrary arrests, and the denial of the right of trial

[38] *Tribune Almanac,* 1863, election returns.

by jury and called it one of the greatest revolutions in history.[39]

Republicans sought to explain the vote by pointing to the fact that they had been too absorbed in war and too politically indifferent. They said that the defeat in Indiana was due to the fact that the soldiers absent on the field were not allowed to vote. Governor Morton, feeling that the fate of the North was trembling in the balance, wrote to Lincoln and pleaded for a vigorous military movement to open the Mississippi River, claiming that only by recognizing the unity of economic interests of the Middle West and the lower Mississippi valley and seeking by an advance action to reëstablish this unity, could the situation in Illinois, Indiana, and Ohio be saved.[40] Other Republicans, more stern and critical, attacked not only the administration but Lincoln himself. The President needed "something of the old Jacksonian passion"; only "true Republicans" should conduct the war.[41] Early in the year an ultra-Republican Methodist paper had severely attacked Lincoln when it said, "We want to hear of no more balls at the White House, no more carousing over flowing bowls of punch while the enemy is in sight of the capitol." If facts do not merit such censure, still less do they support the following boast. "If nothing is ever going to be done on the Potomac farther than to defend the capitol, the great West and Northwest stand ready to take the job of putting down the Rebellion." [42] The vote in the election showed that in so far as it is possible to speak by the ballot, the "Great West" had spoken against Lincoln and his conduct of the war.

After the election the Democrats were much more aggressive, and the administration seemed to weaken itself by releasing several prisoners. Many Republicans pointed out what they considered the inconsistency in such arbitrary and violent seizures followed by unconditional release.[43] Though the arrest of the editor of the New Albany *Ledger* occurred at this time, there were in general fewer arrests in November and December.[44] "Where are your bastilles now, your arbitrary arrests?" asked Vallandigham boldly. A more definite

[39] In support of these statements see: The Columbus *Crisis*, Oct. 22, 1862; Cole, *op. cit.*, p. 297; Porter, *Ohio Politics*, pp. 144, 145; *Enquirer*, Oct. 22, 1862; Indianapolis *Sentinel*, Nov. 8, 1862.

[40] Cincinnati *Daily Commercial*, Oct. 4, 1864; Indianapolis *Journal*, Nov. 17, 1862; Foulke, *Morton*, I, 209.

[41] Cincinnati *Gazette*, Nov. 10, 1862; Ashtabula *Sentinel*, Dec. 3, 1862.

[42] *Western Christian Advocate*, Feb. 19, 1862.

[43] Indianapolis *Journal*, Nov. 27, 1862.

[44] Columbus *Crisis*, Nov. 19, 26, 1862; Indianapolis *Journal*, Nov. 29, 1862.

peace movement appeared, the opposition papers advocating the restoration of the "Union as it was" by means of a peace conference
with the South.[45]

Where a thousand men a year ago, expected the South to be thrashed
back into the Union, now scarcely one can be found. . . . The war . . .
is a monstrosity in every sense. . . . We find apparently endless war on
our hands, the resources of half the old Union fastened up and half the materials of progress for the North isolated; . . . the precious metals out of
circulation . . . prices of commodities doubled, taxation more than quad-
rupled, . . . hundreds of thousands of negroes seduced or stolen from their
lawful owners, . . . and the bastard government administered but on the
caprices of reckless wire-pullers.[16]

Dr. Olds of Lancaster, Ohio, now released from prison "where he
had been in solitary confinement and was denied the use of his Bible,"
was received with great rejoicing and spoke to great audiences re-
citing his experiences in Ft. LaFayette, New York; his trip with a
citizen escort through three counties in Ohio to the capitol at Columbus was a triumphal procession and his release a "great victory for
constitutional liberty." [47] The newly elected Legislatures of Indiana
and Illinois, ruled by their Democratic majorities, began to lay plans
for control of the coming winter session and for forms of obstructive
tactics which were to result in little less than legislative and administrative chaos.[48] On the last day of the year Sam Medary of the *Crisis*
published the following summary of its events as he saw them. "The
year 1862 has been a year of blood and plunder, of carnage and con-
flagration, . . . of falsehood and corruption, . . . of bastilles, perse-
cutions and tears, . . . of despotism, desolation and death." [49] Only
a little less bitter was extreme Republican and Unionist criticism of
the conduct of the war. The editor of the *Ladies' Repository,* a popular
monthly periodical "devoted to literature and religion," said in the
last issue of 1862: "And then to feel that so much of all this sacrifice
and suffering has been rendered ineffective by a toothless policy and
incompetent or heartless generals! The picture is too sad to look
upon! Let us draw the curtain and silently wait, hoping even in the
midst of despair!" [50] Although we cannot escape their note of sadness,

[45] Indianapolis *Sentinel,* Dec. 8, 1862.
[46] *The Crisis,* Dec. 3, 1862.
[47] *Ibid.,* Dec. 31, 1862; Jan. 7, 1863; Porter, *Ohio Politics,* p. 149.
[48] Foulke, *Morton,* I, 213; Cole, *op. cit.,* p. 298.
[49] Columbus *Crisis,* Dec. 31, 1862; see also *The Enquirer,* Jan. 16, 1863.
[50] *The Ladies' Repository,* Cincinnati, December, 1862.

such statements are none the less harsh and partial judgments of what History in her strange, tragic, and fumbling way was attempting to accomplish by blood and death at Antietam, by Fredericksburg's mistakes and horror, by Lincoln's patience, and by his proclamation of freedom for slaves that was to go into effect the following New Year's day.

CHAPTER XII

Democracy in Convulsion—War Strain, 1863

In 1863 organized protest in the lower West took form in a definite peace movement. It found its most conspicuous expression in Congress and in state elections such as the Vallandigham campaign in Ohio. But the story is only half told if mention is not made of disorganized, chaotic outbreaks and feud down among the masses. In its less serious forms, this was merely neighborhood dispute between Union sympathizers and "sesech," sullenness, verbal threat and counterthreat. But it went far beyond this stage. Restless people, aroused by their reckless local or more intelligent and aggressive national leaders, by what they considered the action of provost marshals in arresting politicians and editors of favorite papers, by the violence of Union soldiers in mobbing presses or by their dislike of the draft or the methods used to carry it out, became involved in bitter quarrels and assault, sometimes resorting to murder and arson. Unionists, in turn, met threat with threat and violence with violence.

The whole record of this will perhaps never be written nor all the truth be known. That there has been, in particular cases, gross exaggeration, and that accounts of these happenings are wordy and profuse, makes a critical estimate of the extent and seriousness of these conditions doubly difficult. It is conceded by special students of the subject that the larger military "conspiracies" in the West which are associated with such secret orders as the Knights of the Golden Circle and Sons of Liberty, which we shall treat later, were ill-conceived and poorly executed. Granting the truth of this, the smaller neighborhood riots were, on the other hand, so intense and frequent as to give the impression that civil and social control were giving way to anarchy, especially in some of the counties of southern Indiana and Illinois. Deserters would resist recapture by fortifying themselves in cabins, swamps, or hills; draft officers would be attacked and killed; Union men would quarrel with their "Copperhead" neighbors and each side would arm for future trouble. On the outskirts of the crowd at political meetings, disputes would arise; the speaker would be arrested, disorder and even death would result.

In Ohio, there occurred at various places violence and the killing of soldiers and civilians.[1] Opposition to the draft in this state centered in the north central portion—Morrow, Richland, Knox, Holmes, and Crawford counties. Here in several localities officers were mobbed, intimidated, or driven off. In Holmes County bands of from twenty to fifty men—popular exaggeration had it that there were as many as seven hundred "Holmes County insurgents"—openly resisted the draft authorities.[2] In Noble County there was a "conspiracy" to induce soldiers to desert and resist capture.[3] In Indiana and Illinois there was much more trouble than in Ohio. In the former of these states disturbances of some kind occurred in as many as nineteen counties—Sullivan, Clay, Rush, Greene, Monroe, Johnson, Blackford, Fulton, Boone, Brown, Fayette, Orange, Daviess, Crawford, Switzerland, Warren, Putnam, Bartholomew and Jay. There were riots in Blackford County, at Danville, at Terre Haute, and—in Brown County—a "civil war." In some cases these activities were directly related to the activities of the mysterious Knights of the Golden Circle.[4]

Official Indiana reports listed instances of resistance to the draft, attacking or killing enrolling officers in many counties including Jay, Boone, Fayette, and Daviess; there was also a Crawford and Orange County "conspiracy," and "outrages, robberies, and incendiary fires were of constant occurrence" as hated abolitionists and despised "Copperheads" retaliated on each other.[5] Our imagination can easily picture conditions in 1863 as suggested by the following report:

The first (disturbance) occurred at Enterprize, in Switzerland County, in consequence of some guns which had been stolen from the . . . Legion. In June a riot and bloodshed took place at Williamsport, Warren County, between furloughed soldiers and citizens; . . . resistance was made to the enrolling officer in Union Township of Bartholomew County. In Rush County, an enrolling officer and his aid were murdered in cold blood; in

---

[1] Cincinnati *Gazette*, Sept. 4, 1863.

[2] F. A. Shannon, *The Organization and Administration of the Union Army*, (1861–1865), II, 228.

[3] Cincinnati *Gazette*, Dec. 1, 1863; Porter, *Ohio Politics*, p. 186.

[4] Mayo Fesler, "Secret Political Societies in the North During the Civil War," *Indiana Magazine of History*, XIV, 207–210; Indianapolis *Sentinel*, Feb. 19, May 2, 1863; Cincinnati *Gazette*, Aug. 27, 1863; Terre Haute *Union* quoted in Cincinnati *Gazette*, Sept. 10, 1863.

[5] *Terrell's Reports*, I, 285–287, 290.

Putnam County a simultaneous attack was made on the enrolling officers of that county; and a similar act was perpetrated in the county of Monroe. . . . During the month of July, large bodies of men assembled in Greene and Sullivan Counties threatening resistance to the draft. An enrolling officer was killed in the latter county. There was also danger of a serious riot at Edinburg, Johnson County, in consequence of some rough treatment given to a fellow who had ornamented himself with butternuts.[6]

Small bands of fifteen or twenty men, others of one hundred or more, surrounded enrolling officers, destroyed draft books, sometimes supported by women, who threw eggs at these obnoxious representatives of a distasteful administration and a war they disliked so much. All accounts agree that in Rush, Sullivan, and Greene counties, there were much larger numbers—several hundred—among them desperate characters, mounted and armed. They resisted the arrest of deserters and sought to kill their victims from ambush. In one case, it was necessary to send three companies of soldiers to enforce enrollment and insure order.[7]

In Illinois certain sections of the southern part were terrorized by armed Union or Copperhead bands. Williamson County, true to the tendencies it had shown before the war and was to exhibit long after, had its quota of riots, and turbulence, quarrels and killings, over questions of desertion, peace, and politics.[8] There were troubles in Franklin, Jackson, Perry, Fulton and Union counties. Draft officials had to be protected by troops, in one case three companies of cavalry. The city of Danville experienced a riot in which five men were killed; the town of Jonesboro had to be "seized" by federal troops; in 1863 guerrilla bands from Missouri and Kentucky were very active; civil war here and elsewhere was demonstrating how degraded it may be when it is prolonged and becomes entangled in local ruffianism, factionalism, and bitterness.[9] In Iowa, in Keokuk County, the killing of Tally, an anti-war agitator, gave rise to the so-called "Tally War" and other riots.[10]

It is clear from this general account that the draft was one of the

---

[6] *Report of Major General John L. Mansfield, Indiana Legion and Minute Men, 1863, 1864, Documents of the General Assembly of Indiana,* Part II, p. 373 (Indianapolis, 1865).

[7] Shannon, *Organization and Administration of the Union Army,* II, 229–231.

[8] Milo Erwin, *The Bloody Vendetta,* pp. 99–103; 269–277.

[9] Cole, *The Era of the Civil War,* pp. 305, 306; Shannon, *op. cit.,* II, 233, 234.

[10] Davenport *Gazette,* Aug. 6, quoted in Cincinnati *Gazette,* Aug. 10, 1863; Keokuk *Gate City,* quoted in Cincinnati *Gazette,* Aug. 31, 1863; *Keokuk County History, passim.*

major causes of these disturbances. The raising of troops by volunteer methods having proved slow and inadequate, the national "Presidential militia draft" of July 17, 1862, was the result. It was but a partial and inadequate effort at conscription. The quotas were apportioned among the states according to population and if a state could not fill its quota of volunteers, the deficiency was to be made up by a special draft of the militia. The names of all liable to draft in a township were written on separate ballots and placed in a wheel or box from which a blind-folded person drew the required number of names.[11] In this and other calls, certain townships and counties needed only the threat of draft and met the required number without resort to actual drafting; this was true of the State of Illinois as a whole in 1862, and in fact of all western states in that year except Indiana and Wisconsin.[12] Even in these states some townships were compelled to raise only a few men—say ten or twelve—by the draft. But widespread discontent was expressed with the method of the draft of 1862 by Republicans as well as by anti-war men. It allowed the state too much control; there were repeated postponements. It permitted the procuring of substitutes and opened the way to many claims for exemption on account of disabilities of a trivial nature. Of this and other drafts, there were complaints that the "weak and wounded, sick and sore" were all too numerous.[13] In fact the draft of 1862 has been considered very defective in its plan and operation, and a failure as a means of raising men. It had some value as a threat or as a stimulation to local patriotic societies.[14] In general, the West was more prompt in responding; the surplus labor population especially in the fall and winter made recruiting more easy there than in the East, where the demand for labor was greater.[15]

As the National Government in the years after 1862 took over greater control of drafting, the anti-war men in the West and elsewhere called for a return to state control of raising men for the

[11] For a lengthy treatment of the complex question of enrollments, drafts, and the evils of substitutes, commutation, bounties, and bounty jumping, see Shannon, *op. cit.,* I, 259–323, II, 11–171.

[12] Cole, *op. cit.,* pp. 275, 276; Shannon, *op. cit.,* I, 290, 291.

[13] Columbus *Crisis,* Apr. 15, 1863; "An unusual number of lame men have been discovered who have all kinds of ruptures, bruises, wounds and latent defects. An immense number have no teeth and hence cannot bite cartridges. Men, who two years ago were thirty and forty now claim to be 'just 46.' " Lancaster *Eagle* (Ohio), Aug. 28, 1862, quoting Mt. Vernon *Banner.*

[14] Shannon, *op. cit.,* I, 289–292.

[15] *Ibid.,* I, 291.

army.[16] Vallandigham and Pendleton of Ohio, Turpie and Voorhees of Indiana, and Richardson of Illinois spoke in Congress against the Enrollment Act of 1863. They said it was unconstitutional, that the provost marshals would be satraps and despots, that a party defeated at the polls the previous fall should not foist on the people a bill that conscripted white men to free Negroes; they said the commutation clause benefited rich men.[17] Such criticism was taken up by the Democratic papers of the West. On this as on so many questions, it was West against East. The poor man, one paper said, could neither furnish a substitute nor pay the three hundred dollar commutation fee; "the poor man . . . must go to the wars"; it complained that wealthy counties, especially in eastern states, purchased entire exemption by paying the money value of their quotas in advance of the draft. Another evil arose from the fact that many men crossed the Canadian border and thus escaped; they were called "skedaddlers." [18] Report had it that many "healthy young men" from the Middle West followed the Federal troops as they went south, gambling and trafficking in the wake of the armies; others sought safe retreat in far western gold-fields.

The system of avoiding the draft by offering bounties to the soldier who would volunteer, in the later years of the war introduced evils into the problem of securing recruits that were especially objectionable. The first act of 1861 offered government bounties of $100 to volunteers; that of October 24, 1863 offered a bounty of $300 to new recruits for three years. A new recruit enlisting October 23 of that year received only $100; one enlisting October 25 received $300. At first, there were few if any additional local bounties, except perhaps to provide for the families of volunteers; later, townships and counties offered bounties, in some cases amounting to several hundred dollars for each man. Some localities offered none, and soldiers would sometimes credit themselves to townships paying the bounties—if possible, those paying the highest—and thus the poorer townships might lose some of their able-bodied men. A soldier who had enlisted in the first call and received $100 and no local bounty might be fighting in the field side by side with another from his own state who had received four or five hundred dollars in bounties or with one

[16] Shannon, *op. cit.,* I, 301.

[17] Columbus *Crisis,* Mar. 11, 1863; Shannon, *op. cit.,* I, 309–323, citing speeches given in *Congressional Globe,* 37 Cong., 3 Sess., 976–1002, 1213–1293, 1363–1391.

[18] Columbus *Crisis,* Apr. 15, 1863; Shannon, *op. cit.,* II, 189, 190.

from some more wealthy community who received even more than this. The average total bounty for a certain Illinois conscription district in 1864 was over one thousand dollars a man.[19]

It was easy for peace men and not hard for some of the soldiers themselves to conclude that the westerner was fighting the war—and an easterner's war at that. As the war dragged on, county debts for bounties grew and grew. Marion County, Indiana, paid over $1,300,-000 in bounties; the aggregate for local bounties in Indiana as a whole during the war was over $15,000,000. The most sordid evil—and the most expensive—was "bounty-jumping." Hundreds of the rougher classes—vagrants and lazy peace men, Irish from the towns, deserters from both northern and southern armies—would assume a patriotic ardor, enlist and receive their bounties, advance pay, and clothing. Then laying aside their uniforms, they would again appear as patriotic citizens at another recruiting station, enlist under another name, and receive the bounty. The quota of that township would be filled by fictitious names, and when the call came, baffled authorities would find an inadequate number reporting at military rendezvous for duty. It is hard for us to believe an official report in Indiana that several thousand names on the muster rolls were nothing but the various aliases of bounty-jumping scoundrels, some of whom enlisted as many as twenty times, one man succeeding in swindling the authorities of eight thousand dollars.[20]

Thus the existence in all parts of Ohio, Indiana, and Illinois of large numbers of deserters was in part due to the temptation to bounty-jumping and reënlisting presented by the offer of large bounties. The officials seemed ready to adapt themselves to a condition of wholesale desertion. Secretary Stanton even issued an order at the request of Governor Tod of Ohio that all soldiers absent "from their respective regiments without leave might be restored without punishment." [21] At one time deserters "were being brought into Columbus, Ohio, by the scores every day." [22] In Indiana nearly every regiment had a considerable number of deserters, it being a frequent thing for

[19] Shannon, op. cit., II, 92.

[20] For evils of the bounty system see J. P. Siddall, Report of Draft Commission, Indianapolis, 1863; Terrell's Reports (Indiana), I, 40–54; 60–70; VIII, 829–831; Indianapolis Journal, Sept. 2, 1862; Western Christian Advocate, Sept. 3, 1862; Rerick, History of Ohio, p. 330; History of Brown County, Ohio (Chicago, 1883), p. 339; Shannon, op. cit., II, 25, 26, 67–75.

[21] Official Records of the Rebellion, Ser. III, Vol. III, pp. 59, 60.

[22] Columbus dispatch to the Cincinnati Gazette, Aug. 13, 1863; History of Brown County, Ohio, p. 339 (Chicago, 1883).

a company to lose 10 or 20 per cent of its men in that way.[23] A provost marshal in southern Illinois rounded up seventy deserters in Williamson and Saline counties in "two days scouring";[24] and this in spite of the evidence that "Egypt" in general was surprisingly responsive to calls for volunteers.[25] Among the regiments raised in this part of the state, one was decimated by desertions; and another from Williamson and Johnson counties became so weakened by desertion and so lukewarm in its hostility to the enemy when engaged on the field of action in the South that it was arrested and disarmed, only one company being considered loyal.[26] In an Irish regiment recruited from Chicago and other cities, as many as one third and one half of some of the companies deserted.[27]

Popular anti-war mass meetings, large and small, were held, it seems, at all times and in almost every county and town. Though often attended by no violence, they aroused the bitterest feeling. One meeting at Springfield, Illinois, attended, it was reported, by forty thousand people, passed resolutions against the further offensive prosecution of the war; others called for peace conventions.[28] A Democratic mass meeting was announced to be held on the twentieth of May at Indianapolis—it was thought to be for the purpose of making an armed demonstration of protest by the Knights. Governor Morton and the authorities made preparations, but when the day came, there proved to be a lack of organization and the plans did not carry, though there is evidence that two or three thousand Democrats were armed. Confusion reigned in the city. Union soldiers without orders marched with fixed bayonets through the crowd to the speaker's stand, "going for Tom Hendricks." The soldiers roughhandled the Democrats they found on the streets. As the crowds left town on outgoing trains in the evening, shots were fired from the car windows, trains were boarded by Union soldiers, and hundreds of revolvers taken away from the disappointed "conspirators."[29]

[23] J. C. Leffel, *History of Posey County, Indiana,* pp. 207, 210 (Chicago, 1913); *History of Pike and Dubois Counties,* p. 531 (Chicago, 1885).

[24] *Cairo Correspondence,* Cincinnati *Gazette,* Aug. 12, 1863.

[25] Cole, *op. cit.,* p. 279.

[26] *Ibid.,* p. 306; *Report Adj. Gen. Illinois,* Vol. VI, *Appendix.* The regiments were the 129th and the 109th Illinois, respectively.

[27] *Report of Adj. Gen. of State of Illinois,* Vol. VI, *Roster of Enlisted Men.* It was the 90th Infantry.

[28] Cole, *op. cit.,* pp. 299, 300.

[29] Foulke, *Morton,* Vol. I, Ch. XXIII; Mayo Fesler, "Secret Political Societies," *loc. cit.,* pp. 211–213.

At Mattoon, Illinois, there was a procession three miles long and thousands of citizens armed with shot-guns, rifles, and muskets, marched to show that they had a constitutional right to bear arms. Vallandigham was cheered.[30] To arouse patriotism and to check disaffection in both southern Illinois and Indiana, prominent generals in the army, some of them War Democrats, came from the field of battle to make speaking tours. General John A. Logan came back to his old neighbors in "Egypt" and pleaded with them to support the war and to write no more grumbling letters to the soldiers in the field urging them to desert. "When a deserter comes to your house, say to him, we keep no place for deserters, we have no food for deserters, instead of saying, . . . go into the woods and hollows, we will bring you provisions in the night. . . . Don't support and sustain deserters." [31] General McClernand was engaged in similar work.[32] The town of Marion, Williamson County, was put under martial law by the provost marshal and a United States Congressman, "Josh" Allen, "the King of the Copperheads," was kept a "prisoner" in it for some time.[33] All through central and southern Illinois civilians took upon themselves the task of holding others to their duty. "Union regulators" by threats, intimidation and violence supported Governor Yates, the provost marshal and the army generals in the difficult work of making all people think alike.[34]

Another event that contributed to the excitement of 1863 was the coming of Morgan the Raider. The border counties of Indiana and Illinois throughout the latter part of the war experienced guerrilla and "bushwhacking" invasions from across the Ohio River. The coming of John Morgan from Kentucky with about two thousand cavalry and some artillery was an event of greater significance, and though it proved in the end to be but a milder type of plundering raid, it nevertheless brought to the stay-at-homes of the West some degree of actual contact with the war that the South was experiencing so bitterly. Morgan crossed the Ohio in July, 1863, and passed through several counties in Indiana and the southern part of Ohio. The whole

[30] Chicago *Times* quoted in the Columbus *Crisis,* Aug. 26, 1863.
[31] Speech given in full in Cincinnati *Gazette,* Aug. 4, 1863.
[32] Cincinnati *Gazette,* Aug. 17, 1863; Generals Hovey, McClernand, and others spoke in Indiana, *Gazette,* Aug. 26, 1863; *Proceedings of the Mass Meetings of the War Democracy, Indiana Pamphlets, Civil War,* Vol. V (Indiana State Library).
[33] *Cairo Dispatch,* Cincinnati *Gazette,* Aug. 3, 1863.
[34] Cole, *op. cit.,* pp. 301, 302.

State of Indiana was aroused. Governor Morton called the Indiana Legion and Minute Men, an organization in the border counties, and other detachments of volunteers—from fifteen to twenty thousand in all. One regiment of the Legion was commanded by Major-General Lew Wallace. Morgan repulsed the Legion in an engagement near Corydon, Indiana, at which several were killed; he took several hundred men prisoners whom he soon paroled. He had little difficulty in evading capture, and his career of robbing stores, stealing horses, and levying demands on mills for flour and grain continued as he crossed the line into Ohio north of Cincinnati.[35] In general, his coming seemed to unify the people of Indiana; there was no concerted uprising in his favor, although the colonel in command of one regiment of militia made this interesting report to Governor Morton:

I am sorry to relate that there were but few points along the line of our march where we did not find men who had been rendering assistance to John Morgan . . . on his expedition of robbery and plunder. Their sympathies were all for Vallandigham, and . . . I suggest the propriety of sending scouts throughout the southern part of our state whose duty it should be to arrest parties who are declaring themselves for Vallandigham and the southern Confederacy.[36]

The raid, though becoming more aimless and less dangerous, caused a panic in all the southern counties of Ohio. Governor Tod called out a far greater number of militia than was needed to cope with it. Morgan continued his plundering; he was unable for some days to recross the Ohio and return south, being thwarted and defeated in a small engagement north of Pomeroy. After several weeks' wandering in southern Ohio he was captured and his followers were taken prisoner or scattered. Peace Democratic papers like the Columbus *Crisis* treated the raid lightly, and Republican papers criticized the expensive and elaborate mobilization of the militia.[37] As late as

---

[35] *Operations of the Indiana Legion and Minute Men*, 1863, 1864. These documents contain reports of officers to Governor Morton. They are found in *Documents of General Assembly of Indiana*, Part II, pp. 369–443 (Indianapolis, 1865); Esarey, *History of Indiana*, II, 771–776; Foulke, *Life of Morton*, I, Ch. XXIII; *Official Records of the Rebellion*, Ser. I, Vol. XXIII, Part I, pp. 395–399, 672–673, 722–729, *et passim;* Ewbank, Louis B., "Morgan's Raid in Indiana," Indiana Historical Society *Publications*, Vol. 7, No. 2.

[36] *Report of Colonel Lawrence S. Shuler commanding 103d Regiment Indiana Militia* found in *Documents of the General Assembly*, Indiana, 1865, Part II, p. 431; L. C. Baird, *History of Clark Co. Indiana*, p. 172 (Indianapolis, 1909).

[37] For Morgan's Raid in Ohio see Henry Howe, *Times of Rebellion in the West*, pp. 13–19; Columbus *Crisis*, July 22, 29, Aug. 26, 1863; P. B. Sarchet, *History of Guernsey Co.*, Ohio, I, 98.

the year 1935 claims were still being presented to the government of Ohio for compensation for losses of horses or other property taken by Morgan's men.

ATTACKS ON THE PRESS, 1862–1864

Another form of popular excitement, indignation, and violence, was attacks on newspaper offices. In the summer of 1862 and in the winter and spring of 1863, after the defeats at Fredericksburg and Chancellorsville, and after the release of several political prisoners, the tone of the opposition press became increasingly bold. The Union men, especially the soldiers, met boldness with boldness. Mob action against newspapers must of course be clearly distinguished from action by the Federal authorities. To the latter class belong the suppression of the Chicago *Times* on the order of General Burnside on June 1, 1863, and the prohibition of the circulation and sale of the Cincinnati *Enquirer* in the Military Department of Kentucky on order of General Palmer. Both of these orders were temporary and that of Burnside aroused a storm of criticism. It was regretted by the President and soon revoked.[38] An important arrest was that of Dennis A. Mahony of the Dubuque (Iowa) *Herald*.[39] Less conspicuous, but cases nevertheless attracting widespread attention, were those of the arrest of J. W. Kees, editor of the Circleville (Ohio) *Watchman* on June 29, 1862 and of A. McGregor, editor of the Stark County (Ohio) *Democrat,* whose press had already been destroyed by a mob the previous year.[40] Rival newspaper editors in every town of considerable size kept the contest up, garbled the issues of the war to fit local, partisan, and personal ends, and even staged fist fights on the street—all of which presents a sorry and discouraging spectacle.[41] In many cases the mob, doing what the Federal military authorities desired but hesitated to do, would destroy the press and the supplies. Soldiers on furlough would attack what they called "treason," "secesh," or "Copperhead" sheets; occasionally the peace men would retaliate and destroy a Republican-Unionist press.

[38] J. G. Randall, *Constitutional Problems under Lincoln,* pp. 493–496, 500.
[39] D. A. Mahony, *The Prisoner of State* (New York, 1863).
[40] Circleville *Democrat,* July 11, 25, 1862; Lancaster *Eagle,* Oct. 23, 1862.
[41] J. F. Bollmeyer, an anti-war editor of the Dayton *Empire* was shot on the streets of Dayton. Republicans said this was due to a dispute about a dog; Democrats called it assassination for political reasons. Lancaster *Eagle,* Nov. 6, 1863; Dayton *Empire,* Nov. 1863, *passim.*

It is impossible to tell how many newspaper editors suffered interference. No doubt the small town presses—and they were often the most outspoken—were hindered in larger numbers than history will ever record. In March, 1863, a hundred or more soldiers in Columbus, Ohio, determined to destroy the Democratic presses of the city. They attacked and damaged the offices of Colonel Medary and scattered copies of the *Crisis* in the streets—"vile files of corruption and treason were sent by thousands in the streets and covered the town." They also attacked the pressroom of the *Ohio Statesman,* a less radical peace journal, but they were stopped by the police. On his return to the city, Medary was met at the station by several hundred sympathizers and carried on their shoulders. "They were freemen," he said in an editorial, "to them it was the birth of a new freedom." [42] Among the other papers whose editors were arrested or officers mobbed or whose publication was in some way hindered, there were, in Ohio, the Mahoning *Sentinel,* the Fremont *Messenger*, the Bellefontaine *Gazette,* the Marion *Mirror,* the Wauseon *Democrat,* the Lancaster *Eagle,* and the Dayton *Empire;* in Indiana, the Indianapolis *Sentinel,* the Rockport *Democrat,* the Terre Haute *Journal;* in Illinois, the Peoria *Demokrat,* the Chester *Picket Guard,* the Quincy *Herald,* the Paris *Democratic Standard,* the Bloomington *Times,* the Jonesboro *Gazette;* in Iowa, the Dubuque *Herald*.[43] There is evidence that some newspapers were edited by incapable and reckless men, but there were so many cases of arbitrary action that it is not hard to understand how the peace Democrats considered that they were victims of tyranny and were fighting the ancient struggle for the freedom of the press. In some cases, Lincoln and Stanton, less rigorous than subordinate officers like Burnside, would revoke the order.[44] The interference being temporary, the persecution resulted in increased circulation for the newspaper; thus it seemed to ardent Republicans that little was gained, while peace Democrats thought that further battles for freedom had been won.

The arrest of local and national political leaders perhaps attracted more attention than that of editors and brought out a greater popular

[42] Columbus *Crisis,* Mar. 11, 1863.

[43] *Ibid.,* Mar. 11, 18, June 10, 1863; Porter, *Ohio Politics,* p. 107; *Indiana Brevier Legislative Reports,* VII, 227; Esarey, *Indiana,* II, 778; Cole, *Era of the Civil War,* pp. 303, 304; J. G. Randall, *Constitutional Problems under Lincoln,* p. 509, note.

[44] Randall, *op. cit.,* pp. 492–507. This account covers interference with the press throughout the North.

protest. After hearing a "treasonous" political speech, some slander of the administration or some act "discouraging enlistments," the Federal troops would seize the offender, try him by martial law and send him to "Old Capitol" at Washington or to some other military prison. The martyred leader was sometimes nominated for office while in prison, or, as the case of Vallandigham, while in exile. So many were arrested just before the election in the fall of 1862, it is difficult to avoid the conclusion that the authorities had the election in mind in what they did. The most prominent instances of arrest, second to that of Vallandigham, were those of Colonel Lambdin B. Milligan of Indiana, Edson B. Olds of Lancaster, Ohio, W. J. Allen, Congressman from Illinois, Henry Clay Dean of Mt. Pleasant, Iowa, and Dennis A. Mahony of the Dubuque *Herald*.[45]

There was in these cases, and in all others, the greatest publicity; a glowing light was turned on them by the vociferous press and by the victims themselves. The *Crisis,* the *Enquirer,* the *Sentinel,* the Dayton *Empire* and a dozen other papers left nothing undone in acquainting the people with their version of the facts. We need to be reminded that we are not dealing with men of obscure careers but with important local heroes. The arrest of Lambdin B. Milligan gave rise to the long drawn out and constitutionally important "Milligan Case"; Mahony and Dean each wrote a book describing his experiences.[46] Accounts of the Olds arrest, his election as a martyr to the State Legislature of Ohio and his spectacular journey after his return from prison from his home in Lancaster, Ohio, through three counties to the meeting of the legislature, were widely circulated. The Vallandigham case, as is well known, attracted wide, even worldwide, attention. Dean in his *Crimes of the Civil War* says of his arrest at Keokuk, Iowa,

I saw the seeds of contention and civil war scattered in every neighborhood of the upper Mississippi Valley. I was arrested because a Democrat, a devoted friend of the Constitution, a sincere lover of the government and union of these states. My arrest had been agreed upon as soon as my name was registered at the Billings House. I could see the Puritans and Roundheads gathering in squads of four or five talking in a low excited whisper . . . the shouting Methodist and the witch burning Puritan, the Universalist and Unitarian with every intervening class of fanatics. I was marched down to the office of the provost marshal and there commanded to strip myself

---

[45] J. H. Marshall, *The American Bastille* (1883).
[46] D. A. Mahony, *The Prisoner of State* (1863); Henry Clay Dean, *The Crimes of the Civil War* (1869).

naked which I had to do in the presence of a large crowd . . . my carpet-bag was searched. I was lodged in the guard house.

There follows a most lurid description of his experience in an "abolition prison." [47] The use of such phrases as "abolition despotism," "American bastilles," and "revolutionary tribunals," was, of course, an exaggeration of conditions. There was little brutality in the treatment of prisoners and sanitary conditions were not as bad as pictured, but authorities on the subject admit that there were some unwarranted arrests and that officers were in some cases over-zealous.[48]

LEGISLATIVE OPPOSITION TO WAR, 1863

More formal opposition to the war came from state legislatures. That of Ohio, it is true, being in the hands of pro-administration forces, did not prove formidable. The Democrats were in a minority and could not prevent the election of Benjamin Wade to the United States Senate. But the session was marked by attempts to prevent military arrests and to inquire into the legality of those of the previous year. Resolutions were offered by Dresel in favor of the rights of states and persons, against emancipation, national banks, military arrests and trials; he was declared by the majority to be a "promoter of sedition and an enemy to his country." [49] But in Indiana and Illinois, the popular revulsion against Lincoln and the war which had been signalized by the elections of 1862 emboldened the victorious Democratic majorities to rash and daring measures. In Indiana the newly elected legislature and state officers, in the winter and spring of 1863, began a career of opposition and delay; this in turn caused Governor Morton to resort to unusual methods, bringing about almost a dissolution of civil government and "executive tyranny"—the "reign of Oliver P. Morton." [50] Democratic majorities in both houses indulged in an excess of resolutions opposing arbitrary arrests, demanding the withdrawal of the Emancipation Proclamation, and asking for an armistice and a peace convention.

[47] Pages 11–15 et seq.

[48] Randall, op. cit., pp. 150–154, 184.

[49] Porter, Ohio Politics, pp. 150–155; Ohio House Journal, 1863, passim; Ohio Senate Journal (1863), p. 222; Rebellion Pamphlets, Vol. II (Ohio State Library).

[50] Foulke, Morton, Vol. I, Chs. XVIII–XXII; William B. Weeden, War Government Federal and State, pp. 233–237 et passim.

There were charges against the "president, governor, abolitionists, negroes and the Massachusetts Yankee, . . . a tumult of words, loud mouthed, dissonant and ungrammatical." [51] In the State Senate, Wolfe offered a resolution opposing a "war for abolitionism," and instructing "our representatives to procure an armistice of at least six months." [52]

When the legislature took up its task of choosing two United States Senators, the Republican minority played a partisan game, and attempted, unsuccessfully, to prevent election by bolting to a nearby town. Thomas A. Hendricks and David Turpie were elected. Charges that Indiana "was not loyal at heart" could not be easily disproved by her aggressive Union Governor Morton at Indianapolis and by Schuyler Colfax in the national House of Representatives. They might point to the War Democrats and the tens of thousands of soldiers in the field, but was not the legislature hostile, and were not her two United States Senators and seven of her eleven Congressmen in opposition?

The Democratic legislature was determined to take military power away from the Governor and place it in the hands of a military board of its own; it refused the necessary appropriations; there resulted a deadlock and an adjournment. Governor Morton by strenuous and extra-legal methods on his own responsibility raised funds or procured them from the national government.[53] By the peace Democrats, he was denounced as a tyrant; by the national administration, he was held to be the strong outpost of the government on this dangerous political front. The student of the relations between the executive and the legislative department of government finds phenomena of special value in Indiana in 1863.[54] Indiana regiments on southern battlefields, aroused by the anti-war resolutions of the legislature sent addresses to it pleading for support. "We petition that you will pour out the treasures of your state as your soldiers have poured out their blood, that you will abstain from heated political discussions and party wrangling, . . . we ask you to adopt resolutions unconditionally and determinedly in favor of Union." In a somewhat less factious tone the "disloyal" legislature replied to the soldiers that they must

[51] Foulke, *Morton*, I, 227; *Report and Evidence of Committee on Arbitrary Arrests* (Indianapolis, 1863).

[52] *Brevier Legislative Reports*, VI, 91 (Jan. 21, 1863).

[53] Foulke, *Morton*, I, 254–255.

[54] Weeden, *War Government, passim*.

have been misinformed, that money had been misapplied, that the emancipation policy of the government had changed the object of the war, adding calmly:

It would be wrong to conceal the fact that there is a growing anxiety in the public mind that this war should be brought to a close. . . . It has lasted nearly two years and with great waste of blood and treasure. . . . Men are not made of iron nor their hearts of steel. . . . There are hearts that will feel and minds that will think even in perilous times like this.[55]

Meantime, in Illinois there was a similar governmental deadlock and a condition among the masses of the people that was ominous. An opposition United States Senator was elected by the legislature; Governor Yates was refused the necessary appropriations and resort was made to private parties to advance money to run the state government.[56] In an attempt to prorogue the legislature, the governor was balked for two weeks by the House. Reckless and partisan members of the Democratic majority, some of whom no doubt belonged to the "Knights of the Golden Circle," [57] voiced grievances in numerous resolutions. Melville W. Fuller of Chicago, a future Chief Justice of the United States, played as intense a part in opposing Lincoln and Yates as did any member from "Egypt." The most notorious of the resolutions of the legislature, after denouncing arbitrary arrests, the suspension of the Writ of Habeas Corpus and the Emancipation Proclamation, and after asserting that the Union could not be preserved by war, expressed itself as in favor of the assembling of a national convention of all the states at Louisville.[58]

VALLANDIGHAM, 1863

By the summer of 1863, all signs pointed to the fact that the new party, the Peace Democracy, was fully formed and aggressive. This party had won great successes in the elections of 1862, had secured several United States Senators and, engaging in obstructive tactics in Congress and western state legislatures, it was arousing a popular discontent of alarming proportions. Its opposition to war and its

[55] *Indiana Senate Journal* (1863), pp. 667–681, 695–700; *Indiana Brevier Legislative Reports*, VI, *passim;* Indianapolis *Journal*, Jan. 26, 1863; Foulke, *Morton*, I, 233–235.

[56] *Message of Richard Yates to the General Assembly* (Springfield, 1865), p. 8.

[57] Mayo Fesler, "Secret Political Societies," *loc. cit.,* p. 219.

[58] *Illinois House Journal* (1863), pp. 76, 372–374, 527, 728 *et passim.*

peace tendencies should not blind us to the fact that it was primarily a western movement; [59] its program was quite sectional; it was far from being simply "pro-southern." The political heir of Jacksonian and Douglas Democracy, it was keeping this democratic tradition alive; it opposed tariffs and was suspicious of banks, a national debt and bondholders; it emphasized the unity of the Mississippi and Ohio valleys and the preservation of trade with the South and of the social and political ties with that section that had existed for half a century. Jeffersonian and Jacksonian ideas of State rights and individualism and pride in "Anglo-Saxon liberties," a love of Union by compromise and concession like that of Henry Clay and Douglas —these were among its tenets. It was an attitude equally out of touch with the extreme secessionists of the far South and what it considered the uncompromising sternness of stiff-necked New England and the lake regions. With the outbreak of war, it had added to its program the opposition tenets we have mentioned—a peace program and a demand for free speech and a free press and for freedom from arbitrary arrest.

Union-loving and non-slaveholding, but geographically located too near the South to resist the undemocratic tendencies in slavery and slave extension, it is an interesting fact, though a historical anomaly that this peace Democracy which constituted in other respects perhaps the most democratic and tolerant—though not the most "intelligent" section in the United States—could not become interested in the prosecution of a war for "freedom and union." The peace Democracy has a distinct place in the political history of the United States. It kept the Middle West from becoming solidly Republican; it helped the Democratic party after the Civil War to retain that national character it has always shown; it kept alive for useful national purposes the tendency of the Middle West and South to ally against the East, against tariffs, capitalism, and corporations—a tendency which later manifested itself in Greenback and Farmers' Alliance movements and other forms of agrarian and insurgent protest. Now that the lake region had allied with "the fanatical East"—Vallandigham attributed this to the influence of the clergy and lecturers—it remained for the lower West to ward off, as the fathers had done, the "war of sec-

[59] On matters pertaining to the war it received support in parts of Pennsylvania, New Jersey and among the Tammany following in New York City, especially among the representatives of these districts in Congress. *Cong. Globe* 37 Cong., 3 Sess., *passim.*

tions" in which it found itself caught as in a vise.[60] If there was associated with it "butternut" ignorance and backwoods localism, clever and designing demagoguery and tactics that taxed to the limit the patience of another great democrat, Abraham Lincoln—himself in large degree a product of this same region—it can only be said that popular democracy has just such crude mediums through which to assert itself and has often conflicting ways of manifesting itself in our plural world and social systems and in a United States so large that sectionalism has shown itself to be inevitable.

In truth Vallandigham's attitude had changed but little since he entered public life. He had belonged to the "progressive Western Democracy" in 1847.[61] He was a bold "Western sectionalist within the Union" before the Civil War. A year and a half before the firing on Sumter, already attracting attention as a western leader in a more unique sense than either Lincoln or Douglas and one of our keenest observers of sectional and group interests, Vallandigham made one of his most important speeches in Congress.

. . . when I came to Washington two years ago, I brought with me an intense nationality; but . . . I learned that without a section to cling to a man was . . . a mere cipher . . . and from that hour I became a Western sectionalist. . . . We of the great valley of the Mississippi are perpetually ignored. . . . But within the Union after the next census we . . . will hold in our hands the political power and destiny of the country. . . .

He charged an abolition North and an aggressive South-East with having conspired for seventy years to control the government while now they were attempting to destroy it. He asked them, "Did you ever dream of a Western Confederacy? . . . We have fed you, we have clothed you, we have paid tribute to you . . . for now these sixty years." [62] In 1863 the same ideas were expressed by him and his followers. Sam Medary in the Columbus *Crisis* sought to come to terms with the "Union" elements in the South in favor of peace, but maintained that southern Union elements were not in favor with the government at Richmond just as the peace Democrats of the North were out of favor with the government at Washington. "War, desperate war, is . . . essential to both governments." [63]

[60] *Cong. Globe,* 36 Cong., 1 Sess., *Appendix* 44.

[61] See his speech on "Constitutional Reform" in the Ohio House of Representatives, Jan. 16, 1847, found in *Speeches, Arguments, Addresses and Letters of C. L. Vallandigham* (New York, 1864), p. 77.

[62] *Cong. Globe,* 36 Cong., 1 Sess., *Appendix,* p. 42, Dec. 15, 1859.

[63] *The Crisis,* Oct. 13, 1863; August 12, 1863, quoting Mobile *Register.*

On January 14, 1863, Vallandigham made his great speech on "The Constitution—Peace—Ruin" in the House of Representatives at Washington. He declared the war for Union a failure, condemned arbitrary arrests as unconstitutional and the rise of centralized government as overthrowing the older individualism and rights of the states. He charged that the large army and navy in two years of war had failed to subdue the ten million "rebels."

Rebels, did I say, . . . your fathers were rebels. . . . (Washington) was a rebel . . . and yet we, who cradled ourselves in rebellion and who have fostered and fraternized with every insurrection in the nineteenth century everywhere throughout the globe . . . would now forsooth make the word rebel a reproach. . . . You have not conquered the South . . . you never will. . . . Money you have expended without limit and blood poured out like water. . . . Defeat, debt, taxation, sepulchers, these are your trophies.

He condemned Puritan domination in "religion or morals or literature or politics"; said the war could only lead to separation and make the banks of the Ohio River the scene of "eternal border warfare" in the future. "Union is consent and good will and fraternal affection, . . . war is force, hate, revenge . . . stop fighting . . . make an armistice, no formal treaty. . . . Buy and sell. . . . Visit the South . . . Migrate. . . . Intermarry. . . . Let time do its office." [64] The speech was "like the speech of Cato" in the Roman Senate, warning the people against "the designs of Caesar" and so great was the demand for it that the *Crisis* could not print sufficient copies.[65] The influence of a man who made such speeches in a day of bitter politics, fervid oratory and war passion, was bound to be great.

Pictures of Clement L. Vallandigham, the unusual, handsome, pure in life, stern in speech and bearing, "cold as ice and hard as iron, a fallen angel defying God," dogmatic and "fanatical" in his insistence on his peculiar peace and reconstruction views, have often been drawn and the story of the Ohio peace movement of 1863 has often been told.[66] The movement has usually been pictured, however,

---

[64] *Cong. Globe,* 37 Cong., 3 Sess., *Appendix,* p. 55.

[65] Columbus *Crisis,* Jan. 28, 1863.

[66] Porter, *Ohio Politics,* Ch. III; E. J. Benton, "The Movement for Peace without Victory during the Civil War," *Collections Western Reserve Hist. Soc.,* Pub. No. 99; T. E. Powell, *The Democratic Party of Ohio,* Vol. I, Ch. XIII; W. H. Van Fossan, "C. L. Vallandigham," *Ohio Arch. and Historical Society Publications,* XXIII, 256; J. L. Vallandigham, *A Life of C. L. Vallandigham* (Baltimore, 1872); *Speeches, Arguments, Addresses and Letters of C. L. Vallandigham* (New York, 1864).

merely as an unpatriotic peace and obstructionist program, its larger political and sectional bearings being neglected. It was, in truth, a thwarted West again asserting itself. The story derives more animation and the picture more distinct colors from the intense war feeling, and from the sense on the part of leaders like Vallandigham of frustrated partisan hopes and personal ambitions and from the exploitation by these same leaders of the dramatic possibilities in the situation, together with no little affectation of persecution and martyrdom.

After Vallandigham's return from Congress to Ohio, in a speech at Mt. Vernon on May 1, 1863, he again made a plea for Union by compromise; he assailed the despotism of the administration and said he "spat upon" such decrees as General Burnside's Order No. 38 (against "declaring sympathy for the enemy"); he took his stand upon "Order No. 1, the Constitution of the United States." Many of his fifteen thousand excited hearers wore copperhead or liberty pins or butternut badges of various kinds. His arrest soon after this, his trial by a military court, now thought by many to have been a blunder and perhaps illegal, his "banishment," at President Lincoln's suggestion, to the Confederacy,[67] his refusal to identify himself with the South, and his later sojourn in Canada as an exile, are all well-known events. Become now a popular hero, his followers met in a huge noisy convention at Columbus to do him honor. There were a thousand wagons in a field south of the city in which thousands of "freemen" slept overnight.[68] In an open air meeting on the State house grounds in the presence of forty or fifty thousand people he was nominated for Governor of Ohio on June 11, 1863.[69] John Brough, a War Democrat, was nominated against him on the Union ticket.

The campaign which followed was turbulent to the last degree, was of national importance and "evoked interest throughout the civilized

[67] J. G. Randall, *Constitutional Problems under Lincoln*, pp. 176–179, 183–185. Lincoln, it is thought, did not order or desire the arrest and sentence of Vallandigham (Porter, *Ohio Politics*, p. 166), but supported his subordinates and later issued his well-known statement, "Must I shoot a simple minded soldier boy who deserts, while I must not touch a hair of a wily agitator who induces him to desert?" (*Reply to Albany Committee of N. Y. Democrats*, Washington, 1863.)

[68] Columbus *Crisis*, June 17, 1863.

[69] Among the best short accounts of the Vallandigham movement are those of G. H. Porter and E. J. Benton, cited above.

world." [70] In Illinois and Indiana, while there were no state elections, there was much sympathy with Vallandigham and the opposition to Governor Morton, to Governor Yates and President Lincoln and to the war, created almost as serious a problem as did the campaign in Ohio. In Iowa, radical peace men like Dennis Mahony and Henry Clay Dean failed in their attempt to control the party and J. M. Tuttle, a moderate War Democrat, ran for Governor.

Vallandigham, like an ostracized Greek statesman, remained in Canada at the Clifton House near Niagara Falls and later at Windsor, sending campaign letters to his frenzied followers through the columns of the *Crisis,* the *Enquirer,* and other peace journals, or making speeches to delegations who came to Canada to honor him.[71] A number of able speakers, called by the Republicans "political hacks," represented his cause in tumultuous meetings in central, southern, and western Ohio, among them, Daniel Voorhees of Indiana, George H. Pendleton of Cincinnati, Samuel Medary of the *Crisis,* Allen G. Thurman and G. E. Pugh. They drew freely from the speeches of their great Douglas in a cause which Douglas himself would probably have repudiated. Voorhees made an extensive tour of the state and the eccentric Henry Clay Dean of Iowa and Dr. Edson B. Olds were called upon to recite the "horrors" of their experiences in "abolition prisons." [72] With unparalleled excitement abroad, the bitter invective of Voorhees and Pugh drew the Copperheads out from the more remote rural districts. If we can believe newspaper reports, they became seething, hissing crowds clamouring loudly but vaguely for their "rights," a "peace convention," a "revolution." They idolized Vallandigham as "the Exile"—as a Kossuth or a William Tell opposing a tyrant—and sang campaign songs, praising him as a "Burke," and a "Tribune of the people," and blaming Lincoln for the "lust of ruthless soldiers" and "the wail of homeless children." The campaign song book [73] contained the following:

> We are coming Abraham Lincoln
> From mountain, wood and glen,
> We are coming, Abraham Lincoln
> With the ghosts of murdered men.

[70] Cincinnati *Daily Commercial,* Oct. 14, 1863.

[71] *The Crisis,* July 22, Aug. 12, Sept. 31, Oct. 21, 1863; Cincinnati *Daily Commercial,* Oct. 1, 1863.

[72] *The Crisis,* Aug. 12, Sept. 16, 30, 1863.

[73] *The Vallandigham Song Book* (Columbus, Ohio, 1863).

Yes, we're coming Abraham Lincoln
With curses loud and deep,
That will haunt you in your waking
And disturb you in your sleep.

There's blood upon your garments,
There's guilt upon your soul
For the lust of ruthless soldiers
You let loose without control.
Your dark and wicked doings
A God of mercy sees,
And the wail of homeless children
Is heard on every breeze.

You may call your black battalions,
To aid your sinking cause;
And substitute your vulgar jokes
For liberty and laws.
No! by the memory of our fathers,
By those green unnumbered graves,
We'll perish on ten thousand fields,
Ere we become your slaves.

These "butternut masses" were the poor and less dominant classes in society—such cutting phrases as the "unwashed" and "the rag-tag and bob-tail of creation" being applied to them by Republicans—and were in close sympathy with similar classes in southern Indiana and Illinois and in Kentucky and Tennessee. Dressed in cheap factory-made clothes or, in remote regions, in butternut-colored homespun, they taunted the Republican home guards as "kid-glove patriots." Republican papers cited proofs of their illiteracy.[74] Aroused by their leaders against the tariff, debt, taxation, and profiteering resulting from the war to free the Negro, they claimed the result would be that the poor white man would be made the poorer and that freed slaves would overrun their Ohio lands. Appeals like the following were effective with them: "It is a contest which will determine the

[74] Cincinnati *Daily Commercial*, Oct. 13, 1863; Jan. 1, 1868; Columbus *Crisis*, July 22, 1863; Ft. Wayne *Times and Union* quoted in *The Crisis*, Aug. 26, 1863. "Butternut was a name dear to backwoodsmen—in the early days butternut trees supplied coloring matter for nearly all the fabrics worn as clothing by the Western people. . . . This costume is still worn in the mountain ranges of Kentucky and Missouri and in southern Illinois. . . . The earlier rebel prisoners were dressed in butternut and the abolitionists by applying it to democrats expected to convey the impression that they were in sympathy with the rebels. The two hearts of the butternut cemented represent the North and South"— *The Crisis*, Feb. 25, 1863, quoting *The Enquirer*.

fate of the West; the East owns the capital and the West feeds the East. . . . (It) will determine whether the free suffrage of the West will be enslaved to the capital of New England." [75] The vagrant and lawless—though there were fewer of these in Ohio than in southern Indiana and Illinois—also joined in. Deserters, bounty-jumpers, and those who were sullen and furtive when volunteers were called for or when the draft was being enforced, became boisterous and bragging at these meetings. However, it seems that there was little direct connection between the Vallandigham movement of 1863 and the "Knights of the Golden Circle." [76]

Another element in the movement were the "old fashioned" peace Methodists, Baptists, and Presbyterians or those church-goers who had opposed the discussion of slavery and "politics in the pulpit." Some of these left their churches and joined the new Christian Union Church, a unique anti-war organization largely composed of proscribed Methodists who became peace Democrats and were, of course, accused of being in sympathy with rebels. The sacrament of the Lord's Supper was denied them in some churches. They claimed that whereas the masses of people, if left alone, would love and respect each other, Republican and Methodist ministers of the gospel were teaching lessons of cruelty and the people "were being misled until their passions were hot as burning sand." [77] So at variance were Christians that while church conferences and presbyteries took action against Vallandigham, many sincere Quakers, appalled by the awfulness of the war, allowed their desire for peace to overcome their desires for the abolition of slavery and supported him as a "practical Christian." [78] Many Irish Catholic workingmen, because of their opposition to conscription and for fear of the competition of free Negro workmen, supported him also.[79]

Against such "renegade" classes of the people, there were arrayed the Union-Republican-War-Democrat groups who supported Brough. They were made up of the respectable, educated, aggressive and

[75] *The Crisis*, Sept. 30, 1863.
[76] Mayo Fesler, "Secret Political Societies," *loc. cit.*, p. 220.
[77] For this difficult problem see H. C. Dean, *Crimes of the Civil War*, p. 9; Faran and McLean, *Politics and the Pulpit;* David Christy, *Pulpit Politics; The Crisis,* Jan. 28, July 29, Oct. 7, 1863; *Western Christian Advocate,* 1863, *passim;* S. F. B. Morse, *An Argument on the Ethical Position of Slavery in the Social System* (Papers from the Society for the Diffusion of Political Knowledge, No. 12, Aug., 1863).
[78] Columbus *Crisis,* Sept. 9, 1863.
[79] Cincinnati *Daily Commercial,* Oct. 6, 8, 13, 1863; *Crisis,* Sept. 16, 23, 1863.

wealthy classes. Though concentrated more largely in the Reserve and in the Miami valleys, they were scattered all over Ohio. They had the moral support of similar classes in Michigan, in the Chicago region and in Iowa, all of whom held Vallandigham in contempt. Republican office-holders, returned army officials and leading business men were of this group, as were also college professors, professional men, and the more prosperous farmers. Their leaders were often prominent laymen in the Methodist, Presbyterian, Congregational, and Unitarian Churches, whose clergy believed in war, advocated "pulpit politics" and prayed for the success of Brough and for northern armies against southern traitors. The Methodist Church was purged of its Democratic members and became, in Ohio and elsewhere, a sort of unofficial State church by its support of the Union and by its intense Republicanism, a party spirit which became so tightly fastened on it that it persists in large degree until to-day.[80] A New England angularity and sternness of mind accompanied the Union war feeling and stood in contrast with the more easy going, tolerant, unaggressive, lower western attitude. Thus the social prestige, the wealth and power that goes with education, culture, and religious leadership, help explain the outcome of the Vallandigham-Brough contest. Patriotism in the form of a war to the uttermost for Union and freedom for the slave became associated with the dominant social classes. They were, of course, bound to win.

The outcome of the election is well known. The vote was large. War Democrats, even though many of them had opposed the Emancipation Proclamation and disapproved the numerous arrests of "ranting editors and broken-down politicians," [81] supported Brough vigorously. Soldiers in the field, now become legal voters, though their vote was light, cast large majorities for Brough. Threats and counter-threats just before the election in October infused fear into the hearts of many voters. Pugh had made his pompous boast that if Vallandigham were elected, fifty thousand armed freemen would escort him from the Canadian line to the State House. This, it was claimed by Brough, would inaugurate civil war in the state. The victories of the Union armies at Vicksburg and Gettysburg help explain the result. The Democratic majority of 1862 was reversed, and Vallandigham was defeated by a large majority, even many southern

---

[80] The prohibition tendencies of the Republicans and the M. E. Church later helped to cement this union.

[81] Speech of S. O. Griswold in Ohio House of Representatives, Jan. 29, 1863.

and western counties voting against him.[82] "We verily believe the spirit of the Lord has moved upon the hearts of many. God has averted a threatened calamity. Let His name be praised," said a Methodist paper.[83]

[82] Porter, *Ohio Politics*, pp. 178–183. His total vote was 187,492; that of Brough 288,374.

[83] *Western Christian Advocate*, Oct. 21, 1863.

CHAPTER XIII

War Prosperity—the Solemnities of 1864

The people of certain parts of central and southern Indiana and Illinois felt the effects of the blockade of the Mississippi and the cutting-off of trade with the South as late as 1863. It has generally been considered that the shift to eastern and European markets and the new demand created by the mobilization and movement of armies along the Ohio and Mississippi rivers solved the problem for all the West within a few months after the beginning of the war. But no such easy solution was forthcoming for the question of a market for the Middle West—then and now the greatest economic problem of that region. Corn was still "at ten cents" or burned for fuel in the more out of the way counties; even Republicans were alarmed at distressing conditions in certain places.[1] Morton wrote to Lincoln admitting that the breaking of social and commercial bonds between the West and the South was one of the causes of the defeat of the Union party in 1862.[2] Furthermore it was felt in the lower West that the eastern railroads were profiting unduly by their growing monopoly of western trade. East-going traffic in 1862 and 1863 was beyond the capacity of the canals, railroads, and lake steamers. Because of the blockade of the Mississippi, the good demand from Europe, the patronage of the railroads by the government for the shipping of troops and war materials, and the subsequent raising of prices, the railroads were enabled to reap great profits, to recover from indebtedness following the Panic of 1857 and to see a marked rise in the value of their stock.[3] They strengthened their position by forming rate combinations which continued until the fall of 1863.[4]

[1] Speeches of Representatives Porter of Indiana and Washburne of Illinois, Feb. 7, 1863. *Cong. Globe,* 37 Cong., 3d Sess., 813; E. D. Fite, *Social and Industrial Conditions in the North during the Civil War,* p. 48; Columbus *Crisis,* Jan. 21, 1863.

[2] Foulke, *Morton,* I, 208, 209.

[3] Fite, *Social and Industrial Conditions,* pp. 42, 43.

[4] *New York Commercial letter* to Cincinnati *Daily Commercial,* Sept. 17, 1862; Fite, *op. cit.,* p. 48; New Albany *Ledger,* August 21, 1863; *Report of Adjutant General of Indiana,* I, 396 (Indianapolis, 1869); Cincinnati *Daily Gazette,* Sept. 15, 1863.

It can easily be understood, then, why Democratic orators continued to predict economic disaster to the West, to say that Cincinnati, which it was claimed had sent 64 per cent of its trade south before the war, would languish, and that owls and bats would flit through its warehouses.[5] Had not the great Douglas said that war would mean final separation? Thus the Ohio would become a boundary line and the new nation to the south might lay tariffs on goods going down the Mississippi; this, together with "the oppressions of the East," would be intolerable. They continued to say, also, that disorder would come even in the Union if the Emancipation Proclamation were allowed to overthrow the plantation system in the South— a system which brought such a great demand for western pork, beef, and grain. Both peace Democrats and Unionists made it clear that the economic connections with the South must be preserved. They differed in method; the former insisting that it could be done only by compromise and peaceful reunion; the latter by war. Governor Morton of Indiana urged Lincoln to recover the Mississippi valley as quickly as possible to quiet the peace Democrats as well as from economic considerations, and Governor Yates of Illinois urged similar action "with the paramount object of keeping those rivers open to the two hundred million dollars of our commerce."[6] There can be no doubt that such considerations, along with pride in the common traditions of the "Great Valley," stirred on Grant's troops at Donelson, Shiloh, and Vicksburg.

WAR PROSPERITY AND EXTRAVAGANCE

But it must be admitted that to most of the West, in spite of the blockade and rate combinations, markets for goods came early in the war. The lake region indeed underwent a very rapid economic development, a typical war "boom." Chicago's fervid patriotism during the years of conflict was accompanied by a growth in population, in grain trade, in wealth, in high rents, and banking business that seems unbelievable.[7] In the first two years of war the population of that city was increased by nearly 27,000. All of northern Illinois was

[5] *Cong. Globe,* 37 Cong., 3 Sess., 812.
[6] Foulke, *Morton,* I, 209–211; *Message of Governor Yates to the General Assembly,* Jan. 5, 1863, p. 8 (Springfield, 1863).
[7] *Message of Governor Yates to the General Assembly,* Jan. 5, 1863; Cincinnati *Daily Commercial,* Nov. 18, 1864, quoting Census of 1860 and the city censuses of 1862 and 1864.

feeling the pulse of new economic forces.[8] The cities of the whole lower West too were experiencing a war prosperity that belied the prediction of peace advocates. Cincinnati never knew such "general prosperity . . . rents advancing . . . brisk demand for city property . . . business profitable." That city and the State of Ohio were becoming industrialized like the East.[9] Indianapolis saw "an immense number of buildings going up. At the end of the war half of the population of the city were newcomers; the farmer in Indiana was making money as never before." The whole state, "in the midst of the fiery ordeal," said Governor Morton, had "unusual prospects spread out before her of prosperity and power."[10] New Albany, Springfield, and other cities were growing rapidly.[11] Across the Ohio into the lower West there occurred a new migration of poorer classes from those parts of the border states that were suffering from disorder and bushwhacking. Into the lake region also, came new streams from the East and from Europe similar to those before the panic of 1857.[12]

Compensation for losses because of high freight rates to the East before the opening of the Mississippi, came in the form of expenditures of the government in the lower West, expenditures attending the advancing operations of the armies in Kentucky, at Cairo and Paducah, and down the Mississippi. This exhilarating influence, together with that of paper inflation, was felt everywhere; merchants, manufacturers, and farmers became "rich while they slept." Farmers paid off millions in mortgages. The river trade as well as that of the railroads going south reached unprecedented proportions. In spite of the blockade of the Mississippi, there was an increase in the building of steamboats in the cities along the Ohio. As the armies advanced southward and new districts were opened to Federal control, the demand for goods increased at Cincinnati, Louisville, and St. Louis; the government let out great contracts for pork, horses, corn, and general army supplies and requisitioned boats wherever government

[8] Cole, *Era of the Civil War*, Ch. XVI.

[9] *Report Commissioner of Statistics*, Ohio (1864), p. 29; Cincinnati *Price Current*, Feb. 18, 1863; Indianapolis *Sentinel*, Feb. 19, 1863.

[10] *Brevier Legislative Reports*, VIII, 32, 36; Indianapolis *Journal*, July 9, 1862; *Indianapolis Correspondence to Cincinnati Gazette*, Aug. 6, 1863; John H. Holliday, "Indianapolis in the Civil War," *Ind. Hist. Soc. Pub.* Vol. IV, no. 9, p. 595.

[11] New Albany *Ledger*, Feb. 28, Mar. 5, 1863; *Compendium of the Ninth Census of the United States*, 42 Cong., 1st Sess., 38, 40–42, 80.

[12] Fite, *op. cit.*, pp. 9, 10, 11, 13, 296.

business required it. St. Louis received shipments from the upper rivers for the use of the armies.[13]

The news of the fall of Vicksburg in July, 1863, was received with celebrations and fireworks in the West—"only peace men refuse to rejoice, they walk cool and solemn."[14] There was rejoicing along the Ohio River towns when the expected opening of the Mississippi brought promise of greater prosperity.[15] Finally came the order from the Treasury Department in September that the great river was formally open and that trade was allowed with certain conquered districts under regulations set down. The Mississippi "ran unvexed to the sea" and higher prices for western produce followed immediately.[16] A victory over the eastern railroads was won at the same time; their monopoly was broken; their directors met at Buffalo, dissolved their combination, permitted competition, and thus brought lower prices for freight going eastward. The West had now high prices, lower rates, and a great demand both from East and South, all at once.[17] The Illinois Central Railroad from Chicago, and the "Terre Haute Road" during the next few months were jammed with traffic for the South; there were not sufficient locomotives and cars to handle the goods, and orders were given that no more freight could be received for Cairo.[18]

The river trade presented opportunities for profiteering and grafting. Steamboat men charged exorbitant rates from soldiers passing up and down the rivers, until General Grant issued orders regulating prices. Merchants in the river cities would violate government regulations regarding trade by smuggling several times the amount of goods they were permitted by government order to ship. It was charged by loyal Republican papers that the seizing within military lines of cotton—now as high as sixty cents a pound in price—and the grant of special permits to trade within and beyond the lines were accompanied by questionable practices, and that such a system "corrupts army officers, encompasses military operations with a horde of

---

[13] *Annual Report, Cincinnati Chamber of Commerce for the Year Ending August 31,* 1863; *Merchants Magazine and Commercial Review,* Vol. 51, p. 396; Rerick, *History of Ohio,* p. 329; Cincinnati *Gazette,* Sept. 30, Aug. 4, 7, 8, Oct., Dec., *passim.* See also *St. Louis Correspondence* to the *Gazette* for the latter part of 1863.

[14] *Western Christian Advocate,* July 15, 1863.

[15] New Albany *Ledger,* July 25, 27, Aug. 25, 1863.

[16] Cincinnati *Gazette,* Sept. 29, 1863.

[17] New Albany *Ledger,* Aug. 21, 1863; Fite, p. 16.

[18] Cincinnati *Gazette,* Sept. 17, Dec. 12, 1863.

plunderers and does not prevent the furnishing of information and supplies of every kind to the enemy." [19]

The new prosperity brought extravagance beyond precedent. At the height of the crisis of war, "the demand for luxuries, for jewels and dress has exceeded anything before thought of. . . . Masses of people in the West before unaccustomed to large amounts of money were spending it profusely." [20] With more money to spend, "the silk and lace period" now dawned for the small towns, while the more wealthy cities began to see the first glimmerings of the post-war "gilded age." The London *Times* correspondent said:

They have money, well or ill-gotten, and must enjoy it. Every fresh bulletin from the battlefield of Chickamauga during my three weeks' stay in Cincinnati brought a long list of the dead and wounded of the Western army yet . . . the noisy gaiety of the town was not abated one jot. Miss Laura Keene, the actress, did not draw a less full house.[21]

Pleasure trips to Niagara Falls were uninterrupted by war, though the gifts to charity, to soldiers' families, to destitute people in the South and to English mill hands thrown out of work, were generous.[22] War was doing its usual work of transforming society in unexpected ways and of creating problems as great as those it sought to solve. A new West was emerging with new interests and new moralities. Indianapolis, for instance, took on "new ideas, new aspirations, new ways." The simple life of the pre-war town was gone forever. Families were broken up; there were alterations in social position and new social cleavages. "Large fortunes [were] made and many families [were being] impoverished. There was more luxurious living and ostentation. Hundreds of young men had become addicted to intemperance and the general moral tone had been lowered. . . . Change was over all." [23]

There were not only moral but grave economic dangers in this war-stimulated prosperity, as the peace Democrats were only too eager to point out. In the national House of Representatives Daniel Voorhees (he and Hendricks of Indiana and Richardson of Illinois

[19] Cincinnati *Gazette,* Aug. 11, 1863; Dec. 1 (*Cairo Correspondence*); Dec. 25, 31, 1863.

[20] *Annual Report Cincinnati Chamber of Commerce,* Cincinnati *Daily Commercial,* Sept. 9, 1863.

[21] London *Times,* Nov. 3, 1863 quoted in Fite, *Social and Industrial Conditions,* p. 259.

[22] *Western Christian Advocate,* Sept. 1863, *passim;* Oct. 14, 1863.

[23] John H. Holliday, "Indianapolis and the Civil War," *Ind. Hist. Soc. Pub.* Vol. IV, No. 9, p. 595.

in the Senate, became the opposition leaders at Washington, after Vallandigham's defeat and exile), held out warnings.

Some superficial observers will point to the appearance of general prosperity. . . . Money is flowing in boundless profusion. . . . Unnatural prices are paid for everything. . . . A meretricious splendor hails us upon the streets, at the rout, the assembly and the theater. The nation seems fattening on blood and carnage. But this high feverish flush . . . is not the genial warmth of health. It is the fierce hectic glow of a swift consumption. What we call money is not money.[24]

S. S. Cox of Ohio said that the prosperity was a delusion, based on greenbacks.

To whom does the money go? To jobbers in stocks, to manufacturers who get twenty-five per cent tariff bounties, to buy up negroes to save sons from the bullet and bonds whose interest is paid in gold. Oh, it is prosperous to run in debt is it? Prosperous to consume and not produce, is it?[25]

In pointing out the rapidly approaching problems of taxes, debt, high prices, and the possibility of repudiation, the Democrats were standing on somewhat firmer ground than when making mere partisan allegations or indulging in loose anti-war talk.

The East fattens on the blood of western men. . . . When the war ends . . . three-fourths of the government debt, about three thousand millions of dollars represented by five and six per cent gold bearing bonds, will be piled up in New England. These bonds, which cost the holders less than forty cents on the dollar and as a consequence pay fifteen per cent interest in gold on the investment, represent New England's profits in a war for the emancipation of the negro.[26]

Thus forebodings of future discontent in the West and a new alliance with the South on the question of Greenbacks and other reconstruction issues, were appearing.

CONSPIRACY—ILL-TIMED AND POORLY EXECUTED, 1863–1864

The prosperity we have described was clearly undermining the opposition of the peace Democrats; the London *Times* correspondent in a keen observation said it was likely to bring defeat for them at elections.[27] Among the other influences at work in the same direction in 1863 and 1864 were the operations of secret orders among the

[24] *Cong. Globe,* 38 Cong., 1 Sess., *Appendix,* 78.
[25] Cincinnati *Daily Commercial,* Oct. 3, 1864.
[26] *The Enquirer,* Nov. 8, 1864 *et passim.*
[27] Cincinnati *Gazette,* Nov. 4, 1863.

western Democrats and attempts at various military conspiracies in favor of the South. Those who read Republican newspapers or who heard speeches of public men could not fail to be alarmed at the vague but startling disclosures that confronted them. But their tense feelings and the passions aroused by war prevented them from taking account of very evident exaggerations, and it is now pretty well conceded that the importance of these movements has been over-stressed; that, far from being a real danger to union sentiment, they resulted in strengthening it and proved a decided element of weakness to the peace Democrats.

With these groups, then, groups whose record was mysterious and darkened with intrigue, among whom may be found in truth some secessionist sympathizers, it is necessary to deal only briefly. They kept alive that direct contact with southern leaders which we have seen characterized the activities of the "Dodge-Jones-Bright" group at an earlier day and indulged in rash and what appeared to be more pro-southern activities than these older men. The leaders were over-zealous, over-irritated, or reckless, second, or third-rate politicians— most of the prominent peace Democrats refused to be identified with them—and their followers were largely ignorant or vagrant and seem to have been uninformed as to the purposes of the little clique at their head. They had, since 1861, been forming or introducing from other sections the secret order of the Knights of the Golden Circle or the Order of American Knights and Sons of Liberty, which with their mummery and passwords, seem to have appealed greatly to certain classes. Indeed fraternal organizations, both indoor and outdoor, have since had this appeal in the Middle West. While the mass of the membership did little more than attend lodge meetings and support the peace Democrats in political matters, the few at the center were rather "direct actionists," given to plans of a far-flown and apparently threatening nature, which however, ill-timed and poorly executed, proved disastrous in the end.[28]

The Knights of the Golden Circle had been organized in Cincin-

[28] Mayo Fesler: "Secret Political Societies in the North during the Civil War," *Indiana Magazine of History*, Vol. XIV, No. 3, pp. 183–286. This convincing treatment is made the basis of what the author has to say on this subject. See also Elbert J. Benton, "The Movement for Peace without Victory during the Civil War," *Publication No. 99, Western Reserve Historical Society*, pp. 1–72; Foulke, *Morton*, I, Chs. 28–30; Benj. Pitman, *Trials for Treason at Indianapolis; Official Records, War of the Rebellion*, Series II, Vol. II, pp. 228–378 *passim*.

nati in 1854 and spread southward and southwestward, becoming very strong in Texas. At first it had for its object the annexation of territory to the United States at the expense of Mexico; it was associated in the public mind with filibustering imperialistic desires in Central America and belongs in the long chain of movements with similar objects going back as far as the "Burr Conspiracy." It later became identified with the cause of slavery, of white supremacy, with State rights and the Democratic party, in so far as that party represented these interests. Later, under various names and with a loose organization and a weak leadership, it spread among the peace Democrats of the West and became strong in southern Indiana and Illinois; its total membership north of the Ohio was, however, probably less than 100,000.[29] In Indiana it had "castles" in all parts of the state. In Illinois it was strong in Williamson and other southern counties and in the lower Illinois River valley rather than in the north.[30] In Ohio it was less important and seems not to have been responsible to any great degree for the Vallandigham enthusiasm.

It was, however, held responsible for the unusually large shipments of arms into Indiana in 1863. Violent outbreaks, resistance to draft and the clash of state and national forces with armed bands which we have noted, occurred in the counties in Indiana and Illinois where the order was strongest. But direct responsibility for the order is hard to establish.[31] It has been considered as a determining element in the success of the Democrats in the elections of 1862. Members of the order gathered in large numbers armed with revolvers at the Indianapolis peace meeting of May, 1863, which proved such a failure. If, as has been charged, they were to coöperate with Morgan in his raid through southern Indiana and Ohio, they failed to do so. There is, in fact, little evidence that any except a few leaders had any idea of directly aiding the South. The order died in some counties and in others changed its form late in 1863.[32] It helped to bring odium on

[29] The estimates vary, those in Republican papers and Government documents are very much larger than this.

[30] Mayo Fesler, op. cit., pp. 214–220.

[31] Ibid., pp. 207–210.

[32] Ibid., pp. 211–214. The following extracts from a letter from Col. H. B. Carrington at Indianapolis to Adj. Gen. Thomas at Washington dated Jan. 24, 1863 shows the attitude of mustering officers and other military men toward the order: "I have been laboriously engaged in the examination of soldiers to detect the operations of the secret society at work to secure desertions. . . . Several organized attempts to do mischief have been frustrated. . . . The evidence involves some quite prominent citizens but I have thought not to make the results public

the name of Democrat and was one of the causes for the formation by Republicans of the "Union League." [33] The newspapers contained many charges against these orders and descriptions of peculiar oaths and gibberish which they ascribed to one society or the other.[34]

The "Order of American Knights" originated in St. Louis in 1863 as a reorganized form of the Knights of the Golden Circle. It spread into Indiana and Illinois, its name later becoming the "Sons of Liberty." More complex, highly organized, and possessing an elaborate ritual, it drew heavily on those districts and those classes that had belonged to the Knights of the Golden Circle. In reality it was little more than a Democratic club, opposed to the administration, and striving to make more impressive the principles of Jeffersonian Democracy, State rights and the Virginia and Kentucky Resolutions by associating them with wordy, cabalistic rites.[35] Some of the leaders, however, and some of the members—how many no one will ever know—had military designs and pro-southern tendencies which made it an instrument for conspiracy. Slavery was a God-ordained institution and the name of Calhoun reversed, *Nuohlac*, was used as a password. In some of the documents uncovered, the objects of the order were to stop war, treat with the South, and make a treaty based on the recognition of grades of civilization and races, Caucasian supremacy and African servitude.[36] Military drill was held in some counties of Indiana and Illinois, and, upon being asked to explain this, the members would say they were training to "protect their rights." [37] Like the Knights of the Golden Circle, its actual

until we push inquiries further. . . . The order is one of the most treasonable character. An apparent improvement is visible in this state growing out of the fact that it is now thought that the Government will deal sternly. . . . Nearly 2,600 deserters and stragglers have been arrested within a few weeks. . . . Most of the deserters true to the oath of their order, desert with their arms, and in one case seventeen fortified themselves in a cabin . . . and were maintained by their neighbors. . . . *Official Records War of Rebellion*, Series III, Vol. III, p. 19.

[33] For "Union Leagues" see *Journal Ill. State Hist. Soc.*, V, 209, 263; *Indiana Brevier Legislative Reports*, V, 84, 85; Columbus *Crisis*, July 1, Sept. 30, 1863; for "Indiana Legion" see Esarey, *Indiana*, II, 764-776.

[34] Columbus *Crisis*, Apr. 22, 1863; Sept. 30, 1863; *Iowa Archives, Reports, Miscellaneous*, G. VIII, p. 175.

[35] Fesler, *op. cit.*, pp. 224, 232; *Official Records War of the Rebellion*, Series II, Vol. VII, pp. 289-295; E. C. Kirkland, *The Peacemakers of 1864* (Macmillan, 1927), pp. 41-45.

[36] Columbus *Crisis*, Aug. 10, 1864 quoting Gen. Carrington's Report to Gov. Morton of Indiana.

[37] J. N. Gridley: "The Husted or Jacksonville Raid," *Journal Illinois State Hist. Soc.*, Vol. V, pp. 209-210.

membership was very small compared to the total number of peace Democrats, though the Republican papers placed it at alarmingly large figures. The aims of the few leaders being ascribed to the whole membership and the size of that membership being exaggerated, the order created no little panic and fear in 1863 and 1864; it was constantly referred to as a treasonous order attempting to unite the Northwest and the South. The Cincinnati *Commercial,* less partisan and more discerning, treated it lightly, ridiculing it as the "Democratic Carbonari" and publishing what purported to be its bombastic ritual and oath.[38] President Lincoln's attitude toward such things, according to John Hay, was one of "good-humored contempt."

A certain H. H. Dodd became Grand Commander in the State of Indiana and Vallandigham in February, 1864, while still in Canada, was prevailed upon to allow his name to be used as Supreme Commander; later he disclaimed any military purpose other than the protection of rights. As military conspiracy became the objects of the leaders, prominent Democratic politicians other than Vallandigham would not allow their names to be used and some even opposed it.[39] Medary of the *Crisis* disclaimed any belief in any form of secret organization,[40] and the *Enquirer* gave it only casual or apologetic treatment.[41] The editor of the Indianapolis *Sentinel,* J. J. Bingham, arrested for complicity in its plots, said that Democratic leaders tried to stop any sort of uprising and that he finally came to consider the order a "humbug." [42]

It was with the secret orders in the West that the southern Confederacy at various times sought to establish connection. While the Confederate Congress at first went little farther than to pass a resolution guaranteeing to the free West the navigation of the Mississippi, the peace newspapers imparted renewed emphasis to the old argument of economic interdependence, western sectionalism, and the desire for separation from New England. All this caused grave concern in administrative circles.[43] It was, no doubt, in these orders also that demands for an armistice and a peace convention received its greatest

[38] Issues of Aug. 2, 1864; Nov. 6, 1868.
[39] Cincinnati *Daily Commercial,* Sept. 23, Oct. 1, 6, 7, 10, 1864.
[40] *The Crisis,* Feb. 18, 1863.
[41] *The Enquirer,* Oct. 9, Nov. 1, 1864; Fesler, *op. cit.,* p. 263.
[42] Indianapolis *Sentinel,* Nov. 8, 1864 quoted in Cincinnati *Daily Commercial.*
[43] New Albany *Ledger,* Jan. 4, Feb. 5, 1863; Indianapolis *Journal,* Jan. 17, 19, 1863; Robert Dale Owen, *The Future of the Northwest* (pamphlet 1863); Mayo Fesler, "Secret Political Societies," *op. cit.,* pp. 242, 243.

support.[44] Finally, in 1864, the Confederacy being ready, it appears, for desperate measures, Jefferson Davis appointed agents who, with nearly a million dollars at their disposal, went to Canada and sought to influence opinion in the Northwest, to purchase arms for the secret orders, to release Confederate prisoners in prison camps at Indianapolis, Chicago, and Rock Island, and to inaugurate such "insurrection" among the peace Democrats as might be possible under the circumstances. There followed various far-flung "northwestern conspiracies." The southern agents apparently becoming over-optimistic, offered money to H. H. Dodd and other leaders of the Sons of Liberty in Indiana. Arms were brought and secreted in Indianapolis awaiting the day for action. Peace meetings were to be called in the West, the southern armies were to make raids in Kentucky and Missouri, and Confederate soldiers from Canada were to coöperate with members of the order. Inklings of all this, published in the newspapers, filled many people in the West with terror. But the concerted movements did not actually occur; "the day" was repeatedly postponed; the leaders of the Sons of Liberty were hesitant; they succeeded in mustering little or no military organization; and secret agents of Governor Morton and the National Government kept in touch with their movements and usually exposed them on the eve of action.[45] The office of H. H. Dodd in Indianapolis was searched, and 135,000 rounds of ammunition and two bushel baskets full of the rituals of the Sons of Liberty were found hidden there; the "plotters" were arrested and held for trial, among them, Bingham, editor of the *Sentinel*. Thus one of the schemes was frustrated.

Leaders of the Sons of Liberty planned to meet at Chicago late in August, 1864, along with the national Democratic convention, to try to capture the convention and to free the Confederate prisoners at Camp Douglas nearby. While the peace Democrats succeeded, as we shall see, in incorporating a peace plank in the national platform, the agents of the Confederacy and their fellow conspirators in the Sons of Liberty failed to dominate the convention and failed to free the prisoners both at Camp Douglas and at Rock Island. The Confederate agents were deceived, and the armed force which the order was to supply proved a broken reed.

When the trial of the Indianapolis conspirators began just before

[44] *Indiana Brevier Legislative Reports*, VI, 21, 91, 92, 142, 169. Indianapolis *Journal*, Jan. 30, 1863; *Sentinel*, Feb. 5, 23, 27, 1863; Columbus *Crisis*, Feb. 18, 1863.
[45] Fesler, *op. cit.*, pp. 276–283.

election day in 1864, the revelations only aided the Unionist cause. H. H. Dodd, one of the most zealous leaders, escaped during the trial and brought further public odium upon himself; [46] he later took refuge in Canada. Even peace Democrats said of him "he was honest, but had a foolish love of the mysterious and a taste for empty sounding titles." [47] "A few hot headed members of the society got up a conspiracy, a mysterious idiosyncrasy of poor half-cracked Mr. Dodd." [48] Vallandigham himself said that Dodd had acted rashly.[49]

Still another attempt was made by the southern agents and certain leaders of the order; this time the plan was to free the prisoners at Camp Douglas. The occasion was to be election night, November 8, 1864 and the excitement that would accompany it in Chicago was expected to add to the chances of success. But the order again failed to produce an organized force; certain bushwhackers from "Egypt" who were imported to give aid accomplished nothing further than to be arrested as suspicious characters. The attempt was exposed before election day and like the other "conspiracies," proved a fiasco.[50]

A famous case in American constitutional law was almost the only result of all these ill-timed projects. In the trials in Indiana held at Indianapolis, after much confusion of testimony and in the face of the complaint that the military court had no jurisdiction, a certain Lambdin B. Milligan was convicted and sentenced to be hanged. The execution of the sentence against Milligan was suspended once by President Johnson, and, after the gallows had been erected at Camp Morton near Indianapolis, the sentence was commuted to life imprisonment. There followed finally the well-known "Milligan case." The Supreme Court, in 1866, in the midst of the bitterness of the reconstruction period, decided that the military court had had no jurisdiction in the case of Milligan, that there was no real invasion in Indiana, and that it was unconstitutional to try him in a "court not ordained by and established by Congress and not composed of judges appointed during good behaviour." [51] Thus, to some extent, the peace Democrats were vindicated at a later day in their opposition to military arrests and trials. However, the secret orders in general

---

[46] Cincinnati *Gazette,* Oct. 8, 1864; Fesler, *op. cit.* pp. 259–261.
[47] *The Enquirer,* Sept. 30, 1864.
[48] *Ibid.,* Nov. 1, 7, 1864.
[49] *Ibid.,* Sept. 27, 1864.
[50] Fesler, *op. cit.,* pp. 270–276.
[51] Samuel Klaus, *The Milligan Case; Ex parte* Milligan, 1867, 4 Wallace, 2; Randall, *Constitutional Problems under Lincoln,* pp. 179–183.

accomplished little. We agree completely with the author of the following summary regarding all their efforts.

> These organizations were singularly lacking in energy and initiative. . . . The President and the authorities at Washington . . . looked upon the machinations of the leaders of these . . . societies with "good humored contempt" and saw in their movements a nearly equal mixture of puerility and malice.[52]

THE WESTERN PEACE BOLT, 1864

During the years 1864 and the first few months of 1865, there were several attempts to bring peace between the North and the South. Some important efforts of this type were associated with the names of Horace Greeley and F. P. Blair, Sr. In February, 1865 there was held the still more significant Hampton Roads Conference, Secretary Seward, President Lincoln, Alexander H. Stephens, and others meeting in a boat near Fortress Monroe to discuss peace and reconstruction. All these efforts were of course failures.[53] Our concern is, in particular, with western peace sentiment as it found expression in the Democratic national convention of 1864, and with the "Ohio Peace Bolt" in the late summer and fall.

Western Democrats had already recognized that the Democrats of the East were more conservative and pro-war and, as the time for the party's national convention approached, there were fears on the part of western peace men that a War Democrat like McClellan would be forced on an unwilling West.[54] Far from representing the anti-war feeling of the Democrats of the lower West, he would be the candidate of "the bankers and bondholders of New York" and would "sell out to eastern monopolists." [55] The action he took in 1861 in giving the order to arrest the members of the Maryland Legislature was held against him. The western peace men favored Long or Pendleton of Ohio or Governor Seymour of New York or Seymour of Connecticut. Ohio Democrats were divided; those in the southern part of the state preferring Vallandigham and those in the northern part, McClellan.[56] Vallandigham had until June, 1864, remained in Canada, still the center of all eyes. On June 15, 1864 he appeared suddenly and dramatically at Hamilton, Ohio, and was

[52] Fesler, *op. cit.*, p. 286.
[53] E. C. Kirkland, *The Peacemakers of 1864*, Chs. II, IV.
[54] Columbus *Crisis*, Aug. 10, 1864.
[55] *Ibid.*, August 17, 24, 1864.
[56] Porter, *Ohio Politics*, p. 192.

elected a delegate to the national Democratic convention which was
to meet at Chicago.[57] There he became the lion of the day.

In late August, 1864, while Sherman was hammering toward
Atlanta, the convention met. As so often happens in conventions of
that party, it was a large, confused, and turbulent body.[58] We have
already shown that the conspirators in the Sons of Liberty were there
planning their "insurrection." The politicians, less inclined to use
force, were there with every variety of opposition and peace program.
There were speeches in the streets for an armistice and peace, "for
free elections, free fights, forcible resistance to the draft and other
measures that taken together constitute a peace that passeth understanding. . . . Many obscure orators desire martyrdom by arrest
and imprisonment in a Lincoln bastille." [59] Vallandigham, the hero
of the hour, in an open-air meeting made this fervent appeal:

If you would have peace abandon that idea of coercion, come back again
to compromise and conciliation; instead of war let us have reason, argument, deliberation; let us have the assemblage of a convention of states.
. . . Let us have an armistice.

Reed of Indiana said: "Resist the draft and shoot down Lincoln's
minions who attempt to enforce it." [60] One of the questions that
divided the delegates was whether, if an armistice were called and
the South refused to come back into the Union, force should be used
against her. It was thought that Vallandigham, Long, Dr. Olds, and
Henry Clay Dean would welcome peace at any price.[61] In reality
there were three groups, the War Democrats of the East and upper
West; the peace Democrats who would consent, though reluctantly,
to McClellan as a candidate on a peace platform; and the extreme
peace group who were very much opposed to McClellan. It was clear
to keen observers that the extreme peace men would insist on a platform on which McClellan could not stand.[62]

Alexander Long, representative from a Cincinnati district, elected to
Congress in the great opposition wave of 1862, became in 1864 a

[57] Porter, *Ohio Politics*, pp. 195, 196. See Vallandigham's speech at Hamilton
in *Official Records War of Rebellion*, Series III, Vol. VII, pp. 328–334.

[58] Cincinnati *Daily Commercial*, Aug. 30, 1864; E. C. Kirkland, *The Peacemakers of 1864*, pp. 129–136.

[59] Cincinnati *Daily Commercial*, Sept. 2, 1864.

[60] *Ibid.*, Aug. 29, 1864.

[61] *Ibid.*, Aug. 29, 1864.

[62] *Ibid.*, Aug. 30, 1864. The correspondent of this paper wrote very discerning
articles on this convention.

leading advocate of peace in the North. He had gone farther than Vallandigham and other peace Democrats who were avowedly for Union and had proclaimed himself ready for separation. He seemed to look upon the war as a contest of the South for nationalism and independence. In a remarkably bold and apparently honest and non-partisan speech in Congress on April 8, 1864 he had said:

The war ought immediately to cease. . . . Land is nothing compared to liberty. . . . We existed as a Republic when the mouth of the Mississippi was held by a foreign power and we could exist again. . . . The union is lost never to be restored. In attempting to preserve our jurisdiction over the Southern states we have lost our constitutional form of government over the Northern. . . . There never was a people on the face of the Earth that demanded an independent government that did not have the sympathy of the American people and ought we now to shrink from the doctrine we have been so willing to apply to others? [63]

To Unionist members of the House this was clearly going too far, and James A. Garfield of the Western Reserve and Schuyler Colfax of northern Indiana took up the fight against the Cincinnatian. Colfax, the speaker, descended from the chair and moved the expulsion of Long from the House. In the debate on the expulsion of Long there was of course much intense partisanship, recrimination, and jingoism, but there was also evidence of manliness and sincerity, on both sides of the House. The tragedy of war was realized. The Republicans were greatly embarrassed by being told that Long's stand was that of leading Republicans in 1861. It was soon clear that the two-thirds vote necessary for expulsion could not be obtained. The resolution was changed to one of censure and Long was declared an "unworthy member." [64]

Long had come to the Chicago convention ready to put a defeatist plank in the platform and to urge State rights and disunion if necessary. But the committee on resolutions did not go that far. Amid great cheering, the convention under Vallandigham's influence adopted the resolution for a cessation of hostilities and peace on the basis of union.[65] Although the extreme peace men of southern Ohio, In-

[63] *Cong. Globe*, 38 Cong., 1 Sess., 1499, 1505.
[64] *Ibid.*, pp. 1505–1593, 1634.
[65] Cincinnati *Daily Commercial*, Aug. 31, 1864. The resolution read: "That after four years of failure to restore the Union by the experiment of war . . . justice, humanity, liberty and the public welfare demand that immediate efforts be made for a cessation of hostilities, with a view to an ultimate convention of the States, or other peaceable means, to the end that at the earliest practicable moment peace may be restored on the basis of the Federal Union of the States."

diana, and Illinois succeeded in putting through this plank, their candidate, Governor Seymour of Connecticut, was not destined to be chosen. General McClellan was nominated with Pendleton of Cincinnati, a more definite peace man, on the ticket as Vice-President. McClellan was opposed by the extreme peace men from Ohio and Indiana; they were in fact preparing for a peace bolt. They said McClellan was guilty of the arrest of the legislature of a sovereign state and was in some respects even less humanitarian than Lincoln. Their rejected candidate, Seymour of Connecticut, was a "pure" peace man. At Columbus, Ohio, on September 14, Medary, Vallandigham, Olds, and Pugh met to consider a bolt. McClellan was deluged with letters from extreme peace men in Ohio and the West asking him to stand for an armistice, "a simple stacking of arms and negotiation." He was told that Medary meant mischief; that Vallandigham would not speak for him; that in southern Ohio, Indiana, and Illinois, the peace men were rampant. Vallandigham pleaded with him, "Do not listen to any of your eastern friends who in an evil hour may advise you to insinuate even a little war in your letter of acceptance." On the other hand War Democrats urged him to favor force if necessary, "force with magnanimity." [66] He came out with his well-known letter of acceptance as a moderate War Democrat, willing to use coercion if necessary. This was too much for Medary and the extremists. They now saw still less difference between Lincoln and McClellan; the people had been "Chicagoed," the peace Democrats "skunked"; they became more and more bitter against Eastern "monopolistic" Democrats and a group of them called a convention of lower western states to be held at Cincinnati.[67] But Vallandigham was not there, and Medary himself was ill and did not attend. This old war horse of the sectional State rights Democrats of the West, a "constitutionalist," a dean of western journalism and a friend of Andrew Jackson, was now failing rapidly and was to die soon after the November election.[68]

The meeting of the bolters was held in Cincinnati late in October. In the building of the Catholic Institute in that city about fifty delegates, coming largely from the lower West, "pro-southern" die hards, and the most extreme western peace men, assembled for a last

[66] McClellan Papers, Manuscript Division, Library of Congress.
[67] Columbus *Crisis*, Sept. 2, 3, 7, 24, 28, Oct. 18. *The Enquirer* opposed the McClellan statement but supported him nevertheless. *The Enquirer*, Sept. 13, 1864.
[68] *The Crisis*, Sept. 14, 1864, November, 1864, *passim*.

futile gesture. Their leaders were Long and Corry of Ohio, Develin
and Jewett of Indiana, and Singleton of Illinois. W. M. Corry was
the leader of a new and vague "labor-peace" movement in Ohio.
Resolutions were adopted favoring peace and State rights, approving
the Virginia and Kentucky resolutions, and repudiating McClellan's
war record and his letter of acceptance. The resolutions considered
the evils of paper money, the protective tariff, debt, the draft, arbitrary arrest and "bayonet elections, padlocked lips, fettered press."
They asserted that the result of a public debt would be to deliver the
agricultural states to bondage and their people to serfdom, and that
for the welfare of labor, Negro slavery among the mingled millions
of southern whites and blacks was the only possible condition of prosperous society. Long, pressed to accept the nomination for President,
refused, and it was considered too late to undertake a campaign.
Thus the whole enterprise collapsed and left little in its train except
thwarted hopes and sullenness.[69]

THE REËLECTION OF LINCOLN, 1864

In our almost exclusive concern with the lower West and, in particular, with the peace Democracy there, we have been doing scant
justice to the Republican-Unionist strength in that region and even
less to the developments around the lakes. There, Republicanism and
Union sentiment was especially strong. In that upper region the factors we saw operating as early as the forties, were still at work. There
were to be found modern intellectual and cultural currents that continued to flow in from the East and from Europe; there, demands
arose for more direct railroad connection with the East; there—in
the Reserve of Ohio, in southern Michigan and in Chicago—was
springing up a veritable surge of capitalism and all the problems of the
industrial civilization it was bringing in. There, the immediate slogan
was, "Lincoln and the War." Agrarianism was receding farther westward and in Iowa, Minnesota and Nebraska, new corn and wheat
belts were emerging. This upper West and the new grain belts looked
to the future; the lower West was about to pass as a major section.
The reëlection of Lincoln affords one proof of this.

But, in 1864, as election day approached, there was much reason for

[69] Elizabeth F. Yager, *The Campaign of 1864 in Ohio* (Ohio State University,
Master's Thesis), pp. 20–22; *Western Christian Advocate*, Oct. 18, 1864; Cincinnati *Daily Commercial*, Oct. 21, 1864.

thinking that Lincoln's administration would be repudiated in the West. The turbulence of the Chicago Peace Convention and the failure of the conspiracies did not mean that the Democratic party had lost its remarkable recuperative power or that McClellan was a candidate unsuited to the moods of 1864.[70] War weariness and despair affected Republicans as well as Democrats; the fearful waste of life by Grant and Sherman was everywhere felt, and the spirit of defeatism prevalent in certain quarters would aid McClellan more than Lincoln. Against the blundering record of the opposition Democrats could be reckoned the mistakes of the Unionist-Republicans. It remained no longer for peace Democrats to point out the "despotism" of the administration forces; it was done by War Democrats and Republicans as well. Senator Trumbull of Illinois and John M. Palmer of that state criticized what they considered the high-handedness of the administration.[71] Many, on the other hand, said the President was too mild. He had often to face the criticism of the Methodist pulpit, pen, and press and of the Cincinnati *Gazette;* moreover, the Chase element in Ohio was opposed to him. A prominent educator in Jacksonville said that the President was reading the New Testament too much and needed the Old Testament warrior spirit of Jackson.[72] Lincoln, indeed, had been renominated, but this had been done in spite of the protests of German and radical Republicans and in accordance with the prevailing feeling that there was nothing else to do. Would the people's patience and trust in Lincoln, the opening of the Mississippi, and the very evident war prosperity, the slow but relentless progress of Sherman in Georgia and Grant in Virginia, would all these factors outweigh the mountain of opposition and turn the balance in Lincoln's favor?

With people's eyes turned rather to the South and the movements of Sherman's army, the Presidential campaign proceeded. It was conducted by Democrats in the West on a peace basis and by the eastern Democrats on a qualified war basis. The more important eastern Democratic papers were moderately pro-war and at no time admitted the doctrines of Long and Vallandigham. In the East, the peace resolution of the Chicago convention, even though McClellan and his eastern followers did so much to override it, proved a millstone on the party's neck. Western Democratic speakers emphasized the resolu-

[70] Cole, *op. cit.,* pp. 319, 322, 323.
[71] Horace White, *Life of Lyman Trumbull,* pp. 206, 207.
[72] Cole, *op. cit.,* p. 314.

tion, continued to call for a convention and pointed out that Pendleton, the candidate for Vice-President, was a moderate peace man.[73]

In Illinois John A. Logan again, as in 1863, was called upon to undertake the task of winning hostile and sullen "Egypt" for the war. He met the Democratic cry of "We must have peace" with a fervid "We must fight on and on." War irritation and demagogism were expressed in his speeches and reconstruction quarrels were foreshadowed.

If the government is restored . . . If I should ever be a member of Congress, I never would sit alongside of Jeff Davis and Benjamin, Slidell, Beauregard and Lee. . . . We want every foot of territory that ever belonged to the United States government and we intend to have it. . . . These gentlemen who are lording it over the people of the South, if we ever get hold of them we will settle the question so effectively with them as to leave them unable to make further disturbance.

As to Vallandigham, he said, "No man will do him honor; . . . patriots and soldiers will spit upon his grave."[74] Equally overwrought Democrats with less of sadness than of venom did not hesitate to taunt Lincoln. "Abraham Lincoln has been the cause of more death and misery than any man of whom history makes mention." "Nero fiddled while Rome was burning and Lincoln called for a comic negro song when he was surrounded by corpses on the battlefield of Antietam."[75] Such leading Democratic papers as *The Enquirer* and Indianapolis *Sentinel* were said to be "fair and gentle" compared to "local copperhead sheets."[76] Lincoln was a "widow-maker"; McClellan would bring reduced taxes and the draft would be no longer needed.[77] Such burning words made impressions and caused local divisions that lasted long after the war. Just before the election in Indiana an armed band of two or three hundred men in Crawford and Orange counties was suppressed—another "miserable failure of an extensive conspiracy." A whole company of the Indiana Legion was disarmed and disbanded as "disloyal."[78] The Republican religious press in pointing to dangers of conspiracies, to the threatened

---

[73] Cincinnati *Daily Commercial*, Nov. 15, 1864.

[74] *Ibid.*, Oct. 5, 1864; Cole, *op. cit.*, p. 327.

[75] *The Enquirer*, Sept. 8, 1864.

[76] In Ohio, the Hamilton *True Telegraph*, the Ashland *Union*, the Chillicothe *Advertizer*, and the *Holmes County Farmer*, were especially violent. Cincinnati *Daily Commercial*, Nov. 7, 1864.

[77] Cincinnati *Daily Commercial*, Nov. 7, 1864; Cole, *op. cit.*, p. 326.

[78] *Report of Brig. General H. Judson, Indiana Legion*, Documents of the General Assembly, Indianapolis (1865), pp. 447, 448.

"burning and sacking of cities, to the assassination of magistrates, bloody revolution itself," did little to allay public excitement.[79] The support given to the war by college presidents and professors, by preachers, and the religious press was criticized by peace Democrats; Bishop Simpson spoke at a conference of Methodist ministers and, it was charged by the anti-war press, turned it into a political mob, bowing before "an idol of war and blood." [80]

But strain and sadness often made men on both sides sober; the "solemnities of the time" softened partisan rancor.[81] The vast drain on resources and men, the continued calls for troops, were bringing a war weariness and nerve strain that might prove more difficult to deal with than Democratic opposition. Indiana, in the course of the war, furnished over 200,000 troops of whom about 25,000 were killed or died of disease and 13,000 were counted as "missing," [82] and Ohio and Illinois each furnished still larger numbers. With these hundreds of thousands torn from their families, quartered in far-off camps, or struggling blindly on southern battle-fields, while their families waited wearily at home—with, in some localities, the supply of men to work in the fields exhausted and the women taking their places—the task at times became so solemn and the grip of war so powerful that men went calmly though vaguely and almost dumbly at their tasks—work they seemed in quieter moments unable to understand but felt they must complete. As in the East and the South, so in the West: hundreds of thousands of lives were being thwarted and twisted by war and family fortunes were being lost or turned in directions little dreamed of in the optimism of the forties. To frontier hardship and tragedy there were now added sorrows of another sort. The West—and American history—still continued frightfully wasteful of human life. The year 1864 was the most solemn and saddening year of the war.

In Indiana bitter and threatening partisan feelings were, in the summer of 1864, quieted somewhat by the calm and serious attitude of the two candidates for governor—Morton and McDonald. They held a series of debates throughout the state. As they sat side by side upon a platform and gravely conversed, Morton said to McDonald, "I am told a great many of your friends have come here armed." Mc-

[79] Western Christian Advocate, November 16, 1864.
[80] The Enquirer, Oct. 5, 1864; Western Christian Advocate, Nov. 23, 1864.
[81] Cincinnati Daily Commercial, Nov. 11, 1864.
[82] Terrell's Reports, Vol. I, Appendix 5.

Donald answered, "I have no doubt three fourths of that audience are armed, but you and I can control these meetings and so long as we do not lose our heads, there will be no trouble." [83]

Although before the November elections, Sherman had been successful around Atlanta and Mobile had been captured, Union men in the West approached the polls with anxiety. Union papers warned authorities to guard the elections, to watch out for "aliens, bounty-jumpers, and deserters." [84] In Indiana, the October state contest, always so important, was considered doubly so this year, for it was felt that in that state, the headquarters of the Sons of Liberty, "treason was most bold" and civil war might be inaugurated. Governor Morton requested Lincoln to allow soldiers to come home to vote and urged an "informal delay" of the draft until after election.[85] When the day finally came, the people went in "almost breathless quiet to the polls; . . . universal quiet everywhere prevailed and peace . . . settled upon all the territory of the loyal states." [86] In Ohio and Indiana "all progressed quietly, Morton was at his home in Indiana, Brough in Ohio . . . Hooker just within call of either, . . . a peaceable election." [87] Some Democrats, however, said that the election was unfair, that the press was muzzled and there was a reign of terror in Indiana, "the most unparalleled and stupendous frauds, ever known, . . . more and more our elections are partaking the character of a French farce under Louis Napoleon." [88]

The outcome of the contest in the West was unmistakable. The wave of Union sentiment and a determination to see the war through which swept Michigan, Wisconsin, and Iowa with overwhelming majorities was almost equaled in the lower West. It was a repetition of 1854 and 1860. Lincoln carried every state. In Ohio, however, the Democratic vote for McClellan made some gains over that for Vallandigham in 1863. Morton was reëlected in Indiana and Oglesby, a Republican, succeeded Yates in Illinois. Union legislatures were elected; this meant that in Illinois a Republican United States Senator would be elected—it proved to be Governor Yates. In Ohio

[83] Foulke, *Morton,* Vol. I, pp. 297–299, 355. See speeches of Dodd, Hendricks, and Perkins, *ibid.*

[84] Cincinnati *Daily Commercial,* Oct. 8, 1864.

[85] Foulke, *op. cit.,* Vol. I, pp. 366–368; Cincinnati *Gazette,* Oct. 11, 1864; Cincinnati *Daily Commercial,* Oct. 4, 11, 1864.

[86] *Message of Governor Yates of Illinois to the General Assembly,* p. 75 (Springfield, 1865) ; Porter, *Ohio Politics,* pp. 125, 126.

[87] *Western Christian Advocate,* Nov. 16, 1864.

[88] *The Enquirer,* Oct. 13, Nov. 4, 9, 1864; Cole, *op. cit.,* p. 326.

fifteen Republican-Union Congressmen were elected from a total of nineteen districts, among them popular army men such as James A. Garfield and Rutherford B. Hayes. Even Cincinnati went for the Union ticket. In Indiana, eight of the eleven districts chose Union men, among them Colfax and Julian. The "Pocket," however, and the lower Wabash remained the Democratic stronghold that it had traditionally been, and Voorhees was returned to Congress. In Illinois, "Egypt" by a violent reversal elected a Union man to displace W. J. Allen, the anti-war Democrat—a result partly due to Logan's efforts. Only three of the thirteen districts went Democratic; they were located in the southern part and in the lower Illinois River valley.[89] Not since the anti-Nebraska wave of 1854 and the popular enthusiasm aroused by the firing on Ft. Sumter, had the stalwart Reserve, unbending Michigan, and patriotic Chicago received such support in the lower West. The combined influence of Lincoln's patience and popularity, of apparently dangerous but really harmless peace conspiracies, of the opening of the Mississippi and war prosperity, and of the military victories of Sherman and other generals, seemed to wipe out the West as a section and, as the Democrats feared, to blend it with the East. The war was being won, but would the West be satisfied with the victory?

[89] Foulke, *Morton,* Vol. I, p. 470; Cole, *op. cit.,* p. 326; *Tribune Almanac* 1865, Election returns for 1864; Porter, *Ohio Politics,* p. 198.

CHAPTER XIV

EXTRAVAGANCE AND PROTEST, 1865–1880

The truth is my fellow citizens, this country belongs to the Republican party (applause). We have redeemed it from rebellion and it is ours. That flag is ours; that Congress of the United States is ours; Ohio is ours; the white loyal men are ours; and the freedmen emancipated in the Providence of God by the Republican party are ours. (A speech, quoted in *Ohio Convention Reporter*, 1870, p. 296.)

REPUBLICANISM TRIUMPHANT

The words quoted above—a typical expression of the post-war psychology of a narrow Republican partisan in Ohio in 1870—may well make us smile to-day. But in very fact the control of the Republican party in the West as in the whole country during the administrations of Grant was formidable and, backed by this type of loyalty, was able to resist all attempts of Democratic or independent political movements to overthrow it. The press of the day was full of boasting by Republicans and of keen, analytical, and bitter criticism by Democrats and independents.

The Republican party has become an organization singularly well disciplined and formidable. It has the tenacity of life, the intolerance of opposition, . . . the pretension to exclusive patriotism that once characterized the Democratic party and it is bound together by the cohesive power of an amount of public plunder exceeding anything of which the Democrats dreamed in the days when they had possession of the government. Its masses are marshalled by an army of office-holders. . . . Grant wields his party like an army and to dispute his supremacy is regarded as an infraction of the laws of war and punished with something of military rigor.

With these words and others accusing the President of exploiting a vulgar popularity and of being disliked by Republican masses but considered a military necessity, the Cincinnati *Daily Commercial* summarized the national political situation in 1872. It noted also that in view of the business depression of that year, a policy of retrenchment should be adopted, taxes should be reduced as much as 50 per cent and there should be a reduction of the war tariff. "Beggars, grabbers and Treasury eaters now in such force at Washington . . . must be gotten rid of; no subsidies should be made; no land grants; no appropriations for new offices, no increases in salaries." Partisanship was denounced as were office-grabbing, and attempts to overthrow the civil service system.[1]

This indictment came from a liberal Republican source, those from Democratic sources were still more outspoken. One of these, a forceful but extravagant expression of lower western Democratic discontent, came from the pen of the intrepid Henry Clay Dean.[2] It pointed to a renewed community of interest between the West and the South, this time between the western and southern small farmer, thus anticipating the Bryan of 1896 with his invective against the East, organized wealth, and industry. In inaccurate, popular fashion, it gives a general survey of post-war political and economic issues in the West. It merits quotation at length.

The pretext for the war was the conflict between northern and southern labor. . . . Its closing legislation has created an issue between the West and the East in which western labor and agricultural industry have allied the South and the West to make common cause against eastern capital and manufacturing machinery. . . . The industrial revolution and the use of farm machinery have added comparatively nothing to the relative wages of labor or the diffusion of increasing prosperity among the agricultural classes of the country, but it may be seen in the more stately mansions, the more arrogant air of the capitalists who own the railroads and steamships which transport grain produce from your door. . . . Eastern capital is a vast sponge dipped into the fountains of western labor to absorb them. . . . Under pretense of freeing black barbarian slaves turned loose to starve, they have enslaved the industrial pursuits of the whole Mississippi Valley.[3] . . . Through the instigation of New England we sent troops to burn up the cotton fields. . . . We . . . ruined our only customers. . . . After destroying our great highway to the markets of the world through the Mississippi, New England drove us into her market to be robbed by her carriers on the way. . . . The East now holds the West in her hand with a deadly grasp. . . . New England owns the railroads, telegraphs and every other means of transportation. She holds mortgages in the new cities of the lakes; . . . the robberies and oppressions of the tariff are oppressions of the West by the East; . . . the robberies and swindles of the bonds are swindles of the East upon the West.[4] . . . If cities are built the extravagant rates of interest must consume the profits of the labor employed; if railroads are built it is upon

[1] Cincinnati *Daily Commercial*, Feb. 15, 19, 20, 21, 1872.
[2] Henry Clay Dean, *Crimes of the Civil War* (1879).
[3] *Ibid.*, pp. 351, 352.
[4] *Ibid.*, p. 358.

some fraudulent scheme as inveigles whole communities to subscribe vast amounts of money to be given in mortgages to these idle usurers and extortioners; . . . if farms are improved the heavy rate of interest consumes the value of the improvement, trenches upon the principal until the sunburnt pioneer grows weary of the vexation and gladly gives up farm and improvement and makes a new trial on the frontier for a home and burial place.[5] . . . You have to pay to keep up a Negro Bureau . . . (and) . . . the standing army appointed to trample down the southern States. . . . You have to keep an army of Congressmen who . . . are giving away the public lands and accepting bribes. . . . Now for the remedy, vote down the present extravagant system of government, vote down standing armies; vote down tariffs, vote down the present system of legislation.[6]

Repudiation of debt, this eccentric man maintained, was a wise provision of Jewish law and was practised by the authors of our government who "never redeemed their continental money."

But neither the frantic boast nor foolish word of Republican partisan nor the bitter protest of western sectionalist nor the keen analysis of the independent gives us as good evidence of the strong position of triumphant Republicanism and the weakness of the demoralized Democracy in the West as do the facts themselves. The succession of losses since 1860, which we have traced—among them the death of Douglas, the defection of War Democrats, the defeat of Vallandigham in 1863, the election of Lincoln in 1864, and finally the winning of the war along lines laid out by more moderate Republicans—rendered opposition futile and factious. The startling successes of the anti-administration forces in the congressional elections in 1862, and their powerful and aggressive activity in Congress during the years 1863 and 1864, and until March, 1865, could not counterbalance their defeats in local, state, and Presidential contests. Another congressional election in 1866 brought another overwhelming defeat. It was getting hard to enlist Democrats to run for office.[7] With their allies in the South defeated and disenfranchised, and their own position so weak, it was a battered party that Allen G. Thurman, William Allen, George H. Pendleton, Thomas A. Hendricks, and Daniel Voorhees sought to revive in the years 1867 and 1868. This group of men whose place in American history is in great need of reappraisal—their reputations being so damaged by "unpatriotic" war activity—now embarked on a task that was to be quite fruitful and historically important.

Difficult as the task was, the opportunity was still afforded for these

[5] Henry Clay Dean, *Crimes of the Civil War*, pp. 336–338.
[6] *Ibid.*, p. 349.
[7] Cole, *Era of the Civil War*, p. 411.

men to do what western Democrats had been doing since the days of
Jackson and the Progressive Democracy of the forties; that is, marshal western men everywhere against those classes whom, in their
eyes, the course of events always seemed to favor—capitalists and
bondholders. To these were now added a still more hated class—war
profiteers. It was still a question whether the Republican party represented the "common man" in any part of the West. There was no doubt
that this man in the lower West distrusted it heartily. Repeated partisan success, eight years of control and manipulation by local professional leaders, post-war prosperity, and overweening pride in saving
the Union, were testing the ideals and standards of the dominant party
and the dominant classes. Rough-shod methods used by Republican
radicals in Congress, the treatment of southern states by Congressmen
and Senators from the East and the lake region, the influence of military men in politics, the methods devised to deal with war debts and
the exploitation of patriotism and of war "psychology" for partisan purposes—there were, in all these national post-war issues, good grounds
for a real opposition of which western Democrats and restless Republicans, too, were soon to avail themselves. A situation which led
western Republicans to say that their states were being consumed
by a tariff favorable to New England and Pennsylvania, and to come
out against increased duties, justified Democrats of the lower West in
extreme denunciation.[8] In Congress, protection was being "run into
the ground" and in Illinois, corporations, contractors, and speculators
were receiving favors from the Republican majority in the legislature,
called "the most disgraceful legislative body that ever convened in the
state." [9] By the strange alchemy of history, the Western Reserve, once
the home of reforms, became intensely partisan in its Republicanism
and even made apology for the questionable practices of the Grant administration, while the lower West became the champions of reform
and of the interests of the poorer, less articulate masses of the whole
South and West.

There was bitter dislike of the thoroughgoing "Jacobin" or "Crom-
wellian" spirit in Congress and the army. Under the plea of "loyalty"
and of conserving hard-won war victories, conscientious Republicans
in the Christian churches of the West were called upon to support their
party in whatever it did. Western Democrats and independent Republicans and various third party movements, though energetic in their

[8] *Ibid.,* p. 409.
[9] *Ibid.,* pp. 406, 407.

demands for reform, were tempted to dull the fighting edge of their sword by taking up financial panaceas of a questionable nature. For several years after 1865 in state, congressional, or national contests, "loyalty" was to win and "reform" was to lose; but a new Democratic party was finally to emerge in the West. Many were to leave the party of Lincoln and join the minor parties, the liberal Republicans, the Greenback, labor, or other movements. The panic years from 1873 to 1876 were to add to the discontent and at last in the late seventies triumphant Republicanism was to find itself seriously undermined throughout the West and to see Ohio, Indiana, and Wisconsin numbered in the doubtful list.

THE REVIVAL OF THE DEMOCRATIC PARTY IN THE WEST
1867–1872

The first marked signs of the revival appeared in Ohio in 1867. In that year a constitutional amendment allowing the Negro to vote was defeated at the polls, twelve counties, usually considered Republican, voting with the Democrats against it.[10] Here and elsewhere in the West, the party now so boldly forcing Negro suffrage on the South had many members who opposed giving Negroes the vote in their own home states.[11] By 1867, western Republicans were even becoming Greenbackers and accepting western Democratic views on bonds and "repudiation." In that year Allen G. Thurman sounded the first clear note in the Democratic revival by conducting a vigorous fight for the governorship of Ohio.[12] His opponent—a military man, Rutherford B. Hayes—defeated him by a very small majority. A Democratic legislature was elected in Ohio, however, and it later undertook the grateful task of electing a United States Senator. The bold, outspoken Vallandigham was passed over for the more available, smooth and cautious Thurman.[13] In both Indiana and Illinois, the Democrats made gains in local elections and even far-off Minnesota refused to follow radical Republican wishes and grant suffrage to Negroes. Early in the next year, the moderate Republican Cincinnati *Commercial* said there was real danger of Democratic success in the presidential contest in 1868.[14]

[10] *Tribune Almanac,* 1868.
[11] E. O. Randall and D. J. Ryan, *History of Ohio,* IV, 293; Cole, *op. cit.,* p. 417, note; Cincinnati *Daily Commercial,* Jan. 20, Nov. 5, 1868.
[12] T. E. Powell, *Democratic Party in Ohio,* Vol. I, Ch. XVI.
[13] Cincinnati *Daily Commercial,* Jan. 13, 1868; *Tribune Almanac,* 1869.
[14] Cincinnati *Daily Commercial,* Jan. 23, 1868.

As the presidential campaign drew near, one of the major questions was whether the spirit of the lower West, and the fear of Democratic success would make the radical Republicans pass over Ben Wade or other men more to their liking and nominate Grant, a popular military man and a former Douglas Democrat, as they had earlier been forced to support a moderate like Lincoln.

Still another factor was at work impelling the Republican convention as it met in Chicago in May, 1868, to exercise care and assure its continued control. President Johnson had just been impeached by the House; his removal had been checked by a group of Senators among them several western Republican insurgents of the type of Lyman Trumbull of Illinois. Chief Justice Salmon P. Chase, it was claimed, was so favorable to Johnson that he was being considered by Democrats as a presidential candidate. Cries went up from stalwarts that these traitors should be punished and be read out of the party. But national conventions do not usually take such reckless steps. Better to nominate the blunt and practical military hero, let him make a few laconic speeches, appeal to "loyal men" to support him, and thus calmly win in November.[15]

As might be expected, the convention that nominated General Grant was a body of respectable, well-dressed, well-behaved men who were little in doubt about the proper thing to do. There was not much swearing and drinking. The platform did not condemn the senatorial traitors and the "recreant" Chief Justice. Schuyler Colfax of Indiana, a moderate like Grant, was nominated for the Vice-Presidency. There was none of the venturesomeness of 1856 or the gravity of 1864. Enthusiasm was lacking, but there was every evidence of the confidence that goes along with respectability, power, and wealth. The Middle West was furnishing candidates that the bondholders of the East and loyal men everywhere would support and who would appeal to doubtful voters in the lower West, as did Lincoln in the two previous contests.[16] What the convention lacked in enthusiasm and candor was amply supplied by a great soldiers' and sailors' convention that met in Chicago at the same time—a kind of military annex to the regular Republican party. Here amid the shouting and flag-waving, John A. Logan and radical military men were heroes. The soldiers said things that many regular Republicans in convention would no doubt have liked to say; Johnson was a

---

[15] *Ibid.*, May 19, 23, 25, 1868.
[16] For a discriminating treatment of the Chicago Convention see *ibid.*, May 16, 18, 20, 21, 22, 1868.

traitor and Trumbull and the independent Senators deserved severe discipline.[17] Moreover, there was another meeting in Chicago at the same time that had great interest in the Republican party taking high ground. Prayers were made and resolutions were presented in the General Conference of the Methodist Church urging the Senate of the United States to be firm in the impeachment trial of President Johnson.[18] And in the nomination of Grant these Methodists had great interest. "Another piece of loyal machinery at the same time," said a paper, "the Methodist Conference, was at work with hearts full 'of sympathy with the great (Republican) convention." [19] We may well ponder seriously the fact that a Christian body was so closely in tune with a convention at which reform liberals like Lyman Trumbull were being supplanted by men of the type of John A. Logan and of General Grant himself.

Meanwhile and for some months previously, the Pendleton movement or the "Ohio idea" had been developing in Ohio, Indiana, Illinois, and Iowa. Here was a young man who could take up the mantle of the great Douglas and oppose the dominant party; this "young eagle" had a following as far West as Kansas and Nebraska. In Democratic State conventions held in several states in January, 1868, Pendleton's name was placed before the people as a candidate for President. Ohio Democrats met January 8 and in a furious convention nominated Pendleton, condemned the usurpations of the radical Republican Congress, demanded the recognition of southern states, opposed Negro suffrage and maintained that the government should not pay a favored class in gold and discharge its debt to all others, including pensions to widows and soldiers, in an inferior currency. Johnson's attitude was upheld. The Indiana convention demanded that bonds should be taxed and should be redeemed in greenbacks; the tariff laws should be repealed; incoming foreigners should be protected; and all attempts to regulate "moral ideas and appetites by legislation," were declared unwise and despotic.[20] But would eastern Democrats like August Belmont accept a western champion? Doubt also attached to Hendricks of Indiana. How would he, a bondholder and an owner of stock in a national bank, stand on greenbacks? Indiana politicians were tricky and had often made deals with southern or eastern leaders and been untrue to the West. There

[17] Cincinnati *Daily Commercial*, May 20, 1868.
[18] *Ibid.*, May 23, 1868; *General Conference Journal*, M. E. Church, 1868, p. 158; White, *Trumbull*, p. 317.
[19] Cincinnati *Daily Commercial*, May 25, 1868.
[20] *Ibid.*, Jan. 8, 9, 10, 1868.

was further the two-thirds rule and the fact that the convention was to be held in New York. There was ominous talk about nominating Governor Seymour and even about Justice Chase himself. With considerable misgiving the lower West went to New York in July, 1868, as the followers of Douglas had gone to Charleston in 1860.

The Pendleton delegations from Ohio, Indiana, and Illinois arrived at the convention noisily proclaiming that the West as far out as Kansas was aflame for their young leader.[21] Some of them expected that he would be nominated by acclamation. In the convention there was none of the smoothness of the Grant convention at Chicago. While there was no doubt much manipulation behind closed doors, there was also much traditional Democratic fighting in the open. It was hot, expensive, and long drawn out. There was a great struggle on the greenback plank. Eastern Democrats had no such faith in paper money as these westerners had; some of them held bonds and wanted the national debt paid in "good money." Westerners wanted a statement in the platform that this was a "white man's government"; easterners that it was a "government of the people." The weariness of hot, sweltering sessions was no doubt allayed somewhat by the liquor that flowed freely and by trips to Coney Island. But the hotel bills of westerners were mounting; rumor had it that there was a plan to wear out western delegates by a long convention and by the expense of living in New York.[22] Eastern and southern delegates were early suspected of a willingness to desert the West and "go over to the bondholders." [23]

After much disagreement on the greenback plank, a compromise was arrived at to the effect that bonds were to be paid in greenbacks only when "greenbacks had appreciated to the gold standard"—a solution which was clearly not in accordance with Pendleton's attitude. Nominating ballots followed one after another. The East would not have Pendleton's platform or Pendleton, the man. With New York opposed to Ohio and the West, a deadlock developed. Indiana was among the first to waver, and supported her own Hendricks. Then Ohio led by Vallandigham switched to Seymour of New York to head off Indiana. Seymour was nominated and Indiana was rewarded, and the West supposedly appeased by the nomination of Hendricks as vice-presidential candidate.[24] All in all, New York proved a bad place for

[21] *The Enquirer,* July 8, 1868.
[22] *Ibid.,* July 4–7, 9, 10, 1868.
[23] *Ibid.,* July 7, 1868.
[24] *Ibid.,* July 10, 1868.

western Democrats. The Democratic West had been thwarted by the Democratic East as it had been at Charleston by the extreme Democratic South. *The Enquirer* in disgust summarized the convention, "Expense, crowd, heat, Tammany trickery—a bore." It was already clear that Seymour was destined not to draw out the full Democratic strength in the West.

A Democratic soldiers and sailors convention also met in New York. Among the leaders were the westerners General McClernand and Thomas Ewing. It was called conservative and stood out in clear contrast with the ultra-patriotic military meeting that had been held a few weeks before in Chicago. Soldiers who had fought in the Union army— War Democrats—fraternized with ex-Confederates and listened to speeches that condemned the policy of Congress toward the South. They praised former border state Republicans like General Blair, who opposed Negro suffrage and Congressional reconstruction.[25] They favored the "grand old reconstruction policy of Lincoln," complained that ten states were debarred from their rights and that the markets of the world were closed to the products of southern fields. Sugar, they said, was rotting in the cane; the Mississippi was plunging over broken levees, while boorish plantation Negroes pampered with delusive hopes were sitting in mockeries of conventions in the South.[26] The tone of this meeting was kept up by speakers and newspapers in the campaign that followed in the West. Plunder and corruption in governmental circles, the evils of carpet-bag government, the "beauties of negro rule"—here were issues enough for any campaign.[27] They did not prove, however, to be winning ones. The success of Grant was assured from the first and the details of the campaign need not detain us. In some districts of the West the vote for Grant was overwhelming, and almost everywhere it was large.[28] The revival of the Democracy was proving to be a slow process, and other devices, alliances, and issues were to be tried out before marked success was to be forthcoming.

A feature of the political situation in 1868 was the appearance and activity of the "labor reform movement" in politics. Having become more and more self-conscious in the three or four preceding years, labor was asserting itself in various parts of the country; in the years 1867 and 1868, the agitation came near reaching the proportions of

[25] *The Enquirer,* July 22, 1868.
[26] *Ibid.,* July 4, 6, 1868.
[27] *Ibid.,* July–October, 1868, *passim.*
[28] Cincinnati *Daily Commercial,* Oct. 13, Nov. 1868, *passim;* Cole, *op. cit.,* p. 414.

a nation-wide movement. Prosperity was great in many parts of the country; prices were high, enterprise was booming. There resulted a very sharp demand for labor. Workingmen, feeling their power, demanded concessions, among them the eight-hour day. They organized leagues throughout the country.[29] In the West, the movement was especially strong in Ohio—particularly in Cincinnati. Assuming an attitude on national politics much nearer to that of the Democratic-Greenbackers than to the Republicans, restless under high prices, opposed to "land monopolies and money monopolies," the workers complained that the wealth of the country was locked up in bonds which afforded no employment and were exempt from taxation. Emancipation and Negro suffrage, they maintained, had destroyed the resources of the southern states; since they were no longer raising sugar and rice, southerners had no money with which to come to Cincinnati and buy manufactured goods. In various local elections these "working men" allied with Democrats or "Independent Republican" candidates.[30]

WESTERN PROTESTS AGAINST "GRANTISM"

For years there had been signs of Republican independence in the West. Senators Trumbull of Illinois, Grimes of Iowa, and Doolittle of Wisconsin had been branded as traitors in 1867 and 1868. They or men similarly minded were now ready to take more radical steps.[31] Illinois Republicans were demanding tariff reform and in Indiana and Ohio "reformers" and "independents" were being elected here and there, and were seeking to wield the balance of power in state legislatures.[32] When, in 1871, the "Missouri Movement" led by B. Gratz Brown and Carl Schurz was well started, independent Illinois Republicans soon took up the cause,[33] and Ohio was not long in following.

In fact dominant Republicanism was being opposed on all sides by men within the ranks. Earnest Republicans like Julian of Indiana and Brinkerhoff of Ohio were, with easterners such as Sumner, Adams,

[29] Cincinnati Daily Commercial, Feb. 9, 1872 (An article describing the eight-hour movement in 1868) ; Cole, op. cit., pp. 370, 371.

[30] The Enquirer, July 4, 11, 17, 18, Aug. 14, 1868, et passim; Cincinnati Daily Commercial, Apr. 6, 7, 1868.

[31] White, Trumbull, Ch. XX; Earle Dudley Ross, The Liberal Republican Movement (New York, 1919), pp. 12, 13, 21.

[32] White, Trumbull, Ch. XXII; Bogart and Thompson, The Industrial State, Centennial History of Illinois, IV, 57; Greene, Some Aspects of Politics in the Middle West, 1860–1872 (Madison, 1912), pp. 73, 74; Tribune Almanac, 1870.

[33] Ross, op. cit., p. 24; Bogart and Thompson, 61–67.

and Greeley, turning against Grant; old friends of Lincoln in Illinois were "going over," among them, William L. Herndon. Trumbull and other leaders were ostracized by the administration, like Douglas at the hands of the Buchanan régime in 1857–1858, and like recent middle western insurgents at the hands of conservative Republicans. One by one War Democrats were leaving their Republican-Union allies of ten or twelve years standing, and going back to the Democratic fold; Germans like Koerner and Groesbeck were following Schurz' lead and going independent or Democratic.[34] The historian is compelled to ask the question whether the best men in the party of Lincoln were not leaving it. It need not be pointed out that Vallandigham's followers were ready to welcome all discontented men and encourage Republican divisions. Having for several years struggled along on anti-war and State rights lines, they had met in convention at Dayton on May 18, 1871, had adopted a resolution accepting the thirteenth, fourteenth and fifteenth amendments and by this "new departure" had sought to take a fresh start.[35]

As the western movement of protest led by Gratz Brown, Carl Schurz, and Lyman Trumbull was taken up by eastern liberals, the plan earlier suggested of merely attempting to force the regular Republican party to abandon Grant was given up and a decision to put an independent ticket in the field was made. "Purification and pacification" became catchwords. Democrats were urged to dissolve their party and to support the platform and candidate agreed upon by the Liberal Republicans. Excess of enthusiasm led the Republican insurgent leaders to overlook the smallness of their numbers and to undertake the difficult task of swinging the millions of Democratic voters of the country to their support.[36] In January, 1872, the Liberal Republicans of Ohio approved the call of Missouri Republicans for a meeting to be held at Cincinnati on May 1. Among these was Brinkerhoff of Mansfield, Ohio. He said that he disliked Grant's shameless nepotism, his association with stock jobbers, his project for the purchase of Santo Domingo, his ostracism of prominent Republicans, and his civil service record.[37] If the West could get relief from burdensome taxation,

[34] Ross, *op. cit.*, pp. 12, 63, 69, 76; White, *Trumbull*, p. 356; R. E. Rombauer, *Life of Gustavus Koerner, Pub. No. 9, Ill. St. Hist., Lib.*, p. 301; Cincinnati *Daily Commercial*, May 13, 1872.
[35] Randall and Ryan, *History of Ohio*, IV, 310, 311.
[36] Cincinnati *Daily Commercial*, April 13, 1872.
[37] *Ibid.*, Feb. 3, 14, 1872.

amnesty for southerners, a western type of tariff, and civil service reform, Ohio and Illinois and perhaps Wisconsin and Missouri might be carried for the new movement; but it already appeared that Trumbull and Brown were going to figure less as presidential possibilities than Adams of Massachusetts or Greeley of New York.[38]

With no hurrah and with much earnestness this body of reformers met at Cincinnati, May 1, 1872, coming largely from the states extending from Missouri to New York; old and middle-aged men seemed to be in a majority in this peculiar convention. Pictures of a distracted South under military rule, and of corruption in high places throughout the country were drawn in the opening speeches. The interest of leading editors in the United States such as Henry Watterson of Kentucky, Murat Halstead of Cincinnati, Samuel Bowles of the Springfield, Massachusetts, *Republican* and E. L. Godkin of the *Nation,* gave the convention unusual importance in the newspaper world and able editorial treatment.[39] Susan B. Anthony and other woman suffragists were present. George H. Pendleton and other prominent Democrats looked on smilingly and, on the whole, favorably. Godkin said, "I doubt whether a more respectable, honest, public spirited body of men has ever got together for a similar purpose." But as the forces and influence of the East swelled and the task of framing a platform and nominating a candidate rose before them, there appeared a greater willingness to compromise and manipulate. A desire arose to avoid issues that would interfere with success; Horace Greeley's candidacy became more inexorable; and "Pennsylvania had to be thought of."

With C. F. Adams too cool and intellectual to use for political purposes and with Trumbull not strong in the East, Greeley's chances became very bright. Acceptable to New York and New England liberals as an easterner and a protectionist, the border South too looked upon him favorably as a squatter sovereignty man who had been pro-Douglas in 1858 and had later used the famous words "let the erring sisters depart in peace." In spite of the fact that he was objectionable to Germans, to free traders and to Liberal Republican politicians of Ohio and Illinois, many westerners might reluctantly accept him because he was not a politician and because of his temperance views.[40] Indiana delegates played a decisive rôle in the convention by coming out for Gree-

[38] *Ibid.,* Apr. 22, 1872.
[39] *Ibid.,* May 1, 1872.
[40] Bogart and Thompson, *op. cit.,* pp. 71-73.

ley on the sixth ballot.[41] He was nominated. A convention that was "red hot" against corruption, maladministration, nepotism, and military rule and all that the name of Grant signified, was cool and collected on the tariff and took no further action on it than to submit the question to the people in their congressional districts. Tariff reformers, the supporters of Trumbull and the Germans in the West were bitterly disappointed. But to almost all of them Grant was more objectionable.[42]

The Democratic leaders soon came to the conclusion that all that was left for them was to endorse the Liberal Republican movement. George H. Pendleton came out early in support of Greeley, but Long of Ohio and Voorhees of Indiana were more reluctant.[43] Democratic state conventions in Iowa, Illinois, Indiana and other western states, and finally, the national convention in Baltimore in July were forced to accept the Greeley candidacy as the only hope against the entrenched battalions of Republicanism and President Grant.[44] Even though Greeley might be defeated, perhaps Democratic candidates for state and local office like Thomas A. Hendricks in Indiana, who was running for governor, would come through on the fusion wave. And some independents thought a step would be taken toward the formation of a much needed new political party. The whole procedure afforded amusement to political wags who smiled as they saw in Democratic papers of the West, long, appreciative biographies of Horace Greeley, the self-made man, the "modern Franklin." Many, though unenthusiastic, asserted that he was at least an honest man, with a deep humanity and sympathy with the masses of the people.[45] It was argued that the issues that held Democrats and Liberal Republicans apart lay largely in the past; they agreed and might well coöperate in opposing "imperialism, gift taking, and nepotism, and in favoring civil service and revenue reform, union and peace." [46]

So peculiar had been the turn politics had taken that among both Democrats and Liberal Republicans there was again evident the age-long middle western sense of frustration. Perhaps a few people who read the more enlightened journals would understand the reason for

[41] Cincinnati *Daily Commercial*, May 1, 4, 13 *et passim*, 1872; Ross, *op. cit.*, pp. 121–125.

[42] Cincinnati *Daily Commercial*, May 4, 1872.

[43] *The Enquirer*, May 14, June 12, 13, 14, 1872; Esarey, *Indiana*, II, 857.

[44] *The Enquirer*, May 4, 7, June 12, 13, 27, 28, July 9, 10, 11, 1872.

[45] *Ibid.*, May 7, 9, 14, 1872.

[46] *Ibid.*, June 27, 28, 1872.

this unusual alignment of parties. But Republican farmers were becoming interested in railroad rates and in economic problems affecting the West toward the solution of which the new movement had little to offer; ex-soldiers were almost sure to vote for Grant and Democrats would no doubt stay at home in large numbers on election day rather than vote for Horace Greeley.[47] "Reform" as a vote getting slogan was going to show up poorly in comparison with "loyalty."

Greeley was a pleasing figure but one that lent itself easily to caricature, and the campaign was marked by much bitter personal attack. Grant, conscious of his strong position, doing what uninformed men so often do in the hope that silence might be taken for superior wisdom, refused to be drawn into an extensive campaign of speech-making. His followers, however, did not hesitate to endulge in extreme praise of him and in no little waving of the bloody shirt. "In voting for Grant," said John A. Logan of Illinois, "you vote for prosperity, for peace, for civilization, for Christianity, for the grandest glory that ever shone around a republic in the history of the world." On the other hand it was charged that Greeley was pro-Catholic, and represented "every kind of Democratic, rebellious, Ku-Klux, discontented, hopeful and unreasonable feeling." [48] The Greeley movement was doomed to failure, as the election in November proved. Prosperity still prevailed in large measure in the West and economic and political discontent had not yet reached a high point. However, soon after the election, the specter of hard times was presenting itself and *The Enquirer* called for "greenback relief." [49] The very disappointing election was not without one redeeming feature. Thomas A. Hendricks was elected governor of Indiana, an important Democratic victory.[50]

NEW PARTIES AND NEW ISSUES, 1873–1880

Although the Liberal Republican-Democratic combination of 1872 proved to be a failure, party lines had been at least temporarily dissolved and western polities thrown into solution. Out of this solution there might emerge a political movement of far-reaching consequences. Various small parties were indeed in process of formation, but overtopping all was the possibility that the Democratic party might dissolve and a major new party be formed. Would this be the form that the

[47] Bogart and Thompson, *op. cit.,* pp. 77–82.
[48] Ross, *op. cit.,* pp. 167, 169, 172.
[49] Issues of Nov. 14, 15, 1872.
[50] Esarey, *Indiana,* II, 857, 858.

"Democratic revival" would take? Could Ohio, the state which had done perhaps more than any other to make the Missouri movement of 1871 into the Liberal Republican movement of 1872 and which was furnishing unrelenting foes of "Grantism," be the center of a great national party upheaval in the years 1873 and 1874? Liberal Republicans and independent Democrats were unwilling to step back into old party ranks; indeed such men as Jacob Brinkerhoff, Carl Schurz, George E. Pugh and Thomas Ewing were ready for an entirely new movement. In the powerful Cincinnati *Commercial*, its able editor, Murat Halstead, was again keenly analyzing the national party situation, publishing articles on the evils of old and the need of new parties, on the "physiology of party death" and on "Smash the Democratic Party." "We are weary of old parties and we think the country weary of them. The talk of a Democratic revival is all folly." The demand in Ohio grew and took on state-wide proportions, and a state convention was held in Columbus, July 30. The new movement was called by various names, such as the "Liberal Party," the "New Party," and the "People's Movement." [51] As more and more Democrats came out in its favor, the old Democratic leaders stood aghast.[52]

What would men like Thurman, Hendricks, and Voorhees do? They were no doubt progressive, but they were also very partisan and "Jeffersonian." Thurman jumped into the breach to save the party of Jefferson and Jackson, and called upon his uncle, William Allen, the old leader, to rise up and lead in a campaign for the governorship of Ohio.[53] This rough Jacksonian campaigner aided by the Panic of 1873 and by the public outcry against Republican corruption, won the governorship by a close margin, thus scoring another signal Democratic victory and marking a distinct step in the Democratic post-war revival. He became the hope of western Democrats in the next few years, "rekindled the smouldering fires of the old time Democracy," struck a telling blow at the new party movement, and incidentally helped to keep Greenbackism alive. A Democratic legislature in Ohio later reëlected Thurman to the United States Senate. In 1873, also, in Wisconsin, an alignment of the Grangers, Liberal Republicans, and Democrats carried the governorship and the state legislature; in Iowa an anti-monopoly candidate for governor drew a very large vote and

[51] Cincinnati *Daily Commercial*, July 7, 9, 12, 15, 17, 18, 22, 28, Aug. 2, 4, 1873; Julian, *Political Recollections,* Ch. XV.
[52] Cincinnati *Daily Commercial,* July 31, 1873.
[53] R. C. McGrane, *William Allen: A Study in Western Democracy* published by the Ohio State Archeological and Historical Society (1925) pp. 190–199.

fifty-three "Independents" took their places in the legislature. In the next few years regular Democrats won various legislative, congressional, or gubernatorial contests in the West and with the indirect help of Greenbackers, Grangers, and disinterested Germans put several western states in the doubtful list. When the strong party of Grant won, it was often by such narrow margins as only to give increased zest for the next contest. The Democracy, which had been crippled, ill-led, and ill-used for a decade or more, was again asserting its ancient vitality.

The year 1874, for instance, produced damaging results for the dominant party. In national congressional elections the House went Democratic and in New York Samuel J. Tilden was elected governor. In the West, Democrats, Independent Reformers and the Farmer's "Anti-Monopoly" party carried a majority of the congressional districts in Ohio, Indiana, and Illinois; Cuyahoga County, in which Cleveland is located, went Democratic for the first time in its history as did also certain districts in Chicago.[54] But at the same time the new party movement receded and Greenbackism raised its head again. There were added to the battle-cry of inefficiency and corruption at Washington, the issues of stagnation, the question of resumption of specie payments and of the withdrawal of greenbacks. Since 1865 this kind of money had been in process of being retired by the United States Treasury, and long time bonds were being issued in order that a sound money basis might be reëstablished; during all this time arguments were being piled up that this procedure was wrong. Westerners could not see—with the circulating medium being withdrawn and the amount of this medium, it was feared, dropping below the actual business needs, with resultant increase in the "value of the dollar"—how a section could profit which was constantly in debt and subject to recurrent booms and which was required to pay in "better money" for improvements that had been accumulated in legal tender depreciated greenbacks.[55] On the subtle and difficult question of currency depreciation and appreciation, of hard and soft money, there were those in the West who presumed to speak with authority, many believing that from paper money great blessings would flow.

In 1875, in Ohio, there occurred the greatest political contest since Vallandigham's campaign in 1863—William Allen standing for re-

---

[54] *Tribune Almanac*, 1875; Cincinnati *Daily Commercial,* Oct. 15, Nov. 5, 7, 24, 1874.

[55] Bogart and Thompson, *op. cit.,* pp. 107, 108 *et passim.*

election as governor, his Republican opponent being Rutherford B. Hayes.[56] Allen opposed, as he said, military despotism and moneyed despotism, Grant's cliques of office-holders and government contractors and evil-doers, high and low. In Roman senatorial tones he averred that the flood of corruption would destroy the republic. When his opponents referred to the Civil War and the questionable attitude of peace Democrats he said the "question was not about fighting but about stealing." [57] But he could not avoid the question of greenbacks, a doubly delicate question as the campaign attained national significance and the possibility became apparent of its producing one and perhaps two candidates for the Presidency in 1876. Democrats under Allen's leadership were willing to allow "soft-money" men to think that their party advocated greenbacks, if they chose so to think, but at the same time hard-money men West and East must not be offended. Crude Greenbackism of the Henry Clay Dean type had greater vogue in the newer communities of Iowa, Missouri, and Kansas; it would not be tolerated in Ohio, and Democrats were hard put to it to know where to draw the line. More plausible Greenback arguments that might not prove dangerous at the polls were that the country, which had been "made drunk on paper money" by Republicans during the war, should be allowed to taper off gradually, or the idea of the Republican Oliver P. Morton of Indiana, that they in some way be used to provide more elastic currency for the West and South.[58]

Allen was understood to be more definitely a soft-money man than his more adroit nephew, United States Senator Thurman.[59] A peculiar situation arose, neither Democrats nor Republicans in the West knowing clearly how to stand on the Resumption Act and on the Greenback question in general. In Indiana, the leading Democrat, J. McDonald, was "hard" and Oliver P. Morton, the leading Republican, on the other hand, was "soft." Allen of Ohio was aided by hard-money Democrats who made speeches for him and Hayes by soft money Republicans. The issues were thus confused, and in addition there was injected a question of Catholic opposition to public schools. The business de-

[56] Forrest William Clonts, *The Political Campaign of 1875 in Ohio*. Ohio State University Master's Thesis (1921); R. C. McGrane, "Ohio and the Greenback Movement," *Miss. Valley Hist. Rev.* XI, 529, 530; T. E. Powell, *The Democratic Party in Ohio*, Vol. I, Ch. XX.

[57] William Allen papers, Library of Congress.

[58] Esarey, *Indiana*, II, 866.

[59] R. C. McGrane, *William Allen: A Study in Western Democracy*, pp. 231–245; see also by the same author "Ohio and the Greenback Movement," *Miss. Valley Historical Review*, Vol. XI, pp. 529–530.

pression, too, had its effect; in some regions and in some industries the conditions were even worse than in 1873.[60] The Independents of 1872 looked on this exciting contest with a mixture of anti-Republican feeling and fear that Allen if successful would give a final blow to their cherished new party movement.[61]

Carl Schurz, the chief German Independent, was in this campaign more interested in sound money than in the defeat of the Republican party.[62] His speeches in opposition to the currency vagaries of the Democrats is thought to have had important results. After a bitter contest Rutherford B. Hayes was elected by a very moderate majority, and he became the following year the Republican candidate for President. The followers of Allen, however, would not give up. It was hoped by many westerners that he would be a strong contender for the Democratic nomination against Tilden. He had support in the convention among Greenback Democrats from Kentucky, Missouri, Kansas, and Iowa.[63] But it was all to no avail. Eastern reform represented by Tilden rather than a western brand tinged with inflationism won in the national Democratic convention and Tilden was nominated.[64] The nomination of an eastern candidate did not, however, stop the western Democratic revival. It continued at high tide; old Democrats were reminded of the great days of Douglas.[65]

However much the reviving Democratic party, Liberal Republicanism, or the "New Party" movement of 1873 sought to appeal to local western economic and sectional discontent, there were many thousands of farmers and dwellers in small towns who clamored for more radical action and more distinctly agrarian or Greenback programs. The desire of the western and southern small farmer for agricultural improvement, his restlessness on the question of railroad rates, and his hatred of what he vaguely called monopolies was to produce still other parties in that decade so prolific in third party movements. The railroad, hitherto considered by the westerner as rather indiscriminately a blessing, bringing with it, as it did, the opening of new lands, new markets, and boom times in general, come to be associated with the Panic of 1873 and the depression that followed, with unequal rates and rate-

[60] Forrest William Clonts, *The Political Campaign of 1875 in Ohio* (Master's Thesis, Ohio State University 1921), pp. 4–13.
[61] *Ibid.*, p. 55.
[62] *Ibid.*, p. 57.
[63] Allen Papers, Library of Congress.
[64] Clonts, *op. cit.*, pp. 63–66.
[65] Bogart and Thompson, *op. cit.*, pp. 115, 116.

wars, with absentee ownership and such evils as the "Credit Mobilier" scandal in Congress. In December, 1872, in Illinois, the price of corn was twenty-four cents a bushel and, in some localities, as low as fifteen cents. The railroad rates were so high that it cost as much as the value of five or six bushels of grain to get one bushel to New York. Corn was again, in Illinois, burned as fuel! The farmer blamed the railroads for all his troubles; they were owned by easterners and Englishmen who cared little for the feelings of the West.[66]

It cannot be recounted here how the secret farmer's organization, the "National Grange of Patrons of Husbandry" arose and spread through the upland South, into the old lower and the newer prairie West; how, taking on a semi-political form, though never running a national farmer ticket, it gave great impetus to the election of candidates favorable to the farmer and helped to bring about the passage of state laws dealing with railroad and warehouse legislation and grain inspection. It stood against "railroads, rings, conspiracies, and monopolies." The Illinois laws of 1871 and 1873 and the laws of other states are well-known and justly praised as being among the first steps in the establishment of the principle of public regulation. Illinois and Iowa were especially strong centers of the movement; in addition, Missouri, Indiana, and Ohio were well organized. Now it appeared that rate regulation was becoming a fact without separate political action, and since the latter years of the seventies brought a return of general prosperity, the Grange movement declined somewhat;[67] agrarian discontent was later to express itself in the newer regions of Iowa, Kansas, Nebraska, and the Dakotas—with this we shall not deal.

Out and out Greenbackers were not likely to remain satisfied with what they considered half-hearted attempts of western Democrats and Republicans to espouse their cause. Democrats continued, as we have seen, to flirt with the Greenback idea, but it was an uncertain and doubtful alliance.[68] It is impossible to say just what part Greenbackism played in the election of William Allen in Ohio in 1873 or in his great contest with Hayes for governor in 1875. Daniel Voorhees in Indiana

[66] Solon J. Buck, The Granger Movement (Harvard University Press, 1913), pp. 11–13, 44; A. E. Paine, "The Granger Movement in Illinois," U. of Ill. Studies, I, No. 8, pp. 11, 17; Bogart and Thompson, op. cit., p. 83.

[67] Buck, op. cit., pp. 11–13, 40–57, 61–67, 94–98, and Ch. VI; Journal of Proceedings of the Tenth Session of the National Grange of the Patrons of Husbandry, 1876, pp. 19, 52, 179; Bogart and Thompson, op. cit., pp. 84, 85, 89, 100–105, 121.

[68] Esarey, Indiana, II, 863–865.

was a thoroughgoing believer in paper money—as Allen himself seems also to have become—but western Democrats as a whole were hesitant to endorse a movement that contained so many "bums," "crazy inflationists," and "dilutionists." The Greenback firebrands, in truth, had a flaming evangel.

Burn every United States bond . . . they who hold the bonds, obtained them by taking in and burning the greenbacks, or they term it, retire them. . . . It is infamous for the government to call in its own declared legal tender money and burn it to ashes and then compel people to pay interest on bonds that are not taxed. . . . We had better unite the West and South and secede from a union that benefits only eastern bondholders.[69]

"Eastern masters and money holders . . . have too long held the hot iron of bankruptcy to our backs. . . . Give us back the money of our fathers." [70] Many incendiary pamphlets such as these were published; they advised repudiation and even a class war. In Ohio, miners in the southern part, industrial workers in the northeastern, and farmers in the northwestern part were ready to put out a separate Greenback ticket.[71]

The passage of the Resumption Act of 1875 marked the climax. Illinois Greenbackers met and demanded a repeal.[72] In Indiana, where an "Indiana Plan" and an independent Greenback party had for two or more years been in process of formation, there had already been calls for a national convention. On May 18, 1876, the national Greenback party held its convention at Indianapolis, called for a repeal of the Resumption Act and nominated Peter Cooper for President and S. P. Cary of Ohio for Vice-President. In the election that followed it received about fifty thousand votes in the West. In 1877, the year of a great railroad strike, there was a definite attempt to unite the Greenback and labor vote. In Ohio, the climax of the movement was reached in 1878. So necessary was the Greenback vote considered to Democrats that in that year in Ohio the party came out definitely for greenbacks, and even Allen G. Thurman embraced the "rag baby." [73] In various districts of the lower West in that year, Greenbackers were elected to Congress. But there was already in Ohio the beginning of decline. The revived prosperity again was a factor, and the Bland-

[69] M. Pomeray, *Meat for Men,* p. 3 *et passim.*
[70] Pamphlet, *Hot Drops,* pp. 9, 15.
[71] R. C. McGrane, "Ohio and the Greenback Movement," *Miss. Valley Hist. Rev.,* XI, pp. 531, 533.
[72] Bogart and Thompson, *op. cit.,* pp. 109–110.
[73] McGrane, *op. cit.,* p. 541.

Allison Act of 1878 helped allay discontent. The party, however, continued to receive scattered votes in all the region stretching from Indiana to Kansas and from Tennessee to Iowa.[74]

[74] T. A. Bland, *The Spartan Band,* p. 179; Esarey, *Indiana,* II, 952; O. J. Libby, *The Greenback Movement, 1876–1884.*

CHAPTER XV

The Gilded Age in the West—Social Life

We have already been reminded that the latter years of the Civil War were years of great prosperity and city growth. This condition continued until the year 1873. Chicago almost tripled her population in a decade and by 1869 was "running wild in real estate speculation."[1] Cleveland, Indianapolis and other places more than doubled their numbers in the same period.[2] Smaller towns expanded, extending their building, street grading and paving schemes far beyond their needs. "Paper towns" were laid out especially in Iowa and the newer West; streets and lighting systems were built far out into the country. Bond issues were made that looked forward to indefinite growth in population and in wealth.[3] In Ohio real and personal property increased 87 per cent in value in a decade, while manufacturing estab-

---

[1] Cole, *The Era of the Civil War*, pp. 349, 351.

[2] The population of selected towns in the West in 1860 and 1870, the growth during the decade and the interesting fact that in 1870 it was St. Louis rather than Cincinnati that led Chicago, are shown in the following table: (*Eighth Census of U. S. 1860; Ninth Census, 1870, Population.*)

	1860	1870
Cincinnati	161,044	216,239
St. Louis	160,773	310,864
Chicago	109,260	298,977
Louisville	68,033	100,753
Detroit	45,619	79,577
Milwaukee	45,246	71,440
Cleveland	43,417	92,829
Dayton	20,081	30,473
Indianapolis	18,611	48,244
Columbus	18,554	31,274
Peoria	14,045	22,849
Toledo	13,768	31,584
Quincy	13,718	24,052
Dubuque	13,000	18,434
New Albany	12,647	15,398
Evansville	11,484	21,830
Ft. Wayne	10,388	17,718
Springfield (Ill.)	9,320	17,364

[3] Cincinnati *Daily Commercial*, Oct. 24, 1873; Herbert Quick, *Vandemark's Folly*, p. 133, *et seq.*

lishments and the value of their products increased 100 per cent or over.[4] Merchants sold more goods and laborers received more wages than ever before, and both "wasted their profits on a more extravagant and showy style of living or else put them into speculations and losing enterprises." [5] Railroad construction doubled in a few years and the production of iron, always so accurate a test of general economic conditions, was very large. There was a rapid industrialization, especially in Ohio and in northern Illinois. All this prosperity did little to hinder and much to help the growth of "gilded age" ideals. But the furor of growth and expansion received a check in the Panic of 1873 and the years of depression that followed.

The panic began with bank failures and spread to industry and agriculture. The iron trade fell to a low point and other types of manufacture likewise. For several years after 1873 there was unemployment and low wages for labor; "tramps" roamed the streets of the towns and the country districts of the West in alarming numbers. In the winters following that of 1872–1873, the unemployment led to much suffering of women and children arising from lack of food and clothing. Public and private charitable organizations were taxed to their capacity. In Cincinnati a "lodging and soup house committee" in January, 1874, listed the number of those receiving public relief in two lodging houses as four thousand men and over one hundred women.[6] The sufferings of miners in eastern Ohio and elsewhere were intense; accounts of the pitiable conditions among those engaged in this industry make harrowing reading.[7] Among those not so unfortunate the habits of the earlier period of prosperity could not be easily changed and personal and household economies did not develop to meet the changed conditions. "War prices for work are gone forever" said a report, "but unhappily war extravagancies (sic) remain with us, and this is mainly what is the matter with the finances of all classes now." [8]

The building boom of the late sixties and early seventies resulted in the erection of a great many rapidly constructed, ill designed, cheap and tawdry houses and business blocks. Some of the better homes that had been built before the Civil War possessed a distinction and beauty of line and style suggestive of New England colonial or better south-

[4] First Annual Report Bureau of Labor Statistics, Ohio, 1877, p. 12.
[5] Cincinnati Daily Commercial, Nov. 27, 1874.
[6] Ibid., Oct. 24, Nov. 7, 8, 1873; Jan. 24, 1874.
[7] First Annual Report Bureau of Labor Statistics, Ohio, 1877, pp. 116–192; Report for 1879, pp. 71–106.
[8] Third Annual Report Bureau of Labor Statistics, Ohio, 1879, p. 83.

ern types. But after the war many of the newly rich families built with
little regard to proved architectural values. The "General Grant" mode
came in. French Second Empire influences, meretricious style and
anomalous imperial Roman or Augustan decorations are still evident
in the court houses, city halls, and hotels built in that period. Later,
however, there came some improvement in architecture, and more
beautiful landscape gardening became evident, a change due partly to
the influences of the Philadelphia Exposition of 1876 and the Chicago
Exposition in 1893.[9]

For people in the larger towns, public amusement of the cheaper
sort in the theaters consisted largely of extravaganza and spectacle of
the "Black Crook" variety, or of sentimental melodrama. "Wild West"
shows were attaining a great vogue, and those interested in baseball
were seeing the beginnings of the great clubs like the "White Stock-
ings" of Chicago, that have since played such a part in the public recre-
ational life of our land. Barnum's circus, when it appeared in the
larger cities of the West, drew enormous crowds, as many as twenty-
five thousand witnessing a day's performances in Cincinnati in 1873.[10]
In smaller towns the county fair or the smaller traveling circus never
failed to draw its eager, dusty crowds of tired women and men and
wondering, awe-struck children. But usually, when work gave way to
other interests, it was to rough local sports or to endless discussions of
politics and religion and, among veterans of the Civil War, to re-
counting memories of that conflict. Camp meetings in summer and
revival meetings in winter drew vast crowds and seemed to strike
responsive chords in the hearts of harried, uncouth older men and
women and of impressionable young people. Though at first they
might hesitate, they would finally eagerly respond and be converted.
In later years they might discount "revival methods," but they were
also likely to admit the impetus and direction given to their lives by
this stirring emotional experience. There were many who, sure to be
converted at meetings, were, in turn, sure to "back-slide" and the
process was repeated several times. The preacher in the local Methodist, Baptist, or Presbyterian church was often a stern exacting man
who spoke plainly, coarsely, and mercilessly to his people of sin, repentance, and the straight and narrow way. Human frailty and need

[9] Cincinnati *Daily Commercial*, Apr. 22, 1872; Bogart and Thompson, *The Industrial State, 1870–1893*, pp. 193, 213.
[10] Bogart and Thompson, *op. cit.*, pp. 196, 203, 204; Cincinnati *Daily Commercial*, July 24, 1873.

were frankly recognized, and it was felt that an adequate salvation was near at hand to anyone who sought truly and with his whole heart.[11]

And indeed the world from which the repentant sinner sought to be saved was full of pitfalls and temptations. The low tone of public morality was not confined to the Federal Government. The sessions of the Illinois Legislature in those years were marked by aggressive contests of rival interests, sections, corporations, and individuals for spoils, privileges, and concessions. Lobbying and log-rolling were notorious, and the activity of soldiers and of popular Civil War generals was far from wholesome.[12] If the prosperity of the late sixties and early seventies did not encourage high ethical standards, neither did the depression that followed after 1873. A newspaper summary for the year 1873 contained the following: "The world of morality has little to boast of. Crime has increased rapidly; corruption has left its taint all over the land. Defalcations, embezzlements, frauds, murders, swindles, violence, riots, and thefts are and have been the order of the day." In Cairo, it was reported, one man a week was killed; in Chicago, there were gamblers, murderers, and confidence men; in Springfield "bullies, strumpets, vagrants, and sneak-thieves." [13] In Ohio there was a conscious feeling that a "crime wave" was spreading over the land —a murder mania and general insecurity of life—a condition not improved by legal delays and the poor jury system. Newspaper editors used very strong, perhaps extravagant, language in describing how the previous era of speculation and "bubble blowing" brought in its train an age of defalcations, governmental corruption, free passes, extravagance, "Grantism," laxity and fraud among state and county officials, merchants and traders.[14] The Henry Ward Beecher "Plymouth" or "Brooklyn scandal" was accorded between fifty and a hundred columns in the leading paper in the West, and the public mind for two or three months was keenly whetted for the fact, rumor, or lying recrimination that such a case afforded.[15]

It was an age of widespread intemperance and drunkenness; no survey of the records leaves us in any doubt about that. The temper-

[11] Cincinnati *Daily Commercial*, Dec.–Apr., 1873, 1874, *passim;* Cole, *op. cit.*, p. 424.

[12] Cole, *op. cit.*, pp. 396, 399, 403, 405–407, 415, 419.

[13] Bogart and Thompson, *op. cit.*, pp. 28, 29, quoting the Chicago *Tribune* and other Illinois papers.

[14] Cincinnati *Gazette,* Feb. 2, 1874; Cincinnati *Daily Commercial,* Jan. 31, Feb. 2, 1874.

[15] Cincinnati *Daily Commercial,* July 3, 11, 20–24, 28–30, Aug., Sept., *passim,* 1874.

ance reform wave of the fifties which had resulted in experiments with the "Maine Law" or other types of regulation had largely spent its force in the following years. The all absorbing slavery question and the years of terrible war had caused a cessation of interest in regulation;[16] in fact, the war and the upsetting of accepted standards and ways of life had brought, in the sixties, a new wave of intemperance and drunkenness, with which the inadequate license or local option laws of Ohio, Indiana, Illinois and other states were unable to cope.[17] Public men became notorious drunkards, and the question of their indulgences and attempts at reformation became subjects of popular discussion.[18] But protest against these conditions was not long in coming. A more rigorous licensing bill was passed in Illinois in 1872, and all over the state there were formed temperance clubs and organizations including a "Catholic Total Abstinence Union."[19]

In Ohio the revived war on liquor took an unusual and dramatic form. In Washington Court House, Hillsboro, Wilmington, and other towns in the southwestern part of the state, another "Ohio Movement" broke out in the winter of 1873–1874. Called by various names, this "Women's Whiskey War" or "Women's Crusade" was perhaps the most unique temperance movement in our history. Springing up during a winter marked by stirring revivals, it sought by religious and moral fervor not only to destroy the drink demon and close the saloon but to induce the saloon keeper to sign the pledge and become converted. Bands of fearless, keyed-up women, supported by other bands at prayer in the churches, would venture forth on the streets of the town, kneel in prayer on the pavement or curbstone or, if admitted into the drugstore or saloon, would sing, pray, and plead within the doors of the iniquitous place itself.[20] Many of the saloon keepers yielded at once, but even so great importunity did not move the hearts of the more obdurate. In Washington Court House, the women, upon being denied admittance, stood out of doors on a very cold winter day from early noon until eleven o'clock at night singing and praying for the hard-hearted keeper. At Hillsboro, a conservative place where the "old Virginia blood still dominated" and where many old gentlemen

[16] Esarey, *Indiana,* II, 614–617; Cole, *op. cit.,* 207, 209, 219; Beveridge, *Lincoln,* II, 228, 229, 293, 294.
[17] Cincinnati *Daily Commercial,* Jan. 15, 1874; Bogart and Thompson, *op. cit.,* pp. 42, 43.
[18] Cole, *op. cit.,* p. 422.
[19] Bogart and Thompson, *op. cit.,* pp. 44, 46, 48.
[20] E. O. Randall and D. J. Ryan, *History of Ohio,* IV, 330.

still took their regular dram, "the war" continued for many weeks.[21]

The immediate results of the movement were remarkable; small towns readily took it up and soon it spread to larger places in Ohio, like Springfield, Dayton, and Columbus. It reached the northern part of the state, and over into Indiana and Illinois and other states.[22] The devoted crusaders were even ready to tackle such large cities as Cincinnati where beer and whiskey drinking was very widespread and the liquor interests very strong.

The press treated the movement with widely varying degrees of criticism, approval, and scorn. The Chicago *Tribune* remarked after several weeks of the campaign had passed:

. . . the fervor of the intemperate temperance women is abating, and yet . . . saloons are as numerous. . . . The volume of orisons made a momentary impression on the air, excited the ridicule of the anti-religious world, awakening regret in the breasts of those whose religion is not wholly irrational and sensational . . . and these are the only results which have been produced by the "praying women." [23]

On the other hand the earnestness of the women crusaders elicited favorable comment from many sources. Their success in the smaller towns was conceded.[24] *Harper's Weekly,* the eastern journal, said, "underneath all the mean phenomena is the inexpressible and far-reaching sorrow of suffering women." [25] It might here be added that legislative regulation of the liquor traffic was given impetus by the revived temperance feeling of the seventies and that the National Prohibition party soon made its appearance.

"SPOON RIVER" IN THE SEVENTIES AND EIGHTIES

In the most comprehensive treatment of American life written as yet, the authors describe the post-war period as one marked by "the politics of acquisition and enjoyment" and by "gilded age culture." [26] Another writer laments the passing of the pre-war "Golden Day." [27]

[21] Cincinnati *Daily Commercial,* Jan. 19, 23, 29, Feb. 2, 6, *et passim,* March, 1874, *passim.*
[22] *Ibid.,* Feb. 16, 20, 23, 1874.
[23] Quoted in Bogart and Thompson, *op. cit.,* p. 50.
[24] Cincinnati *Daily Commercial,* Feb. 10, 1874.
[25] Quoted in the *Commercial,* March 2, 1874.
[26] Charles and Mary Beard, *The Rise of American Civilization,* Vol. II, Chs. XXIII, XXV.
[27] Lewis Mumford, *The Golden Day.*

We must ask the question whether the artificial, materialistic, and even sinister forces that such writers ascribe to American life as a whole, were at work in the West. What has already been put down in this and other chapters would suggest that they were—how completely, when the whole of western life is taken into consideration, it would be impossible to say. So hard a task is it to plumb the deeper currents of life that the American historian rarely goes farther than an analysis of political, sectional or economic conditions, adding perhaps a brief treatment of surface social life and manners, but avoiding "behavior" and the deep springs that underlie it. To do more would be to attempt the rôle of psychologist, social philosopher or literary artist. A group of novelists, poets, and journalists, however, have not hesitated to treat these deeper currents of western life; their "realism" and their depth of discernment of vital issues help to fill the gap left by the historian.[28] Certainly the reader could well afford to neglect a portion of the endless story of middle western partisan politics and read this remarkable series of novels, memoirs and poems, which, beginning with stories of the river towns of Missouri, Indiana, and Illinois, given us by Mark Twain, Edward Eggleston and John Hay, is continued in the pictures of Iowa and Wisconsin by Herbert Quick and Hamlin Garland, is further continued in the harsh outlines of small-town life drawn by Edgar W. Howe and revealed in the stark epitaphs on the "Spoon River" tombstones of Edgar Lee Masters. The list is completed by the "sagas" of the prairies of Iowa, Nebraska, and the Dakotas that come from the pens of Willa Cather, Glenway Wescott, O. E. Rolvaag, Ruth Suckow and others. Edward Eggleston with James Whitcomb Riley and Booth Tarkington are leaders in "the Indiana school" of sentiment and local color; Mark Twain and Hamlin Garland, Rolvaag and the prairie writers exhibit a more vigorous descriptive realism touched with wonder and romance, while Edgar Lee Masters heads a rebellious school in its determined "revolt from the village." Although certain of these writers go too far in stressing the drab and sordid, or in trying to deal with western life in terms of the new psychology of repression, frustration, and reckless abnormal outlet, or in imitating European novelists by describing the western

[28] Dorothy Dondore, "Points of Contact between History and Literature in the Mississippi Valley," *Miss. Valley Hist. Rev.* Vol. XI, pp. 227–236; also, *The Prairie and the Making of Middle America*, Chs. VI–VIII, by the same author; Carl Van Doren, *Contemporary American Novelists* (1922).

farmer in terms which continental writers apply to the European peasant, nevertheless, their work, taken as a whole, is already assuming an epic and monumental character.[29]

In these books, and in a thousand unwritten family histories, we see the sons and daughters of the "hardy yeomanry of the forties" now approaching middle or old age. Almost all of them had passed through the experience of civil war. They had suffered broken families, death, disease, or some other vital change in their lives. Young men had gone to war and returned now to find changes in their own fortunes, in the family, or on the farm so great that they must start life anew. There still remained that alluring and often deceptive appeal of the West, and many of them, joining the movement of the newly arriving Scandinavians and Germans, sought again to enact the romance or, more likely, the tragedy of the frontier on a stage stretching from Kansas to the Dakotas. Such an undertaking brought to them as it had brought to their fathers in Ohio, Indiana, and Illinois, a nervous drive and overstrain of hard work, a fight with drought and grasshoppers, and a struggle with debt and mortgage. New attempts had to be made also to settle for their new frontier standing problems of access to market, adequate prices for corn and wheat, and fair railroad rates.

Their brothers, sisters, cousins, or neighbors who had remained in the older cities, towns, and rural districts of Ohio, Indiana, Illinois, and Michigan had had far different fortunes. Many of the older families in Cincinnati, in Indianapolis, and in Chicago, and others similarly situated in Peoria and St. Louis had now become the leading families in the West, reflecting in some instances substantial culture and refinement. Many less noted families in town and country had also risen

---

[29] It is of course recognized that only those works dealing with the earlier period and with the older West apply to the subject-matter of this book. Any list that attempted to cover the whole Middle West would include: by Mark Twain, *Life on the Mississippi, Huckleberry Finn, Tom Sawyer,* and *The Gilded Age;* by Edward Eggleston, *The Hoosier School-Master,* and *The Greysons;* by Booth Tarkington, *A Gentleman from Indiana* and *The Magnificent Ambersons;* by Edgar Lee Masters, *Spoon River Anthology, Mitch Miller,* and *Skeeters Kirby;* by Herbert Quick, *Vandemark's Folly, The Hawkeye* and *One Man's Life;* by Hamlin Garland, *Main Travelled Roads* and *A Son of the Middle Border;* by Edgar Howe, *The Story of a Country Town;* by William Allen White, *A Certain Rich Man;* by Willa Cather, *O Pioneers* and *My Antonia;* by Ruth Suckow, *Country People;* by Glenway Wescott, *The Grandmothers;* by O. E. Rolvaag, *Giants in the Earth* and *Peder Victorious.* Sherwood Anderson's *Poor White* should be mentioned, as should also his *Winesburg Ohio*— a completely "behavioristic" but rather unconvincing treatment of small town life in the northern part of that state.

in the social scale. Thanks to hard-working mothers and fathers, they had become prosperous merchants or owners of valuable farm lands— their "acres" numbering, in some cases, several hundred in the matchless corn counties of Indiana, Illinois, and Iowa. They soon left the farm and as "retired farmers" set up a landed aristocracy in hundreds of small towns in these states. They enjoyed a short heyday, little realizing how, in the course of time, their magnificent land holdings would dwindle in value and how their children would come to regret their parents' frenzied adding of quarter section after quarter section to the patrimony.

To many of these families the transition from frontier barrenness, privation, and economy to newer conditions of well-being, from older religious dogmatism or evangelical piety to newer conditions of religious ease or liberalism, was very difficult and brought much family division and personal unhappiness, but their lives were none the less marked by a certain steadiness and growth. Sons of these families went to college and often became the better type of preachers, politicians, lawyers, doctors, or college teachers, and they or their descendants represent much of what is most valid in middle western life to-day. For other families of retired farmers, less fortunate experiences were in store. The parents were ill-adapted to their new social environment and became dissatisfied, and with the children the nervous western tension took on new forms. They became restless real estate speculators, driving lawyers or politicians, owners of banks or waterworks or other growing public utilities, and many fell into questionable schemes and practices. They committed their fortunes to the uncertain tide of business success and social climbing in their restricted home communities. Now they would sail on the high waves of public favor, and now plunge down into utter failure and material and moral collapse. They supply a gilded culture for the small town as more spectacular and venturesome families of the same general type did for the cities.

Along with these more articulate and prominent classes in town and country, but distinctly not a part of either, there was another less happy class. The grim battle with frontier or post-frontier conditions brought to their fathers and to them discouragement and defeat. In hundreds of "Spoon Rivers" these men and women, likewise children or grandchildren of the hardy yeomen of the forties, were living unsuccessful, thwarted and twisted lives. Of their unfulfilled destinies the historian can never have documentary proof; only in the grim epitaphs of a poet's imagination or on the dim ungraven tablets of family memory and tradition are they revealed. Edgar Lee Masters in his *Spoon River Anthology*, presents a remarkable gallery of small town types. Too much stress on sordidness and despair make the pervading mystery and fatalism and the epic elevation of the references to Lincoln, to old pioneers, to Anne Rutledge and to the stronger Spoon River characters, all the more effective. The following are portions of the epitaphs of the Sunday School superintendent and the photographer who made pictures of the pioneers.

HENRY PHIPPS

I was the Sunday school superintendent,
The dummy president of the wagon works
And the canning factory,
Acting for Thomas Rhodes and the banking clique;
My son the cashier of the Bank,
Wedded to Rhodes' daughter,
My week days spent in making money,
My Sundays at church and in prayer.
In everything a cog in the wheel of things-as-they-are:
Of money, master and man, made white
With the paint of the Christian creed.
And then:
The bank collapsed. I stood and looked at the wrecked machine—
The wheels with blow-holes stopped with putty and painted;
The rotten bolts, the broken rods;
And only the hopper for souls fit to be used again
In a new devourer of life, when newspapers, judges and money-magicians
Build over again.

.   .   .   .

RUTHERFORD McDOWELL

They brought me ambrotypes
Of the old pioneers to enlarge.
And sometimes one sat for me—
Some one who was in being
When giant hands from the womb of the world
Tore the republic.
What was it in their eyes—
For I could never fathom
That mystical pathos of drooped eyelids,
And the serene sorrow of their eyes.

.   .   .   .

And these grand-children and great grand-children
Of the pioneers!

Truly did my camera record their faces, too,
With so much of the old strength gone,
And the old faith gone,
And the old mastery of life gone,
And the old courage gone,
Which labors and loves and suffers and sings
Under the sun! [30]

PROGRESS IN HIGHER LIVING

But to contend that the millions of westerners in 1880 were living a drab existence of repressive Puritanism, thwarted desires and furtive concealments is to make indiscriminate statements and to be guilty of indicting a whole people. For many thousands of families there had been for decades the steady increment of higher values and the stimulations that come from world currents of thought and activity. Even in the prairie regions, the recurrent periods of boom and prosperity and the work of building up the civilization of a new area provided an objective task which, though approached with a too frenzied drive, often brought enthusiasm and wholesome, satisfying results. And then, too, hard work, privations and suffering did not necessarily preclude a sense of well-being. The defects and shortcomings of middle western life were rather incidents or the social waste incurred in the vast processes of mass living and of political, sectional, and economic development. Nor were there lacking cultural achievements—certainly the material foundations for what might later be a higher life were laid.

By the seventies the public school system had become well developed. On the basis laid down before the Civil War, and after the settlement of many questions relating to the raising of state school funds, the powers of state and county superintendents, the foundation of high schools, and the furnishing of educational facilities for colored children, a remarkable superstructure was raised. Some opposition had, it is true, been voiced by Catholics, and in some places it was felt that Democrats were less interested in educational progress than were Republicans. In the cities, especially, there had been great progress, and in the country, the district school era was here in full force. The little red or white school-house, the country school-teacher, often able and versatile, the "literary" and the spelling school—these institutions mark a distinct period in the educational history of the West. To only

[30] Pages 183, 200.

a few was it apparent that the district system would have to give way to better types of organization. In the seventies there were twenty or thirty thousand district schools in the Middle West.[31]

The western state university was coming into its own. Having been founded in Indiana and Michigan two or three decades before the Civil War, in Wisconsin and Iowa on the eve of that struggle, and in Illinois, Kansas and Ohio in the years immediately following, it was destined to become an institution of unique importance in the educational world.[32] The movement for this type of education had received great impetus from the efforts of Jonathan B. Turner of Jacksonville, Illinois, and from the passage by Congress of the Morrill Bill in 1862 providing for land-grant endowment for agricultural and industrial education.[33] The establishment of these universities, together with the state normal schools, based on government aid in the form of land or tax appropriations or other forms of public support, marks an epoch in middle western, and indeed American, education. They proved to be influential factors in the introduction in successful forms of industrial, agricultural, technical, and scientific training. Along with the public elementary and secondary schools they promoted the secularization of education in the West. It should be added here that there was developing outside the doors of these schools, also, an interest in scientific agriculture and many local horticultural societies were being formed. And everywhere the use of agricultural machinery and labor-saving devices of all sorts was on the increase.

It was fortunate that the private or denominational academies, seminaries and colleges which we have seen were founded before the Civil War in all the states north of the Ohio, continued to dwindle in numbers. But it was still more fortunate that a few in each state survived—a result due to the self-sacrificing labor of their faculties, to denominational zeal, and to the fact that in most of these colleges there was a New England influence that kept the fires of learning burning in the midst of storms that would quench and clouds of indifference that would stifle. Thus in spite of trial, poverty, and civil war, there were saved for the future Middle West, Oberlin, Denison, Ohio

[31] *American Journal of Education*, Edited by Henry Barnard, Vol. XXIV, pp. 244–248, 250, 304–305, 379 *et passim;* E. P. Cubberley, *Public Education in the United States*, Chs. V, VI, VII.
[32] Cubberley, *op. cit.*, pp. 200–212; N. M. Butler, *Education in the United States*, pp. 276–279; Esarey, *Indiana*, I, 282, 331, II, 997–1016.
[33] Burt E. Powell, *The Movement for Industrial Education and the Establishment of the University*, Chs. I, II, IV, VIII, X.

Wesleyan, DePauw, Wabash, Illinois College, Knox, Northwestern, Beloit, Grinnell, Notre Dame, and several others. After the war there was in many of these schools, it is true, slow progress; a real renaissance was not to come until a later day. In some respects, narrow sectarian control and the presence of the long-coated, clerical professors exercised a deterrent effect, as did also perhaps the pseudoculture we have already described. But if the professors were not great scholars or specialists, they were often shrewd judges of human nature, keen observers, and unique personalities. If the interest in learning was often partial and sentimental, if physical science, social science, and modern languages were neglected, nevertheless, Greek, Latin, Moral Philosophy, and the prevailing evangelical and missionary fervor were not without their broadening influence; a certain type of social idealism and literary refinement was the result. In vigorous though imperfect ways, the idea of "general culture" was kept alive.[34]

In religion the reign of dogmatism and "long prayers and long sermons" did not continue unchallenged. "Either the churches will have to change much or the coming man will not attend them," said an outspoken critic in 1874.[35] There was a continuation in many places of that tolerance and indifference we saw in the pre-war period. The Lincoln tradition of religious liberalism, and heterodoxy of the Unitarian and Universalist variety, though they claimed only a few declared adherents, were vigorous and active.[36] Robert G. Ingersoll, of Illinois, by the arts of the rhetorician rather than the logical reasoner, was proclaiming a gospel of attractive but somewhat superficial "infidelism." His speeches and lectures were being published in the seventies under the headings *Heretics and Heresies, The Gods and other Lectures,* and *Some Mistakes of Moses.* The theory of evolution or natural selection was being widely discussed in the newspapers;[37] in 1879 a student chose "Theistic Evolution" as the subject of his graduation essay in Ohio Wesleyan University.

Music and the drama of the best type received attention in the cities; this was especially true of Cincinnati, Chicago, and St. Louis, where concerts, opera, symphony, and plays were available for the

---

[34] See catalogues of these colleges 1860–1880 *passim;* Webster, *Seventy-five Significant Years, The Story of Knox College,* 1837–1912; E. T. Nelson, *Fifty Years of Ohio Wesleyan;* Wilde, *Northwestern University;* Esarey, *Indiana,* II, 987–995.

[35] Cincinnati *Daily Commercial,* Nov. 6, 1874.

[36] Cole, *op. cit.,* pp. 426, 427.

[37] Cincinnati *Daily Commercial,* July 11, Nov. 9, 1874.

people in the surrounding regions. If Salvini, the great Italian actor, made a wide popular appeal in his somewhat too physical portrayal of the parts of "Spartacus," "Samson," and "Othello," greater refinement and subtlety was portrayed by Booth, Barrett, the elder Sothern, and Fanny Janauschek.[38] The lecture courses or lyceums characteristic of pre-war days continued on into the seventies. "What delightful people I met in that Western tour," said one of the lecturers, "studious, educated, hospitable, they gave an impression that a new and nobler America was arising in the West."[39] In Marietta and Chillicothe, Ohio, Vevay, Madison and New Harmony, Indiana, and in the college towns scattered here and there, standards of living far removed from frontier roughness and rigor were being achieved. Such living reflected neither gilded age falseness nor the sordidness of "Spoon River."

The most important forms of advanced social thought in the West were associated with the reform, Greenback, and Granger movements already noted. In addition, Socialism was making its first appearance on any considerable scale, being associated usually with German "radicalism." Labor, too, was becoming awakened. The formation of unions had received great impetus in the sixties, and labor, as we have seen, had figured in the election of 1868 and in various third party movements.[40] Workmen had, of course, received high wages and had participated in the general extravagance that marked the period up to 1873. Then, in turn, the several years of depression, low wages and unemployment were followed by the revival of business in 1878 and 1879, and by high prices and a higher cost of living. Labor, again becoming powerful and aggressive, inaugurated a new period of discontent, organization, and strikes. With this development we shall not deal. It, along with the appearance of the industrial revival in Ohio, Illinois, and other states, signifies the definite emergence of a new industrial epoch centered particularly in the lake region—now clearly the dominant part of the West. If we add to the industrial lake district, its tributaries, the newer corn and wheat belts of the Missouri and upper Mississippi valleys, we have before us a newer Middle West whose history from 1880 to the present would call for separate treatment.

[38] Cincinnati *Daily Commercial*, May 10, 1872, Jan. 20, Dec. 18, 1874 *et passim;* Bogart and Thompson, *op. cit.*, pp. 201–203.
[39] M. D. Conway, *Autobiography*, II, 307.
[40] *First Annual Report, Bureau of Labor Statistics*, Ohio, 1877, p. 34.

The spirit of the older West—the West of the forties and fifties—which has been one of the main themes of this book, was to be perpetuated in parts of the newer corn and wheat belts—in Missouri, Kansas, Nebraska, and the Dakotas. If here a new agricultural boom occurred in the late seventies and early eighties, it was only to be followed by later gloom. Here the alliance between the lower West and the South continued to show itself in various economic and political forms. But to describe it in detail lies far beyond our purpose. Perhaps careful study would reveal that in the person of William Jennings Bryan and in the Populist and Democratic protest movements of the nineties, we would find a further outcropping of the themes we have been treating. Bryan, the son of a Virginian, himself born in the lower West, at Salem, Illinois, moved to Nebraska and there renewed in modified form the political tradition that, coming down through Allen, Douglas, Vallandigham, Thurman and Pendleton, traces back to the Progressive Democracy of the forties, and through Andrew Jackson, back to Thomas Jefferson himself.[41] But more important and valid than the career of one man or the record of any movement would be the wider story of the life and achievements of the whole people in this new Middle West.

THE SOURCES AND VALIDITY OF MIDDLE WESTERN CULTURE

The question has been asked, was middle western culture derivative and merely imitative of eastern and European patterns or was it itself original and contributory to the life of the East and indeed to all American life? Frederick J. Turner's work, claiming for the frontier and the West great contributions to American democracy, political reform, individualism and national characteristics, and profoundly influencing the writing of American history during the last forty years, has been called in question. The counter claim has been made that in its governmental forms, state and local, the Middle West has been imitative of the East,[42] that its spirit has been too individualistic, and that, cul-

---

[41] In 1893, Lyman Trumbull, now an old man, entertained Bryan in his Chicago home. This staunch western Republican insurgent had, after 1872, turned back to Democracy, but later became a Populist; he was interested in free silver and socialism and volunteered to defend Eugene V. Debs in the great injunction case. That the careers of these two men thus converged was prophetic of more recent Democratic and insurgent Republican alliances in the Middle West. White, *Trumbull*, pp. 413, 414, 425.

[42] Dixon Ryan Fox (ed.), *Sources of Culture in the Middle West, Backgrounds versus Frontier* (D. Appleton-Century Company, 1934).

turally the older American and European civilizations with their accumulated amenities and refinements, coming in contact with the roughness of the frontier, have been only disintegrated and degraded.[43] The romantic idealization of the frontier as the place where the return to nature and the simple life might be realized on a continental scale,[44] as well as the claim that life on the western farm and in the small country town was hardy, wholesome and fine—all such ideas have been held up to ridicule.[45] In reality, it is said, the Middle West has been drab and commonplace, an uninteresting, conforming "Bible belt," if not, indeed, sordid and vicious.[46]

There was, of course, much that was far from romantic in western life, much struggle and sadness. The glowing anticipation and the dream of opportunity that lured the settler and his family all too often turned to a tale of defeat and despair. The fluidity, change, and lack of stability that has marked American life in general was accentuated here. People indeed became culturally uprooted and detached. A frenzied absorption in the earlier and rougher tasks of civilization building left less time and inclination for polite forms. The disintegration of the only stable culture that Western Europe has produced— medieval Christian civilization—was already well along its course as a result of the Renaissance, the Reformation, and the industrial and political revolutions in Europe; it was carried further by dissenting American colonists in the East, and still further by restless pioneers in the West. Individualism, already so strongly marked in European Protestantism, in the *laissez faire* eighteenth and early nineteenth century economic thought and practice in Europe and the eastern part of the United States, was indeed intensified under western conditions. An exception might be made in the case of the ravages caused by competitive industrial capitalism, which reached a much more extensive and devastating state in Europe and eastern America than in the Middle West. But, in general, the heritage that the middle westerner received was itself already shot through with disintegrating elements; for this he is not to blame. It was the *milieu* in which he lived.

But comparisons between civilizations may be stressed too much

[43] Lewis Mumford, *The Golden Day.*

[44] V. S. Parrington, *The Romantic Revolution in America (Main Currents of American Life,* Volume II).

[45] See Edgar Lee Masters, *Spoon River Anthology;* Edgar Howe, *The Story of a Country Town;* Sinclair Lewis, *Main Street.*

[46] H. L. Mencken, in the *American Mercury, passim;* Sherwood Anderson, *Winesburg Ohio.*

and become not only odious but historically and culturally useless. Alternatives may easily be too sharply drawn. The life of any people derives from the past and is imitative of earlier culture patterns, but it is likewise, in turn, contributory to the main stream. It is, above all, *sui generis* and in itself valid. The Middle West from 1840 to the present day has constituted a section, a civilization, a people, and to indict a whole people is, we are told, a highly futile task. Each civilization is self-verifying, has its own validities, and is primarily to be estimated in terms of itself. The universal endeavor and struggle of human life expressed itself in a new local habitation in the Middle West and took on new local forms.

Viewed in this wider compass, apologies are not necessary. The very opening of the vast stretch of new land bounded by the Ohio, the Missouri, and the great lakes, considered only in its physical aspects such as the clearing of forests, the draining of swamps, the taming of a wild soil, the building of roads, canals, and railroads, was itself a significant task accomplished only by an unsurpassed energy and by a great toll of flesh and blood. The introduction of English and eastern American forms of government and law, of Christianity and the higher thought and art forms that the world had developed, was in itself a great achievement. The part the Middle West played in national politics on matters involving slavery extension, union, Civil War, railroad control, agrarian legislation, and general social reform—these were major themes in American history from 1840 to the present day. The democracy and humanity of Abraham Lincoln was, itself, a contribution to the whole world. The decent human life made possible for millions of human beings in this broad central valley— this too is self-validating; and, in recent years, the appearance here of unique schools of writers only adds to the significance of the older Middle West in American and human history.

BIBLIOGRAPHY

The materials from which this study has been prepared were found in the following places: The Newberry Library in Chicago; The Chicago Historical Society; The University of Chicago Library; The Historical Department of Iowa, Des Moines; The Iowa Historical Society, and The Library of Iowa University, Iowa City; The Wisconsin State Historical Society Library, Madison; The Indiana State Library, Indianapolis; The Ohio State Library and the Library of the Ohio Archeological and Historical Society, Columbus; The Library of the Historical and Philosophical Society of Ohio and the Mercantile Library, Cincinnati; The Library of Congress, Washington, D. C.

I. Guides to Source Material and Bibliographies

There is, of course, no general bibliographical guide for the study of the Middle West as a whole nor for the lower West in particular. The most valuable guides to newspaper materials are:

Galbreath, C. B. *Newspapers and Periodicals in the Ohio State Library.* (The newspaper files are now to be found in the Library of the Ohio Archeological and Historical Society, Columbus.)

Scott, F. W., *Newspapers and Periodicals of Illinois, 1814–1879,* in *Collections of the Illinois State Historical Library,* Vol. VI.

Griswold, Ada Tyng, *Annotated Catalogue of Newspaper Files in the Library of the State Historical Society of Wisconsin* (Madison, 1911).

Bradley, I. S., *Bibliography of Available Documentary and Newspaper Material for the Old Northwest, Am. Hist. Ass'n. Report, 1896,* Vol. I, pp. 296–319.

Other general bibliographical guides of value are:

Bowker, R. R., *State Publications* (New York, 1908).

Buck, Solon Justus, *Travel and Description 1765–1865, Illinois. Collections* of the Illinois State Library, Vol IX, Bibliographical Series Vol. II.

Griffin, H. P. C., *Index of Articles upon American Local History.* Bibliographies of Special Subjects No. 3, Boston Public Library.

Hasse, Adelaide R., *Index to Economic Material in the Documents of States —Illinois* (Carnegie Institution, 1909) ; *Index to Economic Material in the Documents of the States—Ohio.* Vol. II (Carnegie Institution, 1912).

Stevenson, R. T., "A Preliminary Report on the Ohio Archives," *American Historical Association Report,* 1906, Vol. II, p. 165.

Lindley, Harlow, "Report on the Archives of the State of Indiana," *American Historical Association Report,* 1910, p. 315.
Alvord, C. W. and Pease, T. C., "The Archives of the State of Illinois," *American Historical Association Report,* 1909, p. 379.
Shambaugh, Benj., *A Second Report on the Iowa Public Archives* (Des Moines, 1907).
Pease, T. C. *The County Archives of Illinois* (Illinois State Historical Library, 1915).
Ryan, Daniel J., *The Civil War Literature of Ohio* (Cleveland, 1911).
Thomson, P. G., *A Bibliography of Ohio* (Cincinnati, 1880).
Thwaites, R. G., *Descriptive List of Manuscript Collections of the State Historical Society of Wisconsin, together with Reports on other Collections of Manuscripts in Adjacent States* (Madison, 1906).

II. Official Publications, National and State

Of the official publications of the United States Government the most useful for this study proved to be *The Congressional Globe;* the *United States Census* for the years 1840, 1850, 1860 and 1870; the numerous volumes of the *Official Record of the Rebellion; Senate and House Executive Documents* that contain reports of the Land Office; reports on River and Lake Commerce issued by the Secretaries of the Treasury and War and the Corps of Topographical Engineers. Of the documents of the states, the *Senate* and *House Journals* of Ohio, Indiana, Illinois and Iowa are indispensable. Of great value on economic, social and political conditions in the lower West are *Debates of the Ohio Convention 1850–1851, 2* vols.; *The Report of the Debate and Proceedings of the Convention for the Revision of the Constitution of the State of Indiana,* 1850, 2 vols. (Indianapolis 1850); the *Journal of the Convention of the People of the State of Indiana* (Indianapolis, 1850); the *Journal of the Convention assembled at Springfield* (Illinois, June 7, 1847); *The Constitutional Debates of 1847, Collections, Illinois State Historical Library,* Vol. XIV (Springfield, 1919, edited by A. C. Cole); *A Contemporary Account of the Debates of the Illinois State Constitutional Convention of 1847,* found in the *Illinois State Register,* June, July and August of that year; the *Debates of the Constitutional Convention of the State of Iowa at Iowa City,* 1857. Other official material of use includes:—
Report on the Internal Commerce of the United States. Bureau of Statistics, Treasury Department (Government Printing Office, 1888).
Report of the Commissioner of Statistics of Ohio, 1857–1865 *et seq.* (later called *Ohio Statistics*).
Annual Report, Bureau of Labor Statistics, Ohio, 1877–1880 *et seq.*
Annual Report, Sup't. of Public Instruction, Indiana, 1852–1857 *et seq.*
Indiana Brevier Legislative Reports, Vols. I–VIII. These contain the most useful record of the debates in the Indiana Legislature from 1857 to 1865, and afford valuable material on Indiana social life, politics, sectional divergence, etc.

Terrell, W. H. H., *Report of Adj. General,* Indiana, Vol. I. *War of Rebellion,* 1861–1865 (Indianapolis, 1869).
Executive Documents, Legislative Documents, Reports, etc., of the various states on various matters.

III. Newspapers

The materials for the book were drawn from local newspapers more largely than from any other source. The danger in the use of such material must not close our eyes to the fact of our absolute dependence on it for information regarding local facts, tendencies, and "color." Some of the papers, for instance the Cincinnati *Commercial,* which was much less partisan than most of the others, are in fact very valuable sources of information. The author is again and again dependent on the interpretation of events given by Murat Halstead and others in the *Commercial.*

The newspapers which most clearly represent the spirit of the lower West before, during, and after the war may be said to have been: the Cincinnati *Enquirer,* the Columbus *Crisis,* the Dayton *Empire,* the New Albany *Ledger,* the Vevay *News,* the Indianapolis *Sentinel,* the Terre Haute *Journal,* the Springfield *Illinois State Register,* the Alton *Courier,* the Chicago *Times,* the Chicago *Herald* and the Dubuque *Herald.* These papers were the organs of Douglas, Buchanan or Breckinridge before the war and from 1861–1864 were allied with the various forms of the peace Democracy. The editors of several of them were subjected to arrest and imprisonment during the war for alleged disloyalty. There were many smaller town or country newspapers that showed a more "pro-southern" attitude than these. Many have disappeared, but the few that remain are uniquely important and afford intensely interesting material.

The Cincinnati *Enquirer* was edited by J. J. Faran. The editor of the Columbus *Crisis* was Samuel Medary, ex-Governor of Kansas under Buchanan; this paper was in many respects the most violent in its attacks on the Lincoln administration. The Dayton *Empire* reflected the spirit of Vallandigham who lived in that city. The editor of the Indianapolis *Sentinel* was J. J. Bingham. The paper followed Douglas until 1861, but after his death veered more and more toward the Vallandigham movement. The Springfield, Illinois, *State Register* was edited by Charles H. Lamphier. The Chicago *Herald* was an administration paper under Buchanan and was even more conservatively Democratic than the *Times,* which was edited by James W. Sheahan and controlled largely by Cyrus McCormick. Dennis Mahony, the editor of the Dubuque *Herald,* was one of the most conspicuous of the newspaper editors who were imprisoned during the war.

The opposing tendencies at work in the upper West throughout the period from 1845–1865 are shown by the Ashtabula *Sentinel,* a Western Reserve Free Soil paper, the *St. Joseph Valley Reporter* (South Bend) edited by Schuyler Colfax, the Chicago *Journal,* and the Chicago *Tribune.* Conservative and Whiggish Republicanism is well represented by the Indianapolis *Journal* and the New Albany *Tribune.*

Among the most prominent newspapers in addition to those already mentioned were: the Cincinnati *Gazette*, the Logansport *Pharos*, the *Illinois State Journal*, the Keokuk *Gate City*, the Iowa City *Democratic Press*, the St. Louis *Democrat*, the St. Louis *Reveille* and the St. Louis *Republican*.

IV. CONTEMPORARY PERIODICALS, YEAR BOOKS, ETC.

The American Encyclopedia, 1860–1865.
DeBow's Review.
DeBow, J. D. B., *Industrial Resources of the South and West*, 1853.
Democratic Monthly Magazine: B. B. Taylor, editor, 1844.
The Dial, Cincinnati, 1860.
Genius of the West, 4 vols., 1851–1855.
Hunt's Merchants' Magazine, 1845–1865.
Medary, *The New Constitution*, 1849 (Columbus, Ohio).
Niles' National Register, Baltimore, during the years 1845–1849.
Ohio Convention Reporter, 1870–1871 (Columbus, Ohio).
The Tribune Almanac, 1856–1865.
The Western Christian Advocate, (Methodist Episcopal, Cincinnati).
The Western Messenger (Cincinnati, 1840).
Western Monthly Magazine, 1831–1836, 5 vols. (Cincinnati, edited by James Hall.)
Western Quarterly Review, 1849 (Cincinnati).
The Western Review, 1846 (Columbus).
The Whig Almanac, 1844–1856 (later the *Tribune Almanac*).

V. MEMOIRS, LETTERS, SPEECHES, ETC.

A list of the most representative materials of a personal nature such as memoirs and letters would include:
Sidney Breese Correspondence. Reprint in *Journal Illinois State Historical Society*, October, 1909.
William Allen Papers, Library of Congress.
Diary and Correspondence of Salmon P. Chase. Report American Historical Association, 1902, Vol. II.
Conway, Moncure Daniel, *Autobiography*, 2 vols. (Riverside Press, 1904).
Dodge, Grenville, M., *Memoirs.*
Drake, Daniel, *Memoir*, edited by Beverly Bond, Jr., *Quart. Pub. Hist. and Phil. Society of Ohio*, Vol. XVIII, Nos. 2, 3.
Foster, Lillian, *Wayside Glimpses, North and South.* Reprint in *Journal Illinois State Historical Society*, Vol. V.
French, William M., *Life, Speeches, State Papers and Public Services of Governor Oliver P. Morton* (Cincinnati, 1864).
Grant, Ulysses S., *Personal Memoirs*, 2 vols. (New York, 1885–1886).
Grierson, Francis, *The Valley of the Shadows, Recollections of the Lincoln Country 1859–1863* (Boston, 1909).

Halstead, Murat, *Caucuses of 1860, a History of the National Political Conventions of the Current Presidential Campaign* (Columbus, 1860).

Julian, George W., *Political Recollections* (Chicago, 1884).

Letters of Governor Kirkwood. Iowa Historical Record, Vols. I–III.

Koerner, Gustave, *Memoirs*, 2 vols. T. G. McCormick (ed.), (Cedar Rapids, 1907).

Nicolay and Hay, *Abraham Lincoln, Complete Works* (The Century Co., 1894).

Logan, John A., *The Great Conspiracy, Its Origin and History* (New York, 1886).

Marston, Francis W., *After Eighty Years* (Columbus, 1886).

Palmer, John M., *Personal Recollections* (Cincinnati, 1901).

McClellan Papers, Manuscript Division, Library of Congress.

Polk, James K., *Diary*, edited by Milo M. Quaife (McClurg, 1910).

Powers, Hiram, *Letters to Nicholas Longworth. Hist. and Phil. Soc. of Ohio, Quarterly Publications*, 1906, Volume I.

Reynolds, John, *My Own Times* (Chicago, 1879).

Richardson, J. D., *Messages and Papers of the Presidents* (Washington, 1896–1899).

Roberts, Isaac Phillips, *Autobiography of a Farm Boy* (Albany, 1916).

Russell, W. H., *My Diary North and South* (Boston, 1863).

Schurz, Carl, *Reminiscences*, 3 vols., (New York, 1907).

Sherman, William Tecumseh, *Memoirs*, 2 vols. (New York, 1875).

"The Diary of a Public Man." *North American Review*, Vol. 129.

Correspondence of Robert Toombs, Alexander H. Stephens and Howell Cobb. Edited by U. B. Phillips. *Report American Historical Association*, 1911. Vol. II.

The Lyman G. Trumbull Manuscripts, Library of Congress.

Vallandigham, C. L., *Speeches, Arguments, Addresses and Letters* (New York, 1864).

The Record of Hon. C. L. Vallandigham (Columbus, Ohio, 1863).

Venable, W. H., *A Buckeye Boyhood* (Cincinnati, 1911).

Voorhees, Daniel W., *Speeches.* Compiled by C. S. Voorhees.

Wallace, Lew, *An Autobiography* (New York, 1906).

Of the foregoing, special mention may be made of the *Memoirs* of Gustave Koerner which show the peculiar position of the Belleville District in southern Illinois and reflect an intimate knowledge of many public men in the lower West, of the *Sidney Breese Correspondence*, the Trumbull Manuscripts and the Allen Papers.

VI. Contemporary Political Pamphlets, Books, etc.

There appeared during times of intense political bitterness large numbers of partisan political pamphlets, "exposures," etc. Some of the important publications of this sort follow:

Ayer, J. W., *The Great Northwestern Conspiracy in all its startling details.* Indiana, Adjutant General. *Indiana and the War*, Vol. V., No. 5.

Reports and Evidence of the Committee on Arbitrary Arrests. Indiana and the War, Vol. III, No. 12.

Bland, T. A., *The Spartan Band,* 1879 (biographies of Greenback leaders).

Bowles, W. A., *Analytical View of the testimony given on the part of the Government in the cases vs. H. H. Dodd and against W. A. Bowles and others before a military commission at Indianapolis,* 1864.

Coatsworth, Stella C., *Loyal People of the Northwest* (Chicago, 1869).

Funk, Isaac, *Copperheads under the Heel of an Illinois Farmer* (New York, 1864).

Dean, Henry Clay, *The Crimes of the Civil War* (1868).

Record of Disloyal Democracy. Indiana Political Pamphlets, Vol. III, No. 13.

Appeal to the Democrats of Indiana, 1863.

Letter of Rosecrans to the Democrats of Indiana. *Civil War Pamphlets, Indiana State Library,* Vol. III, No. 13.

The Draft in Indiana. Adjutant General, *Indiana and the War,* Vol. II, No. 13.

Ewing, Thos. and Stewart, L. W., *Joint Discussion of the Finance Question,* 1876.

Indiana Draft Commissions Report, Adjutant General, *Indiana and the War,* Vol. II, No. 9.

Report of the Committee on Federal Relations, Indiana Adjutant General, *Indiana and the War,* Vol. III, No. 11.

Honest Money League of the Northwest, Extracts from some of the Communistic, Inflammatory and Treasonable Documents circulated by the National Greenback Party (Chicago, 1878).

Hot Drops (A Greenback pamphlet).

Howe, Henry, *Tories of the Rebellion in Illinois* (Cincinnati, 1867).

Indiana. *Civil War Pamphlets,* Indiana State Library.

Authentic Exposition of the Knights of the Golden Circle, 1861.

United States Judge Administrator General's Report on the Order of American Knights or Sons of Liberty, 1864.

Mahony, Dennis, *The Prisoner of State* (New York, 1863).

Marshall, John A., *American Bastille, A History of the Illegal Arrests and Imprisonment of American Citizens in the Northern and Border States* (Philadelphia, 1883). An important but prejudiced and exaggerated treatment.

McConnell, J. P., *Address to Fellow Democrats.*

Owen, Robert Dale, *The Future of the Northwest,* 1863.

——, *Conditions of Reconstruction,* 1863.

George H. Pendleton, The Copperhead Candidate for Vice President, 1864.

Pitman, B. (Editor), *Trials for Treason at Indianapolis,* disclosing a plan for establishing a Northwestern Confederacy (Cincinnati, 1865).

Pomeray, M., *Meat for Men* (A Greenback pamphlet).

Republican Conspiracy to divide the Union.

284 BIBLIOGRAPHY

Stidger, F. G., *Treason History of the Order of Sons of Liberty.*
Treason in Indiana Exposed.
The Three Voices; the Soldier, the Farmer, and the Poet of the Copper-head (New York, 1863).
The Trial of Hon. Clement L. Vallandigham by a Military Commission (Cincinnati, 1863).
The Congressional Record of Vallandigham. His Course on the War. (Cincinnati, 1863).
Whitney, W., *Military Arrests in 1863.*
——, *War Powers of the President and the Legislative Power of Congress.*
Wilson, George, *The Greenbackers and their Doctrines,* 1878.

VII. Biography

Appleton's Cyclopedia of American Biography (New York, 1887).
Beveridge, A. J., *Abraham Lincoln, 1809–1858,* 2 vols. (Riverside Press, 1928).
Bingham, John, *James Harlan* (Iowa City, 1913).
Biographical Congressional Dictionary, Government Printing Office, 1913.
Biographical Encyclopedia of Illinois in the Nineteenth Century (Phila-delphia).
Biography of Ohio, Biographical Annals of Ohio, 3 vols. (Springfield, 1902–1908).
Bloss, G. M. D., *Life and Speeches of George H. Pendleton.*
Clark, Dan Elbert, *Samuel Jordan Kirkwood* (Iowa City, 1917).
Dawson, G. F., *Life and Services of General John A. Logan* (Chicago, 1887).
The Eccentric Preacher or a Sketch of the Life of Lorenzo Dow, 1841.
Forney, J. W., *A Succinct Biographical Sketch of William H. English.*
Foulke, W. D., *Life of Oliver P. Morton,* 2 vols. (Indianapolis, 1899).
Holcombe, John W., *Life and Public Services of Thomas A. Hendricks with Selected Speeches and Writings* (Indianapolis, 1886).
Hollister, O. J., *Life of Schuyler Colfax* (Funk and Wagnalls, 1886).
James, Davis L., "Judge James Hall," *Ohio Arch. and Hist. Society Pub-lications,* Vol. XVIII, pp. 468–483.
Johnson, Allen, *Stephen A Douglas* (New York, 1908).
Jordan, Henry D., "Daniel W. Voorhees." *Mississippi Valley Hist. Re-view,* Vol. VI, pp. 532–555.
Lamb's Biographical Dictionary of the United States (Boston, 1900).
McGrane, R. C., *William Allen, A Study in Western Democracy.* Published by Ohio State Archeological and Historical Society, 1925.
McLaughlin, Andrew Cunningham, *Lewis Cass,* American Statesman Series.
Milton, George Fort, *The Eve of Conflict: Stephen A. Douglas and the Needless War* (Houghton Mifflin Company, 1934).
Parish, J. C., *George Wallace Jones* (Iowa City, 1912).
Pelzer, Louis, *Augustus Cæsar Dodge* (Iowa City, 1908).

——, *Henry Dodge* (Iowa City, 1911).
Robertson, A. H., *Career of Lyman Trumbull* (Master's thesis).
Rombauer, R. E., *Life of Hon. Gustavus Koerner. Transactions of Ill. State Hist. Soc.* (1904) Pub. No. 9, Ill. State Hist. Library.
Sheahan, J. W., *Life of Stephen A. Douglas* (New York, 1860).
Sutherland, James, *Biographical Sketches of the Members of the Forty-first General Assembly* (Indianapolis, 1861).
Vallandigham, James L., *Life of Clement L. Vallandigham* (Baltimore, 1872).
White, Horace, *The Life of Lyman Trumbull* (Boston, 1913).

VIII. Monographs, Works on Special Subjects, etc.

A large number of scholarly monographs have been written which bear directly or indirectly on the history of the older Middle West. The author has drawn repeatedly from one or another of the following:

GENERAL

Barnes, Gilbert Hobbs, *The Antislavery Impulse* (New York, D. Appleton-Century Company, 1933).
Benton, Elbert J., *The Movement for Peace without a Victory During the Civil War.* Western Reserve Historical Society, *Collections,* Publication No. 99, pp. 1–72.
Brownson, H. G., *History of the Illinois Central to 1870.* University of Illinois *Studies in the Social Sciences,* IV, 1915, Nos. 3, 4.
Buck, Solon Justus, *The Granger Movement, 1870–1880* (Harvard University Press, 1913).
Callahan, J. M., "The Northern Lake Frontier during the Civil War." *Report American Historical Association,* 1896, I, 335–359.
Callender, G. S., "Early Transportation and Banking Enterprises with Relation to the Growth of Corporations." *Quarterly Journal of Economics,* XVII, p. 111 (Nov., 1902).
Catterall, R. S., "The National Railroad Convention in St. Louis, 1849." *Missouri Historical Review,* Vol. XII, No. 4 (July, 1918).
Clark, O. B., *The Politics of Iowa during the Civil War.*
Cole, Arthur Charles, "The Constitutional Debates of 1847." *Collections of Illinois State Historical Library,* Vol. XIV (Springfield, 1919).
Coulter, E. Merton, "Effects of Secession Upon the Commerce of the Mississippi Valley." *Mississippi Valley Historical Review,* Vol. III, pp. 275–300 (1916–1917).
Davis, W. W., "Ante-Bellum Southern Commercial Conventions." *Transactions Alabama Historical Society,* 1904, Vol. V, pp. 153 *et seq.*
Dickerson, O. M., "The Illinois Constitutional Convention of 1862." *University of Illinois Studies,* Vol. I, No. 9.
Dodd, W. E., "The West and the Mexican War," *Journal Illinois State Historical Society,* V, No. 2, p. 159.
"The Fight for the Northwest, 1860," *American Historical Review,* XVI, 774 (July, 1911).

Robert J. Walker, Imperialist (booklet) Chicago Literary Club.

Fesler, Mayo, "Secret Political Societies in the North during the Civil War." *Indiana Magazine of History,* Vol. XIV, No. 3 (Sept., 1918), pp. 183–286.

Fish, Carl Russell, "The Decision of the Ohio Valley." *Report American Historical Association,* 1910, p. 153.

Fite, Emerson D., *The Presidential Campaign of 1860* (New York, 1911). *Social and Industrial Conditions in the North during the Civil War* (New York, 1910).

Fox, Dixon Ryan, (ed.) *Sources of Culture in the Middle West* (New York, D. Appleton-Century Company, 1934).

Gephart, W. F., *Transportation and Industrial Development of the Middle West,* Columbia University *Studies,* Vol. 34, pp. 1–273 (1909).

Greene, E. B., *Some Aspects of Politics in the Middle West, 1860–1872,* (Madison, 1912).

Hodder, F. H., "The Genesis of the Kansas Nebraska Act," *Wisconsin Historical Society Proceedings,* 1912.
"Some Aspects of the English Bill for the Admission of Kansas," *Report Am. Hist. Ass'n,* 1906, I, 201.
"Some Phases of the Dred Scott Case," *The Mississippi Valley Historical Review,* Vol. XVI, pp. 3–22 (June 1929).

Hubbart, H. C., " 'Pro-Southern' Influences in the Free West, 1840–1865." *Miss. Valley Hist. Rev.,* Vol. XX (June, 1933), 45–62.
"Revisionist Interpretations of Stephen A. Douglas and Popular Sovereignty." *The Social Studies,* Vol. XXV (March, 1934), 103–107.

Kirkland, E. C., *The Peacemakers of 1864* (New York, The Macmillan Company, 1927).

Kline, A. M., "The Attitude of Congress toward the Pacific Railway, 1856–1862." *Report American Historical Association,* 1910, p. 191.

Libby, O. G., "A Study of the Greenback Movement, 1876–1884." *Transactions of the Wisconsin Academy of Sciences, Arts, and Letters,* Vol. XII, Part II, 1899, p. 530.

Lowrey, L. T., *Northern Opinion of Approaching Secession* (Columbia University, 1917).

Lynch, William O., "Anti-Slavery Tendencies of the Democratic Party in the Northwest, 1848–50." *Mississippi Valley Historical Review,* XI, 319–331 (December, 1924).

Lyons, John F., "The Attitude of the Presbyterians in Ohio, Indiana and Illinois toward Slavery, 1825–1861." *Journal of Presbyterian Historical Society,* Vol. XI, p. 69 (1921–1923).

Macy, Jesse, *Institutional Beginnings in a Western State. Johns Hopkins University Studies in Historical and Political Science,* Second Series, VII.

Matthews, Albert, "The Origin of Butternut and Copperhead." *Colonial Society, Massachusetts, Publications* XX, 205–237.

Murphy, J. L., "Alabama and the Charleston Convention of 1860." *Transactions Alabama Historical Society,* V, 239 *et seq.* (1904).

Persinger, C. E., "The Bargain of 1844 as the Origin of the Wilmot

Proviso." *Report of the American Historical Association,* 1911, Vol. I, p. 189.

Randall, J. G., *Constitutional Problems under Lincoln* (New York, 1926).

Ray, Ormond P., *The Repeal of the Missouri Compromise.*

Russel, Robert R., "Economic Aspects of Southern Sectionalism, 1840–1861," University of Illinois, *Studies in the Social Sciences,* Vol. XI, Nos. I and II.

Sanborn, J. B., "Some Political Aspects of Homestead Legislation," *American Historical Review,* VI, 19 (October, 1900).

Scrugham, Mary, "The Peaceable Americans of 1860–1861," *Columbia University Studies in History, Economics and Public Law,* Vol. XCVI, No. 3, Whole No. 219 (1921).

Shannon, F. A., *The Organization and Administration of the Union Army,* 2 Vols. (1928).

Siebert, W. H., *The Underground Railroad from Slavery to Freedom* (The Macmillan Company, 1898).
"Light on the Underground Railway," *American Historical Review,* I, 455–463 (1895–1896).

Smith, Paul S., "First Use of the Term 'Copperhead,' " *American Historical Review,* XXXII, 799–800 (1926–1927).

Smith, Theodore Clark, *The Liberty and Free Soil Parties in the Northwest.* Harvard Historical Studies, VI (New York, 1897).

Sweet, W. W., "The Methodist Episcopal Church and Reconstruction," *Journal Illinois State Historical Society,* Vol. VII, No. 3, p. 147.

Turner, Frederick J., "The Place of the Ohio Valley in American History," *Ohio Archeological and Historical Society Publications,* XX, 32–47.
The Significance of Sections in American History (New York, Henry Holt and Company, 1932).
The United States 1830–1850, The Nation and Its Sections (New York, Henry Holt and Company, 1935).

Weeden, W. B., *War Government Federal and State* (1906).

Webster, H. J., *History of Democratic Party Organization in the Northwest (1824–1840)* (Columbus, 1915).

ILLINOIS

Boggess, Arthur Clinton, *The Settlement of Illinois, 1778–1830* (Chicago, 1908).

Cole, Arthur C., "President Lincoln and the Illinois Radical Republicans, 1858–1861," *Mississippi Valley Historical Review,* Vol. IV, pp. 417–436 (1917–1918).

Dickerson, O. M., "The Illinois Constitutional Convention of 1862," *University of Illinois Studies,* Vol. I, No. 9.

Greene, E. B., "Sectional Forces in the History of Illinois," *Publication No. 8, of the Historical Library, Illinois* (1903), pp. 75–83.
The Government of Illinois (New York, 1904).

Hand, John P., *Negro Slavery in Illinois. Transactions of the Illinois State Historical Society* (1910).

Harris, N. D., *Negro Servitude in Illinois.*
Martin, A. S., *Illinois and the Civil War* (University of Illinois, Master's Thesis).
Newell, Mason N., *Township Government in Illinois. Publication No. 9, of the Historical Library, Illinois 1904,* p. 467.
Paine, A. E., "The Granger Movement in Illinois." *Illinois University Studies,* Vol. I, No. 8, p. 335 (Sept., 1904).
Pooley, William Vipond, *The Settlement of Illinois from 1830–1850* (Madison, 1908).
Putnam, James William, *The Illinois and Michigan Canal.* Chicago Historical Society *Collections,* Vol. X.
Shaw, Albert, *Local Government in Illinois.* Johns Hopkins University *Studies in Historical and Political Science,* First Series, Vol. I, No. 3.
Thompson, Charles Manfred, *The Illinois Whigs before 1846.* University of Illinois *Studies in the Social Sciences,* Vol. IV, No. I.
"A Study of the Administration of Gov. Thomas Ford," *Collections of Illinois State Historical Library,* Vol. VII, pp. lvi, lvii, lix.

INDIANA

Esarey, Logan, *Internal Improvements in Early Indiana.* Indiana Historical Society *Publications,* Vol. V, No. 2.
Henry, W. E., *Some Elements of Indiana's Population.* Indiana Historical Society *Publications,* Vol. IV, No. 6.
Kettleborough, Charles, *Constitution Making in Indiana,* 2 Vols. (Indianapolis Historical Commission, 1916).
Woodburn, J. A., *Indiana Politics during the Civil War.* Indiana Historical Society *Publications,* Vol. V.

IOWA

Clark, O. B., *The Politics of Iowa during the Civil War and Reconstruction Period* (Iowa City, 1911).
Herriott, F. J., *The Transfusion of Political Ideas and Institutions in Iowa, Annals of Iowa,* 3 Series, VI. 46.
Whence Came the Pioneers of Iowa. Annals of Iowa, 3 Series, VII.
Lathrop, H. W., *The Tally War. Iowa Historical Record,* Vols. VII, IX.

OHIO

Campbell, James Edwin, *Ohio Democracy in the Civil War.*
Clonts, F. W., *The Political Campaign of 1875 in Ohio* (Ohio State University Master's Thesis, 1921).
MacFarland, R. W., *The Morgan Raid in Ohio.* Ohio Archeological and Historical Society. *Pub.* Vol. XVIII, p. 243.
McGrane, R. C., "Ohio and the Greenback Movement," *Mississippi Valley Historical Review,* Vol. XI, 526–542 (March, 1925).
Porter, G. H., *Ohio Politics During the Civil War Period,* Columbia Uni-

versity *Studies in History, Economics and Public Law*, Vol. XL, No. 2 (New York, 1911).

Quillen, F. U., *The Color Line in Ohio* (Ann Arbor, 1913).

Shilling, David Carl, *Relations of Southern Ohio to the South during the Decade preceding the Civil War, Quarterly Publication of Historical and Philosophical Society, Ohio* (Cincinnati, 1913).

Wilgus, J. A., "The Evolution of Township Government in Ohio," *Annual Report, American Historical Association*, 1894, pp. 403–412.

Yager, Elizabeth F., *The Campaign of 1864 in Ohio* (Ohio State University Master's Thesis, 1925).

WISCONSIN

Paxson, Frederick, L., "A Constitution of Democracy, Wisconsin, 1847," *Mississippi Valley Historical Review*, II, 3–24 (June, 1915).

IX. General Works, State Histories, etc.

County histories, too numerous to mention, afford another class of material. Of state histories and the numerous works of a general nature the following may be especially noted:

Davidson, Alexander, and Stuve, Bernard, *A Complete History of Illinois from 1693 to 1873* (Springfield, 1867).

Bogart, E. L. and Thompson, C. M., *The Industrial State, 1870–1893, Centennial History of Illinois*, Vol. IV (Chicago, 1922). A work of the better type.

Cole, Arthur Charles, *The Era of the Civil War, 1848–1870, Centennial History of Illinois*, Vol. III (Chicago, 1922). An unusually good state history.

Dillon, J. B., *History of Indiana.*

Donaldson, Thomas, *The Public Domain* (Government Printing Office, 1884).

Dunn, J. P., *Indiana, A Redemption from Slavery*, American Commonwealth Series (Boston, 1900).

Eddy, T. M., *The Patriotism of Illinois*. 2 vols. (Chicago, 1865).

Esarey, Logan, *A History of Indiana*, 2 vols. (Indianapolis, 1918).

Ford, H. A. and Ford, K. B. (editors), *A History of Cincinnati, Ohio* (Cleveland, 1881).

Ford, Gov. Thos., *History of Illinois* (1849).

Galbreath, C. B., *History of Ohio*, 5 vols. (1925).

Haley, J. J., *Debates That have made History* (St. Louis, 1920).

Hinsdale, B. A., *The Old Northwest* (New York, 1888).

Howe, Henry, *Historical Collections of Ohio* (Cincinnati, 1847).

Johnson, Emory (and collaborators), *History of the Domestic and Foreign Commerce of the United States*, 2 vols. (Carnegie Institution, 1915).

Pease, Theodore Calvin, *The Frontier State 1818–1848, Centennial History of Illinois*, Vol. II (Springfield, 1918).

Pike, J. O., *First Blows of the Civil War.*
Powell, T. E., *Democratic Party of Ohio.*
Randall, E. O. and Ryan, D. J., *History of Ohio,* 5 vols.
Rerick, R. H., *History of Ohio* (Madison, 1902).
Ross, Earle Dudley, *The Liberal Republican Movement* (New York, 1919).
Smith, Edward Conrad, *The Borderland in the Civil War* (The Macmillan Company, 1927).
Weeden, William Babcock, *War Government, Federal and State* (Boston, 1906).

X. SOCIAL LIFE, TRAVEL, DESCRIPTION, ETC.

Barnard, Henry (Editor), "Common Schools and Public Instruction," *The American Journal of Education,* Vol. XXIV pp. 225–336 (1873).
Barnhardt, J. D., "Rise of the Methodist Episcopal Church in Illinois," *Journal Illinois State Historical Society,* Vol. XII, No. 2.
Batchelder, James L., *The United States, the West and Ohio as Missionary Fields.*
Belting, Paul E., "The Development of the Free Public High School in Illinois before 1860," *Journal Illinois State Historical Society,* Vol. XI, Nos. 3, 4.
Bennett, Milo, "The Building of a State," *Journal Illinois State Historical Society,* Vol. XIII, No. 3, pp. 324–354.
Cist, Charles, *Sketches and Statistics of Cincinnati, 1851.*
Cubberley, E. P., *Public Education in the United States* (Houghton Mifflin Company, 1919).
Ditzler, J., *Philosophy of the History of the Church* (St. Louis, 1866). Contains an account of the "Christian Union Church," 1862–1864.
Erwin, Milo, *The Bloody Vendetta, embracing the early history of Williamson County, Illinois* (Marion, Illinois, 1876). Republished (1914) by the Herrin *News,* Herrin, Illinois.
Doctrines and Discipline of the Methodist Episcopal Church, 1844.
Fite, Emerson David, *Social and Industrial Conditions in the North during the Civil War* (The Macmillan Company, 1910).
Hall, James, *Statistics of the West* (Cincinnati, 1837).
Sketches of the History, Life and Manners of the West, 2 vols., (Philadelphia, 1855).
Romance of Western History (Cincinnati, 1857).
The West, Its Soil, Surface and Productions (Cincinnati, 1848).
The West, Its Commerce and Navigation (Cincinnati, 1848).
Johnson, Charles B., *Illinois in the Fifties* (Champaign, Illinois, 1918).
Journal of the General Conference of the Methodist Episcopal Church, 1860.
King, I. F., *The Introduction of Methodism in Ohio.*
Kofoid, Carrie Prudence, "Puritan Influences in the Formative Years of Illinois History," *Pub. No. 10 of the Illinois State Historical Library,* 1905, pp. 261–347.

Latta, S. A. *The Cholera in Cincinnati, 1850.*
Lloyd, James T., *Lloyd's Steamboat Directory and Disasters on the Western Waters* (Cincinnati, 1856).
Maclean, J. P., "Rise, Progress and Extinction of the Society of Shakers at Cleveland," *Ohio Archeological and Historical Society Publications,* Vol. IX, pp. 32–124.
"The Shaker Community of Warren County," *Ohio Archeological and Historical Society Publications,* Vol. X, pp. 251–304.
Miller, E. A., *History of Educational Legislation in Ohio, 1803–1850.*
Nicholson, Meredith, *The Hoosiers* (The Macmillan Company, 1900).
Owen, R. and Campbell, Alexander, *Debate on the Evidences of Christianity* (London, 1839).
Randall, E. O., "The Separatist Society of Zoar," *Ohio Archeological and Historical Society Publications,* Vol. VIII, pp. 1–105.
The Roman Catholic Church and Free Thought (Cincinnati, 1868).
Shaw, Rev. James, *Twelve Years in America* (London, 1867). One of the best descriptions of social and religious conditions in Illinois before and during the Civil War.
Smith, O. H., *Early Indiana Trials and Sketches.*
Smith, W. H., "Old Time Campaigns." *Journal Illinois State Historical Society,* Vol. XIII, 23–32.
Stock, H. T., "Protestantism in Illinois before 1835," *Journal Illinois State Historical Society,* Vol. XII, pp. 1–31, April, 1919.
Sweet, W. W., *The Methodist Church and the Civil War.*
Thrapp, R. F., "Early Religious Beginnings in Illinois," *Journal Illinois State Historical Society,* Vol. IV.
Trollope, Mrs. T. A., *Domestic Manners of the Americans* (New York, 1904).
Vallandigham Song Book (Columbus, 1863).

XI. LITERATURE AND NOVELS, CRITICISM, ETC.

Anderson, Sherwood, *Poor White* (The Viking Press, 1920).
Atkeson, May Meek, "Study of the Local Literature of the Upper Ohio Valley (1820–1840)," *Ohio State University Bulletin,* Vol. XXV, No. 3.
Cather, Willa, *My Antonia* (The Houghton Mifflin Company, 1926).
O Pioneers! (The Houghton Mifflin Company, 1913).
Chandler, Josephine Craven, *The Spoon River Country* (Reprinted from *Journal Illinois State Historical Society,* Vol. XIV, Nos. 3, 4).
Clemens, S. L. (Mark Twain), *Adventures of Huckleberry Finn,* 1884; *Adventures of Tom Sawyer,* 1876; *The Gilded Age,* 1873; *Life on the Mississippi,* 1883.
Coggeshall, W. R., *The Poets and Poetry of the West* (Columbus, 1860).
Dondore, Dorothy, "Points of Contact Between History and Literature in the Mississippi Valley," *Mississippi Valley Historical Review,* Vol. XI, pp. 227–236 (1924–1925).

The Prairie and the Making of Middle America (1926).

Eggleston, Edward, *The Hoosier School-Master* (Orange Judd Publishing Company, 1892).

The Graysons (The Century Company, 1904).

Esarey, Logan, "The Literary Spirit Among the Early Ohio Valley Settlers," *Mississippi Valley Historical Review,* Vol. V, pp. 143–157 (September, 1918).

Gallagher, William Davis, *Selections from the Poetical Literature of the West* (Cincinnati, 1841).

Gale, Zona, *Friendship Village* (The Macmillan Company, 1908).

Garland, Hamlin, *Main-travelled Roads* (Harper and Brothers, 1891).

Rose of Dutcher's Coolly (Harper and Brothers, 1899).

Son of the Middle Border (The Macmillan Company, 1917).

Hay, John, *Pike County Ballads* (Osgood and Company, 1871).

Howe, Edgar Watson, *The Story of a Country Town* (Harper and Brothers, 1917).

Howells, William Cooper, *Recollections of Life in Ohio* (Cincinnati, 1895).

Masters, Edgar Lee, *Spoon River Anthology* (1915).

Skeeters Kirby (The Macmillan Company, 1923).

Mitch Miller (The Macmillan Company, 1920).

Children of the Market Place (New York, 1922).

Mumford, Lewis, *The Golden Day* (Boni and Liveright, 1926).

Quick, Herbert, *The Hawkeye* (The Bobbs-Merrill Company, 1923).

Vandemark's Folly (The Bobbs-Merrill Company, 1922).

Quick, Herbert and Edward, *Mississippi Steamboatin'* (Henry Holt and Company, 1926).

Rolvaag, Ole Edvart, (Paal Morck), *Giants in the Earth* (Harper and Brothers, 1927).

Peder Victorious (Harper and Brothers, 1928).

Rusk, R. Leslie, *The Literature of the Middle Western Frontier,* 2 vols. (Columbia University Press, 1925).

Saxon, Lyle, *Father Mississippi* (The Century Company, 1927).

Suckow, Ruth, *Country People* (Alfred A. Knopf, 1924).

Iowa Interiors (Alfred A. Knopf, 1926).

Van Doren, Carl. *Contemporary American Novelists,* 1900–1920 (The Macmillan Company, 1922).

Venable, Emerson, *Poets of Ohio* (Cincinnati, 1912).

Venable, W. H., *Beginnings of Literary Culture in the Ohio Valley.*

Welder, Martin, *Farm Life in Central Ohio Sixty Years Ago.*

Wescott, Glenway, *The Grandmothers; a Family Portrait* (Harper and Brothers, 1927).

White, William Allen, *A Certain Rich Man* (The Macmillan Company, 1909).

INDEX

"Abolition prisons," 206, 213
Abolitionism, 49, 63, 108, 120, 151, 170, 195
Academies, 69
Adventists, 63
Age of Reason, 67
Agrarian discontent, 241, 242; *see* Granger movement
"Alabama platform," 134
Albion, Illinois, 6
Allen, William, 13, 15, 16, 17, 18; and revival of the Democratic party, 242, 254, 255, 256, 257
Alton, Illinois, 4, 39, 40
"American Knights, Order of," 226, 227, 230; *see* "Sons of Liberty"
American party, 106, 111, 112, 139
Amusements, popular, 35, 60, 62, 263
Antioch College, 68, 70, 71
"Appeal of Independent Democrats," 99, 100
Appleseed, Johnny, 42
Architectural standards, 262, 263
Armistice with South, proposed, 206, 207, 231
Arrests, arbitrary, 184, 185, 191, 204-206, 208, 209, 229, 234
Art, 60, 61
Athens, Ohio, 69
Atlanta campaign, 238

Banks and banking, 11, 15, 31; bad conditions, 110; opposition to eastern bankers, 230; in *Spoon River Anthology,* 270
"Banner district," 105, 147
Baptists, 44; "peace Baptists," 215
Beecher family, 54, 56; Henry Ward, 264; Lyman, 60
Bell, John, 138, 144, 183
Belleville, Illinois, 6, 172, 173
Beloit College, 70, 273
Beveridge, Albert J., 33, 102
Birney, James, 39
"Black Codes," 44, 48; see Negro, Ohio, Indiana, Illinois

Blair, F. P., 114, 230
Bland-Allison Act, 260
Bonds, government, 223, 249; attacks on bondholders, 230, 246, 247, 259
Border state "reconstruction" (1860-1861), 161-165
Bounties and bounty jumpers, 198, 199, 215; *see* Draft, Deserters
Boy's Town, A, 45
Breckinridge, J. C., 138, 144, 183
Bright, Jesse D., 15, 107, 146; opposes Douglas, 119; letter to Jefferson Davis, 164, 176; expelled from United States Senate, 179
Brinkerhoff, Jacob, 20, 24, 26, 27, 249
Brough, John, 212-216; *see* Vallandigham
Brown, B. Gratz, 249
Bryan, William Jennings, 11, 275
Buchanan, James, 111, 112; charges against (1856), 112, 113; election of, 114; and Lecompton constitution, 117, 118; "partyism," 139; indecision, 168, 169
Burnet, Jacob, 54
Burnside, General Ambrose E., 204
Bushwhacking, 41, 220, 229
"Butternut masses," 214; *see* "Copperheads"

Calhoun, John C., 18, 19; speech on the unifying influence of the western rivers, 85
Camp meetings, 263
Campbell, Alexander, 64, 65; "Campbellites," 44, 65
Canada, as a center of conspiracy, 228
Canals, 14; construction of, 22; Wabash and Erie, 23, 96; Illinois-Michigan, 23; Erie, 96; eastern trade by, 74, 96
Capitalism, 241-243
Carpet-bag rule, 248
Cartwright, Peter, 42

293

Cary, Alice, 57, 60

Cary, Phoebe, 57

Cass, Lewis, 15, 16; and popular sovereignty, 89; loses senatorial seat, 115

Cather, Willa, 267

Catholicism, 60, 65, 66, 253, 256; Catholic Total Abstinence Union, 265

"Central Republic," 162

Chandler, Zachariah, 108, 115; and the "rugged issue," 172

Charity, 222, 262

Charleston convention (1860), 132-138

Chase, Salmon P., 48, 99, 100, 245; governor, 109; approves "real popular sovereignty," 143; and Lincoln, 235

Chicago, 5, 17, 20-23, 50; Germans in, 63; trade connection with New Orleans, 87; increase in population, 91, 219; and grain trade, 96; and tariff, 97; eastern influences in, 97; Republicans strong in, 108, 239; Republican national convention (1860), 138-141; "pork packers desire southern trade," 153; "submissionists" in, 154; Tribune for peaceable secession, 171; and use of force to save the Union, 172; suppression of Times, 203; war prosperity in, 219

Chickamauga, Battle of, 222

Chillicothe, Ohio, 4, 52

Cholera, the, 36

Churches, protestant, extreme loyalty of, 216, 246, 263; the Church college, 272, 273; liberalism and indifference, 273; Christian Union church, 215; see Religion, Methodists

Cincinnati, 6, 14, 36; culture center, 53, 55, 59, 61; the Mirror, 54; printing and publishing center, 55; newspapers, 55; school of writers, 56, 57; Germans in, 63; trade with the South, 78, 79, 81, 180, 249; as the "South Carolina of the North," 105; greatest city in the West, 78; "platform," 134; The Commercial, 142, 152, 227; The Enquirer, 149, 156, 173, 203, 213, 248; relations with South, 156, 180, 219, 220; economic distress in (1861), 180; war prosperity, 220; votes for Lincoln, 239

Circus, the travelling, 263

Clary's Grove boys, 39

Clay, Henry, 13, 90

Cleveland, Ohio, 23, 91

Clevenger, Shobal V., 60

Coercion, use of, to save the Union, 166-177; peaceable, 167; opposed by local Democratic conventions, 167; resolution against, 169; upper West favors, 171-173; after firing on Ft. Sumter, 173, 174; sentiment sweeps West, 173, 174

Colfax, Schuyler, 110, 127, 232, 245

Colleges, 69, 70, 272; curriculum, 70, 71, 273; classicism, 70, 71; religious atmosphere, 71; expenses, 71; sectarian control, 273

Confederacy, 157, 160; seeks to establish connection with "Sons of Liberty," 227; guarantees free navigation of Mississippi, 227; appoints agents to conspire in West, 228

Communities, social, 62

Compromise, of 1850, 88; demands for, 146-154; Crittenden, 147, 149, 153; border state (1860-1861), 148, 149, 151

Congregational church, 97, 216

Congressional election (1862), 188-193; issues and outcome, 188-190; map, 189; called a revolution, 191; Lincoln repudiated, 190

Conscription, see Draft

"Conspiracies," anti-draft, etc., 195, 200, 223-230; leaders, 224; "Knights of the Golden Circle," 176, 177, 194, 195, 215, 224 ff.; Indianapolis riot, 225; "Order of American Knights," 226; to unite West and South, 227-229; in Chicago, 228, 229; final estimate of, 230

Constitution (of the United States), 147, 162, 211, 212

Constitutional conventions, 12; in Ohio, 46; in Indiana, 46, 48; in Illinois, 50, 182

Constitutional Union party, 138

Convulsion, democracy in, 187, 194-217

Conway, Moncure C., 66, 68, 274 (note)

"Copperheads," 183, 194, 195, 200, 201; bands, 196; in Vallandigham campaign, 213, 214; attacks on Lincoln, 236; *see* Peace Democracy, Vallandigham, Western Peace Bolt

Corn, production of, 75, 80; price of, 33, 218; new corn belt, 234; burned as fuel, 33, 258

Corruption, governmental, 240-243, 248, 256, 264

Corydon, Indiana, 4

Cox, S. S., 223

Crime, 110, 264

Crimes of the Civil War, 205, 241, 242

Crisis, The, 149

Culture, middle western, 52-72; writers, 56, 57, 268-271, 274; the college, 273; sources and validity of, 275-277; *see* Liberalism

Cumberland Road, 24

Dakotas, the, 275

Darwinism, 67, 68, 273

Daviess, Jo, 44

Dayton, Ohio, 10

Dean, Henry Clay, 183; description of his arrest, 205, 206; in Vallandigham campaign, 213; his attack on eastern capital, debt, taxation, bondholders, tariff, 241, 242; his Greenbackism, 256

Death rate, 33

Debt, 31; fear of bankruptcy in Illinois and Indiana, 75; financial bondage of West to East, 76, 223; moratorium proposed, 180; national, 234, 241, 242; repudiation proposed, 242; mortgages, 268

Declaration of Independence, 47, 49, 111, 141

Democracy, Progressive Western, 3, 9, 11, 12, 14, 16, 18, 63, 107, 130, 243, 275

Democratic Monthly Magazine, 3, 11

Democratic party, 11, 13, 21; dominant party in the Middle West, 14; Germans and, 94; Douglas and, 104, 107, 173, 174; pro-southern faction in West, 107, 164, 183; platform (1856), 111; split over

Lecompton constitution, 122; defections from, 131, 188; local party convention described, 131, 132; Charleston convention (1860), 132-138; break with southern leaders, 137, 138; "McCormick-Times-Egypt" branch, 154; leaders in upper West vigorous pro-war men, 172, 173; in congressional elections of 1862, 188; Peace Democrats, 181 ff., 208 ff., national convention (1864), 230; eastern Democrats more pro-war, 230, 235; demoralization of, 242; attempts to revive, 242, 244-249, 250, 254; convention (1868), 247, 248; western Democrats thwarted by eastern, 248; fusion with Liberal Republicans, 250, 252; revival (1873-1874), 254, 255; *see* Progressive Western Democracy, Peace Democrats, War Democrats, Douglas.

Denison University, 70, 272

DePauw University, 70, 273

Deserters, 199, 200, 215, 226 (note), 238

Detroit, 23, 91, 115

Dial, The (Cincinnati), 55, 60, 68

Disease, 36

Dodd, H. H., 227-229

Dodge, A. C., 4, 15

Doubtful counties of Illinois, Indiana, Ohio, 104, 105, 112, 136, 138; in Lincoln-Douglas contest, 128; map, 135; in election of 1860, 140, 142; in Indiana, 142 (note)

Douglas, Stephen A., 13, 15, 16; on Oregon, 16, 18; and popular sovereignty, 28, 89, 118, 123; break with South, 29; as representative of West, 35; author of Kansas-Nebraska Act, 99-101; motives, personal ambition, 100, 116-118; newspaper support of, 107, 109; pro-southern faction in West opposes, 107; western insurgent, 116-129; the problem of interpretation, 116, 117; break with Buchanan, 118; votes with Republicans, 119, 120; opposes Lecompton constitution, 121; Dred Scott Decision, 123; views not greatly different from Lincoln's, 124, 127, 142; the great debate, 125-129; Charleston convention, 132, 133; and Republican convention, 140, 141; health declining, 142; for compromise and against war, 147, 166; favors use of force after Sumter, 172, 173; unfortunate death, 175; Douglas War Democrats, a minority, 178

Dow, Lorenzo, 42

Draft, 184, 197; opposition to and violence against, 195, 196, 231; Act of 1863, 198; exemptions from, 198; bounties and bounty jumping, 198; Peace Democrats and, 231, 234, 238; see Deserters, Arbitrary arrests

Drake, Daniel, 36, 53; patron of culture, 56

Drama, see Stage

Dred Scott Decision, 123

Dress, 35, 36; the "silk and lace period," 222

Drunkenness, 37, 222, 264, 265, 266

Dubuque, 5, 22; trade with East, 86

Earlham College, 70

Eastern influences, 52; see Upper West, Lake region, etc.

Economic conditions, see Banking, Capitalism, Debt, Extravagance, Panic, Prosperity, Railroads, Trade

Education, see Schools, Colleges, Universities

Edwards, Ninian, 4

Edwardsville, Illinois, 6

Eggleston, Edward, 267

"Egypt," 14, 37; attitude on Negro, 50; favors Kansas-Nebraska Bill, 100; opposes coercion, 169; danger of civil war in, 176; economic distress in (1861-1862), 181; response to call for volunteers, 200; deserters in, 200; in election of 1864, 236

Election, of 1856, 111-114, 130; of 1860, 141-145; congressional, of 1862, 181-193, 189 (map); of 1864, 234, 239; of 1868, 245-248; of 1872, 249-252; see Politics, "Partyism"

Emancipation Proclamation, 48, 51, 181, 183, 208, 249

Emerson, Ralph Waldo, 68

English, William H., 120-122; English Bill, 121, 122

Enquirer, The (Cincinnati), "pro-southern," 149; and southern trade, 156; supports war, 173; prohibition of circulation of, 203; supports Vallandigham, 213; criticizes Tammany and the East, 248

Epic Age of the West, 34, 58

Erie Canal, 5, 74, 76; see Canals

European influences, 52, 53; see Upper West, Germans

Expansion, territorial, 12, 16, 17, 19

Extravagance, 103, 110, 222, 223, 240-243, 261, 262

Farmer, western, struggle and overstrain, 31, 33, 268; prosperity, 220; interest in railroad rates, 253, 257, 258; Greenback interests, 257; his children, 268, 269; the "retired," 269

Feud and disorder, 39, 40, 194, 200

"Fifty-four forty or fight," 17

Fillmore, Millard, 111, 112, 139

Finley, J. B., 113

Fitch, Graham N., 146

Flint, Timothy, 54, 57

Foote, J. P., 53

Ford, Governor Thomas, 41

Free silver, 13, 260

Free Soil party, 14, 19, 21, 46, 48, 63, 96

Fremont, John C., 111-113, 139

Frontier, struggle, 31, 33, 276; tasks of civilization building, 31, 52, 271, 277; romance and tragedy of, 8, 268, 269; cultural degradation, 276

Frustration, middle western sense of, 252, 267, 269

Fugitive Slave Law, 40, 88

Fuller, Melville W., 182, 208

Galena, Illinois, 76, 94

Gallagher, W. D., 54, 57

Gallipolis, Ohio, 6

Garfield, James A., 232, 239

Garland, Hamlin, 267

Gazette, The (Cincinnati), 159

Genius of the West, The, 52

Geology, 67

Germans, 6, 22, 63; agnosticism, 64, 68;

immigration of, 92, 268; idealism, 94; and Democratic party, 94, 106, 107; and free soil, 97; dislike of anti-foreign tendency of Whigs and Republicans, 94, 106, 107; in Republican party, 131; belief in use of force, 172, 173; opposition to Lincoln, 235; and Liberal Republican movement, 251, 252

"Gerrymandering," 107, 108, 114, 168, 182

Gettysburg, Battle of, 216

Giddings, Joshua, 141; and the "rugged issue," 172

"Gilded Age," 222, 261-277, 269

Granger movement, 254, 255, 258; laws, 258; see Farmer, Greenbacks

Grant, U. S., 221, 235, 240, 245, 246, 253

"Grantism," 249-253, 256, 264

Greeley, Horace, 113, 230; and Douglas, 128, 250; nominated by Liberal Republicans, 250-253

Greenbacks, 13, 220, 223, 244, 246, 247, 255-259

Grinnell College, 70, 273

Guerilla bands, 196, 201, 202

Habaes Corpus Writ, 178, 208

Hall, James, 10, 13, 53, 57

Halstead, Murat, 137; "squatter sovereignty" man, 139; and the Liberal Republicans, 251; critic of "partyism," 254; see Charleston convention (Democratic party), Chicago convention (Republican party)

Hampton Roads Conference, 230

Hanks, Nancy, 42

Hannegan, Edward A., 15, 16, 18

Hard Times, see Panic

Harrison, William Henry, 4

Hay, John, 59

Hayes, Rutherford B., 239, 244, 256, 257

Heathenism, 42, 43

Heffron, Horace, 151, 168-170

Hendricks, Thomas A., 13, 182, 186, 200, 222; and revival of Democratic party, 242; as candidate (1868), 246, 247; elected governor of Indiana, 252, 253; and the Democratic revival, 254

Herald (Dubuque), 152

"Higher law," 142, 143

Hillsboro, Ohio, 265

Homesteads, 133

Hoosier School-Master, The, 37

Howells, William Dean, 45, 57, 68

Huckleberry Finn, 83

Illinois, Negro suffrage in, 46, 182; "Black Code" in, 48, 50, 51, 182; production of corn, 75; trade with South, 76, 80, 180; doubtful central counties, 104, 105, 112; election of Buchanan, 114; apportionment of districts, 125; Lincoln-Douglas debates, 125-127; doubtful in election of 1860, 141, 142; sympathy with South, 151, 176; Republicans moderate and compromising, 153; many Democrats influenced by Douglas to support war, 173; economic distress, 180; constitutional convention of 1862, 182; "gerrymandered," 182; congressional election of 1862 in, 188, 190; opposition to draft in, 195, 196; Granger laws, 258; crime and governmental corruption in, 264; "Spoon River," 266, 270

Illinois Central Railroad, 120, 156, 221

Illinois College, 70

Illinois Monthly Magazine, 54

Illinois River, 5; trade of, 80, 82

Illiteracy, 37-39; in Indiana, 38; in Illinois, 38

Immigration, see Lower West, Upper West, Germans, Irish

Immorality, social, 36, 42, 264

Imperialism, democratic, 12, 17

Indiana, Negro suffrage in, 46; civil rights of Negro in, 48; low prices in, 75; trade with South, 76, 79, 180; Republicans in Quaker and "Yankee" counties, 108; prevention of quorum in legislature, 110, 207; prohibition law, 110; doubtful central counties, 104, 105, 112; and election of Buchanan, 114; "bogus" Senators, 114; doubtful in election of 1860, 141, 142; southern part "pro-southern," 150, 157; economic distress in (1861-1862), 180; congressional election of 1862 in, 188, 189, 190; opposition to draft in, 195, 196 ff.; Morgan's raid in, 201, 202; legislative opposition to war, 206, 207; "disloyal" legislature, 207; war prosperity, 220; Legion, 236; war weariness in, 237; politicians "tricky," 246; school of writers, 267

Indianapolis, 79, 81, 200, 220

Indians, 4

Individualism, 275, 276; as a disintegrating tendency in modern history, 276

"Infidelism," 64, 67, 131, 273

Inflation, 220, 223, 257-259; see Greenbacks

Ingersoll, Robert G., 64, 273

Insanity, Civil War and, 187

Intemperance, 35, 36, 222, 264-266; see Prohibition, "Maine Law"

Iowa, 5, 15, 16, 22, 108; opposition to Negro suffrage in, 46, 47; trade with South, 76, 80; compromise with South urged, 151; congressional election of 1862 in, 189, 190; "Tally War," 196; and reëlection of Lincoln, 238

Irish, 22, 40, 115; in Chicago and the lake cities, 92; and Democratic party, 94; in the election of 1860, 142; support Vallandigham, 215

"Irrepressible conflict," deprived of revolutionary meaning, 142-144

Jacksonian Democracy, 9, 11, 13, 40, 137; gives way to Douglas Democracy, 107; Peace Democrats attempt to revive, 182; persistence of, 275

Jefferson, Thomas, 11, 13, 137, 182, 275

Johnson, Andrew, 245

Jones, G. W., dispute with Douglas, 119; "dough face," 120; letter to Jefferson Davis, 164; arrest of, 181, 182

Journal (Indianapolis), 152

Julian, George W., 100, 249

Kansas, 98, 99, 121, 122, 127, 268, 272, 275

Kansas-Nebraska Bill, 98-101

Kaskaskia, Illinois, 4

Kees, J. W., 185

Kellogg, W. B., 108; and Republican-

Douglas entente, 128; proposes compromise on slavery, 153

Kentucky, 3, 4, 5, 31; "neutrality" of, 161

"Knights of the Golden Circle," 176, 177, 194, 195, 215; "puerility" of, 230

Know Nothing Party, see American Party

Knox College, 70, 273

Koerner, Gustav, 51, 172, 173, 250

Labor movements, 234, 244, 248, 249, 259, 274

Ladies' Repository, The, 55, 192

Laissez faire theory, 63, 107

Lake region, 5, 12, 13, 14, 20, 21, 26, 28; Chicago convention of 1847, 86; desire to set boundaries of slavery, 88; favorable to Wilmot Proviso, 88; against Fugitive Slave Law, 88; trade with East, 96; and homesteads, 96; reluctantly accepts Lincoln, 138-141; see Upper West

Lane, Henry S., 139-141

Lane Seminary, 72

Leaves of Grass, 68

Lecompton constitution, 117, 119, 121

Lexington, Kentucky, 69

Liberal Republicans, 249-253; leaders, 249, 250; demands, 251; Cincinnati convention, 251

Liberalism, 11-13, 62, 63, 66-68, 249-253, 271-274

Life on the Mississippi, 83

Lincoln, Abraham, 4, 33, 39, 58, 66; on slavery in the West, 90; in the election of 1856, 111; and the old line Whigs of central Illinois, 112, 125; slow to join the Republican Party, 124, 125; debate with Douglas, 125-129; attitude near to that of Douglas, 127, 142; reluctantly accepted by lakes and the East, 138-141; repudiated by the free West, 178-193; criticism of, as President, 183, 185, 213, 214, 235; his patience, 193, 210, 239; reëlected, 234-238; his contribution, 277

Liquor traffic, control of, 102, 264, 265, 266

Literary Gazette, 53
Literature, 53 ff., 267, 270, 277
Logan, John A., 50, 115, 147, 148; and South, 176; urges "Egypt" to be patriotic, 201, 236; demagogism, 236, 245, 253
"Logan's Black Law" (Illinois), 50
Long, Alexander, 230, 231, 232; "Peace Bolt," 232
Longworth, Nicholas, grape culture, 36, 79; patron of arts, 53, 61; lawyer, speculator, 78
Lovejoy, Elijah P., 39, 40
Lovejoy, Owen, 109
Lower West, 5, 6, 20, 21; population growth, 22; votes with South, 25, 26; social attitudes, 30-51, 182; on civil rights of Negro, 47; immigration into, 47, 182, 220; relations with South, 47, 73-87, 105, 154, 156, 180, 176, 177; polite society in, 52; opposition to Wilmot Proviso, personal liberty laws, temperance reform, 88, 97; favors Fugitive Slave Law, Kansas-Nebraska Act, 88, 101; votes for Douglas (1860), 144; compromise, anti-coercion attitude, 146, 161, 166, 168; many Democrats in, influenced by Douglas to support war, 173, 174; economic distress in (1861-1862), 180; opposes Emancipation Proclamation, 183, 184; in election of 1862, 190; passing as a major section, 234, 239; champions "reform," 243; disappointment at attitude of eastern Democrats, 247; spirit of, persists in prairie West, 275
Lyceums, 60, 72, 274

Madison, Indiana, 80
Mahony, Dennis, 152; leader in early peace movement, 175, 181; arrest of, 184; defeated for Congress, 190
Main Street, 8
"Maine Law," 102, 265
Mann, Horace, 68, 71
Marietta, Ohio, 6; College, 70
Mark Twain, 8, 37, 59, 66, 83, 267
Mass meetings, political, 9, 10; *see* Politics
"Massac War," 41

Massie, Nathaniel, 4
Masters, Edgar Lee, 8, 34, 267, 270
Materialism, 103; *see* Extravagance
McClellan, General G. B., 230, 231, 233
McClernand, John A., 15, 147; Land Graduation Bill, 92
McCormick, Cyrus, 87
Medary, Samuel, 12, 17, 113, 164; founds Columbus *Crisis,* 149; leader in early peace movement, 175; opposes Emancipation Proclamation, 184; calls election of 1862 a revolution, 190, 192; desires to unite with Union elements in South, 210; in Vallandigham campaign, 213; and Peace Bolt (1864), 233; death, 233
Medicine, 36
Medieval civilization, 276
Memphis trade convention (1845), 85
Methodist church, 44, 191, 216, 263; accused by "peace Methodists" of fomenting hate and cruelty, 215; criticism of Lincoln by, 235, 237; opposes Johnson, favors Grant, 246; the preacher of, 263, 264; revivals, 263; *see Western Christian Advocate*
Mexican War, 19
Miami University, 69, 70, 72
Michigan, 5, 21; opposition to Negro suffrage in, 46; personal liberty law, 89; population increase, 91; in election of 1860, 133, 140, 141; coercion spirit in, 108, 115, 172, 239; congressional election of 1862 in, 189, 190; and reëlection of Lincoln, 238
Middle West, 3; national political battle-ground, 6, 9, 103-115; economic developments in, 8; "sagas" of, 8; southern trading interest of, 8, 73-87, 154, 156, 180; immigration into, 8, 91, 92; money crazes in, 8; discontent, 8, 223, 234; cultural life, 8, 52-72; sectionalism in, 100, 103, 104, 190; challenge to the East and South, 131, 132; repudiates Lincoln, 188-193; thwarted, 209, 211; extravagance in, 219-223; East "fattening" on, 223; bondage to East, 234; waste of human life in, 237; votes with

East in 1864, 239; lake region the dominant part of, 274; a new Middle West, 274; sources and validity of culture of, 275-277; a "Bible belt," 276; see Lower West, Upper West
Militia Bill, in Illinois, 167, 168; in Indiana, 168; passed after Sumter, 174
Millerites, 63, 187
Milligan Case, 205, 229
Milwaukee, 22, 23, 91, 115
Minnesota, 115, 244
Mississippi River, trade, 73, 74, 79, 80, 82; steamboats on, 81, 82; the "epic" of, 82; unity of the valley of, 159, 164, 191, 209, 219; blockade of, 160, 218; need of recovery of, 219; opened, 221, 235
Missouri, 19, 22, 37, 123, 147, 249; Compromise, 123, 147; "movement," 249
Monopolies, 230, 233, 249; anti-monopoly parties, 254, 255, 257
Morality, state of, 36, 42, 222, 223, 240-242, 264, 269
Morgan's Raid, 201, 202
Mormons, 40, 41, 62
Morrill Tariff, 160
Morton, Oliver P., 120, 188, 200, 206, 228, 237, 238, 356; see Indiana
Music, 53, 60-62, 273
Muskingum River, 5

National Road, 4, 5, 167; "despotic majority" north of, 167-169
Naturalism, 64, 65
Nauvoo, Illinois, 40
Nebraska, 98, 99, 101, 102, 275
Negro, the, 11, 13, 28, 45; right to vote, 45-47, 244, 249; civil rights, 47-50; exclusion of, from Indiana, 49; "Logan's Black Law," 50; "inferiority of," 49, 151, 152; "equality," 51, 71; Republicans and, 152
New Albany, Indiana, 81; Ledger, 157
New Constitution, The, 11
"New Departure," 250
New England, 6; influences in West, 30, 52, 53, 97; "fattening" on West, 223
New Harmony, 62, 67, 70
New Orleans, Battle of, 44, 52, 74

"New Party" movement, 257
New Salem, Illinois, 33
New York, 6
Newspapers, 55, 56; leading, in West, 55; rage for local and party sheets, 55, 56
Northwest, old, 52
"Northwestern Confederacy," 162
"Northwestern Conspiracy," 162
Northwestern University, 273
Notre Dame University, 70, 273
Novel, the middle western, 8; local color, 267; "Indiana school," 267; descriptive realism, 267; "revolt from village," 267; monumental character, 268, 277
Nueces boundary, 18, 19

Oberlin College, 70, 72, 97, 272
Ohio, Negro suffrage in, 46; "Black Code," 48; trade with South, 78, 79; election of 1862 in, 188; opposition to draft in, 195; Morgan's raid in, 202; Vallandigham-Brough campaign, 208-217; election of 1864 in, 238; "Ohio idea," 246, 247; "New Party" movement in, 254; see Vallandigham, Western Reserve, Cincinnati
Ohio Wesleyan University, 70, 71, 273
Olds, Edson B., 184, 185, 192; in Vallandigham campaign, 213; and the "Peace Bolt" of 1864, 233
Ordinance of 1787, 45
Oregon question, 16-19, 20
Origin of Species, 68
Owen, David Dale, 67
Owen, Robert, 62, 64, 65
Owen, Robert Dale, 67, 150

Paganism, 35, 42, 64, 66
Paine, Thomas, 67
Panic, of 1837, 14, 31; of 1857, 154; of 1873, 240, 244, 253, 262
"Partyism," 112, 114, 130-132, 139; triumphant Republicanism, 240-242; in the seventies, 254
Patriotism, among Republicans and War Democrats, 186-188, 191; in 1864, 237
"Peace Bolt" (1864), 230 ff.; leaders, 234

Peace convention proposed, 206, 207, 226, 227, 230

Peace Democracy, origin of, 174, 175, 178, 181; membership of, 178; opposes Emancipation Proclamation, Lincoln, war, conscription, tariff, debt, taxation and profiteering, 183-185, 192, 198, 200, 201, 214; defends freedom of speech and press, 184; estimate of, 186; successes in 1862, 189, 190; extravagant claims of, 190; more definite movement, 191-194, 208; anti-war mass meetings, 200, 201; represents a thwarted West, 209, 211; on opening of Mississippi, 219; undermined by war prosperity, plots and "conspiracies," 223, 224; opposes McClellan, 230; "Peace Bolt," 233 ff.; extreme peace men, 231, 233, 234; "labor-peace" movement, 234; collapse of extreme peace movement, 234; see "Copperheads," Vallandigham

Pendleton, George H., 13, 147-149; in Vallandigham campaign, 213; as Vice-Presidential candidate, 233; and revival of Democratic party, 242; "Ohio idea," 246-248; and Democratic convention (1868), 247

Pennsylvania, 3, 4, 5, 45

Pike County Ballads, 59

Pioneers, 33, 34, 270, 271; conditions of life of, 35, 36

Pittsburgh, trade with South, 76, 78

Plain Dealer (Cleveland), 20, 26

Pluralism, 162

"Pocket," the, 105, 239

Poetry, the "Cincinnati school," 58, 60; James Whitcomb Riley and sentiment and local color, 267; Edgar Lee Masters and "realism," 267

Politics, the excesses of middle western, 9, 10, 58, 188; in Indiana, 110, 114; "in the pulpit," 215, 216; spirit of, in the period of Grant, 240 ff., 249 ff.; "of acquisition and enjoyment," 266; endless story of middle western, 267; see Republican party, Democratic party, Peace Democracy

Polk, James K., 14, 16, 18, 19

Poor whites, 182

Popular sovereignty, 28, 89, 137; Kansas-Nebraska Bill, 98-101; popularity of, 109; appears to be bringing freedom to the West, 109, 120, 136, 139; attracts former anti-Nebraska men, 112; Republicans attempt to use, 142; see Stephen A. Douglas

Population of Middle West, 4, 56; distribution of (1840), 7; growth of, in lake region, 22; movement to Illinois, 87

Poverty, 222

Powers, Hiram, 53, 60, 61

Preparedness for war with South, 166; opposed by lower West, 167; favored by upper West, 166, 167

Presbyterian church, 44, 65, 97, 215, 216

Press, freedom of, 184; attacks on, 203-206; mob action against, 203; suppression of, by Federal authorities, 203; arrest of editors, 203, 204; attack on Columbus Crisis, 204; violence against in Ohio, Indiana and Illinois, 204; "Copperhead," 205; "ranting editors," 216

Profiteering, 221, 223, 243

Prohibition of liquor traffic, 11, 12, 29, 246; favored in lake district, 97; "Maine Law," 102; German dislike of, 106, 107; in Illinois, checked by Democrats, Germans, and Irish, 109, 110; "Women's Crusade," 265, 266

Prosperity, 14, 31, 110; spurious, 180; war stimulated, 219, 220, 222, 223, 235; post-war, 261, 262

Pugh, George E., 113, 133, 134, 146, 147, 213, 216, 233

Purcell, Bishop, 65

Puritanism, 59, 66, 271

Quakers, 46, 48; become Republicans, 108; many support Vallandigham, 215

Railroads, 5, 21, 74; and trade with East, 79, 90; and trade with South, 86, 87; Illinois Central, 86, 87, 120; development of (1850-1857), 94 ff.;

in 1850 (map), 93; in 1860 (map), 95; building craze, 241, 242; prosperous (1862-1863), 218; monopoly, 218, 258; combination broken, 221; corruption, 241, 242; opposition to, 254, 257, 258; Credit Mobilier, 258; and Granger movement, 258; and Panic of 1873, 262
Raisin, River, 3, 44
Reconstruction, "border state," 161-165
Reconstruction of South, 248, 249
Regionalism, 161, 162; Douglas and, 117, 118
Regulators, 40, 41; Union, 201
Religion, 42; revivals, 43, 64, 263; theological debate, 64; orthodoxy, 66; religious ease and liberalism, 269, 273; see Camp meetings, Revivals, Methodist Church
Representation, apportionment of, 107, 108, 114, 168; see "Gerrymandering"
Republican party, 14, 20; economic origins of, 21, 28; in upper West, 100, 101, 108, 109; Lincoln Republicans moderate, 108; certain Republicans favor Douglas, and popular sovereignty, 112, 120, 121, 127, 129; difference between Republicans and Douglas not great, 120; local party convention described, 131, 132; national convention (1860), 138-141; in need of issues, 109, 139; "Blacks" vs "Mulattoes" in 1863, 140; conservative spirit on border, 140; fear of Douglas in Lincoln convention, 140, 141; platform (1860), 140, 141; in "popular sovereignty garb," 139, 142, 143; coercion sentiment in, 166, 167, 171, 172; war patriotism, 168, 188; criticism of Lincoln, 191; forms "Union Leagues," 226; triumphant Republicanism, 240 ff.; pride and power, 243, 253; nominates Grant, 245; insurgents, 245, 246, 250; Liberal Republicans, 249-253; great leaders leaving, 250
Resumption Act, 256, 259
Revivals, religious, see Religion, Churches
"Revolt from the village," 8, 59, 267

Reynolds, John, 108
Rice, Dr. Nathan, 65
Richardson, William A., 99, 100, 133, 134, 190, 222
Riley, James Whitcomb, 267
Riots, draft, 195; see Draft, Deserters
River Improvement, Harbor and River Bill of 1847, 21-26; Memphis Convention, 85; Harbor and River Bill (1854), 96
River Trade, see Trade
Rolvaag, O. E., 267
Romanticism, 6, 8, 17, 58; of the frontier, 276

"Sagas" of the prairie, 8, 267
St. Louis, 23; manufactures, 81; southern river trade, 81; population, 81; war prosperity, 220
Scandinavians, 268
Schools, public, 38; teachers, 38, 53; state-wide system, 39; opposition of Catholics, 271; district school, 271
Schurz, Carl, 106, 249, 257
Scioto River, 5
Secession of South, 146, 151, 155; Cincinnati Commercial and Indianapolis Journal and peaceable, 170; Republicans not opposed, 171; upper West later opposes, 171; sympathy with, in North, 224; see Compromise, Coercion
Secret orders, 223 ff.
Sectionalism, 3, 4, 9, 13, 19, 21, 25, 28, 29, 88 ff., 97, 103, 104, 116 ff., 138 ff., 161, 223, 243
Seminaries, 69
Seward, W. H., 140, 141
Seymour, Governor, 247
Shakers, 62
Sherman, John, 143
Sherman, W. T., 231, 235, 238
Skepticism, 66, 67
Slavery, 12, 16, 19, 45, 66, 72, 234
Smith, Caleb B., 108
Smith, Joseph, 40
Smuggling, 221
Social attitudes, 30-51, 66
Social conditions, 30-51, 62, 63, 194-217, 219-224, 261-275
Social radicalism, 11, 274

Soldier vote, 191, 216, 238
"Sons of Liberty," 226, 228, 230, 231
South, natives of, in West, 3, 4, 6
Southern influences in West, 3, 4, 6, 13, 21, 44, 45; cultural, 52, 69; trade relationships, 74, 75, 85, 87; "pro-slavery" men in West, 108, 119, 144, 224; Douglas Democracy not pro-southern, 134; in election of 1860, 145; in lower West (1860), 146; Cincinnati *Enquirer* and, 149; South-West "alliance," 150; West the child of the South, 166, 167, 209
Speculation, 110, 111, 261, 264, 269
Speech, freedom of, 184, 209; arrest of editors, 184; *see* Press, Arbitrary Arrests
Spiritualism, 187
"Spoon River," 34, 266-271, 274
Spoon River Anthology, 8, 59, 270, 271
Springfield, Illinois, 5, 10, 52
Stage, the, 53, 60-62, 222, 223, 263, 273, 274
State rights, 149, 226, 232-234, 250
State Sentinel (Indiana), 152
State universities, 272
Steamboats, engaged in southern trade, 79, 81, 82; romance of steamboat days, 85; Mark Twain and, 83; social life on, 83; disasters, 84, 85; increase of during war, 220; exorbitant rates, 221
Suckow, Ruth, 267
Suffrage, woman, 12, 29, 97; demands for in lake region, 97
Sumner, Charles, 113
Sumter, Fort, effect of firing on, 173, 174

Tariff, of 1846, 20; protective, 97, 223; Morrill, 160; opposition to, 234; Western Republicans oppose, 243, 249; Liberal Republicans and, 251, 252
Taylor, B. B., 3
Temperance reform, *see* Intemperance, Prohibition, "Women's Crusade"
Texas, Annexation of, 16, 19
Thayer, Eli, 143
Theological debate, 64-66
Third party movements, 257

Thurman, Allen G., 113, 213; and revival of the Democratic party, 242, 244, 254, 259
Tilden, Samuel J., 257
Tippecanoe, Battle of, 3, 44
Toledo, grain shipments, 96
Trade, convention at Chicago (1847), 15, 23, 27; convention at Memphis (1845), 85, 86; with the East, 8, 21, 28, 74, 86, 96, 218; with the South, 8, 21, 73-87, 154-160; golden age of river trade, 82; resultant political influences, 82, 209; New Orleans trade, 155; railroad trade with South, 155, 156, 158; trade of river cities, 61, 155, 156; after firing on Sumter, 160; increase during war, 220; profiteering, 221; *see* Lower West, Upper West
Trade with the South, *see* Trade
Transylvania University, 52, 69
Trollope, Mrs. Frances, 35, 53
Trumbull, Lyman, 102; elected U. S. Senator, 109; against Lecompton constitution, 121; Republican insurgent, 245, 246; "ostracized," 250; and W. J. Bryan, 275 (note)
Turner, Frederick J., 275
Turner, Jonathan B., 70

Uncle Tom's Cabin, 113
Unemployment, 262
Union, the, 151, 162, 163; Union meetings, 149, 150; sentiment for, 192, 194, 224, 238; Union bands, 196; Peace Democracy and, 209, 232; preservation of, by war, 216; Alexander Long and, 232
"Union League," the, 226
Unitarianism, 64, 68, 71, 216
Universities, State, 69, 272
Upper Northwest, 5, 21
Upper West, 5, 6, 12, 20-26; and homesteads, 44, 96; and Chicago convention (1847), 86; and Wilmot Proviso, 27, 88; and Fugitive Slave law, 88; and personal liberty laws, 89; development, 90-97; trade with East, 96; other bonds with East, 97, 171; breaks from Democratic South (1854-1855),

97-101; neglect of interests of, 98; opposition to Kansas-Nebraska Bill, 99; lake Democrats break with party, 100; fusion of anti-slavery elements in, 100-102; wave of moral feeling, 102; Republicans of, uncompromising, 108, 109; reluctantly accepts Lincoln, 138-141; and coercion, 166, 167, 168-172, 209; in election of 1862, 190; war prosperity in, 219; new immigration into, 220; and reëlection of Lincoln, 234, 239; dominant part of West, 274; see Lower West, Sectionalism, Middle West

Validity of middle western history and life, 277
Vallandigham, Clement L., 11, 113, 147, 244; proposal to divide the Union into four parts, 162; leader in Peace party, 175, 211, 232, 233; policies, 179, 184, 185; western sectionalist, 210; speeches against prosecution of war, 211, 212; campaign against Brough, 212-217; campaign song, 213, 214; defeat, 216; and "Sons of Liberty," 227, 229; at Chicago convention (1864), 230-232; and "Peace Bolt," 233
Vandalia, Illinois, 45, 53
Vicksburg, Mississippi, 158, 159, 216, 221
Vincennes, 3, 6
Virginia, 3, 4, 5; influences in West, 30, 31
Volunteer forces, 186
Voorhees, Daniel W., leader in early Peace movement, 175; in Vallandigham campaign, 213; in House of Representatives, 222, 223; and revival of the Democratic party, 242, 254; a Greenbacker, 259

Wabash River, 5, 150
Wabash College, 70
Wade, Benjamin, 172
Wallace, Lew, 164, 202
War, Civil, "psychological" justification of, 187; attack on, by Peace Democrats, 191, 192; opposition to, 207, 208; profiteering, 221, 223, 243; carnage, 223; solemnities, 232,

235, 237; war weariness, 234; waste of human life, 237; effect on family fortunes, 268
War Democrats, 173, 178, 248; patriotism of, 186, 188; called upon to check "Copperheads," 201; John Brough, 212, 215, 216; in 1864, 230, 231, 233; see Democratic party
Washington Court House, Ohio, 265
Webster, Daniel, 89, 90
Weld, Theodore, 63
Wentworth, John, 20, 25, 27; threatens the South, 173
Wescott, Glenway, 267
West, bondage to East, 215; see Middle West, Upper West, Lower West
Western Christian Advocate, criticizes Lincoln, 191; comment on Vallandigham's defeat, 217; in election of 1864, 236, 237
Western "Peace Bolt" (1864), 233, 234
Western Quarterly Review, 63
Western Reserve, 5, 20, 24, 27, 28, 37; Negro suffrage in, 49; and tariff, 97; furnishes Republican leaders, 105; rigid Republicanism of, 108, 152, 190, 232, 239; ready to use force against South, 172; extreme partisans in, excuse public evils, 243
Wheat, production of, 75; new wheat belt, 234; see Trade
Whig party, 13, 14, 15, 40, 48; "conscience Whigs," 50; lack of appeal to foreigner, 94; and tariff, 97; of lower West, 105; in Ohio and Illinois, 105, 106; and American party, 106; many join Peace Democrats, 183
Whitman, Walt, 68
Williamson County, Illinois, feud and disorder, 196, 200, 201
Wilmington, Ohio, 265
Wilmot Proviso, 20, 27, 143
Wisconsin, 5, 15, 16, 22, 28, 115; Negro suffrage opposed, 46, 114; personal liberty law, 89; population increase, 91; in election of 1860, 140, 141; congressional election of 1862 in, 188, 189, 190; reëlection of Lincoln, 238; fusion movement in (1873), 254
"Women's Crusade," 265, 266

Yancey, William L., bolt at Charleston against Western Democrats, 134, 136, 137; favors free navigation of Mississippi, 160

Yankees, 31, 45
Yates, Governor Richard, 51, 188, 219, 238; *see* Illinois
Young, Brigham, 41

(1)